ARNT COBBERS / OLIVER JAHN
Edited by PETER GÖSSEL

PREFAB HOUSES

TASCHEN

CONTENTS

Above: Cover of the magazine *Popular Science*, 1946

Oben: Titelseite der Zeitschrift „Popular Science" von 1946

En haut: Couverture du magazin *Popular Science* de 1946

Opposite page: Richard Buckminster Fuller with the model of the Dymaxion House, c. 1929

Linke Seite: Richard Buckminster Fuller mit dem Modell des Dymaxion-Hauses, um 1929

Page de gauche: Richard Buckminster Fuller avec la maquette de la maison Dymaxion, vers 1929

Page 1: Still from Buster Keatons' famous short film *One Week*, 1920

Seite 1: Szene aus Buster Keatons berühmtem Kurzfilm „One Week", 1920

Page 1: Scène du fameux court métrage de Buster Keaton *One Week* (*La Maison démontable*), 1920

Page 2: A heavy-duty Sikorsky S-64 Skycrane lifting a complete prefabricated house, measuring 28 feet by 44 feet, from the factory to its destination.

Seite 2: Ein komplettes, 8,50 m x 13,50 m großes Fertighaus wird mit einem Sikorsky S-64 Skycrane Transporthubschrauber von der Fabrik zum Aufstellungsort verfrachtet

Page 2: Une grande maison préfabriquée complète de 8,50 m x 13,50 m est transportée par hélicoptère depuis l'usine jusqu'au lieu de montage.

FACTORY-MADE HOUSES

HÄUSER AUS DER FABRIK / DES MAISONS SORTIES DE L'USINE

Opposite page: A portable town for Australia, erected at Hemming's Patent Portable House Manufactory, Clift House, Bristol, c. 1853

Rechte Seite: Eine transportable Stadt für Australien, aufgebaut in Hemming's Patent Portable House Manufactory, Clift House, Bristol, um 1853

Page de droite: Une ville portable pour l'Australie, montée à la Hemming's Patent Portable House Manufactory, Clift House, Bristol, vers 1853

A young couple receives a house as a wedding present. A prefabricated house. Still dressed in a tuxedo and bridal gown, the couple drives to the building site. A truck driver tosses the last of several casket-like boxes from the deck of his truck and races away. What then begins is an ill-begotten attempt on the part of the groom to put the numbered pieces of wood spilling out of the wooden boxes together to build an attractive little house. *One Week* is the title of this 1920 film classic, with Buster Keaton in the role of the young man. He saws, hammers, and stacks, and in the end he and his wife are completely perplexed when they take stock of the structure, which is more reminiscent of a Cubist sculpture—with its slanted walls, crooked windows, and entrance on the upper floor—than of a house. With this film Buster Keaton not only created a masterpiece of slapstick comedy, he also satirized a topic widely discussed in the United States and many other countries in the early 1920s: the prefabricated house. All over the world, innovative architects were developing concepts for houses that could be produced in assembly-line style.

However, not everything that looks like a prefabricated house, really is a prefabricated house. A prefabricated house, in the narrower sense, is either produced in a factory and set on the building site as a complete unit, or it consists completely of components that are industrially prefabricated before they are delivered to the building site, where the final assembly of the house is completed. Because more effort is involved in the preliminary planning, it makes sense to produce building components in standardized sizes beforehand. The boundary between prefabricated houses, in the narrower sense, and building methods that make only partial use of prefabricated elements cannot be clearly drawn.

Building block systems are usually used to ensure that building components are prefabricated at low prices, and that construction on site is as quick and as easy as possible. Hence, most prefabricated housing

Ein junges Paar bekommt zur Hochzeit ein Haus geschenkt. Ein Fertighaus. Noch in Frack und Brautkleid fahren die beiden zur Baustelle. Vom Deck eines Lastwagens knallt ihnen ein Arbeiter die letzte einer Reihe sarggroßer Kisten vor die Füße und rast davon. Was dann beginnt, ist der von Pannen begleitete Versuch des Bräutigams, die aus den Kisten quellenden nummerierten Holzteile zu einem schmucken kleinen Wohnhaus zusammenzusetzen. „One Week" heißt der Filmklassiker aus dem Jahr 1920, der junge Mann wird gespielt von Buster Keaton. Er sägt und hämmert und stapelt, und am Ende bestaunen er und seine Frau ratlos ein Gebilde, das mit seinen schrägen Wänden, schiefen Fenstern und einer Eingangstür im ersten Stock mehr einer kubistischen Skulptur ähnelt als einem Wohnhaus. Buster Keaton liefert mit seinem kleinen Film nicht nur ein Kabinettstück slapstickhafter Komik, sondern nimmt auch aufs Korn, was zu Beginn der 1920er Jahre in den USA und vielen anderen Ländern in aller Munde war: das Fertighaus. Überall auf der Welt entwickelten innovationsfreudige Architekten Konzepte für Häuser, die gleichsam wie am Fließband produziert werden konnten.

Nicht alles, was wie ein Fertighaus aussieht, ist auch eines. Ein Fertighaus im engeren Sinne wird entweder in einer Fabrik gefertigt und als ganzes am „Bauplatz" aufgestellt, oder es besteht aus industriell vorgefertigten Komponenten, die an die Baustelle angeliefert und dort endmontiert werden. Aufgrund des erhöhten Planungsaufwandes im Vorfeld liegt es nahe, die Baukomponenten in standardisierten Maßen vorzufertigen. Die Grenze zwischen Fertighäusern im engeren Sinne und Bauweisen, die nur zum Teil auf vorgefertigte Elemente zurückgreifen, ist jedoch nicht eindeutig zu ziehen.

Zumeist sollen Baukastensysteme für eine kostengünstige Vorfabrikation der Baukomponenten und eine schnelle und möglichst einfache Montage vor Ort sorgen. Die meisten Fertighaus-Systeme beruhen daher auf

Un jeune couple reçoit une maison en cadeau de mariage. Une maison préfabriquée. Encore en tenue de mariés, ils se rendent sur le chantier dans leur décapotable. De la remorque d'un poids lourd, un ouvrier leur lance la dernière de toute une série de caisses, de la taille d'un cercueil, et déguerpit. S'ensuit la tentative chaotique du marié d'assembler les éléments de bois numérotés et entassés dans les caisses pour en faire une jolie petite maison. Ce classique des années vingt où le jeune homme est incarné par Buster Keaton s'intitule *One Week* (*La Maison démontable*). Le voilà qui scie, martèle, empile pour finalement contempler avec son épouse un résultat aux murs obliques, aux fenêtres de guingois, avec la porte d'entrée au premier étage. Autrement dit : une sculpture cubiste plutôt qu'une habitation. Avec son court métrage, Buster Keaton livre non seulement une perle rare du comique burlesque, mais prend aussi pour cible ce qui faisait l'actualité du début des années vingt aux États-Unis comme dans beaucoup d'autres pays : la maison préfabriquée. Partout dans le monde, des architectes innovateurs et dynamiques développaient des concepts de maisons adaptées à la production en série.

Pourtant n'est pas maison préfabriquée tout ce qui en a l'air. Une maison préfabriquée, au sens strict du terme, peut soit être fabriquée en usine puis installée sous sa forme intégrale sur le « terrain à bâtir », soit se composer d'éléments préfabriqués produits industriellement, livrés sur le chantier et assemblés sur place. En raison de l'investissement élevé qu'implique la planification en amont, il est judicieux de préfabriquer les éléments de construction dans des dimensions standardisées. La limite entre des maisons préfabriquées au sens strict et des méthodes de construction qui n'ont recours qu'en partie à des éléments préfabriqués n'est toutefois pas évidente à tracer.

D'ordinaire, les systèmes de construction modulaire devaient permettre une préfabrication économique des éléments de construction, ainsi qu'un

A PORTABLE TOWN FOR AUSTRALIA,

ERECTED at HEMMING'S PATENT PORTABLE HOUSE MANUFACTORY, CLIFT HOUSE, BRISTOL,

Shewing the CHURCH and PARSONAGE HOUSE as ordered to be sent out to THE BISHOP of MELBOURNE.

construction was based on wood or steel frames enclosed using prefabricated panels made of the most diverse materials. However, there were many experiments with the industrial production of complete units, including even the interior fixtures, that were arranged side by side on the building site.

Prefabrication is a child of nineteenth-century industrialization. The use of mass-produced nails, rather than expensive hand-wrought nails, made it possible to construct a house solely out of boards that any sawmill could deliver by using nailed joints. Mortise and tenon joints, as used in timber-frame houses, were no longer necessary. The emergence and spread of prefabrication is also closely related to the life of pioneers in those days, i.e. the occupation of extensive areas of land by European settlers. This gave rise to a need for houses that could be built quickly and at low cost, transported easily, and, considering the lack of trained craftsmen, built by people with no special skills. Hence, prefabrication was initially more common in North America and Australia.

The year 1833 was destined to mark a milestone in prefabrication; it was when the first historically documented prefabricated house was produced in Great Britain. The London carpenter Herbert Manning developed a complete building kit for emigrants headed for Australia, which could be assembled in one day. His Portable Colonial Cottage for Emigrants would eventually become famous.

This was also the year that "balloon frame" construction, which is still common in North America, was developed, presumably by the Chicago master builder Augustine Taylor. It was a precursor of prefabrication. The structures consist of narrowly placed studs and correspondingly arranged horizontal ceiling beams, with their broader sides in the vertical, encased in wooden boards on the outside and paneled on the inside. Basically it was a case of the re-adoption and adaptation of the traditional form of

Rahmenkonstruktionen aus Holz oder Stahl und einer Beplankung mit vorgefertigten Paneelen aus unterschiedlichen Materialien. Immer wieder wurde jedoch auch damit experimentiert, komplette Raumzellen samt Innenausstattung industriell vorzufertigen und vor Ort aneinanderzureihen. Die Fertigbauweise ist ein Kind der Industrialisierung des 19. Jahrhunderts. Durch die Verwendung maschinell hergestellter Drahtstifte anstelle handgeschmiedeter Nägel war es möglich geworden, ein Haus zu konstruieren, das nur aus Brettern, wie sie jedes Sägewerk maßgerecht liefern konnte, und aus genagelten Verbindungen bestand. Verzapfungen wie beim Fachwerkbau entfielen. Die Entstehung und Verbreitung des Fertigbauverfahrens sind zudem eng mit dem Pionierleben jener Tage verbunden, d.h. mit der Landnahme weiter Regionen durch europäische Siedler. Damit einher ging die Notwendigkeit, auf schnelle und kostengünstige Weise Wohnbauten zu schaffen, die einfach zu transportieren und angesichts des Mangels an geschulten Fachkräften durch Nichtspezialisten errichtet werden konnten. Dementsprechend war die Fertigbauweise in ihren Anfängen insbesondere in Nordamerika und in Australien verbreitet.

Das Jahr 1833 sollte das Stichdatum für das Aufkommen der Fertigbauweise bilden: In diesem Jahr entstand in Großbritannien das erste nachweisbare Fertighaus, nachdem der Londoner Zimmermann Herbert Manning für Australien-Auswanderer einen kompletten Hausbausatz entwickelt hatte, der innerhalb eines Tages zusammengebaut werden konnte. Sein Portable Colonial Cottage for Emigrants sollte Berühmtheit erlangen.

Im selben Jahr wurde – wahrscheinlich durch den Chicagoer Baumeister Augustine Taylor – die bis heute in Nordamerika weit verbreitete Holzleichtbauweise „Balloon Frame" entwickelt, die eine Vorstufe des Fertigbaus darstellte. Diese Konstruktion bestand aus enggestellten Brettpfosten, entsprechend angeordneten, hochkant liegenden Brettern als Deckenbalken, einer Brettschalung außen und einer Vertäfelung innen.

montage sur site rapide et aussi simple que possible. C'est pourquoi la plupart de ces systèmes reposaient sur des constructions à ossature de bois ou d'acier et à revêtement en panneaux préfabriqués en matériaux divers. Ces systèmes donnèrent toutefois sans cesse lieu à des expérimentations de production en série de modules complets, aménagement intérieur compris, à juxtaposer sur site.

La préfabrication est héritière de l'industrialisation du XIXᵉ siècle. Remplaçant les coûteux clous en fer forgé façonnés à la main, l'utilisation de pointes produites en usine permet de construire une maison uniquement composée de planches fabricables par toute scierie aux dimensions prescrites et de raccords à clouer ensemble. Les mortaises et les tenons des colombages disparaissent. L'apparition et la diffusion du procédé de préfabrication sont en outre étroitement liées à la vie des pionniers de cette époque, à savoir la conquête de régions lointaines par des colons européens. Elle s'accompagnait de la nécessité de produire des habitations rapidement et à bas coûts, faciles à transporter et, au vu du manque de main d'œuvre qualifiée, assemblables par des non spécialistes. C'est pourquoi la construction préfabriquée fut tout particulièrement répandue à ses débuts en Amérique du Nord et en Australie.

1833 devint l'année de référence de l'apparition de la construction préfabriquée. En effet, c'est à cette date-là que la première maison préfabriquée recensée vit le jour en Grande-Bretagne, lorsque le charpentier londonien Herbert Manning conçut un kit de construction complet pour les émigrants partant pour l'Australie, kit pouvant être assemblé en une journée. Son Portable Colonial Cottage for Emigrants gagna de la notoriété.

Sans doute par l'intermédiaire de l'architecte de Chicago Augustine Taylor, la même année vit l'apparition de la *Balloon frame* (charpente ballon), une structure de bois légère largement répandue en Amérique du Nord, qui constituait un premier pas vers la construction préfabriquée. Cette

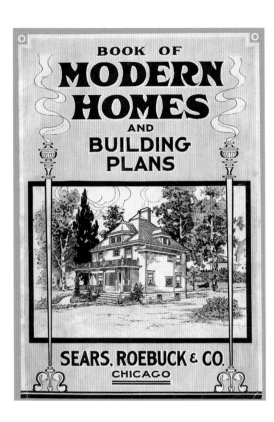

timber-frame construction with continuous studs previously used in Europe for centuries. The system was based on partial prefabrication; it still required considerable work at the building site, but this could be performed by untrained laborers.

The construction method based on this wooden skeleton was derisively referred to as "balloon frame" since it seemed as if a strong gust could blow the houses away. However, the system was practical and cheap, and the result was a permanent structure that was still highly variable in size and layout. It soon became widespread and contributed to a boom in the American wood industry. In the second half of the nineteenth century, a large proportion of all houses built in the United States had balloon frames. In the Western United States, entire cities were built using this type of house.

When the Glaswegian company Thomas Eddington and Sons developed a rolling process to produce corrugated sheet metal in 1844, a new material began to compete with all wood prefabricated post-and-beam construction. In order to produce housing for the hundreds of thousands of gold-diggers who came to California between 1848 and 1854 to try their luck during the gold rush, entrepreneurs like Peter Naylor, from New York, made use of English corrugated sheet metal technology. Companies like Edward Bellhouse in Manchester, Charles Young in Glasgow, and Samuel Hemming in Bristol produced thousands of prefabricated houses out of corrugated sheet metal for California, Australia, and South Africa. The number of prefabricated houses only began to decline when an indigenous building industry began to emerge in the colonies around 1860.

At the beginning of the twentieth century, companies in the United States, like Sears, Roebuck and Co., Gordon van Tine, Montgomery Ward, The Hodgson Company, and Aladdin, began to market prefabricated houses through mail-order catalogues. Cut-to-measure wooden beams, as well as

Im Grunde handelte es sich also um eine Wiederaufnahme und Anpassung traditioneller Ständerbauweisen, wie man sie in Europa jahrhundertelang praktiziert hatte. Das System beruhte auf einer Teilvorfertigung und beanspruchte auf der Baustelle zwar noch ein erhebliches Maß an Arbeit, diese konnte jedoch auch von ungelernten Kräften bewältigt werden.

Diese hölzernen Rippenkonstruktionen wurden spöttisch „Balloon Frames" genannt, weil sie wirkten, als könne ein starker Windstoß sie hinwegfegen. Doch das System war praktisch und billig und das Ergebnis ein ortsfestes Haus, das in Größe und Grundriss variabel war. Diese Bauweise verbreitete sich rasch und bildete alsbald eine der Grundlagen für den Boom der amerikanischen Holzindustrie. In der zweiten Hälfte des 19. Jahrhunderts war ein hoher Anteil der gesamten Wohnbausubstanz in den Vereinigten Staaten Balloon-Frame-Häuser. Insbesondere im amerikanischen Westen entstanden ganze Städte aus diesen Häusern.

Als 1844 die Glasgower Firma Thomas Eddington and Sons ein Walzverfahren zur Herstellung von Wellblech entwickelt hatte, bekam die rein hölzerne Pfosten-Balken-Konstruktion im Fertighausbau Konkurrenz. Die britische Wellblech-Technik machten sich Unternehmer wie Peter Naylor aus New York zunutze, um Unterkünfte für die Goldgräber zu schaffen, die während des kalifornischen Goldrauschs zwischen 1848 und 1854 zu Hunderttausenden ihr Glück versuchten. Firmen wie Edward Bellhouse in Manchester, Charles Young in Glasgow oder Samuel Hemming in Bristol produzierten Tausende von Fertighäusern aus Wellblech, die nach Kalifornien, Australien oder Südafrika geliefert wurden. Erst als um 1860 in den Kolonien ein eigenes Baugewerbe entstand, gingen die Verkaufszahlen vorgefertigter Wohnhäuser wieder zurück.

Zu Beginn des 20. Jahrhunderts begannen in den Vereinigten Staaten Firmen wie Sears, Roebuck and Co., Gordon van Tine, Montgomery Ward, The Hodgson Company oder Aladdin, vorgefertigte Häuser per Versand-

construction était composée de montants très rapprochés et de planches verticales servant de solives, disposées avec le même écart, d'un planchéiage à l'extérieur et de lambris à l'intérieur. Il s'agissait au fond d'une reprise et d'une adaptation des constructions à poutres et à poteaux traditionnelles telles qu'elles avaient été réalisées en Europe pendant des siècles. Le système reposait sur une préfabrication partielle et nécessitait encore une quantité considérable de travail sur le chantier, qui pouvait toutefois être effectué par des ouvriers non qualifiés.

Par dérision, ces ossatures en bois à nervures étaient qualifiées de *Balloon frame*, parce qu'elles donnaient l'impression de pouvoir être balayées d'un fort coup de vent. Mais ce système était pratique et économique. Il en résultait une maison en dur, dont le plan et la taille étaient toutefois modulables. Il se répandit rapidement et constitua bientôt le fondement de l'exceptionnelle productivité de l'industrie du bois américaine. Dans la deuxième partie du XIXᵉ siècle, les maisons *Balloon frame* représentaient une grande partie du parc d'habitation des États-Unis. L'Ouest américain assista tout particulièrement à l'apparition de villes entières composées de ce type de maisons.

Lorsqu'en 1844, l'entreprise de Glasgow Thomas Eddington and Sons développa son procédé de laminage pour la fabrication de tôle ondulée, les constructions poteaux-poutres en bois connurent une véritable concurrence dans le secteur des maisons préfabriquées. Pour loger les chercheurs d'or qui partirent par centaines de milliers chercher fortune en Californie au cours de la ruée vers l'or entre 1848 et 1854, des entrepreneurs comme Peter Naylor de New York mirent à profit la technique anglaise de tôle ondulée. Des entreprises comme Edward Bellhouse à Manchester, Charles Young à Glasgow ou Samuel Hemming à Bristol produisirent des milliers de maisons en tôle ondulée qui furent expédiées vers la Californie, l'Australie ou l'Afrique du Sud. Ce n'est qu'avec l'apparition dans les

GREATER ECONOMY=BIGGER PROFITS

By Building Two or More Houses at the Same Time.   All Live Real Estate Operators and Contractors Are Now Building on a Larger Scale Wherever Possible.

DO LIKE THE LARGEST REAL ESTATE OPERATORS ARE NOW DOING. Improve your property by building on a little larger scale and reap the big benefits either in the way of increasing your profits or doubling percentage of earnings on your investment. Houses built one at a time under ordinary conditions which would earn you 10 per cent would easily earn you 15 or 50 per cent more profit if the same quality of house was built six at one time.

THERE ARE MANY REASONS WHY YOU CAN LOWER YOUR BUILDING COSTS by this procedure. Here are just a few illustrations. For instance, excavating. While laborers, horses, scoops and other implements are on the ground, six basements can be excavated at a slight advance over a lesser number. As much as 25 per cent can be saved on this procedure alone. The cost of foundation walls, especially when made of concrete, can be considerably reduced in price when the forms for concrete work can be used for a number of houses, as the cost of lumber for making the forms, and the labor, can be entirely saved for all additional houses, and by placing a larger order for concrete or masonry work, any up to date contractor is willing to make big concessions in price.

BUILDING ON A LARGER SCALE enables the various contractors and subcontractors to proceed from one building to the next without loss or delay. Carpenters can lay out their framing work for six houses at one time. While one house is in the course of framing, another house will be under its roof, and carpenters during inclement weather can always be worked to the very best possible advantage, which means low building cost for carpenter labor. Plasterers and painters proceed in a like manner, all of them doing the work to the very best advantage and at the very lowest cost. Furthermore, much closer supervision can be had when a number of houses are built close together at one time, as the contractor or foreman can carefully watch the work as it progresses, making every penny paid for labor count to the very best advantage.

WE ARE SELLING MANY OF THE HOUSES SHOWN IN THIS BOOK in lots of fifteen to twenty-five houses, all of which are built in numbers of five to ten at one time. Realty operators and contractors building in this manner claim an actual saving of from 10 to 25 per cent, and claim to give the owner far better satisfaction than would be possible if building one house at a time. On pages 100 and 101 we show these very same houses separately with a larger illustration and quote a

total price for all the material to complete these houses. In designing these houses it has been our aim to have Modern Homes No. 193, No. 194 and No. 196 with foundations of exactly the same dimensions, thus enabling a contractor when laying out his work and making his form to use the same forms on the three different houses, all different in design from an exterior viewpoint yet similar in foundation and arrangement on the inside. We also have planned Modern Homes No. 192, No. 195 and No. 197 in a similar manner, which enables realty operators or individuals who are building on a larger scale for the purpose of renting, speculation or selling, to do the work in the most economical manner at the very lowest possible cost and still be in position to erect the six houses one next to the other without being confronted with the monotony that is found in many localities where the same scheme has been followed out by making slight changes in the front elevation, but not sufficient to make the house look as though each one was an entirely different pattern or design, as we aim to do, and as illustrated above. The above illustration shows six modern homes shown on pages 100 and 101 erected one next to the other on adjoining lots. One can see at a glance that there is no monotony or similarity in their appearance, yet they are constructed on similar foundations and three of each have identical interior arrangements.

IMPROVE YOUR VACANT PROPERTY. If you adopt this scheme of building two or more houses at a time your houses will be sold long before they are completed or, if rented, they will double the interest on your money. Investments of this kind are readily financed by banking institutions or money lenders, as they realize that the security is the best that can be had.

DON'T FORGET that when building in this manner you are cutting out all delays, you are saving in the cost of bringing the scaffolding and tools from one job to the other, you are practically building six houses with the same amount of trouble and attention that is necessary when building one.

TO THOSE WHO ONLY WANT TO BUILD ONE HOUSE FOR RESIDENCE OR OTHER PURPOSES, you can make no mistake in selecting any one of the designs on the following pages. Each one of them is considered very good, of a convenient arrangement, and the excellent material used puts these houses on a par with any other house we show in this book. We simply have pointed out the advantages of building more than one house at a time, which is now being practiced by all the largest and most up to date realty operators in this country.

SEARS, ROEBUCK AND CO.   **CHICAGO, ILLINOIS**

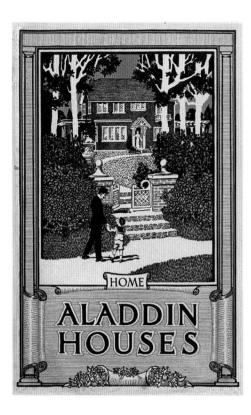

façade and roofing elements, were offered for houses built using the balloon frame widely accepted in the New World; customers could also opt for plumbing and heating, while the nails and paint were even included. Everything was precisely numbered and delivered, along with the assembly instructions, by rail or truck. The first product sold in this manner was the Readi-Cut House by Aladdin in 1906. Aladdin offered a total of 450 different models, and a total of roughly 65,000 houses were sold.

However, Sears, Roebuck and Co. enjoyed the greatest success. Between 1908 and 1940, the company was able to sell between 70,000 and 100,000 houses through its catalogue and sales offices. The first catalogue, printed in 1908, already offered 22 different models at prices between $650 and $2,500. Sears' strongest point was its ability to offer precision-built components for a surprisingly wide range of house models, all of which were packed and shipped along with simple assembly instructions. A Sears house was delivered by rail, packed in two freight cars. Most of the customers took advantage of the opportunity to seek advice in local sales offices. This enabled them to select a model, clarify the question of financing, and decide whether they wanted to order furniture from the Sears Roebuck catalogue all at the same time. The company even offered maintenance contracts.

The house kit essentially consisted of the pre-cut, marked wooden beams out of which the supporting frame was constructed according to the plan. The windows, doors, cladding elements, roofing shingles, nails, and paint were included; plumbing and electrical installations came at additional cost. The company advertised that roughly 40 % of the labor costs incurred in conjunction with traditional housing construction was saved in the production of their prefabricated houses, while the quality was considerably better. No architect was ever named for any of the roughly 450 different

katalog zu vermarkten. Auf der Grundlage der Balloon-Frame-Konstruktion, die sich in der Neuen Welt weithin durchgesetzt hatte, wurden zugeschnittene Holzbalken, Fassaden- und Dachelemente angeboten, nach Wahl auch die komplette Haustechnik, sogar die Nägel und die Farben. Alles wurde penibel durchnummeriert und inklusive Aufbauanleitung als Bahnfracht oder per Lastwagen angeliefert. Das erste auf diesem Wege verkaufte Produkt war 1906 das „Readi-Cut House" von Aladdin. Das Angebot Aladdins umfasste 450 verschiedene Modelle, von denen insgesamt rund 65 000 Stück verkauft wurden.

Am weitaus erfolgreichsten war jedoch die Firma Sears, Roebuck and Co. Zwischen 1908 und 1940 verkaufte das Unternehmen über seine Kataloge und Verkaufsbüros zwischen 70 000 und 100 000 Hauseinheiten. Im ersten Katalog von 1908 wurden bereits 22 verschiedene Modelle angeboten, die zwischen 650 $ und 2 500 $ kosteten. Die Stärke von Sears lag vor allem in der Kompetenz, für eine erstaunlich große Reihe verschiedener Haustypen sehr präzise gearbeitete Bauteile anzubieten, die zusammen mit einer einfachen Aufbauanleitung verpackt und versendet wurden. Ein Sears-Haus wurde, verteilt auf zwei Güterwaggons, mit der Bahn ausgeliefert. Die meisten Kunden nutzten die Möglichkeit, sich in den lokalen Verkaufsbüros beraten zu lassen. Hier konnten sie ein Modell auswählen, die Finanzierungsfrage klären und gleich noch entscheiden, ob sie auch die Möbel von Sears Roebuck bestellen sollten. Sogar einen Wartungsvertrag bot die Firma an.

Der Fertighaus-Bausatz bestand im Wesentlichen aus den zugeschnittenen und gekennzeichneten Holzbalken, aus denen nach Plan das Tragskelett aufgebaut wurde. Im Preis inbegriffen waren die Fenster, Türen, Verkleidungselemente, Dachschindeln, Nägel und Farbe; die sanitären und elektrischen Installationen mussten extra bezahlt werden. Die Firma warb damit, dass bei der Herstellung ihrer Fertighäuser gegenüber vergleichbaren,

colonies d'un secteur du bâtiment local, vers 1860, que le nombre de ventes de maisons préfabriquées recula.

Au début du XXᵉ siècle, aux États-Unis, des entreprises comme Sears, Roebuck and Co., Gordon van Tine, Montgomery Ward, The Hodgson Company ou Aladdin, commencèrent à commercialiser des maisons préfabriquées par correspondance. Sur le modèle largement répandu des *Balloon frames*, des poutres de bois, des éléments de façades et de toitures taillés sur mesure furent proposés sur catalogue, ainsi que la domotique, la visserie et les couleurs. Tout était méticuleusement numéroté et livré par voie ferrée ou par poids lourd, accompagné du mode d'emploi. Le premier produit vendu de la sorte fut la Readi-Cut-House d'Aladdin en 1906. L'offre d'Aladdin regroupait 450 modèles différents dont il vendit 65 000 exemplaires.

L'entreprise Sears, Roebuck and Co. était de loin la plus connue. De 1908 à 1940, elle vendit entre 70 000 et 100 000 maisons à travers ses catalogues et ses bureaux de vente. Dans le premier catalogue de 1908, 22 modèles différents étaient déjà proposés, à des prix allant de 650 $ à 2 500 $. La force de Sears résidait surtout dans son aptitude à offrir des éléments préfabriqués façonnés avec minutie pour une quantité étonnante de types de maisons préfabriquées, emballées et envoyées avec une notice d'installation accessible. Répartie sur deux wagons de marchandises, une maison Sears était livrée par voie ferroviaire. La plupart des clients profitaient de la possibilité de se faire conseiller dans les bureaux de vente locaux. Ils pouvaient y choisir un modèle, régler les questions financières et même commander des meubles Sears Roebuck. Qui plus est, la société proposait un service d'entretien.

Le kit de construction de maison préfabriquée était essentiellement composé de poutres de bois taillées sur mesure et identifiées, permettant l'assemblage de l'ossature porteuse à partir d'un plan. Le prix comprenait fenêtres,

Page from the Hodgson Houses
catalog, 1920

Seite aus einem Katalog für Hodgson
Houses von 1920

Page d'un catalogue pour les maisons
Hodgson de 1920

models offered by Sears Roebuck, although the company did have an architecture department, directed by David S. Betcone, while a woman named E. L. Meyer was responsible for interior decorating components for a certain period.

Since there was a shortage of housing in the vicinity of expanding production facilities, it made sense for many companies to build their own housing estates, thus enabling them, in times of labor shortages, to attract employees and tie them to the company. For example, after Standard Oil purchased a coal mine in Carlinville, Illinois, in 1917, the company ordered building kits for a million dollars from Sears—which was, at the time, the largest order in the history of mail-order sales. Railway tracks were even laid down solely for the purpose of unloading the freight cars that carried the 156 houses to this location.

An important step in the development of prefabricated houses was marked by the emergence of mass production at the beginning of the twentieth century, which was closely connected to the invention of the automobile and the assembly line. This process was made famous by the production of Henry Ford's Model T, which had been produced on an assembly line since 1913. The new production method did not result in advantages in terms of the quality or durability of automobiles, when compared with traditional assembly methods. However, the production costs could be reduced and the volume of production considerably increased. In terms of production, the focus was shifted from the optimization of the individual product to the optimization of the production process. Industrial production processes also opened up new possibilities for the building industry.

At the beginning of the twentieth century prefabrication had already attracted the interest of the young architectural avant-garde. Frank Lloyd Wright and Walter Gropius associated prefabricated building techniques not only with a new lifestyle, but also with the solution of social questions.

in herkömmlicher Weise errichteten Gebäuden rund 40 % der Arbeitskosten eingespart würden und die Qualität der Konstruktion deutlich höher sei.

Da in der Nähe wachsender Großbetriebe oft ein Mangel an Wohnraum herrschte, bot es sich für viele Unternehmen an, eigene Werkssiedlungen zu errichten, womit nicht zuletzt in Zeiten des Arbeitskräftemangels die Attraktivität des Arbeitsplatzes gesteigert und die Bindung an die Firma gestärkt wurde. Nachdem beispielsweise Standard Oil 1917 die Kohlenmine in Carlinville, Illinois, aufgekauft hatte, bestellte das Unternehmen Hausbausätze für eine Million Dollar bei Sears – die bis dahin größte Bestellung im Versandgeschäft. Um die zahlreichen Güterwaggons für die insgesamt 156 Häuser zu entladen, wurde sogar eigens ein Gleisanschluss an den Bauplatz verlegt.

Ein bedeutender Schritt in der Entwicklung des Fertighauses ist durch das Aufkommen der Massenfertigung zu Beginn des 20. Jahrhunderts markiert, das eng mit der Erfindung des Automobils und des Fließbandes verbunden war. Berühmt wurde dieses Verfahren durch die Produktion von Henry Fords Modell T, das seit 1913 am Fließband montiert wurde. Zwar erbrachte die neue Fertigungsmethode im Hinblick auf Qualität und Langlebigkeit der Autos keinen Vorteil gegenüber der herkömmlichen Montage. Doch konnten die Fertigungskosten gesenkt und die Stückzahlen deutlich erhöht werden. Herstellungstechnisch verschob sich der Schwerpunkt von der Optimierung des Einzelprodukts hin zur Optimierung des Fertigungsverfahrens. Auch der Bauwirtschaft boten die industriellen Produktionsverfahren ganz neue Möglichkeiten.

Bereits zu Beginn des 20. Jahrhunderts kam die Fertigbauweise auch ins Visier der jungen Architekten-Avantgarde. Frank Lloyd Wright oder Walter Gropius verbanden die Fertigbautechnik nicht nur mit neuen Lebensformen, sondern auch mit der Lösung sozialer Fragen. Wright war der Ansicht, dass

portes, éléments de revêtement, bardeaux du toit, clous et peinture; les installations sanitaires et électriques étaient en sus. L'argument publicitaire de la société consistait à dire que, par rapport à des bâtiments similaires bâtis de manière traditionnelle, la fabrication de leurs maisons préfabriquées faisait économiser près de 40 pour cent des coûts de main d'œuvre, et permettait une hausse notable de la qualité de la construction. Étant donné le manque de logements régnant à proximité des grandes sociétés en expansion, de nombreuses entreprises furent amenées à construire leurs propres cités ouvrières. En ces temps de pénurie de main-d'œuvre, cette initiative contribua à accroître l'attractivité des emplois et l'attachement des ouvriers à l'entreprise. Après avoir acheté en 1917 les mines de charbon à Carlinville, Illinois, la Standard Oil commanda pour un million de dollars de kits de maisons chez Sears, la plus grosse commande par correspondance jusque-là. Afin de décharger les 156 maisons des nombreux wagons de marchandises, un raccordement de voie ferrée fut même tout spécialement posé jusqu'au chantier.

Un pas majeur dans l'évolution de la préfabrication de maisons est franchi au début du XXe siècle avec l'avènement de la fabrication en série, étroitement liée à l'invention de l'automobile et de la chaîne de montage. Ce procédé devient célèbre avec la production du Modell T d'Henry Ford, assemblé à la chaîne depuis 1913. Cette nouvelle méthode de fabrication n'apporte certes aucun avantage en termes de qualité et de durabilité des automobiles par rapport à l'assemblage traditionnel. Les coûts de production sont toutefois réduits et le nombre d'exemplaires considérablement augmenté. D'un point de vue technique, l'optimisation du produit fait place à l'optimisation du procédé de fabrication. Ces nouvelles méthodes de production industrielle offriront également de nouvelles perspectives à l'industrie du bâtiment.

Dès le début du XXe siècle, la préfabrication attira également l'attention

Wright believed that every American was entitled to own a house that fulfilled high aesthetic standards, but was still affordable. In 1911 he designed American System Built Houses for the real estate developer Arthur L. Richards of Milwaukee. His "Ready Cut" prefabricated house, designed as a simple building kit in 1915 and based on the balloon frame system, is also worth mentioning.

After the First World War prefabricated construction also finally reached the European Continent. Almost over night, architects of the still young Modernist movement became enthusiastic about new building materials and what seemed like unlimited technological progress. Industrial production became a model, both in terms of material aesthetics as well as production technology. The machine became one of the central metaphors of modernism. It dominated design practice of architects and designers to the smallest detail. It is no wonder that innovations in the field of industrial mass production piqued the interest of architects.

One of the pioneers in this context was the German architect Walter Gropius. While working in Peter Behrens' office as a young architect he had already planned to establish a building company in order to both reduce costs by means of industrial prefabrication and to improve the quality of the buildings through meticulous development and extensive testing. As the director of the Bauhaus, he collaborated with Fred Forbat and Adolf Meyer between 1920 and 1923 in developing the *Baukasten* (building block) system of residential units based on concrete elements that would make it possible to build standardized flat-roofed houses—a concept that was not widely accepted. The *Metalltypenhaus* (metal model house) designed by Bauhaus artist Georg Muche and the architectural student Richard Paulick—a steel skeleton to which 3 mm steel plates were affixed—was only built as a prototype by a company in Leipzig that built safes, the Carl Kästner AG. The metal house can still be seen today in Dessau. The plans

jeder Amerikaner ein Recht darauf habe, ein Haus zu besitzen, das auch höheren ästhetischen Ansprüchen genüge und dennoch erschwinglich sei. Für die Firma Arthur L. Richards aus Milwaukee entwarf er 1911 die American System-Built Houses. Erwähnenswert ist auch sein „Ready-Cut"-Fertighaus von 1915, das auf der Basis des Balloon-Frame-Systems als einfacher Baukasten konzipiert war.

Nach dem Ersten Weltkrieg erreichte die Fertigbauweise auch endgültig den europäischen Kontinent. Fast über Nacht begeisterten sich die Architekten der noch jungen Moderne für neue Baumaterialien und den scheinbar unbegrenzten technischen Fortschritt. Sowohl in materialästhetischer als auch in produktionstechnischer Hinsicht war die industrielle Fertigung das Vorbild. Die Maschine wurde zu einer der Zentralmetaphern der Moderne. Sie beherrschte die Entwurfspraxis der Architekten und Designer bis ins kleinste Detail. Kein Wunder also, dass Innovationen auf dem Feld industrieller Massenfertigung das Interesse der Architekten weckten. Einer der ersten der Stunde war hier der Deutsche Walter Gropius. Schon als junger Architekt im Büro von Peter Behrens hatte er sich mit dem Gedanken getragen, eine Baugesellschaft zu gründen, um durch industrielle Vorfertigung nicht nur die Kosten zu senken, sondern auch die Qualität des Gebauten durch minutiöse Entwicklungsarbeit und massenhafte Erprobung zu verbessern. Als Direktor des 1919 gegründeten Bauhauses entwickelte Gropius zusammen mit Fred Forbat und Adolf Meyer in den Jahren 1920 bis 1923 den „Baukasten", ein Raumzellensystem auf der Basis von standardisierten Beton-Elementen, mit denen sich normierte Häuser errichten ließen – das Konzept setzte sich jedoch nicht durch. Auch von dem „Metalltypenhaus" des Bauhaus-Künstlers Georg Muche und des Architekturstudenten Richard Paulick – ein Stahlskelett, auf das 3 mm dicke Stahltafeln montiert waren – wurde nur ein Prototyp gebaut, der noch heute in Dessau zu besichtigen ist. Auch die Pläne des jungen Architekten

des jeunes architectes avant-gardistes. Frank Lloyd Wright ou Walter Gropius associèrent non seulement les techniques de la préfabrication à de nouveaux modes de vie, mais aussi à la résolution de questions sociales. Pour Wright, chaque Américain avait le droit de posséder une maison répondant aussi à de hautes aspirations esthétiques, tout en restant abordable. En 1911, il conçut les American System-Built Houses pour l'entreprise Arthur L. Richards de Milwaukee. Conçue sur la base des *Balloon frames* comme un simple kit de construction, sa maison préfabriquée de 1915, dite «Ready-Cut», est digne d'être mentionnée.

Après la Première Guerre mondiale, la préfabrication atteint aussi définitivement le continent européen. Quasiment du jour au lendemain, les architectes du mouvement moderne encore jeune s'enthousiasmèrent pour de nouveaux matériaux et pour un progrès technique apparemment illimité. Tant du point de vue de l'esthétique des matériaux que des techniques de production, la fabrication industrielle avait valeur de modèle. La machine devint la métaphore centrale de la modernité: elle dominait l'élaboration des projets des architectes et des designers, jusque dans les moindres détails. Rien d'étonnant à ce que les innovations du secteur de la production industrielle aient éveillé l'intérêt des architectes.

L'Allemand Walter Gropius appartenait à l'avant-garde de la première heure. Jeune architecte travaillant dans le cabinet de Peter Behrens, Walter Gropius projetait déjà la création d'une société de construction ayant non seulement pour objectif de diminuer les coûts de production grâce à la fabrication industrielle, mais aussi d'améliorer la qualité des bâtiments par un travail d'étude minutieux et une expérimentation de masse. En tant que directeur du Bauhaus fondé en 1919, Gropius développa le *Baukasten*, mode de construction en kit, avec Fred Forbat et Adolf Meyer entre 1920 et 1923, un système modulaire basé sur des éléments de béton avec lesquels on aurait pu construire des maisons standardisées si l'invention s'était

Walter Gropius, "Large-scale
Building Blocks", 1923

Walter Gropius, „Baukasten im
Großen", 1923

Walter Gropius, « Kit de construction
en grand », 1923

by the young architect Philipp Tolziner to expand the Törten Estate by building steel houses also failed. Nevertheless, all of these projects brought the Bauhaus the reputation of being one of the pioneers of the modern prefabricated house movement.

Another pioneer in the field of prefabricated construction was the French architect Jean Prouvé. In the mid-1930s he designed prefabricated buildings made of sheet metal that were never reproduced, but nevertheless represented a milestone. This included his building for the Aeroclub "Roland Garros" in Buc (Yvelines), which was prefabricated in Prouvé's workshop and can be seen as a manifesto of modernism. Prouvé recognized the need to restructure the building industry and called for buildings to be produced like automobiles or airplanes in a process subject to continual refinement, optimization and renewal.

The European avant-garde approach was transported to America in 1930 by the Swiss architect Albert Frey, who had worked on the Villa Savoye in Le Corbusier's Paris office, thus gaining familiarity with the design vocabulary of the movement from direct experience. At the *Architectural and Allied Arts Exhibition* in 1931, he presented his Aluminaire, a three-story house made of aluminum, glass, and steel, which he had designed in collaboration with Alfred Lawrence Kocher. Companies like Bethlehem Steel, Alcoa (Aluminum Company of America), Westinghouse, and Pittsburgh Plate Glass made the materials used for the steel frames, the corrugated aluminum panels, as well as other components, available for the sake of advertising.

In the United States Frey encountered an increasingly prosperous market. After the World Economic Crisis in 1929, and the subsequent Great Depression, hope was burgeoning that the production of prefabricated houses would help to revive the desolate economy. With much aplomb, the architect Howard T. Fisher established the General Houses Corporation in

Philipp Tolziner, die Siedlung Törten mit Stahlhäusern zu erweitern, scheiterten. Gleichwohl brachten all diese Projekte dem Bauhaus den Ruf ein, einer der Pioniere der modernen Fertighaus-Bewegung zu sein.

Ein Pionier auf dem Gebiet vorgefertigten Bauens war auch der Franzose Jean Prouvé. Der Konstrukteur entwickelte Mitte der 1930er Jahre Gebäude aus Stahlblech in vorgefertigter Bauweise, die zwar Unikate blieben, aber wegweisend wurden. Dazu gehörte das Gebäude des Fliegerclubs „Roland Garros" in Buc (Yvelines), das in den Werkstätten Prouvés vorgefertigt wurde und geradezu als Manifest der Moderne galt. Prouvé erkannte die Notwendigkeit einer Umstrukturierung der Bauindustrie und forderte, dass die Konstruktion von Gebäuden, ebenso wie die von Autos oder Flugzeugen, einem Prozess fortwährender Weiterentwicklung, Optimierung und Erneuerung unterworfen werden müsse.

Der europäische avantgardistische Ansatz wurde 1930 durch den Schweizer Architekten Albert Frey, der im Pariser Büro von Le Corbusier an der Realisierung der Villa Savoye mitgearbeitet hatte und dessen Formensprache aus direkter Anschauung kannte, nach Amerika vermittelt. Auf der „Architectural and Allied Arts Exhibition" präsentierte er 1931 sein zusammen mit Alfred Lawrence Kocher entworfenes dreistöckiges Haus aus Aluminium, Glas und Stahl mit dem Namen „Aluminaire". Das Material für den Stahlrahmen, die Wellblechpaneele aus Aluminium und die anderen Elemente wurde von Firmen wie Bethlehem Steel, Alcoa (The Aluminum Company of America), Westinghouse und Pittsburgh Plate Glass zu Werbezwecken zur Verfügung gestellt.

In der Tat traf Frey in den Vereinigten Staaten auf einen zunehmend prosperierenden Markt. Nach der Weltwirtschaftskrise von 1929 und der sich daran anschließenden Großen Depression war hier die Hoffnung aufgekeimt, dass die Herstellung von Fertighäusern der darniederliegenden Wirtschaft wieder auf die Beine helfen würde. Mit großem Aplomb gründete

imposée. Même la Metalltypenhaus (maison-témoin métallique) de l'artiste du Bauhaus Georg Muche et de l'étudiant en architecture Richard Paulick, une ossature métallique avec des panneaux d'acier de 3 mm d'épaisseur, se limita à la construction d'un seul prototype que l'on peut encore voir à Dessau aujourd'hui. Néanmoins, tous ces projets contribuèrent à la réputation du Bauhaus comme pionnier du mouvement moderne de la maison préfabriquée.

Le Français Jean Prouvé était également un pionnier dans le domaine de la construction préfabriquée. Au milieu des années trente, le constructeur conçut des bâtiments en tôle d'acier selon la méthode de la préfabrication, qui restèrent certes des pièces uniques, mais ouvrirent toutefois la voie à cette pratique. Parmi ces derniers, on compte le bâtiment du Club d'aviation *Roland Garros* à Buc (Yvelines), qui fut préfabriqué dans les ateliers de Prouvé et qui fut pour ainsi dire considéré comme le manifeste du mouvement moderne. Prouvé reconnaissait la nécessité d'une restructuration de l'industrie du bâtiment et exigeait que la construction d'édifices soit soumise à un processus continu de perfectionnement, d'optimisation et de renouvellement, à l'instar des voitures ou des avions.

En 1930, l'architecte suisse Albert Frey, qui avait travaillé dans l'agence parisienne de Le Corbusier à la réalisation de la Villa Savoye et dont il connaissait le langage formel pour l'avoir pratiqué, fut le médiateur de l'approche avant-gardiste européenne aux États-Unis. En 1931, lors de l'*Architectural and Allied Arts Exhibition*, il présenta son projet développé avec Alfred Lawrence Kocher, l'Aluminaire, une maison en aluminium, verre et acier de trois étages. Le matériau pour l'ossature d'acier, les panneaux de tôle ondulée en aluminium et les autres composants furent mis à disposition par des entreprises comme Bethlehem Steel, Alcoa (The Aluminum Company of America), Westinghouse et Pittsburgh Plate Glass à des fins publicitaires.

1932, which cooperated with diverse supply companies in their intention to play a leading role in the market for prefabricated houses. Companies like General Electric, Pittsburgh Plate Glass, or Pullman Car & Manufacturing were taken on board in order to be able to offer houses at prices of between $3,000 and $4,500. Fisher simply applied the production processes of the automobile industry to the production of prefabricated houses.

In the United States, the cooperation between innovative architects and the steel industry led to the development of remarkable ideas. One of the most experimental designers was the autodidactic engineer, architect, and futurist Richard Buckminster Fuller, who ceaselessly developed visions of new ways of living. Fuller's first model of a prefabricated housing unit was presented to the public at a Chicago department store in 1929; it was destined to make history as the Dymaxion House. The design was nothing less than an attack on every traditional concept of what houses should look like: Fuller proposed a central mast in the middle of the hexagonal floor plan that would support the entire structure via high-tension steel cables, thus rendering load-bearing walls unnecessary. The house was planned with a living room, dining room, two bedrooms, two bathrooms, a library, and even a sun terrace on the roof, but no one was interested in buying it. In 1936, he had a prefabricated bathroom patented under the name Dymaxion Bathroom. However, the only version to ever be produced was a living capsule, designed in 1944, called the Dymaxion Deployment Unit; it was deployed, in relatively small numbers, by the United States armed forces as officers' quarters, radar barracks, and infirmaries.

The "House of Tomorrow", designed by George and William Keck for the 1933 *Century of Progress Exhibition* in Chicago was a product of the collaboration between architects and industry. Some 750,000 visitors viewed the prototype, which had been erected as a three-story steel skeleton structure clad in sheet steel in only three days. People marveled at features such as

der Architekt Howard T. Fisher 1932 die General Houses Corporation, die mit verschiedenen Zulieferbetrieben zusammenarbeitete und den Markt für vorgefertigte Häuser bestimmen sollte. Firmen wie General Electric, die Pittsburgh Plate Glass Company oder Pullman Car and Manufacturing wurden an Bord geholt, um standardisierte Wohnhäuser zu Preisen zwischen 3000$ und 4500$ anbieten zu können. Für die Herstellung der Fertighäuser übernahm Fisher die Fertigungsweise der Autoindustrie.

Die Kooperationen zwischen innovativen Architekten und der Stahlindustrie sollten in den Vereinigten Staaten zu einigen bemerkenswerten Ergebnissen führen. Einer der experimentierfreudigsten Entwerfer war der Ingenieur, Architekt und Zukunftsforscher Richard Buckminster Fuller, der unermüdlich Visionen für ein neues Wohnen und Leben entwickelte. In einem Kaufhaus in Chicago wurde 1929 Fullers erstes Modell einer vorgefertigten Wohneinheit der Öffentlichkeit vorgestellt; unter dem Namen Dymaxion House sollte es Geschichte machen. Der Entwurf war ein Angriff auf das althergebrachte Verständnis dessen, wie ein Wohnhaus auszusehen habe: Auf einem sechseckigen Grundriss dachte sich Fuller einen zentralen Mast, der über eine Zugspannung die gesamte Konstruktion halten sollte, wodurch auf tragende Wände verzichtet werden konnte. Das Haus sollte über einen Wohn- und Essbereich, zwei Schlafzimmer, zwei Nasszellen, eine Bibliothek und sogar eine Sonnenterrasse auf dem Dach verfügen. Kaufinteressenten fanden sich jedoch keine. 1936 ließ Fuller sich eine vorgefertigte Nasszelle unter dem Namen Dymaxion Bathroom patentieren. Doch erst die als Dymaxion Deployment Unit bezeichnete Wohnkapsel aus dem Jahr 1944 wurde zumindest in geringer Stückzahl tatsächlich hergestellt und vom US-amerikanischen Militär als Offiziersbehausung, Radarbaracke und Krankenstation eingesetzt.

Ein Produkt der Zusammenarbeit zwischen Architekt und Industrie stellte auch das von George und William Keck für die Ausstellung „Century of

Aux États-Unis, Frey arriva effectivement sur un marché en pleine expansion. Après la crise économique de 1929 et la Grande dépression qui s'était ensuivie, l'espoir avait germé de voir la fabrication de maisons préfabriquées remettre à flot l'économie mal en point. Avec une grande audace, l'architecte Howard T. Fisher fonda en 1932 la General Houses Corporation, qui travaillait avec plusieurs sous-traitants et entendait dominer le marché des maisons préfabriquées. Des entreprises telles que General Electric, Pittsburgh Plate Glass ou Pullman Car and Manufacturing furent mises à contribution pour proposer des habitations standardisées à des prix allant de 3000$ à 4500$. Fisher ne fit qu'appliquer les procédés de fabrication de l'industrie automobile à la production de maisons préfabriquées.

Aux États-Unis, les coopérations entre des architectes innovateurs et l'industrie de l'acier donnèrent le jour à des concepts remarquables. L'un des concepteurs les plus passionnés d'expérimentations était l'ingénieur, architecte et futurologue Richard Buckminster Fuller, qui développait inlassablement des visions d'une nouvelle façon d'habiter et de vivre. En 1929, le premier modèle d'une unité d'habitation préfabriquée de Fuller fut exposé dans un grand magasin de Chicago sous le nom de Dymaxion House. Il allait faire date. Ce projet audacieux était une offensive contre toute conception traditionnelle de l'apparence de la maison individuelle. Sur un plan hexagonal, Fuller avait inventé un mât central auquel était suspendue l'ossature, rendant les murs porteurs caducs. La maison prévoyait un espace séjour et salle à manger, deux chambres, deux salles d'eau, une bibliothèque, et même une terrasse sur le toit. Pourtant, aucun acquéreur ne se présenta. En 1936, Fuller fit breveter une salle d'eau préfabriquée sous le nom de Dymaxion Bathroom. Ce fut pourtant la capsule d'habitation dite Dymaxion Deployment Unit de 1944 qui fut effectivement fabriquée – tout au moins en petite quantité – et utilisée par les militaires américains comme logement pour officiers, baraque à radar ou infirmerie.

The Armco-Ferro-Mayflower House, a steel structure designed by Robert Smith Jr. and presented at the *Century of Progress Exhibition* in Chicago, 1933, was presumably the first house to feature porcelain enamel siding.

Das von Robert Smith Jr. entworfene und in Stahlkonstruktion ausgeführte Armco-Ferro-Mayflower House auf der Ausstellung „Century of Progress" in Chicago 1933 war vermutlich das erste Haus mit einer Stahlblechemaillierung als Hausverkleidung.

La maison à ossature en acier Armco-Ferro-Mayflower conçue par Robert Smith Jr. et vue à l'exposition Century of Progress en 1933 à Chicago, fut probablement la première à utiliser un émaillage de la tôle d'acier en guise de revêtement extérieur.

air conditioning and custom installations, which included a dishwasher in the kitchen and an aquarium in the children's room, but still no one wanted to buy the house.

The Chicago real estate tycoon Robert Bartlett purchased the prototype of the Keck House in 1935, along with four other models shown at the fair, and had them reassembled in Beverly Shores, where he intended to market premium building sites to his wealthy clientele. The plan backfired, but the former exhibition houses are still standing and now being restored: the Keck House can be found alongside a two-story flat-roofed building with a roof terrace by Robert Law Weed, the Florida Tropical House, a house made completely of cypress by Murray D. Heatherington, the Cypress Log Cabin, and a steel skeleton building by Walter Scholer, the Wieboldt-Rostone-House, which was clad in a material called Rostone (a mixture of slate, limestone and alkali). The only house to fulfil the exhibition organizers' criteria of being low enough in cost for the average American family and suited for serial production was the Armco-Ferro House by Robert Smith Jr. His façade, made of riveted and enameled corrugated metal panels, served as a model for the Lustron Homes, produced from 1948 to 1950.

The designs by Fuller, Gropius, Frey, Weed and the Kecks were examples of Modernism. However the public at large in America was not willing to accept factory-built houses, thus orders were rare. The idea of building a house out of metal, as if it were a car chassis, was something new that people were not used to. It is therefore not surprising that a critic for the *New York Sun* snidely referred to it as a "canned house", arguing, "If father wants a new door cut through to his room he doesn't get a saw. He gets a can opener." Innovative companies founded in the 1930s, like American Homes, American Houses, Inc., or the Homosote Company, soon went bankrupt. The building industry in those years focused mainly on the task

Progress" von 1933 in Chicago entworfene „House of Tomorrow" dar. 750 000 Besucher besichtigten den Prototyp, der in nur drei Tagen als mit Stahlblech verkleideter dreistöckiger Stahlskelettbau errichtet worden war. Man staunte über Extras wie die Klimaanlage und Einbauten wie den Geschirrspüler in der Küche oder das Aquarium im Kinderzimmer, aber kaufen wollte das Haus niemand.

Der Chicagoer Immobilien-Tycoon Robert Bartlett erwarb 1935 den Prototyp des Keck-Hauses ebenso wie vier andere auf der „Century of Progress" gezeigte Modelle und ließ diese in den Beverly Shores als Mustersiedlung wieder aufstellen. Zwar schlug sein damit verbundener Plan, das dortige Gelände als Premium-Baugrund für eine wohlhabende Klientel zu vermarkten, fehl; die „Ausstellungsstücke" stehen aber noch heute und werden derzeit restauriert. Neben dem Keck-Haus finden sich hier das Florida Tropical House von Robert Law Weed, ein zweistöckiger Flachdachbau mit Dachterrasse, die ganz aus Zypressenholz gefertigte Cypress Log Cabin von Murray D. Heatherington sowie das Wieboldt-Rostone-House von Walter Scholer, ein Stahlskelettbau, der mit einem Werkstoff namens Rostone (einem Gemisch aus Schiefer, Kalkstein und Alkali) verkleidet war. Nur das Armco-Ferro House von Robert Smith Jr. erfüllte übrigens die von den Ausstellungsveranstaltern vorgegebenen Kriterien für ein kostengünstig in Serienproduktion herstellbares Haus für eine durchschnittliche amerikanische Familie. Seine Fassade aus vernieteten und emaillierten Wellblechpaneelen wurde zum Vorbild für die Lustron Homes, die von 1948 bis 1950 produziert wurden.

Die Entwürfe von Fuller, Gropius, Frey, Weed oder der Kecks waren zwar Demonstrationen der Moderne, doch das amerikanische Publikum konnte sich mit einem Wohnhaus aus der Fabrik zunächst nicht anfreunden, und so blieben Bestellungen die Ausnahme. Die Idee, ein Haus wie eine Autokarosserie ganz aus Metall zu fertigen, war zum damaligen Zeitpunkt für

Le projet House of Tomorrow conçu pour l'exposition Century of Progress de 1933 à Chicago par George et William Keck était également le fruit de la collaboration entre architectes et industrie. 750 000 visiteurs découvrirent le prototype de trois étages à revêtement de tôle et squelette d'acier édifié en seulement trois jours. Des options telles que la climatisation et des éléments encastrés comme un lave-vaisselle dans la cuisine ou l'aquarium dans la chambre d'enfants firent l'admiration de tous, mais la maison ne trouva pas preneur.

En 1935, le magnat de l'immobilier de Chicago Robert Bartlett acheta le prototype de la maison Keck, ainsi que quatre autres modèles exposés sur le salon, et les reconstruisit en un lotissement modèle près de Beverly Shores. Il avait l'intention de vendre l'emplacement à une clientèle aisée comme terrain à bâtir de standing. Son plan échoua. Les modèles d'exposition de l'époque s'y trouvent toujours et sont actuellement en cours de restauration. À côté de la maison Keck se trouvent aussi la Florida Tropical House de Robert Law Weed, un bâtiment à toit plat de deux étages avec toit-terrasse, la Cypress Log Cabin de Murray D. Heatherington à revêtement intégral en bois de cyprès, ainsi que la Wieboldt-Rostone House de Walter Scholer, un bâtiment à ossature d'acier dont le revêtement est en Rostone (un mélange d'ardoise, de calcaire et d'alcali). Seule la Armco-Ferro House de Robert Smith Jr. avait rempli les critères imposés par les organisateurs d'une maison économique et fabricable en série pour une famille américaine moyenne. Sa façade à panneaux de tôle ondulée émaillés et rivetés devint le modèle des Lustron Homes qui furent produites entre 1948 et 1950.

Les concepts de Fuller, Gropius, Frey, Weed ou des frères Keck étaient certes emblématiques de l'époque moderne. Toutefois le public américain avait du mal à se faire aux maisons individuelles tout droit sorties de l'usine, et les commandes restèrent exceptionnelles. À l'époque, l'idée de

Prefabricated houses for workers on a dam in Victoria, Australia, 1947

Fertighäuser für die Arbeiter eines Staudammprojekts in Victoria, Australien, 1947

Maison préfabriquées pour les ouvriers d'un projet de barrage à Victoria, Australie, 1947

of erecting living space as quickly, cheaply, and simply as possible. The order books of Sears and Aladdin were full, and they saw no need to adapt the traditional formal language of their house models to Modernism. While the prefabricated steel house continued to play a subordinate role in private residential construction, the situation in the military context was quite different. In order to create easily transportable housing for the troops of the United States Army, the engineers Peter Dejongh and Otto Brandenberger designed the so-called Quonset Hut for the George A. Fuller Construction Company in 1941. Reminiscent in its tunnel-like shape of the Nissen Huts used by the British military in the First World War, it was named after the naval air base at Quonset Point, Rhode Island, where it was originally produced. The prefabricated hut consisted of a skeleton of round arches, clad in galvanized corrugated sheet metal, and had a plywood floor. Many of the roughly 170,000 housing units that were produced have survived to this day in the United States: as factory halls, simple churches, or shops. The concept was never accepted for the construction of private houses. However, the modernistic church that Bruce Goff designed in 1945 on the basis of one of them in Camp Parks, California, did become famous, as did the studio house that the French avant-garde architect Pierre Chareau designed for the American painter Robert Motherwell on the basis of two Quonset building kits in 1946, which featured full-length windows flooded with light.

The prefabricated housing industry received tremendous impetus after President Roosevelt established the Federal Housing Agency in 1942, which was responsible for creating housing for the many workers in the defense industry who were deployed at locations far from home. After the war, the agency was responsible for promoting building programs to satisfy the demand for living space on the part of soldiers returning from Europe and the Far East. This is where the two German architects Walter

das Publikum zu neu und ungewohnt. Bezeichnend ist beispielsweise, wie der Kommentator der „New York Sun" Freys und Kochers „Aluminaire" als „Konservendosenhaus" verspottete: „Wenn Papa eine neue Türöffnung für sein Zimmer haben will, greift er nicht zur Säge, sondern zum Dosenöffner." So verschwanden viele der in den 1930er Jahren gegründeten Firmen wie American Homes, American Houses Inc. oder die Homosote Company alsbald wieder vom Markt. Die Bauindustrie jener Jahre war vor allem darauf bedacht, Wohnraum so schnell, billig und einfach wie möglich zu schaffen. Sears und Aladdin hatten volle Auftragsbücher und sahen keine Notwendigkeit, die traditionelle Formensprache ihrer Hausmodelle an die der Moderne anzupassen.

Spielte das vorgefertigte Stahlhaus im privaten Wohnhausbau nach wie vor nur eine untergeordnete Rolle, so war die Situation im militärischen Bereich völlig anders. Um leicht transportierbare Truppenbehausungen für die US-amerikanische Armee zu schaffen, entwarfen die Ingenieure Peter Dejongh und Otto Brandenberger 1941 für die George A. Fuller Construction Company die sogenannte Quonset-Hütte. Sie geht in ihrer halbrunden Form auf die vom Britischen Militär während des Ersten Weltkriegs eingesetzten Nissen-Hütten zurück, und war nach dem Produktionsstandort am Luft- und Marinestützpunkt Quonset Point in Rhode Island benannt. Die Hütte bestand aus einem Skelett aus Rundbögen, die mit einer Fassade aus verzinkten Wellblechpaneelen verkleidet und mit Schichtholzböden ausgestattet wurden. In den USA stehen viele der rund 170 000 produzierten Behausungen bis auf den heutigen Tag: als Fabrikhallen, einfache Kirchen oder Ladenlokale. Für den privaten Hausbau konnte sich das Konzept jedoch nicht durchsetzen. Berühmt wurden die modernistische Kirche, die Bruce Goff 1945 im kalifornischen Camp Parks baute, sowie das mit seinen raumhohen Fenstern lichtdurchflutete Atelierhaus, das der französische Avantgarde-Architekt Pierre Chareau 1946 für den amerikanischen Maler

réaliser une maison intégralement en métal, tel un châssis de voiture, était totalement neuve pour le public. Rien d'étonnant à ce que le commentateur du *New York Sun* déclarât, fielleux, au sujet de la « maison boîte de conserve »: « Lorsqu'un père de famille veut découper une nouvelle porte dans sa chambre, ce n'est pas une scie qu'il utilise, mais un ouvre-boîte. » Dans les années trente, des entreprises comme American Homes, American Houses Inc. ou la Homosote Company firent rapidement faillite. Pendant ces années, l'industrie du bâtiment était surtout soucieuse de bâtir des logements aussi rapidement, simplement et à bas prix que possible. Les carnets de commande de Sears et Aladdin étaient pleins et ils ne voyaient pas la nécessité d'adapter le langage formel de leurs modèles à celui de la modernité.

Si la maison d'acier préfabriquée ne jouait encore qu'un rôle mineur dans le domaine de la construction de logements privés, la situation en était tout autrement dans le domaine militaire. Pour proposer aux troupes de l'armée américaine des logements facilement transportables, les ingénieurs Peter Dejongh et Otto Brandenberger créèrent en 1941 lesdites cabanes Quonset pour la George A. Fuller Construction Company. Tirant son nom du site de production situé près de la base navale et aérienne Quonset Point à Rhode Island, la cabane préfabriquée était composée d'une ossature d'arcs en plein cintre à revêtement de panneaux de tôle ondulée galvanisée et dotée de planchers en contreplaqué. Parmi les 170 000 logements produits, dont la forme semi-sphérique rappelait les cabanes Nissen utilisées par les militaires britanniques lors de la Première Guerre mondiale, nombreux sont ceux qui ont survécu aux États-Unis, sous la forme de hangars, de simples églises ou de locaux commerciaux. Toutefois, le concept ne s'imposa pas sur le marché de la construction privée. Résultat de la transformation d'une de ces cabanes, l'église moderniste de 1945 de Bruce Goff à Camp Parks en Californie acquit de la notoriété. Il en fut de même de l'atelier inondé de

Gropius and Konrad Wachsmann saw a chance for the panel system they had developed in the early 1930s for Christoph & Unmack, one of the largest producers of wooden barracks in Europe. After emigrating to the United States, they had developed a prefabricated house out of preassembled panel elements for General Panel Corporation, a company they jointly founded in 1941. However, the hope that they would be able to sell 10,000 units per year was never fulfilled. Fewer than 200 houses were produced, and even fewer of them were sold.

After the Second World War there was a regular prefabricated housing boom in the United States. Some 70 companies were active in this market segment in the post-war era, ultimately leading to the construction of roughly 200,000 prefabricated houses. However companies such as Vultee, Lustron, and the Spartan Aircraft Company, which offered buildings built on the basis of steel frames or clad in sheet metal, were still not able to survive. Companies that limited themselves to more conventional forms and materials were more successful, and, correspondingly, most of the prefabricated houses were clad in shingles and had pitched roofs. When Gropius's student Carl Koch developed his first prefabricated house in 1948, he equipped it in the best Bauhaus tradition with a flat roof. When it failed to sell, he developed his Techbuilt House, this time of course with a pitched roof—and he was soon successful.

The situation in Europe was more difficult: although millions of people had no place to live on the Old Continent due to the destruction of the Second World War, people were reluctant to accept prefabricated construction. In Germany, which had not only lost 25 % of its entire housing stock to bombing, but also had to integrate 12 million refugees from former German territories in Eastern Europe, one form of prefabricated housing was used extensively: the Nissen Hut. This was a barracks-like emergency shelter made of corrugated sheet metal with an arched roof, which had already

Robert Motherwell unter Verwendung zweier ausrangierter Quonset-Einheiten entwarf.

Einen gewaltigen Auftrieb erhielt die Fertigbaubranche, nachdem Präsident Roosevelt 1942 eine Bundesbaubehörde (Federal Housing Agency) geschaffen hatte, zu deren Aufgaben die Schaffung von Wohnraum für die vielen Arbeiter in der Rüstungsindustrie gehörte, die an Standorten fern der Heimat eingesetzt waren. Nach dem Krieg bestand ihre Aufgabe in der Förderung von Bauprogrammen, um den Bedarf an Wohnraum für die aus Europa und Fernost heimkehrenden Soldaten zu decken. Hier sahen die beiden deutschen Architekten Walter Gropius und Konrad Wachsmann, die Anfang der 1930er Jahre für Christoph & Unmack, einen der größten Holzbaracken-Hersteller Europas, Paneelsysteme entwickelt hatten, ihre Stunde gekommen. Nach ihrer Emigration in die USA hatten sie für ihre 1941 gegründete gemeinsame Firma General Panel Corporation ein Fertighaus aus vorgefertigten Tafelelementen entwickelt. Doch die Hoffnung, davon 10 000 Stück jährlich abzusetzen, sollte sich nicht verwirklichen. Nicht einmal 200 Häuser wurden produziert, von denen nur wenige verkauft wurden.

Nach dem Zweiten Weltkrieg kam es in den USA zu einem regelrechten Fertighaus-Boom. In diesem Marktsegment waren in der Nachkriegszeit rund 70 Firmen präsent, und immerhin rund 200 000 vorgefertigte Häuser wurden gebaut. Nach wie vor konnten sich hier jedoch Firmen wie Vultee, Lustron oder die Spartan Aircraft Company, die auf der Basis von Stahlrahmen und Stahlblechverkleidungen konstruierte Gebäude anboten, nicht halten. Erfolgreicher waren Unternehmen, die sich auf konventionellere Formen und Materialien beschränkten, und dementsprechend verfügte das Gros der Fertighäuser über Schindelverkleidung und Satteldach. Als der Gropius-Schüler Carl Koch 1948 sein erstes Fertighaus entwickelte, versah er es in bester Bauhaus-Tradition mit einem Flachdach. Nachdem es sich

lumière par ses fenêtres toute hauteur conçu par l'architecte français d'avant-garde Pierre Chareau en 1946 pour le peintre américain Robert Motherwell à partir de deux éléments Quonset abandonnés.

Suite à la création par le président Roosevelt en 1942 de la Federal Housing Agency (administration fédérale du bâtiment) destinée à fournir des habitations aux nombreux ouvriers de l'industrie de l'armement contraints de travailler loin de leur pays, le secteur de la préfabrication connut un essor considérable. Après la guerre, elle avait pour mission de subventionner les programmes de construction afin de couvrir les besoins des soldats de retour d'Europe et d'Extrême-Orient. Les deux architectes allemands qui, au début des années trente, avaient développé des systèmes de panneaux pour Christoph & Unmack, l'un des plus gros fabricants de cabanes en bois d'Europe, virent là leur heure venue. Après leur émigration aux États-Unis, ils avaient développé une maison préfabriquée faite de panneaux préfabriqués pour l'entreprise qu'ils avaient créée ensemble en 1941, la General Panel Corporation. Leur espoir d'en écouler 10 000 par an fut déçu et, dans les faits, pas plus de 200 ne furent produites, dont seuls quelques exemplaires furent vendus.

Après la Deuxième Guerre mondiale, on assista aux États-Unis à un véritable essor des maisons préfabriquées. Au cours de la période d'après-guerre, près de 70 entreprises occupaient ce segment de marché et environ 200 000 maisons préfabriquées furent construites. Des entreprises comme Vultee, Lustron ou la Spartan Aircraft Company qui proposaient des bâtiments à ossatures d'acier et revêtements de tôle d'acier ne purent toutefois pas se maintenir. Les entreprises qui s'en tenaient à des formes et des matériaux plus traditionnels étaient plus prisées, raison pour laquelle la majorité des maisons préfabriquées possédaient un revêtement à bardeaux et un toit en pente. Lorsque l'ancien élève de Gropius Carl Koch conçut sa première maison préfabriquée en 1948, il la dota d'un toit plat, dans la pure

Demountable employee housing by the Tennessee Valley Authority: Houses were constructed in fully equipped slices, which were transported individually and are connected to each other on the site.

Zerlegbare Häuser für Angestellte der Tennessee Valley Authority: Die bereits komplett ausgestatteten Bauelemente der Häuser konnten einzeln transportiert und am Zielort wieder zusammengesetzt werden.

Maisons démontables pour employés de la Tennessee Valley Authority: les éléments constructifs complètement équipés pouvaient être acheminés individuellement puis réassemblés sur le site.

been developed during the First World War by the Canadian engineer Peter Norman Nissen. Thousands of them were erected on the periphery of cities and towns and became the architectural symbol of the misery of post-war Germany. A sense of the provisional and of desperation associated with those years is possibly what later prevented people in Germany from believing in prefabricated houses—people wanted nothing more than a secure roof over their heads and to be surrounded by sturdy walls.

An attempt was also made in post-war France to combat housing shortages with the help of prefabricated houses. In 1944, Jean Prouvé was already commissioned by the Ministry of Reconstruction and Urban Planning to build 800 houses as emergency shelters that could be easily disassembled. However, only 400 of these "Maisons à portique", which were equipped with an axial steel frame, were ever erected. Again commissioned by the government, Prouvé developed a series of aluminum clad lightweight steel houses based on the same principle, but only a few were ever erected because they were more expensive than expected. Prouvé's Alba houses, developed for the Abbey Pierre's homeless organization in 1956, were also not a success.

The 1960s were a period of social transition in which attitudes towards prefabricated housing also changed. During this era, which was marked by space travel, the moon landing, and even children's books that predicted weekend trips to distant galaxies, prefabricated construction was discovered both as a form of artistic expression and as a technical means of creating houses to provide a basis for new lifestyles, which seemed to be imminent in a society characterized by an extremely optimistic view of progress. One of the houses of the era of space travel was La Bulle six coques by the French architect Jean Maneval, which was used for an entire colony of holiday homes in the Pyrenean Mountains in 1967, literally making it look like the site of an invasion from outer space. The space ship-like

nicht verkaufte, entwickelte er sein Techbuilt-Haus, diesmal natürlich mit Satteldach – der Erfolg ließ nicht auf sich warten.

Schwieriger verlief die Entwicklung in Europa: Obwohl auf dem Alten Kontinent durch die Zerstörungen des Zweiten Weltkriegs Millionen von Menschen ohne Obdach waren, ließ man sich nur zögerlich auf die Fertigbauweise ein. In Deutschland, das nicht nur allein 25 % seines gesamten Wohnungsbestandes im Bombenkrieg verlor, sondern zudem 12 Millionen Vertriebene aus den deutschen Ostgebieten zu integrieren hatte, kam es zu einem massenweisen Einsatz vorgefertigter Behausungen: den Nissenhütten. Es handelte sich um barackenartige Notunterkünfte aus Wellblech mit halbzylindrischer Dachform, die bereits während des Ersten Weltkriegs durch den kanadischen Ingenieur Peter Norman Nissen entwickelt worden waren. Sie wurden zu Tausenden an den Rändern der Städte und Gemeinden errichtet und avancierten zum architektonischen Symbol des Elends der deutschen Nachkriegszeit. Der Ruch des Provisorischen und der Not jener Jahre war es möglicherweise, der die Menschen in Deutschland auch später davon abhielt, in vorgefertigte Häuser Vertrauen zu fassen – wünschte man sich doch nichts sehnlicher, als ein festes Dach über dem Kopf und solides Mauerwerk um sich zu haben.

Auch im Nachkriegs-Frankreich versuchte man, der Wohnungsnot mit Hilfe von vorgefertigten Häusern Herr zu werden. Bereits 1944 erhielt Jean Prouvé vom Ministerium für Wiederaufbau und Städtebau den Auftrag, 800 demontierbare Häuser als Notunterkünfte zu schaffen. Von den mit einer axialen Metallrahmenkonstruktion versehenen „Maisons à portique" wurden allerdings nur etwa 400 aufgestellt. Auf demselben Prinzip beruhend entwickelte Prouvé Anfang der 1950er Jahre – ebenfalls im Regierungsauftrag – eine Serie aluminiumverkleideter Stahlleichtbauhäuser, von denen allerdings nur ein paar wenige aufgestellt wurden, da sie teurer waren als erwartet. Auch den Häusern des Typs Alba, die Prouvé 1956 für

tradition du Bauhaus. Voyant qu'elle ne se vendait pas, il développa sa Techbuilt House, possédant bien évidemment, cette fois-ci, un toit en pente: le succès ne se fit pas attendre.

Sa progression en Europe s'avéra quant à elle plus difficile. Bien que, sur le vieux continent, des millions de personnes se soient retrouvées sans toit suite aux destructions de la Deuxième Guerre mondiale, les constructions préfabriquées se heurtaient encore à une certaine hésitation. En Allemagne, où 25 % du parc de logement total avait disparu sous les bombes et où 12 millions de personnes expulsées des territoires d'Allemagne orientale devaient être réintégrées, on eut massivement recours aux habitations préfabriquées provisoires: les cabanes Nissen. Il s'agissait là de baraques provisoires de tôle ondulée à toits semi-cylindriques. Elles avaient été conçues par l'ingénieur canadien Peter Norman Nissen pendant la Première Guerre mondiale. Elles furent construites par milliers à la périphérie des villes et des communes et devinrent le symbole architectonique de la misère de la période d'après-guerre allemande. La mauvaise réputation de ces abris provisoires et la misère de ces années expliquent probablement la réticence ultérieure que manifestèrent les Allemands à l'égard des maisons préfabriquées. Ils ne souhaitaient rien plus ardemment qu'un toit résistant au-dessus de leur tête et un mur solide autour d'eux.

Dans la France d'après-guerre aussi, on essayait de venir à bout de la crise du logement à l'aide de maisons préfabriquées. Dès 1944, Jean Prouvé reçut de la part du ministère de la Reconstruction et de l'Urbanisme une commande de 800 maisons démontables destinées à servir de logements provisoires. Seules 400 unités des «Maisons à portique» dotées d'une ossature métallique axiale furent toutefois montées. Au début des années cinquante – également à la demande du gouvernement –, Prouvé développa une série de maisons à ossature d'acier légère et à revêtement d'aluminium reposant sur le même principe, dont seules quelques-unes furent montées

pavilions, called Futuro, made of fiberglass reinforced polyester and designed by the Finnish architect Matti Suuronen in 1968, also look somehow intergalactic.

These approaches led to the ideal of creating megastructures out of residential capsules: the architect Moshe Safdie, who was only 24 at the time, presented his megastructure Habitat 67 at the Expo 67 in Montreal: 158 housing units consisting of 354 concrete modules assembled as a conglomerate. The British architectural group Archigram developed building structures made of residential capsules as an architectural utopia, which could be expanded at will and joined together to form entire cities. In 1972, the Japanese architect Kisho Kurokawa built the Nakagin Capsule Tower in Tokyo; housing cells were layered around a prefabricated concrete core to form a fourteen-story residential tower. The idea of residential capsule megastructures was repeatedly revived, as in Zvi Hecker's Ramot housing development in Jerusalem in 1974.

In addition, architects given to experimentation developed studies for houses that included elements of prefabricated construction, but which nevertheless remained one of a kind. Representatives of British high-tech architecture such as Alison and Peter Smithson, Richard Rogers, and Norman Foster developed concepts for building techniques aimed at greater flexibility and technical refinement as a result of their fascination with factory-produced metal and plastic components, without seriously being interested in seeing their designs produced in series. This was true of Richard Rogers' Zip-Up House (1968), a bright yellow residential box resting on pink legs, which featured aluminum panels connected by neoprene gaskets and reminded one of the Beatles' "Yellow Submarine". In 1984 Richard Horden adopted the aluminium mast used as a load-bearing element in his Yacht House, a lightweight grid structure, from shipbuilding and suspended the roof and wall panels from it.

die Obdachlosen-Organisation des Geistlichen Abbé Pierre schuf, war kein Erfolg beschieden.

Im Zuge des während der 1960er Jahre einsetzenden gesellschaftlichen Umbruchs wandelte sich auch die Einstellung gegenüber der Fertigbauweise. In einer Ära, die von der Weltraumfahrt und vom Ereignis der Mondlandung geprägt war, in der sogar Kinderbücher bereits für die kommenden Jahre Wochenendtrips zu fernen Galaxien prognostizierten, wurde das Fertigbauverfahren als künstlerische Ausdrucksform entdeckt bzw. als technisches Mittel betrachtet, Häuser als Lebensgrundlage für die neuen Daseinsformen des Menschen zu schaffen, in die man in jenen von einem extremen Fortschrittsoptimismus geprägten Jahren wähnte einzutreten. Zu den Häusern der Raumfahrt-Ära zählen die Bulles six coques des Franzosen Jean Maneval, mit denen 1967 eine komplette Feriensiedlung in den Pyrenäen gebaut wurde und die diesen Ort buchstäblich als Schauplatz einer Invasion der Außerirdischen erscheinen ließen. Auch die 1968 entstandenen raumkapselartigen Pavillons aus glasfaserverstärktem Polyester des Finnen Matti Suuronen, „Futuro" genannt, hatten intergalaktisches Aussehen.

Aus diesen Ansätzen entwickelte sich die Idee, mit Wohnkapseln Megastrukturen zu schaffen. 1967 stellte der erst 24-jährige Architekt Moshe Safdie auf der Weltausstellung in Montreal seine Megastruktur Habitat 67 vor: 158 Hauseinheiten aus 354 Beton-Modulen sind zu einem gigantischen amorphen Gebilde zusammengesetzt. Die britische Architektengruppe Archigram entwickelte als Architekturutopie Gebäudestrukturen aus Wohnkapseln, die sich beliebig erweitern und zu ganzen Städten zusammenstecken lassen sollten. 1972 realisierte der japanische Architekt Kisho Kurokawa in Tokio den Nakagin Capsule Tower: Um einen Betonkern wurden vorgefertigte Raumzellen zu einem 14-stöckigen Wohnturm geschichtet. Die Idee der Wohnkapsel-Megastrukturen erfuhr noch einige

en raison de leur coût dépassant les prévisions. De même, les maisons du type Alba que Prouvé avait conçues pour l'organisation des sans-abri de l'abbé Pierre en 1956 ne remportèrent pas de succès.

Parallèlement aux bouleversements de société qui survinrent dans les années soixante, la perception de la préfabrication évolua aussi. À une période marquée par la navigation spatiale et l'atterrissage sur la lune, dans laquelle les livres pour enfants pronostiquaient déjà des week-ends sur de lointaines galaxies dans les années à venir, on découvrit le procédé de préfabrication comme forme expression artistique, voire on le considéra comme un moyen technique de créer des maisons offrant des conditions de vie à de nouvelles formes d'existence des individus, auxquelles on pensait accéder, à cette époque de croyance débridée dans le progrès. Parmi les maisons de la période de la conquête spatiale, on compte la Bulle six coques du Français Jean Maneval, avec laquelle un lotissement de vacances entier fut conçu en 1967 dans les Pyrénées et qui sembla littéralement faire de ce lieu le théâtre d'une invasion extra-terrestre. Ressemblant à des navettes spatiales, les pavillons Futuro en polyester renforcé de fibres de verre du Finnois Matti Suuronen datant de 1968 avaient eux aussi une apparence intergalactique.

L'idée de créer des mégastructures à partir de capsules d'habitation prit là son origine. En 1967, l'architecte Moshe Safdie à peine âgé de 24 ans présenta à l'Exposition universelle à Montréal sa mégastructure Habitat 67: 158 unités d'habitation composées de 354 modules de béton assemblés en une agglomération. Véritables utopies architecturales, des structures de bâtiments constituées de capsules d'habitation pouvant être agrandies et assemblées à volonté afin de constituer des villes entières furent développées par le groupe d'architectes britanniques Archigram. En 1972, l'architecte japonais Kisho Kurokawa réalisa à Tokyo la Nakagin Capsule Tower: des cellules préfabriquées furent empilées circulairement autour

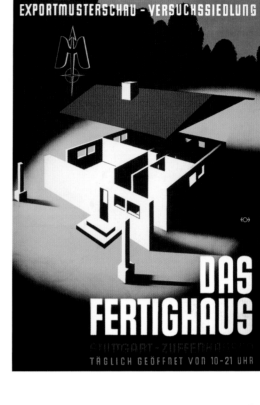

The ecology movement of the 1970s brought an end to this euphoria with regard to technological progress and futuristic architectural dreams. Now, highly modern building materials that did not seem to be in harmony with a return to nature—such as plastic or aluminum—fell into disrepute. This was further exacerbated by the fact that prefabricated elements had often been used to build high-density housing, which was now generally viewed negatively. Hence, prefabricated building now came to be associated with the aesthetic and social failure of de-individualized, megalomaniac, prefabricated slab housing blocks clustered on the periphery of large cities. Thus, the acceptance of the prefabricated house in large parts of Europe remained low up until the 1990s. Nevertheless, many very successful prefabricated houses were built. Manufacturers of prefabricated homes in Germany repeatedly hired ambitious architects for individual series, such as Otto Leitner, who developed the Ideal Haus for the Kaufhof chain of department stores in 1961. It was built by the Johann Huf carpentry workshop as a flat-roofed building resting on supports, clad in wood, with a panorama window, a porch swing seat, and an outdoor pool. Manfred Adam, a student of Sep Ruf's, also designed the equally successful and timelessly beautiful model for Huf, in 1972, called the Fachwerkhaus 2000. The prefabricated house called Tanja, designed in 1970 by Heinrich B. Hellmuth for the Schneckenburger company in Rottenburg, represented an interesting approach with its spacious layout and expressive pitched-roof. However, such ambitious prestige projects cannot conceal the fact that many prefabricated houses seemed provisional, banal or akin to barracks; the producers often attempted to make the product appear to be unique by adding elements that seemed to be individual.

Prefabricated construction only gradually began to again emancipate itself from a homespun, cheap, mass-produced image during the 1990s. This is mainly due to the use of computer-operated programs in the design and

Fortsetzungen, etwa in Zvi Heckers Siedlung Ramot in Jerusalem von 1974.

Darüber hinaus entwickelten experimentierfreudige Architekten Studien von Häusern, die Elemente der Fertigbauweise beinhalteten, aber gleichwohl Unikate blieben. Vertreter der britischen High-Tech-Architektur wie Alison und Peter Smithson, Richard Rogers oder Norman Foster entwickelten Ende der 1960er Jahre, fasziniert von der Idee fabrikgefertigter Metall- und Kunststoffkomponenten, Konzepte für eine auf Flexibilität und technische Verfeinerung abzielende Baupraxis, hatten aber kein ernsthaftes Interesse daran, ihre Entwürfe einer seriellen Fertigung zuzuführen. Dies galt etwa für das Zip-Up House von Richard Rogers (1968), eine auf pinkfarbenen Stützen ruhende knallgelbe Wohnbox, deren Aluminium-Paneele durch Gummidichtungen verbunden waren und die an das „Yellow Submarine" der Beatles erinnerte.

Die ökologische Bewegung der 1970er Jahre bereitete dieser Zukunfts- und Technikeuphorie und den futuristischen Architekturträumen ein Ende. Nun waren plötzlich hochmoderne Baumaterialien, die nicht in Einklang zu stehen schienen mit einer Rückkehr in den Schoß von Mutter Natur – wie etwa Kunststoff oder Aluminium –, schlecht beleumundet. Erschwerend kam noch hinzu, dass durch den Einsatz der Fertigbauweise im Massenwohnungsbau deren Idee generell in Verruf gebracht worden war. Vorgefertigtes Bauen wurde nun mit dem ästhetischen und sozialen Scheitern der entindividualisierten, megalomanen Plattenbauquartiere in den Speckgürteln der Großstädte in Verbindung gebracht.

Die gesellschaftliche Akzeptanz des Fertighauses sollte bis in die 1990er Jahre hinein gering bleiben. Und doch entstand eine große Zahl sehr erfolgreicher Fertighäuser. Deutsche Fertighaushersteller engagierten immer wieder ambitionierte Architekten für einzelne Serien: So entwickelte Otto Leitner 1961 für die Kaufhof-Kette das von der Firma Huf Haus gebaute

d'un noyau de béton sur une tour de 14 étages. L'idée de mégastructures de capsules d'habitation trouva son prolongement en 1974 dans le lotissement Ramot de Zvi Hecker à Jérusalem.

Par ailleurs, des architectes passionnés d'expérimentations développèrent des études de maisons comportant des éléments préfabriqués tout en restant des réalisations uniques. Fascinés par l'idée de composants métalliques ou plastiques préfabriqués en usine, des représentants de l'architecture high-tech britannique comme Alison et Peter Smithson, Richard Rogers ou Norman Foster inventèrent des concepts pour une pratique de l'architecture axée sur la flexibilité et le progrès technique, sans toutefois porter un intérêt sérieux à la production en série de leurs projets. Ceci valut par exemple pour la Zip-Up House de Richard Rogers (1968) – une boîte à habiter jaune vif sur des poteaux roses, aux panneaux d'aluminium raccordés par des joints de caoutchouc –, qui rappelait le fameux *Yellow Submarine* des Beatles.

Le mouvement écologique des années soixante-dix mit un terme à cette euphorie du futur et de la technique, ainsi qu'aux rêves d'une architecture futuriste. Tout à coup, les matériaux de construction les plus modernes qui ne semblaient pas en harmonie avec le retour vers mère Nature – tels que le plastique ou l'aluminium – avaient mauvaise réputation. Pour couronner le tout, l'utilisation de la préfabrication dans la construction massive de logements sociaux avait jeté le discrédit sur cette idée. La construction préfabriquée fut alors associée à un échec esthétique et social des logements mégalomanes désindividualisés des pourtours des grandes villes.

Ainsi l'adhésion sociale au concept des maisons préfabriquées resta-t-elle faible jusque dans les années quatre-vingt-dix. Malgré cela, un grand nombre de maisons préfabriquées couronnées de succès virent le jour. Des fabricants allemands du secteur engagèrent sans cesse des architectes ambitieux pour des séries particulières: en 1961, Otto Leitner conçut pour

The "House of the Future" at Disneyland in Anaheim, California, 1957, was an experiment in building with plastics.

Das „House of the Future" in Disneyland, Anaheim, Kalifornien von 1957 stellte den Versuch dar, Plastik als hauptsächliches Baumaterial zu verwenden.

La «House of the Future» à Disneyland, Anaheim, Californie, en 1957, est une tentative d'utilisation du plastique comme matériau de construction principal.

production processes. The prefabricated housing industry now stands at a juncture reminiscent of the dynamism of the 1920s and 1930s. In the meantime, even star architects such as Daniel Libeskind have designed prefabricated houses, and these are produced and equipped according to state-of-the-art ecological criteria. Unlike the case during the early Modernist period, planners' visions are now no longer threatened by failure due to inadequate building technology. Today it is a very short path from Computer Aided Design (CAD) to the computer-controlled production of building components with previously unimaginable precision. It is now impossible to build a passive house, for example, without using prefabricated components that can only be produced within tolerances of less than a millimeter by using CAD. The tools used in industrial production are so flexible that the components no longer need to be slavishly standardized as was the case in traditional production, and measurements can now be easily varied.

In the meantime, houses are emerging in Europe, Asia, and in North and South America, that are particularly interesting in terms of design. Rocio Romero's LV House (2000) for instance, or the weeHouse by Alchemy Architects (2003), appear to be the most recent re-interpretations of Ludwig Mies van der Rohe's Farnsworth House. For many years now, companies like Muji in Japan or BoKlok in Scandinavia—and more recently also in Poland and England—have been supplying prefabricated houses in large numbers. In Sweden alone, with only nine million inhabitants, 14,000 units are sold every year. Muji offers models designed by Kengo Kuma and Kazuhiko Namba that are as simple as they are elegant, and far more interesting than the building-kit houses offered by the multinational concerns Mitsubishi, Toyota, and Panasonic. Katsu Umebayashi of F.O.B. Architects in Kyoto established the company F.O.B. Homes along with his colleague Kazu Kobayashi in Tokyo in 1999 in order to develop a modernistic prefab-

„Ideal-Haus", einen aufgeständerten, holzlattenverkleideten Flachdachbau mit Panoramafenstern, Hollywoodschaukel und Außenpool. Manfred Adam, ein Schüler Sep Rufs, entwarf 1972, ebenfalls für die Firma Huf Haus, das ebenso erfolgreiche wie zeitlos-schöne „Fachwerkhaus 2000" – ein Modell, das bis heute in Deutschland sehr erfolgreich ist und unlängst sogar nach China exportiert wurde. Auch das von Heinrich B. Hellmuth 1970 konzipierte Fertighaus „Tanja" für das Rottenburger Unternehmen Schneckenburger bot mit sehr großzügigem Raumprogramm und expressiver Satteldachform interessante Ansätze. Doch solche ambitionierte Vorzeigeprojekte können nicht darüber hinwegtäuschen, dass viele Fertigbauhäuser provisorisch, banal und barackenhaft wirkten; häufig versuchten die Hersteller das Produkt durch Hinzufügung individuell wirkender Elemente mit dem Anschein eines Unikats zu versehen.

Erst seit den 1990er Jahren emanzipiert sich die Fertigbauweise allmählich wieder vom Ruf des hausbackenen, billigen Massenprodukts. Und das verdankt sie vor allem dem Einsatz von computergesteuerten Programmen im Entwurf- und Fertigungsverfahren. Die Fertighausbranche steht mittlerweile vor einem Aufbruch, der an die Dynamik der 1920er und 1920er Jahre denken lässt. Inzwischen entwerfen selbst Star-Architekten wie Daniel Libeskind Häuser in Fertigbauweise, die nach neuesten ökologischen Kriterien hergestellt und eingerichtet sind. Denn anders als in den Zeiten der jungen Moderne muss heute planerische Phantasie nicht mehr an mangelhafter Bautechnik scheitern. Der Weg vom computergestützten Entwurf (CAD) zur computergesteuerten Fertigung der Elemente in nie dagewesener Präzision ist kurz geworden. Passivhäuser etwa lassen sich heute gar nicht anders realisieren als unter Einsatz vorgefertigter Teile, die nur durch das CAD-Verfahren millimetergenau hergestellt werden können. Die Fertigungsmaschinen der Industrie sind darüber hinaus so flexibel, dass, anders als in traditioneller Vorfertigung, die Bauteile nicht mehr dem

la chaîne Kaufhof l'Ideal-Haus construite par la menuiserie Johann Huf, un bâtiment surélevé à toit plat, à revêtement de lattes de bois, avec fenêtres panoramiques, balancelle et piscine extérieure. En 1972, Manfred Adam, élève de Sep Ruf, projeta pour Huf également la maison à colombage Huf 2000, tout aussi connue et d'une beauté intemporelle. La maison préfabriquée Tanja de H.B. Hellmuth conçue en 1970 pour l'entreprise Schneckenburger de Rottenburg offrait également une approche intéressante. Pourtant, ce genre de modèles ambitieux ne parvint pas à occulter l'aspect provisoire, banal, l'air de bicoque de nombreuses maisons préfabriquées. Pour toutes ces raisons, les fabricants essayaient souvent de les doter d'éléments individuels, afin de leur donner une apparence unique. Ce n'est que depuis les années quatre-vingt-dix que la construction préfabriquée s'émancipe peu à peu de cette réputation de produit de masse fade et de mauvaise qualité. Et ce, grâce au recours aux programmes de conception assistés par ordinateur pour la création et la réalisation. Entre-temps, le secteur des maisons préfabriquées est au seuil d'un nouveau départ, rappelant la dynamique des années vingt et trente. Et même les architectes de renom comme Daniel Libeskind projettent des maisons préfabriquées, produites et équipées selon les tous derniers standards écologiques. Contrairement à l'époque des jeunes modernes, l'imagination dans la planification ne doit plus échouer devant une technologie défaillante. Du plan esquissé sur ordinateur à la fabrication informatisée des éléments d'une précision jamais égalée jusque-là, le chemin est devenu plus court. Les maisons passives, par exemple, ne sont plus réalisées aujourd'hui sans le recours à des éléments préfabriqués produits au millimètre près par des procédés CAO. Les machines de production industrielles sont d'une telle flexibilité que, contrairement à la préfabrication traditionnelle, les éléments de construction n'ont plus besoin d'être strictement standardisés, étant donné que les dimensions peuvent varier sans problème.

ricated house that can be individually adapted to the clients' requirements, in terms of both the building's volume and the layout of the rooms, by the company's own team of designers.

In view of questions regarding energy consumption, recycling, sustainability, and cost efficiency, ideas like Adam Kalkin's emerge of constructing houses entirely out of decommissioned shipping containers. The basic version of his Quik House consists of six reusable cargo containers. The individual modules are assembled using a crane in one day; the house is ready for habitation within three months. The perforations required for doors and windows are made beforehand in consultation with the customer. Including heating and plumbing fixtures, the basic version of the Quik House, with three bedrooms, two bathrooms, and a total of 2,000 sq.ft. of floor space, costs roughly $184,000. Kalkin does not really act as an architect, but instead offers the customer a system that allows them to assemble their own living containers. However, concepts of this type have their limits. A decommissioned container can be purchased for roughly €2,000, while a new one from the factory costs roughly €4,000. An old container intended for conversion is dented and rusty and requires extensive refurbishment: doors and windows must be cut out and sufficient insulation must be provided. Transportation ultimately costs roughly €9.00 per mile, and a crane is needed to install the container modules on site. This is a clear indication of how an idea, which is interesting from the standpoint of recycling, becomes problematic not only in economic terms, but also ecologically, in terms of the carbon footprint made by refurbishment and transport.

What will the prefabricated house of the future look like? Will it have a steel frame or be a wooden structure, built as a skeleton or panel system? Or will there be yet again a greater tendency to shift to the old idea of the "residential cell" and to favor residential units that can be easily moved

Diktat der Standardisierung unterworfen sind, sondern sich in ihren Größen problemlos variieren lassen.

In Europa, Asien und Amerika entstehen mittlerweile Fertighäuser von hoher gestalterischer Qualität. Rocio Romeros LV-Haus (2000) oder das weeHouse von Alchemy Architects (2003) erscheinen wie aktuelle Neuinterpretationen von Mies van der Rohes Farnsworth-Haus. Schon seit vielen Jahren bedienen Firmen wie Muji in Japan oder BoKlok in Skandinavien und seit kurzem auch in Polen und England den Markt der Fertighäuser in größerem Umfang. Allein in Schweden mit seinen neun Millionen Einwohnern werden jedes Jahr 14000 Hauseinheiten verkauft. Muji hat mit ebenso schlichten wie eleganten Entwürfen von Kengo Kuma oder Kazuhiko Namba Modelle im Angebot, die weit interessanter sind als die Baukastenhäuser von Multis wie Mitsubishi, Toyota oder Panasonic. Katsu Umebayashi vom Büro F.O.B. Architects in Kyoto und sein Kollege Kazu Kobayashi gründeten 1999 in Tokio die Firma F.O.B. Homes, um ein modernistisches Fertighaus zu entwickeln, dessen Gebäudevolumen und Raumaufteilung vom hauseigenen Designerteam individuellen Kundenansprüchen angepasst werden kann.

Vor dem Hintergrund von Fragen zur Energiebilanz, Wiederverwertbarkeit, Nachhaltigkeit und Kosteneffizienz entstanden Ideen wie die von Adam Kalkin, ein Haus allein aus ausgedienten Schiffscontainern zu bauen. Sein Quik-Haus besteht in der Basis-Version aus sechs wiederverwerteten Frachtcontainern. Die einzelnen Module werden vor Ort an einem Tag mit einem Kran zusammengesetzt, bezugsfertig ist das Haus dann nach knapp drei Monaten. Die für Fenster und Türen notwendigen Einschnitte in den Boxen werden in Abstimmung mit dem Kunden vorab vorgenommen. Inklusive der Heizung und Sanitäranlagen kostet die Grundversion des Quik-Hauses mit drei Schlafzimmern und zwei Bädern auf einer Fläche von 185 m² rund 184000 $. Kalkin betätigt sich im Grunde nicht wirklich

Entre-temps, des solutions de grande qualité créative voient le jour en Europe, en Asie et en Amérique du Nord ou du Sud. La LV-Home (2000) de Rocio Romero ou la weeHouse des Alchemy Architects (2003) apparaissent comme des réinterprétations contemporaines de la maison Farnsworth de Mies van der Rohe. Depuis plusieurs années déjà, des entreprises comme Muji au Japon ou BoKlok en Scandinavie, et depuis peu également en Pologne et en Angleterre, fournissent en grande quantité le marché des maisons préfabriquées. Rien que pour la Suède et ses neuf millions d'habitants, 14000 unités sont vendues par an. Avec ses modèles sobres et élégants de Kengo Kuma ou de Kazuhiko Namba, Muji a une offre bien plus intéressante que les maisons modulaires des multinationales telles que Mitsubishi, Toyota ou Panasonic. Katsu Umebayashi du cabinet F.O.B. Architects à Kyoto et son collègue Kazu Kobayashi ont créé en 1999 l'entreprise F.O.B. Homes à Tokyo, ayant pour but la conception d'une maison préfabriquée moderniste dont le volume et la disposition des pièces peuvent être adaptés aux exigences individuelles du client par l'équipe de designers de l'entreprise.

En matière de bilan énergétique, de recyclabilité, de durabilité et de rapport coût/efficacité, on rencontre des idées comme celles d'Adam Kalkin de construire une maison à partir de simples containers maritimes recyclés. Les différents modules sont assemblés sur site en une journée à l'aide d'une grue. La maison est prête à être occupée au bout de trois mois à peine. En accord avec le client, les ouvertures nécessaires pour les fenêtres et les portes sont pratiquées au préalable dans les boîtes. Chauffage et sanitaires compris, la version de base de la maison Quik à trois chambres et deux salles de bains et une surface avoisinant les 185 m² coûte environ 184000 $. Kalkin n'agit pas vraiment ici en tant qu'architecte, mais propose un système grâce auquel le client peut composer son propre container d'habitation. Mais ce type de concept a ses limites. Un container au rebut coûte environ

and quickly deployed anywhere? The Modernist ideals of producing intelligently designed, bright, and low-cost living spaces are currently being revitalized. In 1929, the visionary architect Richard Buckminster Fuller was asked whether the mass production of residential buildings would ultimately lead to architects' losing their jobs. Fuller responded: "The architect's efforts today are spent in the gratification of the individual client. His efforts of tomorrow, like those of the composer, the designer of fabrics, silver, glass and whatnot may be expanded for the enjoyment of vast numbers of unseen clients. Industrial production of housing, as contrasted with the present industrial production of raw materials and miscellaneous accessories, calls for more skill and a higher development of the design element, not its cessation."

als Architekt, sondern bietet ein System an, mit dem der Kunde sich seinen eigenen Wohncontainer zusammenstellen kann. Derartige Konzepte haben jedoch ihre Grenzen. Ein ausgesonderter Container ist für etwa 2 000 € zu bekommen, während ein neuer ab Werk etwa 4 000 € kostet. Der zum Umbau vorgesehene alte Container ist verbeult und verrostet und muss aufwendig bearbeitet werden: Tür- und Fenstereinschnitte müssen vorgenommen, eine ausreichende Wärmedämmung gewährleistet werden. Für den Transport fallen Kosten von etwa 300 € pro 50 km an, und auf dem Grundstück ist ein Kran erforderlich, der die Container-Module zu einem Haus vereint. Hier wird deutlich, wie eine vom ökologischen Standpunkt der Wiederverwertbarkeit interessante Idee nicht nur unter ökonomischen Gesichtspunkten problematisch wird, sondern auch – angesichts der CO_2-Bilanz für Aufarbeitung und Transport – unter ökologischen. Wie wird das Fertighaus der Zukunft aussehen? Wird es eine Stahlrahmen- oder eine Holzkonstruktion sein, errichtet im Skelett- oder Tafelbau? Oder wird man sich doch wieder auf die alte Idee der ‚Raumzelle' verlegen und leicht bewegbare, überall einfach und schnell aufzustellende Wohneinheiten bevorzugen? Die Ideale der Moderne, gestalterisch durchdachte, lichte und kostengünstige Wohnformen zu entwickeln, erneuern sich gegenwärtig mit Macht. 1929 wurde der Architekturvisionär Richard Buckminster Fuller gefragt, ob denn die Massenfertigung von Wohnhäusern den Architekten nicht am Ende arbeitslos machen würde. Fuller verneinte: „Heute bemüht sich der Architekt darum, den Wünschen seines einzelnen Kunden zu genügen. Wie der Designer von Stoffen, Silber, Glas und anderen Dingen seine Entwürfe mit dem Ziel anfertigt, den Lebensgenuss einer möglichst großen Zahl von Menschen zu erhöhen, erfordert die Massenproduktion von Häusern eine Steigerung des architektonischen Könnens und nicht dessen Abschaffung."

2 000 €, alors qu'un nouveau en départ usine en vaut à peu près 4 000 €. Le vieux container destiné à être transformé est cabossé et rouillé et doit faire l'objet de lourdes réparations: les ouvertures des portes et des fenêtres doivent être découpées, une isolation thermique suffisante doit être posée. Pour le transport, on doit compter avec des coûts de l'ordre de 300 € pour 50 km, et sur le terrain, une grue s'impose pour réunir les containers en une maison. Cet exemple montre qu'une idée de recyclage, intéressante du point de vue écologique, peut poser problème sur le plan économique, tout comme sur le plan écologique, au vu de l'émission de CO_2 liée au travail de remise en état et au transport.
À quoi ressemblera la maison préfabriquée du futur? À une construction à ossature d'acier ou de bois, à une construction à ossature ou en panneaux? Ou reviendra-t-on à l'ancienne idée des «cellules d'habitation» et préfèrera-t-on les modules faciles à déplacer et rapides à positionner? Les idéaux des modernes, de créer des formes au design réfléchi, lumineuses et bon marché, connaissent un renouveau puissant. En 1929 l'architecte visionnaire Richard Buckminster Fuller fut interrogé sur les possibles répercussions de la production industrielle d'habitations sur l'activité des architectes. Fuller répondit par la négative: «L'architecte s'efforce aujourd'hui de satisfaire les vœux de chaque client. Tout comme les designers de tissus, de l'argent, du verre et de toute autre chose élaborent leurs projets dans le but d'accroître la joie de vivre du plus grand nombre possible, la production industrielle de maisons exige un accroissement du savoir-faire architectonique, et non pas son éradication.»

MANNING PORTABLE COLONIAL COTTAGE

London, Great Britain
1833–1840

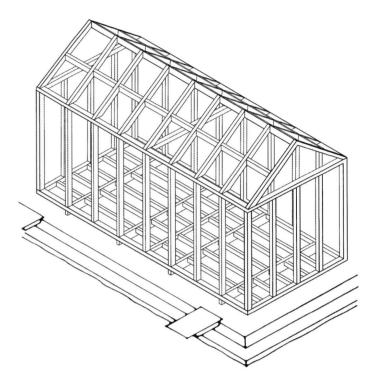

Opposite page: Watercolor of Lieutenant Governor Charles La Trobe's house by R. A. Bastow, 1913

Rechte Seite: Aquarell vom Wohnhaus des Gouverneurs Charles La Trobe, R. A. Bastow, 1913

Page de droite: Aquarelle de la maison d'habitation du gouverneur Charles La Trobe, R. A. Bastow, 1913

Around 1833 a London carpenter named Herbert Manning designed a portable, easy-to-assemble wooden house for his son, who intended to emigrate to Australia. The cottage had a wooden frame and a pitched roof. The supporting posts and beams were already cut to length and could be screwed together on site. The roof was made of tent canvas. Grooves were cut into the posts, which stood about a yard apart, so that the prefabricated full-length wall, door, and window panels could be fitted into them. Since the wave of immigration from England to Australia began to swell in the years after 1833, there was suddenly a great demand for portable, easy-to-assemble housing of the type that Manning had developed. An advertisement for Manning's "Portable Colonial Cottages" published in the *South Australian Record* on November 27, 1837, is the first evidence of his entrepreneurial initiative, and Manning actually did ship dozens of prefabricated cottages to Australia in subsequent years. The fact that the building components could be easily transported over great distances contributed to the success of the cottages. In the Australian city of Melbourne, the Manning Cottage built in 1839 for Charles La Trobe, who later became the Lieutenant Governor of Victoria, can still be viewed with many of its original furnishings.

Long before the word "prefabrication" even existed, Manning had developed a system that worked by precisely adhering to standard measurements. With panels, posts, and plates that each had the same length, breadth and thickness, and thus could be easily installed, Manning created the prototype of the modern prefabricated house.

Um 1833 entwarf ein Londoner Zimmermann namens Herbert Manning ein transportables und leicht zu montierendes Holzhaus für seinen Sohn, der nach Australien auswandern wollte. Das Cottage war eine Holzrahmenkonstruktion mit Satteldach, deren Stützpfosten und Querbalken bereits zugeschnitten waren und vor Ort verschraubt werden konnten. Das Dach bestand aus Zeltleinwand. Die Pfosten hatten einen Abstand von knapp 1 m und waren mit Nuten versehen, in die vorgefertigte raumhohe Wand-, Tür- und Fensterpaneele eingesetzt wurden.

Da in den Jahren nach 1833 eine regelrechte Auswanderungswelle von England nach Australien einsetzte, entstand plötzlich ein Bedarf nach transportablem und leicht montierbarem Wohnraum, wie ihn Manning entwickelt hatte. Eine Werbeanzeige für Mannings „Portable Colonial Cottages", die am 27. November 1837 im „South Australian Record" erschien, ist der erste Beleg für seine unternehmerische Initiative, und tatsächlich ließ Manning in den folgenden Jahren Dutzende seiner vorgefertigten Cottages nach Australien verschiffen. Zum Erfolg trug bei, dass die Bauteile auch über größere Distanzen problemlos transportiert werden konnten. Im australischen Melbourne kann man bis heute jenes Manning Cottage, das der spätere britische Generalgouverneur Charles La Trobe 1839 aufgebaut hatte, mit Teilen der Originaleinrichtung besichtigen.

Lange bevor das Wort „Vorfertigung" überhaupt existierte, hatte Manning ein System entwickelt, das mit präzise eingehaltenen Standardmaßen arbeitete. Mit Paneelen, Pfosten und Platten, die alle jeweils die gleiche Länge, Breite und Dicke hatten und ohne große Schwierigkeiten installiert werden konnten, schuf Manning den Prototyp des modernen Fertighausbaus.

En 1833, un charpentier londonien du nom de Herbert Manning inventa une maison en bois transportable et facile à monter pour son fils qui projetait d'émigrer en Australie. Le cottage à toit en bâtière avait une ossature de bois. Ses poteaux et poutres étaient déjà taillés sur mesure et pouvaient être assemblés sur site à l'aide de vis. Le toit était en toile de tente. Les poteaux espacés d'à peine 1 m comportaient des rainures dans lesquelles étaient insérés les panneaux de cloisons, portes et fenêtres de toute hauteur.

Les années suivantes connurent une véritable vague d'émigration de l'Angleterre vers l'Australie, entraînant un besoin soudain d'habitations transportables et faciles à assembler qui correspondaient au projet développé par Manning. Une annonce publicitaire pour les Portable Colonial Cottages de Manning, parue le 27 novembre 1837 dans le *South Australian Record*, est la première trace d'une tentative de commercialisation. En effet, les années suivantes, Manning envoya par bateau des douzaines de cottages préfabriqués vers l'Australie. Le transport facile des éléments de construction sur de longues distances contribua à ce succès. On peut encore visiter à Melbourne le cottage de Manning assemblé en 1839 par Charles La Trobe, futur lieutenant-gouverneur britannique en Australie, avec des parties de l'équipement d'origine.

Bien longtemps avant que le terme de « préfabrication » n'existe, Manning avait développé un système fonctionnant avec des mesures standard méticuleusement respectées. À l'aide de panneaux, de poteaux et de dalles, tous respectivement de la même longueur, largeur et épaisseur et pouvant être installés sans grande difficulté, Manning avait créé le prototype de la construction de la maison préfabriquée moderne.

Opposite page: Quaker Meeting House, North Adelaide, 1840

Linke Seite: Quaker Meeting House, North Adelaide, 1840

Page de gauche: Quaker Meeting House, North Adelaide, 1840

Left and below: Lieutenant Governor Charles La Trobe's house, Jolimont (Melbourne), 1839–1840

Links und unten: Wohnhaus des Gouverneurs Charles La Trobe, Jolimont (Melbourne), 1839–1840

En bas à gauche: Maison d'habitation du gouverneur Charles La Trobe, Jolimont (Melbourne), 1839–1840

HODGSON HOUSES

**E.F. Hodgson Company, Dover, Massachusetts, USA
1894–1944**

Opposite page: Hodgson House in Reedsville, West Virginia, around 1936

Rechte Seite: Hodgson-Haus in Reedsville, West Virginia, um 1936

Page de droite: Maison Hodgson à Reedsville, Virginie-Occidentale, vers 1936

Ernest Franklin Hodgson, the son of a farmer from Massachusetts, began breeding poultry at an early age and was soon building his own brooders and chicken coops. In 1891, at the age of 21, Hodgson began producing his "Peep-o'-Day portable coops and brooders" in series on his father's property in the town of Dover, near Boston. Using a simple building system based on prefabricated wooden elements joined by wedge key bolts instead of nails, he soon began building dog houses, pigeon coops, tool sheds, and, finally, the one-room "Hodgson Camp Cottage", which he offered in his first mail order catalogue in 1894. The introduction of a garage that could be built quickly and easily in 1900, the "Hodgson Auto Stable", was particular successful. In 1902, Hodgson brought his "Portable Vacation Cottages" onto the market, and they were soon followed by larger houses.

Despite the rapidly growing competition—e.g. as of 1908 from the Sears Roebuck mail-order catalogue company—business flourished. A Hodgson Bungalow was even depicted in newspaper advertisements published by the Boston Edison Company in 1908, illustrating the advantages of electricity. A year later, Hodgson delivered 20 prefabricated houses to Messina, Sicily, in order to provide shelter for the victims of a flood. Hodgson built hospitals, schools, churches and, above all, residential buildings that were attractively presented to customers in Boston, New York, and other large cities in newspaper advertisements and at exhibitions.

The catalogue ultimately offered four different models with designates that reflected their floor plans, namely I, T, L, and H. They all had one-story and were based on the same system of 6 x 12-ft. wooden elements used for the walls (with a window or a door where needed), the roof, and the floor. The walls and ceilings consisted of red cedar rabbeted boarding backed with a heavy fiber lining, and the floors were of hard pine. All of the elements were either of exposed wood or painted: if the customer did not choose otherwise, the walls were gray, the window frames ivory, and the decorative

Ernest Franklin Hodgson, Bauernsohn aus Massachusetts, züchtete schon als Jugendlicher Geflügel und baute sich dafür seine eigenen Brutkästen und Hühnerställe. 1891, mit 21 Jahren, begann Hodgson auf dem Grundstück seines Vaters in Dover, einem Ort in der Nähe von Boston, mit der Serienproduktion von „Peep-o'-Day portable coops and brooders" („Peep-o'-Day tragbare Ställe und Brutkästen"). Mit seinem simplen Bausystem aus vorgefertigten Holzelementen, die nicht genagelt, sondern mit Keilbolzen verbunden wurden, fertigte er bald auch Hundehütten, Taubenschläge, Geräteschuppen und schließlich das aus einem Zimmer bestehende „Hodgson Camp Cottage", das er 1894 in seinem ersten Versandkatalog anbot. Ein großer Erfolg wurde 1900 der „Hodgson Auto Stable", eine Garage, die schnell und einfach aufzubauen war. 1902 brachte Hodgson die „Portable Vacation Cottages" auf den Markt, denen bald größere Wohnhaustypen folgten.

Trotz der rasch wachsenden Konkurrenz – seit 1908 zum Beispiel durch das Versandhaus Sears Roebuck – florierte das Geschäft. In den Zeitungsanzeigen der Firma Edison, die den Bostonern 1908 den Nutzen der Elektrizität demonstrieren sollten, war ein Hodgson Bungalow abgebildet. Ein Jahr später lieferte Hodgson 20 Fertighäuser nach Messina auf Sizilien, in denen obdachlos gewordene Opfer einer Sturmflut untergebracht werden sollten. Hodgson baute Krankenhäuser, Schulen, Kirchen, vor allem aber Wohnhäuser, die den Kunden durch Zeitungsanzeigen und auf Ausstellungen in Boston, New York und anderen großen Städten schmackhaft gemacht wurden.

Vier Typen, nach der Form ihrer Grundrisse I, T, L und H benannt, bot der Katalog schließlich an. Sie waren alle eingeschossig und basierten auf demselben System: 1,80 x 3,60 m (6 x 12 Fuß) großen Holzelementen für die Wände (wenn nötig mit Fenster oder Tür), das Dach und den Fußboden. Wände und Decken bestanden aus genuteten Zedernbrettern, mit einer

Dès son adolescence, Ernest Franklin Hodgson, fils de fermier du Massachusetts, éleva des volailles et se construisit ses propres couvoirs et poulaillers. En 1891, alors qu'il avait 21 ans, Hodgson lança la production en série des «Peep-o'-Day portable coops and brooders» («couvoirs et poulaillers portables Peep-o'-Day») sur la propriété de son père à Dover, à proximité de Boston. Partant d'un principe de construction élémentaire à partir d'éléments de bois préfabriqués, non pas cloués, mais reliés par des clavettes de serrage, il construisit bientôt également des niches, des pigeonniers, des remises à outils, et, finalement, le «Hodgson Camp Cottage» à une pièce, qu'il proposa en 1894 dans son tout premier catalogue de vente par correspondance. En 1900, le «Hodgson Auto Stable», un garage simple à montage rapide, rencontra un grand succès. En 1902, Hodgson lança sur le marché ses «Portable Vacation Cottages», rapidement suivis de modèles d'immeubles d'habitation plus spacieux.

En dépit de la concurrence croissante, comme celle de l'entreprise de vente par correspondance Sears Roebuck depuis 1908, son commerce prospérait. Dans les petites annonces du journal de l'entreprise Edison qui devait démontrer les bienfaits de l'électricité aux habitants de Boston, un bungalow Hodgson était représenté. Un an plus tard, Hodgson livra vingt maisons préfabriquées à Messine en Sicile, qui devaient abriter les victimes d'un raz de marée privées de domicile. Hodgson construisit des hôpitaux, des écoles, des églises, mais surtout des immeubles d'habitation qui suscitaient l'intérêt des clients en faisant l'objet d'annonces de presse et d'expositions à Boston, New York et dans d'autres grandes villes.

Le catalogue finit par proposer quatre modèles de plain-pied, dénommés en fonction de la forme de leur plan: I, T, L et H. Ils se fondaient tous sur le même système: des éléments en bois de 1,80 m x 3,60 m (6 x 12 pieds) pour les murs (avec fenêtre et porte le cas échéant), le toit et les planchers. Murs et plafonds étaient constitués de panneaux de cèdre à rainures doublés de

Hodgson Unit System

All the 12 foot wide houses shown in this catalog are made up of 6 x 12 ft. units as shown and described here, so that with the porches, ells, valley roofs, etc., it is possible to make up most any arrangement of rooms desired. With the price list in the back of the catalog you can figure out any special combination, or make changes in those shown.

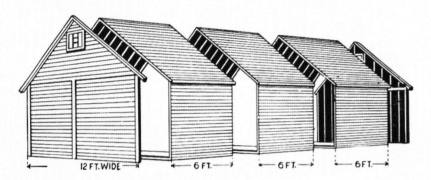

Blank Units (disjointed)

UNITS

This drawing shows three 6 x 12 units and two 12 ft. ends. If put together they would make a house 12 x 18 ft. The prices of these units and ends are in the price list, and to the prices of these blank units should be added the prices of the windows, doors, blinds, etc., these details being shown below. All prices are in the back of the catalog.

PARTITIONS

These 12 ft. partitions can be used at any of the junctions of the 6 ft. units, thereby forming rooms 6, 12, and 18 ft. in length. The opening is furnished with a curtain pole, but if a door is preferred consult the price list. The opening can be at either side or centre of the partition and can be changed at will.

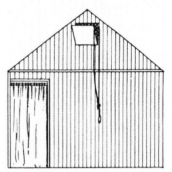

Partitions—See pages 43 and 50

         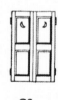

SRW   B W B   DW   CW   DCW   PD   GD   DGD   FGD   SS   CS

These drawings show the different styles of windows, doors, etc. that are used in our houses. These can be located in the units where desired, and the prices will be found in the back of the catalog.

WINDOW AND DOOR DETAIL:—S. R. W.—Sunroom Window; W.—Regular Window; B.—Blinds; D. W.—Diamond Light Window; C. W.—Casement Window; D. C. W.—Casement Window Diamond Lights; T. W.—Transom Window; P. D.—Panel Door; G. D.—Glass Door; D. G. D.—Dutch Glass Door; F. G. D.—French Glass Door; R. D.—Door to roll; S. S.—Solid Shutter to bolt on; C. S. —Crescent shutters hinged like blinds.

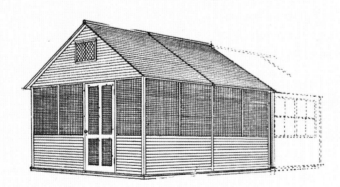

Screened Room Unit 12 x 12 ft.
See pages 26-28-32-50

SCREENED ROOM UNIT

Screened room units are the same size and price as the regular units and the prices include the screens made of galvanized netting. They can be attached to the regular units or made into buildings by themselves as shown on pages 82 and 83. With Storm Awnings, as shown on page 50 will give protection from sun and storms.

PRICES IN BACK OF CATALOG

VALLEY ROOF UNIT

Valley Roof units are used to add rooms at right angles to other rooms. If a house has several rooms it is wise to use a valley roof rather than to run too many rooms in one line. By its use a more practical arrangement of rooms may be had.

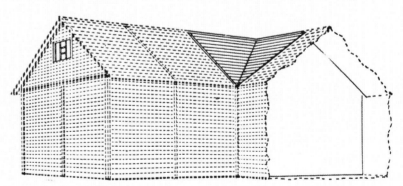

Valley Roof Unit. See pages 34-40-44-46-49
For HIP ROOFS, in place of gables, add $10.00 per end or $20 more for a complete hip roof. (See pages 40-46.)

Pages from the Hodgson Houses
cataloges for 1908 (below) and 1920
(opposite page)

Seiten aus Katalogen der Hodgson-
Häuser von 1908 (unten) und 1920
(linke Seite)

Pages du catalogue des maisons
Hodgson de 1908 (en bas) et de 1920
(page de gauche)

Above: Wedge key bolts used to
assemble a housen

Oben: Keilbolzen, die zur
Hausmontage dienten

En haut: Clavettes de serrage qui
servaient au montage de la maison

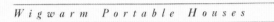

Page Eight **E. F. Hodgson, Dover, Massachusetts**

WIGWARM
CONSTRUCTION

The Wigwarm construction is different from that of other portable houses. Practically speaking, it is a framed house, although lighter than the regularly built house, its frame work is much closer together, making a very strong construction. Washington ceder and fir are used with door and window frames moulded out of heavy fir stock.

Wigwarm Frame Construction

Each house is made up of several sections and they are fastened together with Wigwarm key bolts of special design, and with one blow of a hammer the wedge key tightens up the bolt, saving much time and annoyance during erection or taking apart. The frames are covered with a very heavy waterproof fibre (Wigwarm lining) and then with the Wigwarm special milled, narrow, rabbeted siding not over three to four inches in width. This siding is milled especially for the Wigwarm houses out of California redwood, and is fastened to the frame with Wigwarm galvanized, cement-coated nails. In the construction of one of the small sized Wigwarm houses (10 x 12 feet) over three thousand nails are used. So rigid is its construction that they have withstood gales on the New England coast that have destroyed many staunch buildings about them. Many times sections of the Wigwarm Houses have remained out on the ground unprotected, for three days at a time, with heavy rains, yet when set up they have gone together without the slightest trouble. This construction, although expensive, will not warp or twist, so that a building can be set up any number of times without trouble.

Every house is set up at the factory and the sections stamped, and with the printed directions and plan it is easily put together by unskilled labor without other tools than a screw driver and hammer. All necessary hardware is furnished, and strap irons to fasten them to the foundation. All through the entire construction nothing but the best of lumber, free from defects and knots, is used. In order to make the most perfect portable construction known today practically all the materials entering into the Wigwarm construction are made especially for Wigwarm Houses. Cheaper construction and materials could be used, but the houses would not stand up and would disappoint the person buying them.

Detailed construction of the different sections used to make up a house is given on pages 10 and 11.

Wigwarm Portable Houses *Page Nineteen*

WIGWARM COTTAGES

These two combinations include three large rooms, an ell, and front and side porches. For description of porches and ell, see page 28. Cottage furnishings page 12. Freight rates page 46.

Combination No. 85

One Room 10 x 12 feet	$130
Two Additional Rooms each 10 x 12 feet	220
One Front Porch 6 x 10 feet	35
One Side Porch (one door) 6 x 12 feet	30
One Ell 6 x 6½ feet	40
Total weight, 4,150 lbs. Total,	$455

Combination No. 86

One Room 12 x 12 feet	$155
Two Additional Rooms, each 12 x 12 feet	260
One Front Porch 6 x 12 feet	45
One Side Porch (one door) 6 x 12 feet	30
One Ell 6 x 8½ feet	50
Total weight, 5,050 lbs. Total,	$540

Combination No. 85 *Combination No. 86*

Wigwarm Cottage—Three Rooms, Front and Side Porch and Ell

37

Hodgson Houses in Bristol, Maine

Hodgson-Häuser in Bristol, Maine

Maisons Hodgson à Bristol, Maine

ornaments leaf green. All that was needed to build the house was a hammer in order to connect the building parts by means of the wedge key bolts. Clients could opt to have Hodgson or a local company install heating, bathrooms, toilets or even an open fireplace, features that, even by the 1930s, were by no means considered basic amenities in houses in rural America. Ernest Franklin Hodgson, who proudly referred to himself as "America's First Prefabricator", sold the Hodgson Company in 1944. He died four years later; the company he founded continued to exist under various names until 1995.

Hinterfütterung aus schwerem Textilgewebe, die Böden aus hartem Kiefernholz. Alle Elemente waren holzsichtig oder bemalt: die Wände, wenn vom Kunden nicht anders gewünscht, grau, die Fensterrahmen elfenbeinfarben, die Schmuckornamente laubgrün. Alles, was dem Bauherrn noch zu tun blieb, war, einen Hammer in die Hand zu nehmen und die Bauteile durch Keilbolzen miteinander zu verbinden.
Hodgson oder lokale Firmen vor Ort installierten – je nach Wunsch – Heizung, Badezimmer, Toilette oder auch einen offenen Kamin, alles Elemente, die auch in den 1930er Jahren noch keineswegs zur Grundausstattung eines Hauses im ländlichen Amerika gehörten.
Ernest Franklin Hodgson, der sich stolz „America's First Prefabricator" nannte, verkaufte die Hodgson Company 1944. Er starb vier Jahre später; das von ihm gegründete Unternehmen existierte unter verschiedenen Namen noch bis 1995.

robustes fibres textiles, les planchers de bois de pin dur. Tous les éléments présentaient un revêtement de bois ou étaient peints: les murs – sauf contrordre du client – étaient gris, les cadres de fenêtres, couleur ivoire, les éléments décoratifs vert feuille. Il ne restait plus au fermier qu'à prendre un marteau à la main et à assembler les éléments de construction à l'aide de clavettes de serrage.
Selon les desiderata, Hodgson ou des entreprises locales installèrent le chauffage, la salle de bains, les toilettes et même une cheminée ouverte sur site, autant d'éléments qui, même dans les années trente, n'appartenaient aucunement à l'équipement de base d'une maison de l'Amérique rurale.
Ernest Franklin Hodgson, qui se dénommait fièrement «America's First Prefabricator», vendit la Hodgson Company en 1944. Il mourut quatre années plus tard, mais l'entreprise qu'il avait créée continua d'exister sous diverses appellations jusqu'en 1995.

EINSTEIN HOUSE

Christoph & Unmack AG, Niesky, Germany
1929

Right: Albert Einstein at the window
of his summer house, 1929

Rechts: Albert Einstein am Fenster
seines Sommerhauses, 1929

À droite: Albert Einstein à la fenêtre
de sa maison de campagne, 1929

In early 1929 the City of Berlin launched a plan to honor Albert Einstein on his fiftieth birthday by presenting the avid sailor with a lakefront site, on which he could build a summer house. The young architect Konrad Wachsmann read about the plans in a newspaper, which also reported that the Nobel laureate favored wooden houses. As an employee of Christoph & Unmack, a company in Niesky specialized in the construction of wooden barracks, he saw this as the chance of a lifetime and contacted the Einsteins. He was actually able to win their confidence, and within a few weeks he advanced to the position of their most trusted advisor in questions of building sites and housing construction. While the city fathers' plans to give the famous scientist a building site fell victim to all sorts of infighting, Einstein bought a piece of land on his own on a hill near Caputh, a town south of Potsdam between two of the Havel lakes. In Konrad Wachsmann he already had the architect for his house. Wachsmann's structure combined stationary timber framing with and wooden panel construction. The architect used fir from Galicia for the outer cladding; the interior walls were clad in plywood and panels made with a lignin resin. Slabs of peat were sandwiched in between these two layers as insulation. Particularly striking were the two, 30-ft. supporting beams of Oregon pine, imported from America, that ran through the living room. The full-length, white French doors made the house seem elegant and airy. The house was not one of those produced in series, but essential elements were prefabricated by Christoph & Unmack, assembled in a trial run in a production hall in Niesky, and then taken apart again before being transported to the building site.

In September of 1929 Einstein was able to move into his new abode. Although planned as a summerhouse, Einstein spent more time there than in his city flat, before emigrating to the United States (1932). The Einstein House was recently renovated and now serves as a center for scientific conferences.

Anfang 1929 wollte die Stadt Berlin Albert Einstein zu seinem 50. Geburtstag ein am See gelegenes Grundstück schenken, um dem passionierten Segler darauf ein Sommerhaus zu errichten. Der junge Architekt Konrad Wachsmann erfuhr davon aus der Zeitung, die außerdem zu berichten wusste, der berühmte Nobelpreisträger favorisiere ein Holzhaus. Wachsmann, Angestellter der auf den Holzbarackenbau spezialisierten Firma Christoph & Unmack in Niesky, erkannte darin die Chance seines Lebens und nahm Kontakt zu den Einsteins auf. Er konnte sie tatsächlich für sich gewinnen – und avancierte innerhalb weniger Wochen zu ihrem Vertrauensmann in Grundstücks- und Hausbaufragen. Zwar ging der Plan einer Schenkung der Berliner Stadtoberen an ihren berühmtesten Wissenschaftler in allerlei Gezänk schließlich unter, doch Einstein kaufte sich nun selbst auf einem Hügel bei Caputh, einem zwischen zwei Havelseen gelegenen Ort südlich von Potsdam, ein Grundstück. Den Architekten für sein Haus hatte er ja bereits: Konrad Wachsmann.

Wachsmanns Konstruktion war eine Kombination von ortsfester Fachwerk- und Tafelbauweise. Für die Außenschalung verwendete der Architekt galizisches Tannenholz, die Innenwände verkleidete er mit Sperrholz- und Lignatplatten. Zur Isolierung wurden Torfplatten zwischen die Schalungen gebracht. Markant sind die beiden 9 m langen Trägerbalken aus nordamerikanischer Oregonpinie, die durch das Wohnzimmer liefen. Die bis zum Boden reichenden, weiß gestrichenen französischen Fenster sorgten für einen eleganten und luftigen Eindruck. Das Haus war zwar kein Serienhaus, wesentliche Elemente wurden jedoch von Christoph & Unmack vorgefertigt und in einer Montagehalle in Niesky probeweise aufgestellt, dann wieder zerlegt und zum Bauplatz geschafft.

Im September 1929 konnte Einstein sein neues Domizil beziehen. Obwohl es nur als Sommerhaus gedacht war, verbrachte er die folgenden Jahre bis zu seiner Übersiedlung in die USA 1932 überwiegend hier und nicht in seiner Berliner Stadtwohnung. Das Einsteinhaus ist jüngst renoviert worden und dient heute u.a. als Tagungsort für wissenschaftliche Veranstaltungen.

Début 1929, la ville de Berlin souhaita offrir un terrain près d'un lac à Albert Einstein pour son 50ᵉ anniversaire, afin d'y bâtir une résidence d'été pour ce féru de voile. Le jeune architecte Konrad Wachsmann en entendit parler par la presse, qui révéla également la préférence du fameux prix Nobel pour les maisons en bois. Employé par la société Christoph & Unmack spécialisée dans les constructions de baraques en bois à Niesky, Wachsmann vit là la chance de sa vie et prit contact avec les Einstein. Il réussit effectivement à les convaincre et devint en l'espace de quelques semaines leur homme de confiance, spécialiste des questions relatives aux terrains et à la construction de maisons. Certes, le projet de donation des décideurs municipaux berlinois à leur très renommé scientifique échoua face aux dissensions internes, mais Einstein s'acheta lui-même un terrain situé sur une butte entre deux lacs de la Havel, près de Caputh, au sud de Potsdam. Il avait déjà l'architecte pour sa maison : Konrad Wachsmann. Wachsmann conçut une construction moderne en bois, combinant une structure en dur à colombages avec une construction par panneaux. Pour le revêtement extérieur, l'architecte utilisa du bois de sapin de Galicie, pour l'intérieur, des panneaux en contreplaqué et des dalles Lignat. Des plaques de tourbe furent insérées entre les coffrages pour l'isolation. Longues de 9 m, les deux poutres porteuses en pin d'Orégon d'Amérique du Nord qui traversaient la salle de séjour sont particulièrement remarquables. Les fenêtres à la française peintes en blanc et descendant jusqu'au sol produisaient une impression élégante et aérée. La maison n'était certes pas une maison fabriquée en série, mais des éléments constitutifs furent toutefois préfabriqués par Christoph & Unmack et assemblés à titre d'essai dans un atelier de montage à Niesky, puis redémontés et transportés jusqu'au site. Einstein put s'installer dans son nouveau domicile en septembre 1929. Bien que la maison ait été conçue à l'origine comme résidence d'été, Einstein y passa la plupart de son temps les années qui suivirent, jusqu'à son émigration aux États-Unis en 1932, la préférant à son appartement berlinois. La maison Einstein a été rénovée récemment et sert aujourd'hui, entre autres, de centre de colloque pour des manifestations scientifiques.

Left: View over the terrace
Links: Blick über die Terrasse
À gauche: Vue par-dessus la terrasse

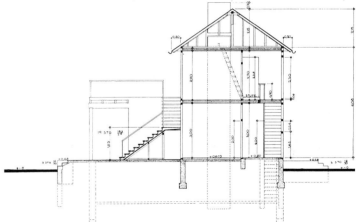

Opposite page: View of the garden
Linke Seite: Gartenansicht
Page de gauche: Vue du jardin

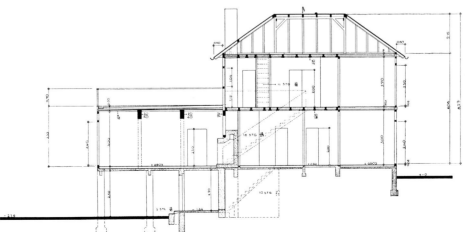

Longitudinal and cross section of the house

Längs- und Querschnitt des Hauses

Coupe longitudinale et coupe transversale de la maison

The kitchen with the serving hatch (above right) and the built-in cupboard in the living room with the serving hatch closed (above) and open (below)

Die Küche mit Durchreiche (oben) und Einbauschrank mit Durchreiche im Wohnzimmer mit geschlossenen und offenen Türen (unten)

La cuisine avec le passe-plat (en haut) et un placard avec passe-plat dans le salon avec porte fermée et porte ouverte (en bas)

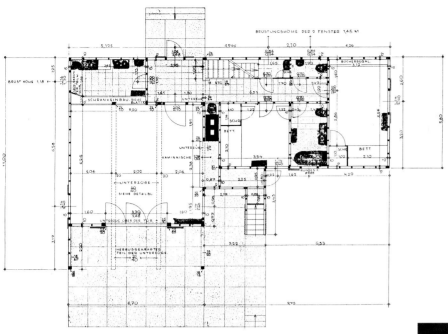

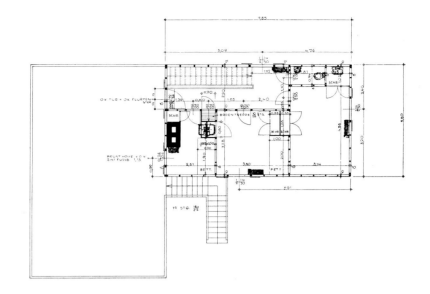

Plans of the ground floor (left) and the upper floor (right)

Grundrisse von Erdgeschosss (links) und Obergeschoss (rechts)

Plans du rez-de-chaussée (à gauche) et de l'étage supérieur (à droite)

Below: View of the terrace from the living room

Unten: Blick vom Wohnraum auf die Terrasse

En bas: Vue du séjour sur la terrasse

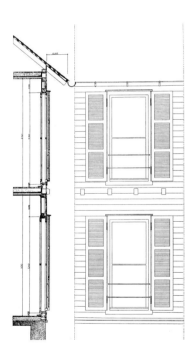

Above: Elevation and section of a façade element

Oben: Ansicht und Schnitt eines Fassadenelements

En haut: Élévation et coupe d'un élément de façade

ALBERT FREY, A. LAWRENCE KOCHER

ALUMINAIRE

New York, New York, USA
1931

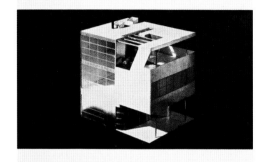

ALUMINAIRE

A House for Contemporary Life

THE ARCHITECTURAL AND ALLIED ARTS EXPOSITION
•
Grand Central Palace, New York City
•
April 18th to 25th, 1931

Right: Brochure presenting the house at the 1931 *Architectural and Allied Arts Exhibition*

Rechts: Broschüre zur Vorstellung des Hauses auf der Ausstellung „Architectural and Allied Arts" 1931

À droite: Brochure de présentation de la maison à l'exposition «Architectural and Allied Arts», en 1931

The Aluminaire house by Albert Frey was first shown in an exhibition hall. The three-story building made of aluminum, glass, and steel was shown at the *Allied Arts and Building Products Exhibition*, which was staged at the Grand Central Palace in New York from April 18-25, 1931. According to contemporary reports, it was the only exciting item exhibited at an otherwise rather boring building trade show.

Albert Frey was born in Switzerland and had worked in Le Corbusier's Paris office between 1928 and 1930, where he also helped to draw the building plans for the Villa Savoye. The creative roots and the experimental character of the Aluminaire are easily recognizable against this background. At the same time, the house was an advertisement for modern building materials from a variety of manufacturers.

The three-story steel skeleton frame structure was clad in low-gauge corrugated aluminum to which panels of insulation were attached. The doors and the frames of the ribbon windows were made of steel, the floors were made of rolled steel plates covered with insulation and black linoleum. The entire load was distributed onto six support pipes, strongly reminiscent of Le Corbusier's "pilotis". The two-story living room on the first floor was particularly impressive: measuring over 16 ft. in height, it was fully glazed on one side.

The Aluminaire was designed as a prefabricated house that—if roughly 10,000 were produced—could be offered at a price of $3,200. However, it never was produced in series. Directly after the exhibition, the New York architect Wallace K. Harrison, who was known for having designed the

Das Aluminaire-Haus von Albert Frey wurde erstmals in einer Messehalle präsentiert. Der dreigeschossige Bau aus Aluminium, Glas und Stahl wurde auf der „Allied Arts and Building Products Exhibition" gezeigt, die vom 18. bis zum 25. April 1931 im Grand Central Palace in New York stattfand. Wenn man zeitgenössischen Berichten glauben darf, war es das einzige aufsehenerregende Exponat einer ansonsten eher langweiligen Baufachmesse.

Albert Frey stammte aus der Schweiz und war zwischen 1928 und 1930 in Le Corbusiers Pariser Büro beschäftigt gewesen, wo er unter anderem Konstruktionszeichnungen für die Villa Savoye angefertigt hatte. Vor diesem Hintergrund werden die kreativen Wurzeln und der experimentelle Charakter des Aluminaire deutlich. Zugleich warb das Gebäude für moderne Baustoffe unterschiedlicher Hersteller.

Der dreistöckige Stahlrahmenbau wurde mit dünnem Aluminiumwellblech verkleidet, das auf Wärmedämmplatten aufgebracht war. Die Türen und die Rahmen der Fensterbänder waren aus Stahl gefertigt, die Böden bestanden aus gewalzten Stahlplatten, die mit Isoliermaterial und schwarzem Linoleum belegt wurden. Die Traglast verteilte sich auf sechs Rohrstützen, die stark an Le Corbusiers „piloti" erinnerten. Beeindruckend war vor allem der gut 5 m hohe, zweigeschossige Wohnraum im ersten Obergeschoss, der zu einer Seite hin komplett verglast war.

Das Aluminaire war so konzipiert, dass man es – bei einer Produktionsserie von etwa 10 000 Stück – zu einem Preis von 3 200 $ hätte anbieten können. Doch es ging nie in Serie. Direkt nach dem Ende der Ausstellung

La maison Aluminaire d'Albert Frey fut présentée pour la première fois dans un hall d'exposition. Ce bâtiment en aluminium, verre et acier de trois étages fut exposé lors de l'*Allied Arts and Building Products Exhibition* (Exposition d'arts connexes et de produits de construction) qui se tint du 18 au 25 avril 1931 au Grand Central Palace à New York. À en croire les comptes rendus de l'époque, ce fut l'unique pièce d'exposition à faire sensation au milieu d'un salon du bâtiment par ailleurs plutôt ennuyeux.

Albert Frey était Suisse et avait travaillé entre 1928 et 1930 dans le cabinet parisien de Le Corbusier, où il avait entre autres réalisé les plans d'exécution de la villa Savoye. Dans ce contexte, les racines créatives et le caractère expérimental de l'Aluminaire apparaissent clairement. Le bâtiment fit aussi de la publicité pour les matériaux modernes de divers fabricants.

Sur ses trois étages, le bâtiment à structure métallique fut revêtu de fines plaques de tôle ondulée en aluminium, posées sur des panneaux d'isolation thermique. Les portes et les cadres des fenêtres en bande étaient en acier, les planchers en dalles d'acier laminé recouvertes de matériaux d'isolation et de linoléum noir. La charge se répartissait sur six supports tubulaires qui rappelaient les pilotis de Le Corbusier. Haute de 5 m et s'étendant sur deux niveaux, la salle de séjour du premier étage était particulièrement impressionnante avec un de ses côtés entièrement vitré.

L'Aluminaire avait été conçue de façon à pouvoir être proposée à un prix de 3 200 $ dans le cas d'une production en série d'environ 10 000 exemplaires. Mais elle ne fit jamais l'objet d'une production sérielle. Aussitôt après l'exposition, l'architecte new-yorkais Wallace K. Harrison – célèbre grâce au

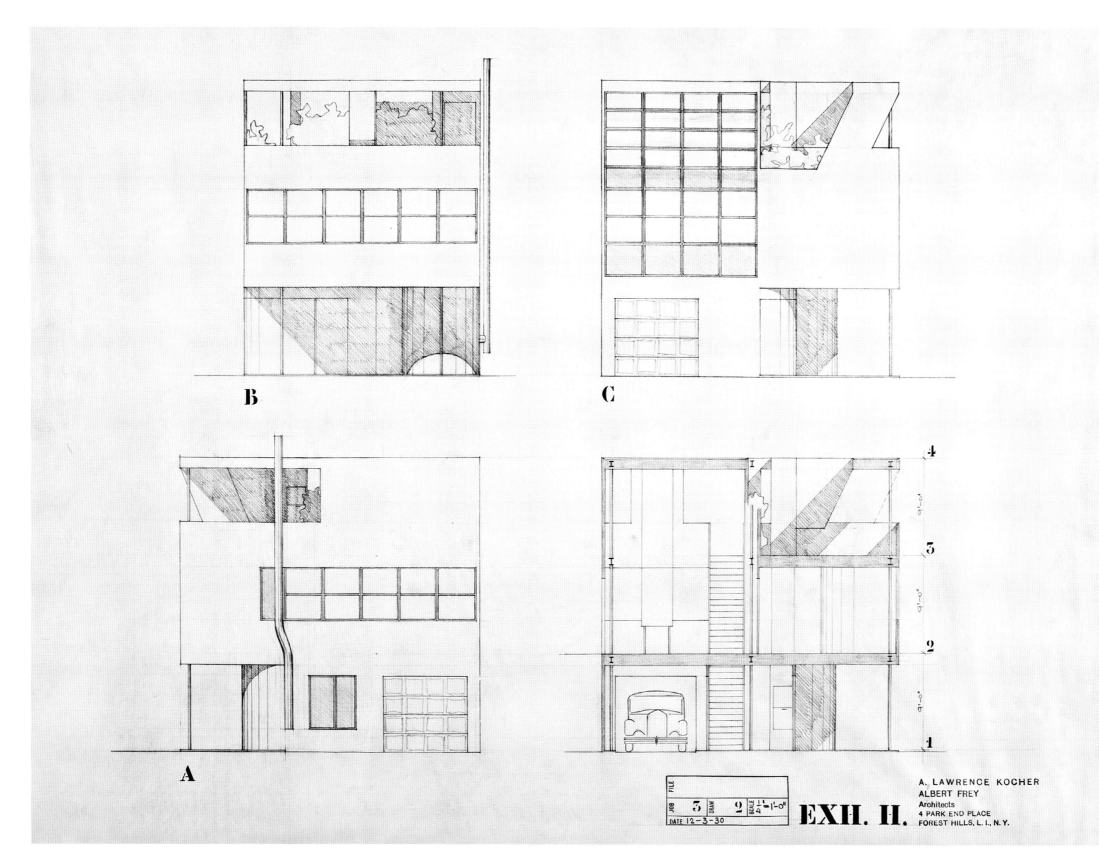

B

C

A

FILE

JOB 3 DRAW 2 SCALE 1/4"=1'-0"

DATE 12-3-30

EXH. II.

A. LAWRENCE KOCHER
ALBERT FREY
Architects
4 PARK END PLACE
FOREST HILLS, L. I., N. Y.

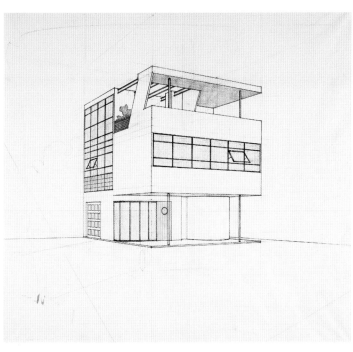

Elevation and cross-section (left page) and a perspective view (above)

Ansichten, Schnitt (linke Seite) und perspektivische Ansicht (oben)

Élévations, coupe (page de gauche) et vue en perspective (en haut)

Sketch of the entryway (above) and the kitchen (below)

Skizzen des Eingangsbereichs (oben) und der Küche (unten)

Esquisses de l'entrée (en haut) et de la cuisine (en bas)

MONEL , WALLS ALUMINUM

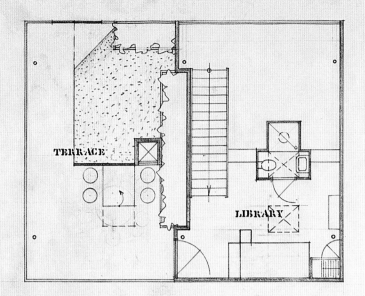

3

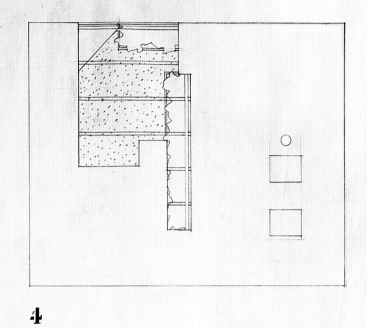

4

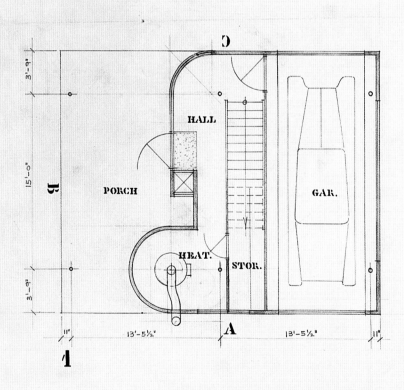

1

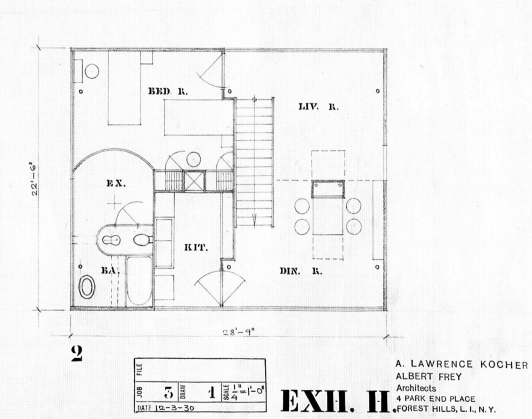

2

FILE			
JOB	3	DRAW	1	SCALE ¼" = 1'-0"
DATE 12-3-30			

A. LAWRENCE KOCHER
ALBERT FREY
Architects
4 PARK END PLACE
FOREST HILLS, L. I., N. Y.

EXH. II.

LIBRARY

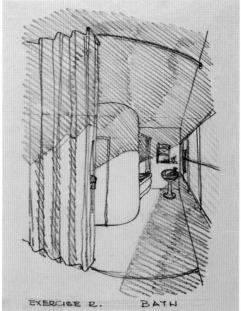

EXERCISE R.   BATH

DINING ROOM

Plans and roof elevation (left page), perspectival sketch of the library, the bathroom and fitness area, and the dining room (above)

Grundrisse und Dachaufsicht (linke Seite), perspektivische Skizzen von Bibliothek, Bad- und Fitnessbereich sowie Esszimmer (oben)

Plans et vue en plan du toit (page de gauche), esquisses en perspective de la bibliothèque, de la salle de bains et de la salle de gymnastique, ainsi que de la salle à manger (en haut)

Rockefeller Center and the Lincoln Center, purchased the prototype for $1,000 and installed it on the grounds of his country home in Syosset on Long Island. A year later, Henry Russell Hitchcock and Philip Johnson presented photographs and drawings of the Aluminaire in their seminal *International Exhibition of Modern Architecture* at the Museum of Modern Art in New York. Along with Richard Neutra's Lovell House (1927–1929), it was one of only two works in the exhibition by an American architect. The house has had a turbulent history. It was repeatedly moved and reconstructed on Harrison's property. After Harrison's death in 1981, his country home was sold and the new owner rented the Aluminaire to tenants who had to be evicted by force five years later so that it could be torn down. On the initiative of the architectural historian Joseph Rosa, who was working on a book about Frey at that time, the house was saved and painstakingly restored on the Central Islip Campus of the New York University of Technology. However, the Aluminaire's odyssey did not end there: in 2003 the architectural department at Central Islip was closed, and the search for a new location still continues.

kaufte der durch das Rockefeller Center und das Lincoln Center bekannt gewordene New Yorker Architekt Wallace K. Harrison den Prototyp für 1000 $ und errichtete ihn auf seinem Landsitz in Syosset auf Long Island. Im Jahr darauf zeigten Henry Russell Hitchcock und Philip Johnson Fotografien und Zeichnungen des Aluminaire in ihrer epochemachenden Ausstellung „International Exhibition of Modern Architecture" im New Yorker Museum of Modern Art – es war neben Richard Neutras Haus Lovell (1927–1929) das einzige Werk eines Amerikaners in der Ausstellung. Das Haus erlebte eine wechselvolle Geschichte. Es wurde auf Harrisons Grundstück mehrfach versetzt und umgebaut. Nach Harrisons Tod im Jahr 1981 wurde sein Landsitz verkauft, der neue Besitzer vermietete das Aluminaire und ließ es fünf Jahre später zwangsweise räumen, um es abzureißen. Auf Initiative des Architekturhistorikers Joseph Rosa, der zu dem Zeitpunkt an einem Buch über Frey arbeitete, konnte das Haus jedoch gerettet und auf dem Central Islip Campus der New York University of Technology liebevoll rekonstruiert werden. Doch die Odyssee des Aluminaire ist noch nicht an ihr Ende gekommen: Im Jahr 2003 wurde die Architekturfakultät in Central Islip geschlossen, und das Haus sucht seither einen neuen Standort.

Rockefeller Center et au Lincoln Center – acquit le prototype pour 1000 $ et l'édifia sur son domaine de Syosset sur Long Island. L'année suivante, Henry Russell Hitchcock et Philip Johnson montrèrent des photographies et des plans de l'Aluminaire lors de leur exposition qui fit date, l'*International Exhibition of Modern Architecture* (Exposition internationale d'architecture moderne) au Museum of Modern Art de New York. De toute l'exposition, ce fut la seule œuvre d'un Américain à côté de la Maison Lovell (1927–1929) de Richard Neutra.

La maison eut une histoire mouvementée : sur le terrain d'Harrison, elle fut déplacée et transformée à plusieurs reprises. À sa mort en 1981, le domaine fut vendu et le nouveau propriétaire la loua avant de l'évacuer de force cinq ans plus tard pour la démolir. À l'initiative de l'historien de l'architecture Joseph Rosa qui travaillait à l'époque à un livre sur Frey, la maison fut toutefois sauvée et reconstruite avec soin sur le campus de Central Islip de la New York University of Technology. L'odyssée de l'Aluminaire n'est pas pour autant terminée : en 2003, la faculté d'architecture de Central Islip a été fermée, et la maison cherche depuis un nouvel emplacement.

The Aluminaire on the grounds of Wallace K. Harrison's country house in Syosset, New York

Das Aluminaire als Landhaus von Wallace K. Harrison in Syosset, New York

L'Aluminaire comme maison de campagne de Wallace K. Harrison à Syosset, New York

The axonometric drawing shows the two-storey living room.

Die Axonometrie zeigt den doppelstöckigen Wohnraum.

L'axonométrie montre la double hauteur du séjour

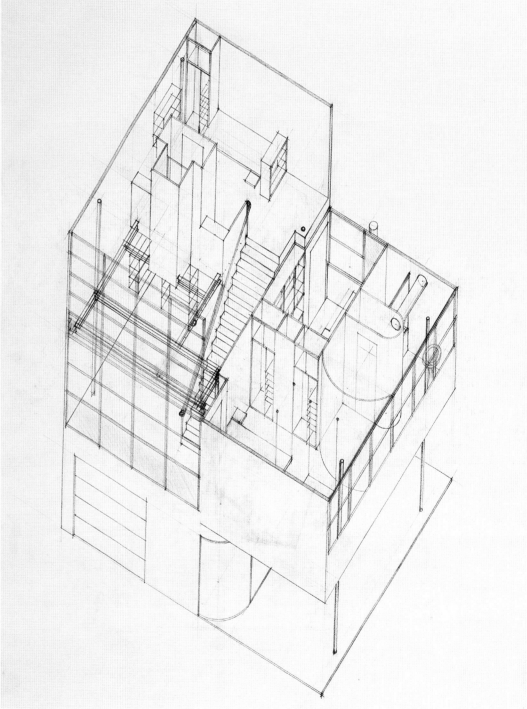

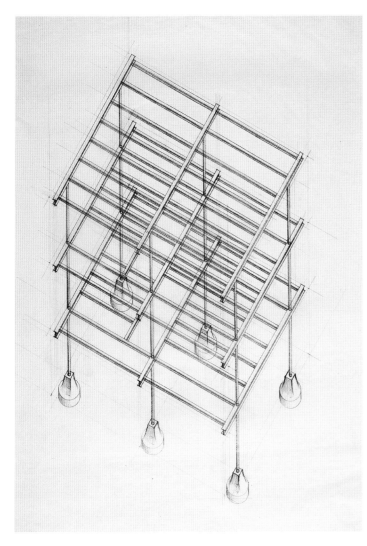

Axonometric drawing showing
structural framework

Axonometrische Darstellung der
Rahmenkonstruktion

Représentation axonométrique
de la construction à ossature

Right: Reconstruction of the
Aluminaire on the Central Islip
Campus of the New York Institute
of Technology in 1991

Rechts: Wiederaufbau des
Aluminaire auf dem Campus
von Central Islip, New York, 1991

À droite: Reconstruction de
l'Aluminaire en 1991 sur le campus
de Central Islip, New York, 1991

ROBERT KRAFFT, FRIEDRICH FÖRSTER, WALTER GROPIUS

KUPFERHAUS

Hirsch Kupfer- und Messingwerke, Eberswalde, Germany
1931–1934

Opposite page: The house models
Juwel (Jewel), *Kupfermärchen* (Copper
Fairy Tale) and *Maienmorgen* (May
Morning) in front of the water tower in
Eberswalde, 1931

Rechte Seite: Die Haustypen „Juwel",
„Kupfermärchen" und „Maienmorgen"
vor dem Wasserturm in Eberswalde,
1931

Page de droite: Les types de maison
Juwel (joyau), *Kupfermärchen* (conte
de cuivre) et *Maienmorgen* (matin de
mai) devant le château d'eau à
Eberswalde, 1931

The Hirsch Kupfer- und Messingwerke (Hirsch Copper and Brass Works) in Eberswalde began producing prefabricated all-copper houses developed by the architect Robert Krafft and the engineer Friedrich Förster in 1930. Because of its relatively light weight and high resistance to fire and corrosion, copper is particularly suitable for prefabricated house construction, and it is as easy to assemble as it is durable. A façade of narrow Eternit panels was built up over wooden framing and then covered with ribbed sheets of copper and insulated with aluminum foil. A patented universal end piece made the panels easy to screw together; the edges were then concealed by copper molding. Originally, sheet copper—with a diamond pattern—was also used for the roof.

The interior walls were clad in embossed sheet metal. The purchasers were able to enjoy a completely furnished kitchen, pre-installed plumbing fixtures, and central heating; they were also able to choose six different diamond patterns embossed into the sheet metal wall cladding in colors such as pastel blue, Nile green, or coral red. The heat build-up originally feared by contemporaries was not a problem, but there was interference with radio reception, since the building acted as a Faraday cage. It also offered little acoustic insulation.

The copper houses cost between 5,000 and 20,000 *Reichsmark*; between 1931 and 1934 fifty-one of them were produced—and ten of these have been preserved in their original form in Berlin. As can be seen in the sales catalogue from 1931, the company advertised its various models with names like *Kupfercastell* (Copper Castle), *Juwel* (Jewel), *Frühlingstraum* (Spring Reverie), *Lebenssonne* (Sunshine) and *Eigenscholle* (Source of Life). The

1930 begann die Eberswalder Firma Hirsch Kupfer- und Messingwerke mit der Produktion eines vorgefertigten Allkupferhauses, das von dem Architekten Robert Krafft und dem Ingenieur Friedrich Förster entwickelt worden war. Kupfer eignet sich aufgrund seiner hohen Feuer- und Korrosionsbeständigkeit hervorragend für die Fassaden eines Fertighauses. Auf der Basis einer Holzrahmenkonstruktion wurde die Fassade aus schmalen Eternitplatten erstellt, die mit geripptem Kupferblech belegt und mit Aluminiumfolie isoliert wurden. Mittels einer patentierten Schraub-Steck-Verbindung konnten die Paneele leicht montiert werden; auf die Kanten kam eine Blende aus Kupferblech. Auch für das Dach wurden ursprünglich Kupferbleche mit einem Rautenmuster verwendet.

Die Käufer kamen in den Genuss einer komplett eingerichteten Küche, fertig installierter Sanitäranlagen und einer Zentralheizung; für die Wandverkleidung konnten sie unter sechs verschiedenen, auf Stahlblech geprägten Rautenmustern in Farben wie Pastellblau, Nilgrün oder Korallenrot wählen. Zwar kam es nicht zu den Hitzestaus, die man seinerzeit befürchtete, dafür aber war der Radioempfang in diesem Faraday'schen Käfig stark beeinträchtigt. Das Haus war außerdem extrem hellhörig.

Die Kupferhäuser kosteten zwischen 5000 und 20000 Reichsmark; zwischen 1931 und 1934 wurden insgesamt 51 Stück produziert – zehn davon haben sich in Berlin in ihrer ursprünglichen Form erhalten. Wie man dem Verkaufskatalog von 1931 entnehmen kann, warb das Unternehmen für seine verschieden großen Modelle mit Namen wie „Kupfercastell", „Juwel", „Frühlingstraum", „Lebenssonne" oder „Eigenscholle". Die Palette reichte von der Gartenlaube bis zum Sechszimmerhaus.

En 1930, la société Hirsch Kupfer- und Messingwerke d'Eberswalde lance la production d'une maison préfabriquée entièrement en cuivre, développée par l'architecte Robert Krafft et l'ingénieur Friedrich Förster. En raison de sa haute résistance au feu et à la corrosion, le cuivre se prête remarquablement bien aux façades d'une maison préfabriquée. Constituée d'étroites plaques de fibrociment, la façade fut montée sur une ossature en bois puis recouverte de tôle de cuivre ondulée et isolée avec de la feuille d'aluminium. Les panneaux pouvaient être facilement montés par assemblage mécanique; un pare-soleil en tôle de cuivre venait se fixer sur les bords. À l'origine, de la tôle de cuivre avec des motifs en losange fut également utilisée pour le toit.

Les acquéreurs bénéficiaient d'une cuisine complètement aménagée, de sanitaires, ainsi que d'un chauffage central. Pour le revêtement mural, ils avaient le choix entre six sortes de motifs en losange gravés sur de la tôle d'acier dans les couleurs bleu pastel, vert Nil ou rouge corail.

L'accumulation de chaleur que l'on craignait à l'époque n'eut pas lieu. En revanche, la réception radio depuis cette cage de Faraday fut considérablement gênée. De plus, la maison était très bruyante.

Les maisons de cuivre coûtaient entre 5000 et 20000 Reichsmark; entre 1931 et 1934, 51 modèles furent produits, dont dix ont été conservés sous leur forme originale à Berlin. Comme on peut le constater dans le catalogue de 1931, l'entreprise proposa ses différents modèles majeurs sous des noms comme *Kupfercastell* (castel de cuivre), *Juwel* (joyau), *Frühlingstraum* (rêve printanier), *Lebenssonne* (soleil de la vie) ou *Eigenscholle* (terre propre). La palette allait de la tonnelle à la maison à six pièces.

ALL KUPFERHAUS

DAS IDEALE EINFAMILIENHAUS

HIRSCH KUPFER- & MESSINGWERKE A.-G. BERLIN

HARDENBERGSTR. 43 / FERNSPR.: SAMMEL-NR. C1 STEINPLATZ 8091 / FÜR FERNVERKEHR: SAMMEL-NR. C1 STEINPLATZ 4536

Ihr Heim!
Haus „Kupfermärchen"

Dieses ist ein wundervolles Kupferhaus
4 Zimmer, Küche, Bad und Kammer . . . . . siehe Seite 10

Eingebaute Schränke sind in allen unseren Häusern vorgesehen. Sie begeistern durch die ökonomische Raumausnutzung und die Ersparnis an Geld und Arbeitskraft die Hausfrau.

Eine unerlässliche Einrichtung für den Haushalt ist unser in die Wand eingelassenes Bügelbrett. Die dauernde Dienstbereitschaft verbunden mit der leichten Handhabung ist in der Tat wirklich praktisch!

In allen unseren Typen ist ein Badezimmer vorgesehen. Wir halten es vom hygienischen Standpunkt aus für unerlässlich und haben es daher zum Prinzip gemacht, dass jedes Haus ein Bad besitzt.

Mit diesem Komfort sind alle unsere Häuser ausgestattet

Opposite page: Catalog of the Hirsch
Copper and Brass Works, 1931

Linke Seite: Katalog der Hirsch
Kupfer- und Messingwerke, 1931

Page de gauche: Catalogue des
Hirsch Kupfer- und Messingwerke,
1931

Section and detail of the external
walls

Schnitt und Detailausbildung der
Außenwände

Coupe et détail des murs extérieurs

range extended from a little garden house to models with six rooms.
In 1932, Walter Gropius was commissioned by the Hirsch Works to design
two prototype houses: Sorgenfrei (Carefree) and Kupferstolz (Copper
Pride). He made a few changes in the appearance of existing models,
substituted aluminum panels for the sheet steel interior cladding, and
optimized the mechanical design of the corner joints.
1933 new models were added with names like *Haifa*, *Jerusalem*, and
Sharon, along with the flagship model *Libanon* (Lebanon). The Jewish company developed these models especially for the Middle East and advertised
among Jews forced to emigrate with the slogan, "Take a copper house with
you to Palestine", claiming that "Even when it's very hot, your rooms will
stay cool!" Fourteen of these houses actually did make their way to the
British Mandate of Palestine, not least because they offered refugees a re-
minder of home. Today there are still eleven of these houses left in Haifa.

1932 wurde Walter Gropius von den Hirsch-Werken damit beauftragt, zwei
weitere Typen zu schaffen: „Sorgenfrei" und „Kupferstolz". Er nahm einige
optische Modifikationen vor, ersetzte die Stahlblechverkleidungen im Innenraum durch Aluminiumtafeln und optimierte die Mechanik der Eckver-
bindungen.
1933 kamen noch Haustypen mit Namen wie „Haifa", „Jerusalem" und
„Scharon" dazu – das Flaggschiff war das „Libanon". Diese Modelle hatte
das jüdische Unternehmen eigens für den Mittleren Osten entwickelt und
warb bei den zur Auswanderung gezwungenen Juden mit den Worten:
„Nehmen Sie ein Kupferhaus mit nach Palästina" – und mit dem schlagen-
den Argument: „Sie wohnen bei größter Hitze in kühlen Räumen!"
Tatsächlich nahmen 14 Exemplare ihren Weg in das damalige britische
Mandatsgebiet Palästina – nicht zuletzt boten sie den Geflüchteten auch
ein Stückchen Heimat. Elf dieser Häuser stehen noch heute in Haifa.

En 1932, Walter Gropius fut chargé par les Hirsch Kupfer- und Messingwerke de concevoir deux autres maisons, *Sorgenfrei* (sans souci) et
Kupferstolz (fierté de cuivre). Il procéda à quelques modifications apparen-
tes sur les modèles existants, remplaça le revêtement intérieur en tôle
d'acier par des panneaux d'aluminium et optimisa la mécanique des assem-
blages d'angle.
En 1933, d'autres modèles de maisons appelés *Haifa*, *Jerusalem* et *Scharon*
virent également le jour, ainsi que le produit phare *Libanon*. L'entreprise
juive avait développé ces derniers spécialement pour le Moyen-Orient et
en faisait la réclame auprès des Juifs forcés à l'émigration en ces termes:
«Emportez une maison en cuivre en Palestine!», avec l'argument implaca-
ble: «Vivez dans des pièces fraîches même par grosse chaleur.»
Effectivement, 14 unités furent acheminées vers l'ancienne Palestine sous
mandat britannique, ce qui offrait surtout la possibilité aux réfugiés d'emporter un souvenir de leur pays. 11 de ces maisons se trouvent encore
aujourd'hui à Haifa.

The *Kupfercastell* (Copper Castle)
model in the company's catalog

Das Modell „Kupfercastell" im
Katalog und als fertiges Musterhaus

Modèle *Kupfercastell* (castel de
cuivre) sur catalogue et comme
maison-modèle réalisée

Haus „Kupfercastell"

Hier ist ein entzückendes zweistöckiges Eigenheim, das durch sein gefälliges Aeussere und seine gelungene Linienführung mit Recht das Ideal eines zweistöckigen Einfamilienhauses genannt wird. Interessant ist die Anlage der Eingangsterrasse, die nach oben hin in einen grossen Balkon endigt, der auch vom Elternschlafzimmer aus zu betreten ist. Die Eingangsterrasse, die eine enge Verbindung mit den Innenräumen herstellt, ist ein beliebter Aufenthaltsort, eine Lebensfreude für den Besitzer. Ueber die Terrasse gelangt man zu dem seitlich gelegenen Eingang. Hier eröffnen sich die unteren grossen Räume. Links von der Diele sieht man eine bequem begehbare Treppe, die zu den oberen Räumlichkeiten führt. Das Esszimmer bietet durch eine reizvolle Oeffnung der Zwischenwand einen wirkungsvollen Durchblick zu dem geräumigen Wohnzimmer mit seiner idyllischen Sitznische. Die Anordnung der Fenster ermöglicht eine rasche Durchlüftung der Räume. Die Küche ist mit allem Komfort ausgestattet, um die häusliche Arbeit so angenehm wie möglich zu gestalten: passend eingebaute Schränke, eingebautes Bügelbrett, ein gut gewählter Platz für Herd und Abwaschtisch sind die besonders auffallenden Vorzüge. In unmittelbarer Nähe des Kücheneingangs bietet sich, falls eine Unterkellerung gewählt wird, die Möglichkeit zur Anlage eines Kellereinganges, der seine Beleuchtung durch ein Fenster von der Terrasse empfängt. Von der im ersten Stock gelegenen Diele führt ein separater Eingang zu den beiden Schlafzimmern, dem grossen Bad und dem Balkon. Einen ganz besonderen Komfort bildet die Ankleidenische im grossen Schlafzimmer mit den beiden eingebauten Wäsche- und Kleiderschränken. Ein Austritt zu dem Balkon ist auch hier vorgesehen. In den Schlafzimmern wie im Bad sind unsere eingebauten Schränke eine sehr willkommene Einrichtung. Der Bodenraum ist mit einer Umklappleiter von dem oberen Flur aus bequem zu erreichen.

BLICK IN DAS WOHNZIMMER

Variations of the expandable
floor plan

Varianten des erweiterbaren
Grundrisses

Variantes du plan extensible

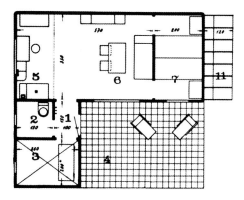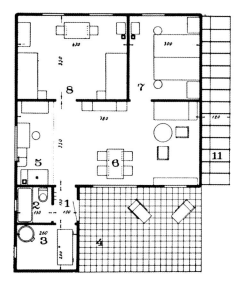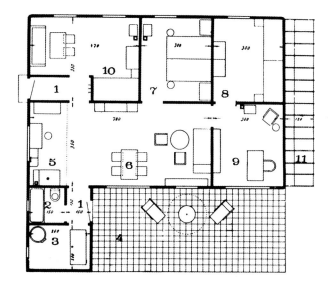

Below: Installation of wall elements
(left), living room interior designed
by Gropius (right)

Unten: Aufstellen der Wandelemente
(links), nach Vorgaben von Gropius
eingerichteter Wohnraum (rechts)

En bas: Montage des éléments de
murs (à gauche); séjour aménagé par
Gropius (à droite)

Haus „Maienmorgen"

Wir sind der Ueberzeugung, dass unser Haus „Maienmorgen" die Erfüllung des Traumes aller derer bedeutet, die bei ihren bescheidenen Mitteln bisher nicht in der Lage waren, an den Kauf eines solchen Hauses zu denken. Wenn man in Betracht zieht, dass bei Verwendung von Ziegeln die Nutzfläche um etwa 20% verkleinert würde, so kann man verstehen, dass auf der verhältnismässig kleinen Baufläche von 37,5 qm viel Raum geschaffen ist. Besonders praktisch und ökonomisch ist der Grundriss angeordnet. Das Wohnzimmer mit der gemütlichen, gut beleuchteten Essnische erweckt einen warmen, behaglichen Eindruck. Für die in letzter Zeit besonders beliebt gewordene Kleinküche mit eingebauten Regalen und einer Abstellkammer sind die Ausmasse dennoch so gewählt, dass der Haushalt bequem versorgt werden kann. W.C. mit Dusche liegen zu ebener Erde. Ueber die separat liegende Treppe erreicht man die oberen Räumlichkeiten. Das lichtdurchflutete Schlafzimmer enthält zwei begehbare eingebaute Schränke und eine Abstellkammer. Der vorgelagerte durchgehende Balkon sowie der Erkerbau geben dem Hause eine reizvolle Note.

Haus „Juwel"

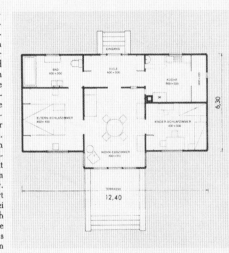

Dieser Dreizimmertyp eines Einfamilienhauses mit den praktisch angelegten grossen Räumen, dem besonders grossen Bad wurde in kurzer Zeit sehr beliebt. Der Eintretende wird von der Individualität und von den Ausmassen der Räume gleichermassen angenehm überrascht sein. In diesem Hause finden Sie, wie in allen unseren Häusern, das Ideal der Hausfrau: eingebaute Schränke. Der Ess-Wohnraum, 5×4 m gross, der von der gut beleuchteten Diele betreten wird, wirkt durch die drei Doppeltüren an der Stirnseite sehr repräsentativ. Der erkerartige Ausbau gewährt einen freien Ausblick nach drei verschiedenen Seiten. — Gleich am Eingang befindet sich eine Telefonnische, durch die das Telefon vom Esszimmer und von der Diele aus bedient werden kann. Eine Durchreiche von der Küche zum Speisezimmer ist eine wirkliche Bequemlichkeit. Vom mittleren Raum gelangt man in die angrenzenden hellen angenehmen Schlafzimmer, deren grösseres direkten Zugang zum Bad und W. C. hat. Eine bemerkenswerte Einrichtung ist das eingebaute Apothekerschränkchen. — Beim Projektieren der Küche waren wir auf Zweckmässigkeit und ökonomische Raumausnutzung besonders bedacht. Die geräumigen Vorratskammern bieten einen vollen Ersatz für einen etwa in Wegfall kommenden Keller und haben den weiteren Vorteil, das lästige Treppensteigen zu ersparen. Der für Abstellzwecke ausnutzbare Bodenraum ist durch eine Luke in der Küchendecke erreichbar.

Wie arbeitet Ihr so angelegtes Kapital? Es bringt die höchsten Zinsen: Gesundheit, Glück und besseres Leben!

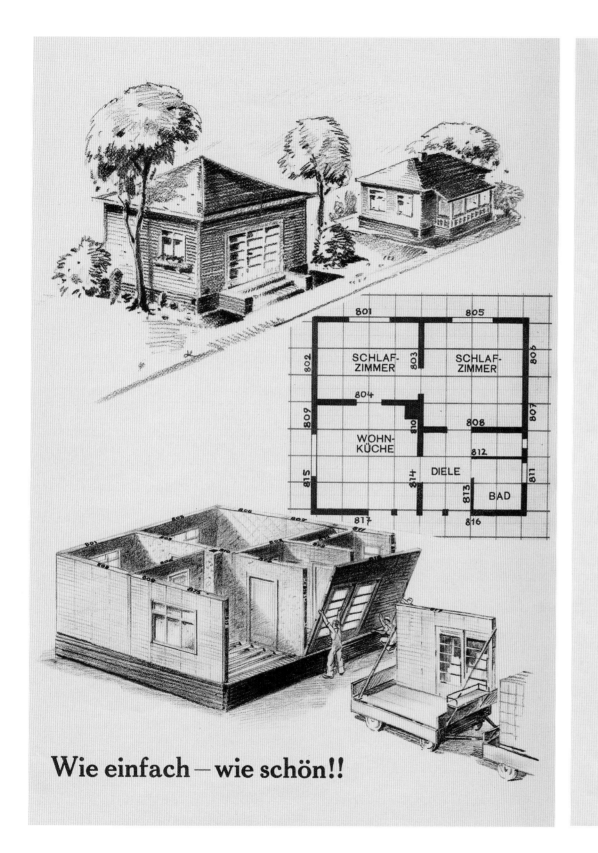

Wie einfach — wie schön!!

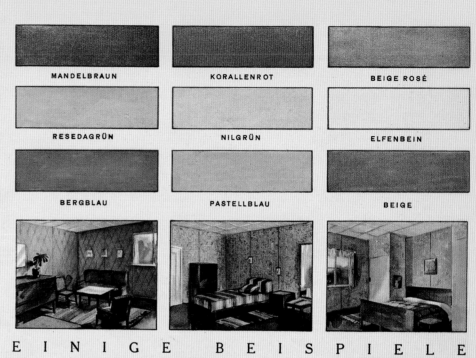
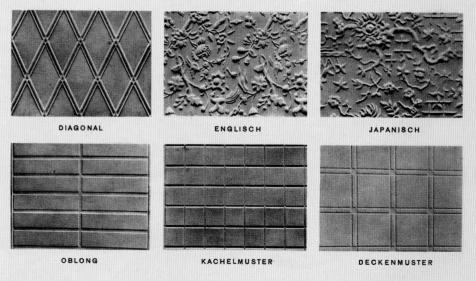

ROBERT W. MCLAUGHLIN JR.

AMERICAN MOTOHOMES

American Houses, Inc. , Kearny, New Jersey, USA
1932–1935

Winslow Ames House in New
London, Connecticut, 1933 (right),
house in Boston, Massachusetts,
1934 (opposite page)

Winslow Ames House in New
London, Connecticut, 1933 (rechts),
Wohnhaus in Boston, Massachusetts,
1934 (rechte Seite)

Winslow Ames House à New
London, Connecticut, 1933 (à droite),
maison d'habitation à Boston, Massachusetts,
1934 (page de droite)

Like many of his colleagues, the American architect Robert McLaughlin believed that he could make money during the Great Depression of the 1930s by building low-cost, prefabricated homes. Hence, he founded American Houses, Inc. in 1932, the year he presented the prototype for a house that would eventually be produced in series under the name American Motohome.

The spectrum of these steel-skeleton houses ranged from a simple four-room model to a spacious version with six bedrooms, four bathrooms, and a two-car garage. The Motohome was clad in panels of asbestos and cement. Heating, plumbing, and electricity were combined in a central "Moto-unit". The house contained countertops made of stainless steel, built-in cabinets, and was equipped with a custom fit stove that included a vent, as well as a refrigerator, and even cigarette lighters.

Each of the homes, as McLaughlin explained, was characterized by "a hitherto unknown level of durability, beauty, economy, and comfort". The components were produced in a factory in New Jersey and assembled on site. The one- or two-story flat-roofed houses paid tribute to International Style. They were advertised as "dwelling machines" and could even be delivered with a supply of food in the kitchen. However, the ostensibly attractive Motohomes did not appeal to a sufficient number of customers, so that the architect and his company turned to the production of more conventional prefabricated homes after barely three years, during which 150 models were delivered.

Wie viele seiner Kollegen hoffte der amerikanische Architekt Robert McLaughlin, während der Großen Depression der 1930er Jahre mit kostengünstiger Fertighaus-Produktion Geld verdienen zu können. 1932 gründete er die American Houses Inc. und stellte im selben Jahr den Prototyp eines Hauses vor, das unter dem Namen „American Motohome" in Serie gehen sollte.

Die Palette dieser Stahlskelett-Häuser reichte vom einfachen Vier-Zimmer-Modell bis hin zu einer großzügig bemessenen Version m it sechs Schlafzimmern, vier Badezimmern und einer Garage für zwei Autos. Das Motohome war mit Paneelen verkleidet, die aus einer Gips-Asbest-Mischung bestanden. Heizung, Sanitärtechnik und Elektrik wurden in einer zentralen „Moto-Einheit" vereint. Das Haus enthielt Arbeitsflächen aus Edelstahl, Einbauschränke, war mit Einbauherd samt Dunstabzugshaube, Kühlschrank und sogar Zigarettenanzünder ausgestattet.

Jedes der Häuser, so erklärte McLaughlin, zeichne sich durch eine „in diesem Ausmaß noch nie dagewesene Langlebigkeit, Schönheit, Wirtschaftlichkeit und Bequemlichkeit" aus. Die Komponenten wurden in einer Fabrik in New Jersey vorgefertigt und vor Ort zusammengesetzt. Die ein- bis zweigeschossigen Flachdachhäuser huldigten dem International Style und wurden als vorgefertigte Wohnmaschinen beworben, die komplett bis zu den Essensvorräten in der Küche ausgeliefert werden würden. Doch der angepriesene Appeal der Motohomes verfing bei den Kunden nicht, so dass sich der Architekt mit seiner Firma nach kaum drei Jahren und etwa 150 ausgelieferten Exemplaren der Produktion konventionellerer Fertighäuser zuwandte.

Comme nombre de ses collègues, l'architecte américain Robert McLaughlin crut pouvoir gagner de l'argent pendant la Grande dépression des années trente en produisant des maisons préfabriquées bon marché. En 1932, il fonda l'American Houses, Inc. et présenta la même année le prototype d'une maison qui allait faire l'objet d'une série appelée American Motohome.

La gamme de ces maisons à ossature d'acier allait du simple modèle de maison à quatre chambres à une version bien plus vaste à six chambres, quatre salles de bains et un garage pour deux voitures. Le revêtement de la Motohome était en panneaux de plâtre-amiante. Le chauffage, la plomberie des sanitaires et l'électricité étaient réunis dans une « unité Moto » centrale. La maison comportait des plans de travail en acier inoxydable, des placards, et était équipée d'une gazinière intégrée avec hotte aspirante, d'un frigidaire et même d'un allume-cigares.

Selon McLaughlin, chacune des maisons se distinguait « par une durabilité, une beauté, une rentabilité et un confort encore jamais égalés dans ces proportions ». Les éléments préfabriqués dans une usine du New Jersey étaient ensuite assemblés sur site. Hommage au Style international, les maisons à toit plat d'un à deux étages étaient présentées comme des machines à habiter préfabriquées, livrées clés en main, avec même des provisions déjà entreposées dans les placards. Toutefois, l'attrait vanté des Motohomes n'eut pas l'effet escompté sur les clients, de sorte qu'après trois ans à peine, et environ 150 modèles livrés, l'architecte voua son entreprise à la production de maisons préfabriquées beaucoup plus conventionnelles.

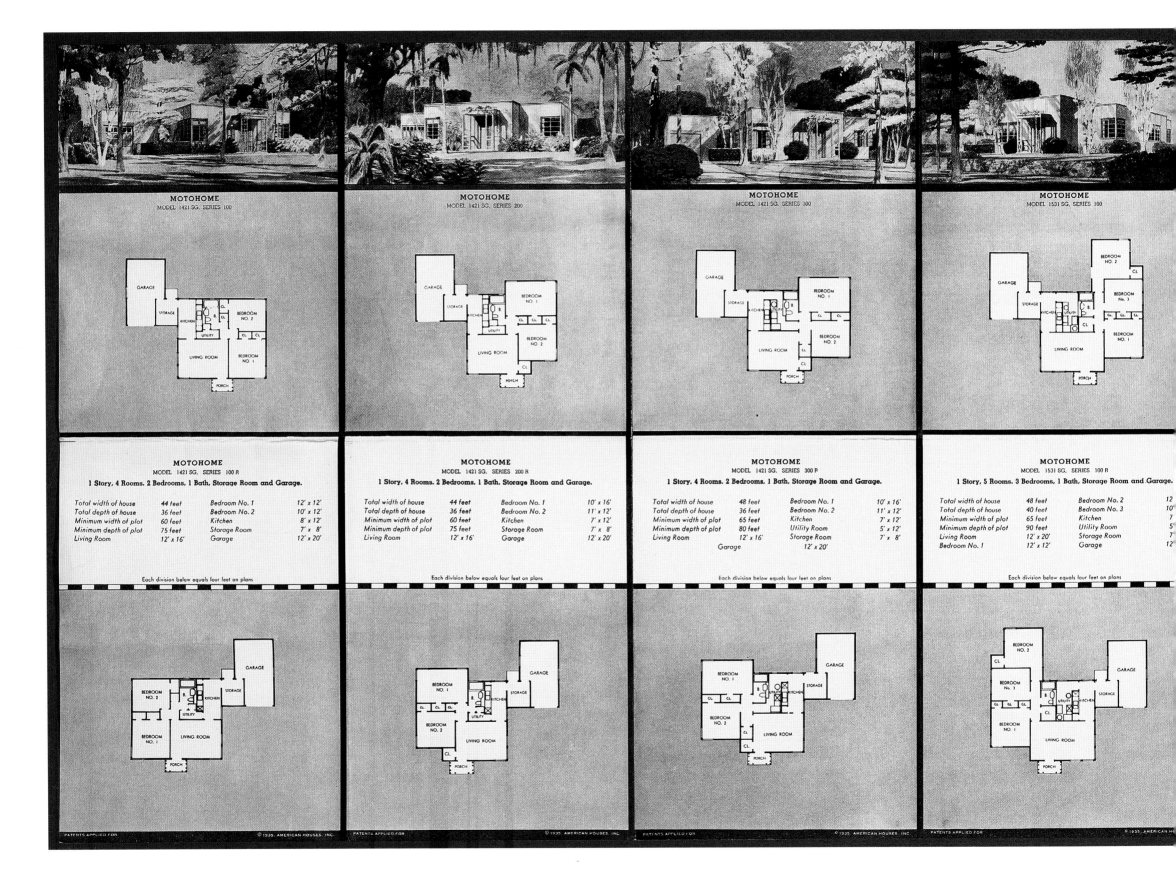

MOTOHOME
MODEL 1421 SG, SERIES 100

MOTOHOME
MODEL 1421 SG, SERIES 200

MOTOHOME
MODEL 1421 SG, SERIES 300

MOTOHOME
MODEL 1531 SG, SERIES 100

MOTOHOME
MODEL 1421 SG, SERIES 100 R

1 Story, 4 Rooms. 2 Bedrooms, 1 Bath, Storage Room and Garage.

Total width of house	44 feet	Bedroom No. 1	12' x 12'
Total depth of house	36 feet	Bedroom No. 2	10' x 12'
Minimum width of plot	60 feet	Kitchen	8' x 12'
Minimum depth of plot	75 feet	Storage Room	7' x 8'
Living Room	12' x 16'	Garage	12' x 20'

Each division below equals four feet on plans

MOTOHOME
MODEL 1421 SG, SERIES 200 R

1 Story, 4 Rooms. 2 Bedrooms, 1 Bath, Storage Room and Garage.

Total width of house	44 feet	Bedroom No. 1	10' x 16'
Total depth of house	36 feet	Bedroom No. 2	11' x 12'
Minimum width of plot	60 feet	Kitchen	7' x 12'
Minimum depth of plot	75 feet	Storage Room	7' x 8'
Living Room	12' x 16'	Garage	12' x 20'

Each division below equals four feet on plans

MOTOHOME
MODEL 1421 SG, SERIES 300 R

1 Story, 4 Rooms. 2 Bedrooms, 1 Bath, Storage Room and Garage.

Total width of house	48 feet	Bedroom No. 1	10' x 16'
Total depth of house	36 feet	Bedroom No. 2	11' x 12'
Minimum width of plot	65 feet	Kitchen	7' x 12'
Minimum depth of plot	80 feet	Utility Room	5' x 12'
Living Room	12' x 16'	Storage Room	7' x 8'
		Garage	12' x 20'

Each division below equals four feet on plans

MOTOHOME
MODEL 1531 SG, SERIES 100 R

1 Story, 5 Rooms. 3 Bedrooms, 1 Bath, Storage Room and Garage.

Total width of house	48 feet	Bedroom No. 2	12'
Total depth of house	40 feet	Bedroom No. 3	10'
Minimum width of plot	65 feet	Kitchen	7'
Minimum depth of plot	90 feet	Utility Room	5'
Living Room	12' x 20'	Storage Room	7'
Bedroom No. 1	12' x 12'	Garage	12'

Each division below equals four feet on plans

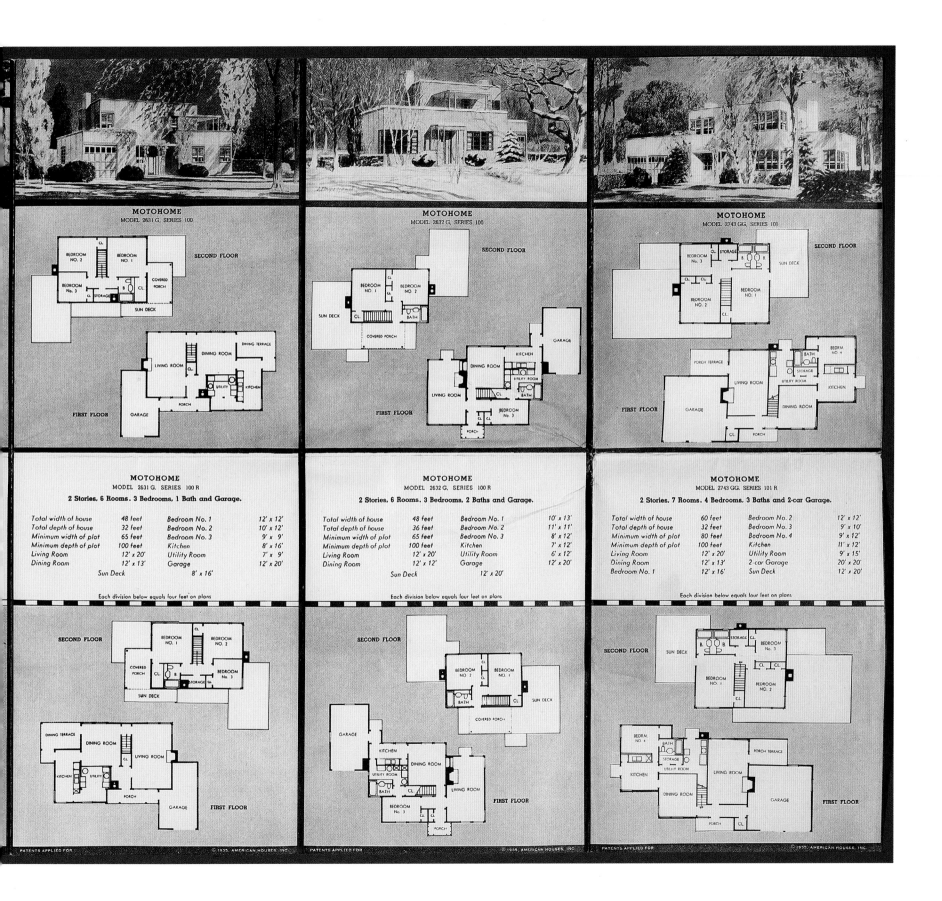

MOTOHOME
MODEL 2631 G, SERIES 100

MOTOHOME
MODEL 2632 G, SERIES 100

MOTOHOME
MODEL 2743 GG, SERIES 101

MOTOHOME
MODEL 2631 G, SERIES 100 R

2 Stories, 6 Rooms, 3 Bedrooms, 1 Bath and Garage.

Total width of house	48 feet	Bedroom No. 1	12' x 12'
Total depth of house	32 feet	Bedroom No. 2	10' x 12'
Minimum width of plot	65 feet	Bedroom No. 3	9' x 9'
Minimum depth of plot	100 feet	Kitchen	8' x 16'
Living Room	12' x 20'	Utility Room	7' x 9'
Dining Room	12' x 13'	Garage	12' x 20'
	Sun Deck	8' x 16'	

Each division below equals four feet on plans

MOTOHOME
MODEL 2632 G, SERIES 100 R

2 Stories, 6 Rooms, 3 Bedrooms, 2 Baths and Garage.

Total width of house	48 feet	Bedroom No. 1	10' x 13'
Total depth of house	36 feet	Bedroom No. 2	11' x 11'
Minimum width of plot	65 feet	Bedroom No. 3	8' x 12'
Minimum depth of plot	100 feet	Kitchen	7' x 12'
Living Room	12' x 20'	Utility Room	6' x 12'
Dining Room	12' x 12'	Garage	12' x 20'
	Sun Deck	12' x 20'	

Each division below equals four feet on plans

MOTOHOME
MODEL 2743 GG, SERIES 101 R

2 Stories, 7 Rooms, 4 Bedrooms, 3 Baths and 2-car Garage.

Total width of house	60 feet	Bedroom No. 2	12' x 12'
Total depth of house	32 feet	Bedroom No. 3	9' x 10'
Minimum width of plot	80 feet	Bedroom No. 4	9' x 12'
Minimum depth of plot	100 feet	Kitchen	11' x 12'
Living Room	12' x 20'	Utility Room	9' x 15'
Dining Room	12' x 13'	2-car Garage	20' x 20'
Bedroom No. 1	12' x 16'	Sun Deck	12' x 20'

Each division below equals four feet on plans

PATENTS APPLIED FOR   © 1935, AMERICAN HOUSES, INC.

"American motohomes: the prefabricated houses that come
complete with food in the kitchen.
Dedicated to the women of America
by Sarah Delano Roosevelt, April 1,
1935." Brochure presenting 14 house
models.

„American Motohomes: Die vorgefertigten Häuser, die komplett bis
zu den Essensvorräten in der Küche
ausgeliefert werden. Den amerikanischen Frauen gewidmet von Sarah
Delano Roosevelt, 1. April 1935." Aus
einer Broschüre, die 14 verschiedene
Modelle der Häuser vorstellt

« American motohomes : les maisons
préfabriquées livrées clés en main,
avec les provisions de bouche dans
la cuisine. Dédiées aux femmes
américaines par Sarah Delano
Roosevelt, le 1er avril 1935.» Extrait
d'une brochure présentant 14
modèles de maisons

HOWARD T. FISHER

GENERAL HOUSES

General Houses, Inc., Chicago, Illinois, USA
1933–1940

Right: Model house at the *Century of Progress Exposition*, 1933
Rechts: Musterhaus auf der Ausstellung „Century of Progress", 1933
À droite: Maison-témoin à l'exposition Century of Progress, 1933

Opposite page: House in Lake Delavan, Wisconsin, 1935
Rechte Seite: Haus in Lake Delavan, Wisconsin, 1935
Page droite: Maison à Lake Delavan, Wisconsin, 1935

The first American architect to consider the idea of producing prefabricated steel houses in series was presumably Howard T. Fisher. As a one-time law student at Harvard, and the son of the former Federal Minister of the Interior and prominent Chicago lawyer Walter Lowrie Fisher, he had excellent contacts. In 1931 he was able to win the support of the president of the Pullman Car Company, which was able to supply the know-how in steel construction for his project. Other wealthy industrialists also joined in when Fisher founded General Houses Inc. in 1932, at the youthful age of twenty-six. The company's name being reminiscent of General Motors is not merely coincidental. Fisher believed that it should be possible to standardize houses, so that they could be produced and sold in large numbers. However, what Fisher envisioned was not the production of houses on a factory assembly line. On the contrary, various parts were to be produced by different companies and put together on the building site. Pullman, for example, would deliver the steel plates for the external walls. General Houses had no production facilities of its own.

In 1933, the first model house was presented during the five-month's of the Chicago *Century of Progress Exhibition*. It aroused considerable interest on the part of the public and the press, but it was not widely accepted. Fisher was, after all, an ambitious architect and had given the house a modern form: a flat-roofed cube without any ornamentation. The walls were made of 4-ft. wide, floor-to-ceiling steel panels, which supported the weight of the roof. The internal walls were also made of exposed steel.

National sales began that same year. Models were offered ranging from a four-room house for $4,500 to a two-story, six-room house with a garage for $8,550 (1934 prices). When the sales volume failed to increase, despite extensive marketing, moderate prices, and easy payment options (installments of $30 per month), the inside was made "cozier" by adding wooden paneling. Later, the outside was also revamped by replacing the flat roof

Der erste amerikanische Architekt, der sich mit der Idee beschäftigte, vorgefertigte Häuser aus Stahl in Serie herzustellen, war vermutlich Howard T. Fisher. Er hatte einige Semester in Harvard studiert, und als Sohn des ehemaligen US-Innenministers und renommierten Chicagoer Rechtsanwalts Walter Lowrie Fisher verfügte er über beste Kontakte. 1931 konnte er den Präsidenten der Waggonbaufirma Pullman, die Know-how im Bereich Stahlbau besaß, für sein Projekt gewinnen. Weitere wohlhabende Industrielle kamen hinzu, und so gründete Fisher 1932, mit gerade mal 26 Jahren, die General Houses Inc. Der Name erinnert nicht zufällig an General Motors: Nach Fishers Vorstellungen sollten Häuser wie Autos standardisiert und in großen Mengen produziert und vertrieben werden können. Was Fisher vorschwebte, war allerdings nicht eine Haus-Fertigung am Fließband einer Fabrik. Vielmehr sollten die einzelnen Teile von verschiedenen Firmen vorgefertigt und auf der Baustelle zusammenmontiert werden. Pullman beispielsweise lieferte die Stahlplatten der Außenwände. General Houses selbst verfügte über keine Produktionsstätte.

1933 wurde ein Prototyp auf der fünf Monate währenden Ausstellung „Century of Progress" in Chicago vorgestellt. Es stieß beim Publikum und bei der Presse zwar auf großes Interesse, insgesamt aber auf wenig Gegenliebe. Denn Fisher war ein Architekt mit Ambitionen und hatte seinem Haus eine moderne Form verliehen: Es war ein ornamentloser Kubus mit Flachdach. Die Wände waren aus 1,20 m (4 Fuß) breiten, geschosshohen Stahlpaneelen zusammengesetzt, die die Last des Dachs trugen. Auch die Innenwände waren stahlsichtig.

Noch im selben Jahr begann der landesweite Verkauf. Angeboten wurden Modelle vom Vier-Zimmer-Haus für 4500 $ bis zum zweigeschossigen Sechs-Zimmer-Haus mit Garage für 8550 $ (Preise von 1934). Als die Absatzzahlen trotz aller Marketingaktivitäten, trotz moderater Preise und trotz günstiger Zahlungsmodalitäten (30 Dollar-Monatsraten) nicht

Le premier Américain qui se pencha sur la question de la fabrication en série de maisons préfabriquées en acier fut sans doute Howard T. Fisher. En tant que fils de l'ancien ministre de l'Intérieur américain et avocat de Chicago réputé Walter Lowrie Fisher, et suite à ses quelques semestres d'études à Harvard, il disposait des meilleurs contacts. En 1931, il réussit à rallier le président de l'entreprise de construction de wagons Pullman à son projet, société qui disposait d'un savoir-faire dans le domaine de la construction métallique. D'autres industriels fortunés s'y associèrent et Fisher – alors à peine âgé de 26 ans – créa en 1932 la General Houses Inc. Le nom ne rappelle pas par hasard la General Motors: pour Fisher, les maisons devaient pouvoir être standardisées et produites en masse puis être commercialisées comme les voitures. Fisher avait non pas dans l'idée de fabriquer des maisons à la chaîne dans une usine, mais bien d'en faire préfabriquer les éléments par différentes entreprises et de les assembler sur le chantier. Ainsi, Pullman livrait les panneaux d'acier pour les murs extérieurs. Quant à General Houses, elle ne disposait elle-même d'aucun atelier de fabrication.

En 1933, un prototype fut présenté lors de l'exposition Century of Progress de Chicago qui durait cinq mois. Il suscita certes un grand intérêt auprès du public et de la presse, mais remporta finalement peu de succès. Fisher étant un architecte ambitieux, il avait doté sa maison d'une forme moderne: on avait là un cube sobre à toit plat. Les murs de 1,20 m (4 pieds) de large étaient faits de panneaux d'acier de la hauteur d'un étage qui portaient le poids du toit. Les murs intérieurs présentaient également un revêtement d'acier.

La même année fut celle du lancement de la vente à l'échelle nationale. L'offre allait de modèles à quatre pièces à un prix de 4500 $ à des maisons de six pièces à deux étages avec garage pour 8550 $ (prix de 1934). Les chiffres des ventes refusant d'augmenter en dépit des efforts marketing,

Opposite page: McDougall
Residence in Riverside, Illinois,
1930s

Linke Seite: McDougall Residenz
in Riverside, Illinois, in den 1930er
Jahren

Page de gauche: Résidence de
McDougall à Riverside, Illinois,
dans les années 1930

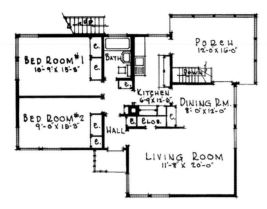

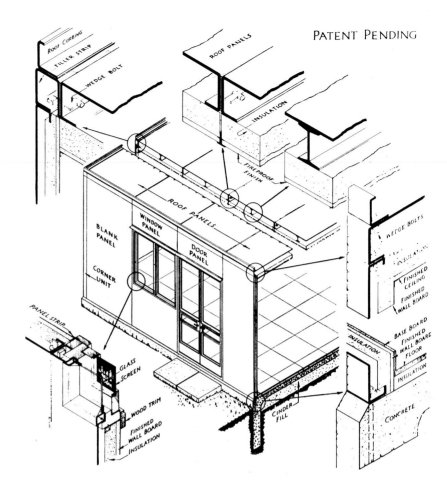

Above: First floor plan of the
exhibition house at the *Century
of Progress Exposition*, 1933

Oben: Erdgeschossgrundriss des
Musterhauses auf der Ausstellung
„Century of Progress", 1933

En haut: Plan du rez-de-chaussée de
la maison-témoin à l'exposition
Century of Progress, 1933

Right: Original design of the wooden
panel as used in houses for the 1933
Century of Progress Exhibition

Rechts: Das originale Design der
Holzverkleidung, wie es 1933 auf der
Ausstellung „Century of Progress"
1933 vorgestellt wurde

À droite: Design d'origine du
revêtement de bois utilisé pour les
maisons de l'exposition Century of
Progress en 1933

with a pitched version. The mail-order catalogue company Sears Roebuck
and Co., which became a partner in the project in 1935, argued that the
taste of the public at large should be taken into consideration. The system
of load-bearing steel plates was first replaced by a steel frame structure fitted out with wood-clad panels of asbestos cement. Later, the entire structure was made of wood.
It is now impossible to determine how many steel houses the company was
ever able to sell, presumably the figure is under one hundred. After Fisher,
the company's founder, left General Houses in 1940, the modern forms
were abandoned completely. The subsequent success was overwhelming:
in 1943 General Houses produced roughly 2,000 prefabricated houses per
month in a traditional style.

steigen wollten, wurde das Innere durch eine Holzverschalung „gemütli-
cher" gemacht. Später änderte man auch das Äußere, indem man zum Beispiel das Flachdach durch ein Satteldach ersetzte. Vor allem das 1935 als
Partner eingestiegene Versandhaus Sears Roebuck and Co. drängte darauf,
auf den Geschmack des breiten Publikums einzugehen. Das System der
lasttragenden Stahlplatten wurde zunächst durch eine Konstruktion aus
Stahlrahmen ersetzt, in die holzverkleidete Asbest-Zement-Platten eingesetzt wurden. Später ging man zu einer kompletten Holzkonstruktion über.
Wie viele Stahl-Häuser General Houses insgesamt verkaufte, ist nicht
mehr zu ermitteln, vermutlich waren es nicht einmal hundert. Nachdem
Unternehmensgründer Fisher die Firma 1940 verlassen hatte, gab man die
modernen Formen gänzlich auf. Der Erfolg war überwältigend: 1943 produ-
zierte General Houses monatlich rund 2000 Fertighäuser in traditionellem
Stil.

des prix modérés et des facilités de paiement (traites de 30 $ mensuelles),
l'intérieur fut rendu plus « confortable » grâce à un revêtement de bois.
L'extérieur fut également modifié ultérieurement, en remplaçant notamment le toit plat par un toit en pente. Mais ce fut surtout l'entreprise de vente par correspondance Sears Roebuck and Co., partenaire à partir de 1935,
qui poussa à s'adapter au goût du grand public. Le système des panneaux
d'acier porteurs fut alors remplacé par une construction à cadre d'acier
dans laquelle furent insérés des panneaux de fibrociment à revêtement de
bois. Puis on passa ultérieurement à une construction intégralement en bois.
Le nombre de maisons d'acier vendu par General Houses au total reste un
mystère, mais sans doute pas plus d'une centaine. Après le départ en 1940
de Fisher, le fondateur de l'entreprise, on renonça totalement à la modernité
des formes. Le succès fut alors écrasant: en 1943, General Houses produi-
sait environ 2000 maisons préfabriquées de style traditionnel par mois.

Below: Living room in a model house from the *Century of Progress Exposition*, 1933

Unten: Wohnzimmer des Musterhauses auf der Ausstellung „Century of Progress", 1933

En dessous: Salon de la maison-témoin de l'exposition Century of Progress, 1933

Above: Kitchen (left) and bedroom (right) in a model house from the *Century of Progress Exposition*, 1933

Oben: Küche (links) und Schlafzimmer (rechts) des Musterhauses auf der Ausstellung „Century of Progress", 1933

Au-dessus: Cuisine (à gauche) et chambre (à droite) de la maison-témoin de l'exposition Century of Progress, 1933

House in Lake Delavan, Wisconsin,
1935
Haus in Lake Delavan, Wisconsin,
1935
Maison à Lake Delavan, Wisconsin,
1935

DYMAXION DEPLOYMENT UNIT

Butler Manufacturing Company, Kansas City, Missouri, USA
1944

Opposite page: Advertising photo promoting the residential use of the Dymaxion Deployment Unit, 1941
Rechte Seite: Werbefoto für die Nutzung der Dymaxion Deployment Unit als Wohnhaus, 1941
Page de droite: Photo publicitaire montrant l'utilisation de la Dymaxion Deployment Unit comme maison d'habitation, 1941

Right: Dymaxion Deployment Unit used as accommodation for troops, 1940
Rechts: Die Dymaxion Deployment Unit als Truppenunterkunft, 1940
À droite: La Dymaxion Deployment Unit comme baraque militaire, 1940

In 1940, Richard Buckminster Fuller was commissioned by the United States government to design low-cost housing for troupes that could be produced efficiently. The housing units were planned as a means of supporting the British forces, then at war with Germany. The multitalented inventor, who had already designed the Dymaxion House in 1927 and presented it in 1929, recognized the project as an opportunity to realize a similar, industrially produced building.

Fuller developed his Dymaxion Deployment Unit (DDU) in collaboration with the Butler Manufacturing Company in Kansas City, which then produced grain silos out of corrugated sheet metal. Using the circular floor plan of a silo, he constructed a housing unit that could be easily erected and taken down and in which the external wall and the supporting structure formed a single unit. The roof was a dome that consisted of convex sheets of steel. The central mast, which had been designed to support the entire Dymaxion House as well as to contain the distribution and supply systems and the triangular lift, served mainly as an assembly aid in the DDU: it could be used to hoist up the cupola after it was assembled on the ground. The plumbing unit was included in a separate cylindrical element. Fuller attempted to use the building's shape to promote air circulation in order to avoid overheating in what was essentially a tin can. Both the wind and installed ventilators played a role here.

The United States military initially ordered thousands of these sheet-metal units in order to use them as radar barracks and emergency housing. However, once metal was classified as a material of strategic importance to arms production after the United States entered the war in 1941, it was 1944 before a small number of these circular buildings were produced for deployment in Alaska, the Near East, and at Fort Monmouth near New York City. Fuller had also designed the DDU for private use, but there was no demand for it by civilians after the war.

1940 wurde Richard Buckminster Fuller von der US-Regierung damit beauftragt, Truppenunterkünfte zu entwerfen, die kostengünstig und effizient zu produzieren sein sollten. Die Behausungen waren zur Unterstützung der britischen Truppen gedacht, die sich im Krieg mit Deutschland befanden. Der multitalentierte Tüftler, der bereits 1927 das Dymaxion-Haus entworfen und 1929 präsentiert hatte, erkannte darin die Chance, ein ähnliches, industriell fertigbares Gebäude zu realisieren.

Seine Dymaxion Deployment Unit (DDU) entwickelte Fuller gemeinsam mit der Butler Manufacturing Company in Kansas City, die damals Getreidesilos aus Wellblech herstellte. Unter Verwendung des kreisrunden Silogrundrisses konstruierte er eine Behausung, die leicht aufzustellen und zu demontieren war, und bei der Außenwand und Tragwerk eine Einheit bildeten. Das Dach wurde durch eine Schale aus konvexen Stahlblechen gebildet. Der zentrale Mast, der beim Dymaxion-Haus noch die komplette Struktur zu tragen hatte und die Verteilungs- und Versorgungssysteme sowie einen dreieckigen Lift enthielt, existierte nur noch als Montagehilfe: An ihm konnte die am Boden zusammengefügte Kuppel emporgezogen werden. In einer separaten zylindrischen Einheit war die Sanitäreinheit untergebracht. Fuller versuchte, die Form des Gebäudes für eine Luftumwälzung zu nutzen, die die übermäßige Aufheizung der Blechdose verhindern sollte. Dabei halfen Wind und auch eingebaute Ventilatoren.

Das US-amerikanische Militär bestellte zunächst Tausende dieser Blecheinheiten, um sie als Radarbaracken und Notunterkünfte einzusetzen. Da aber nach dem Kriegseintritt der USA 1941 Metall als kriegswichtiges Material für die Rüstungsindustrie eingestuft war, konnte erst 1944 eine kleinere Anzahl der Rundbauten hergestellt werden, die in Alaska, im Nahen Osten sowie in Fort Monmouth in der Nähe von New York eingesetzt wurden. Zwar hatte Fuller die DDU auch für den privaten Gebauch konzipiert, dennoch blieb eine zivile Nutzung nach dem Krieg aus.

En 1940, Richard Buckminster Fuller fut chargé par le gouvernement américain de concevoir des logements militaires pouvant être produits à bas coûts et de manière performante. Ces logements provisoires étaient destinés à aider les troupes britanniques en guerre contre l'Allemagne. Ce créateur talentueux qui avait conçu la maison Dymaxion dès 1927 et présentée en 1929, vit là l'occasion de réaliser un bâtiment analogue, pouvant donner lieu à une préfabrication industrielle.

Fuller développa sa Dymaxion Deployment Unit (DDU) en collaboration avec la Butler Manufacturing Company à Kansas City, qui fabriquait à l'époque des silos à grain en tôle ondulée. Se basant sur le plan circulaire de ces silos, il construisit un logement facile à monter et à démonter, dont la paroi extérieure et l'ossature constituaient une unité. Le toit était une coque en tôles d'acier convexes.

Le mât central qui devait aussi porter l'ensemble de la structure de la maison Dymaxion et qui abritait les systèmes de répartition et d'alimentation, ainsi qu'un ascenseur triangulaire, ne servait plus qu'à aider au montage: la coupole assemblée au sol pouvait être hissée en son long. Une unité cylindrique séparée abritait les sanitaires. Fuller tenta d'utiliser la forme du bâtiment pour faire circuler l'air de façon à empêcher l'échauffement excessif de cette boîte en fer-blanc. Le vent ainsi que des ventilateurs intégrés devaient aussi permettre cette régulation.

Les militaires américains commandèrent tout d'abord par milliers ces unités en tôle pour les utiliser comme cabanes à radar et à abris d'urgence. Suite à l'entrée en guerre des États-Unis en 1941, le métal étant devenu un matériau d'importance stratégique pour l'industrie de l'armement, seul un petit nombre de ces bâtiments ronds furent fabriqués à partir de 1944. Ils furent utilisées en Alaska, au Proche-Orient ainsi qu'à Fort Monmouth près de New York. Fuller avait certes également conçu les DDU pour l'usage privé, mais aucune utilisation civile n'eut toutefois lieu après la guerre.

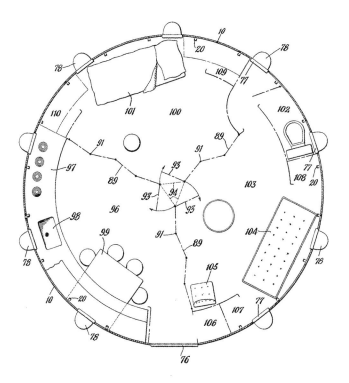

Right und opposite page below:
Drawing for the Patent #2343764
on the Dymaxion Deployment Unit

Rechts und linke Seite unten:
Zeichnungen für das Patent
Nr. 2343764 der Dymaxion
Deployment Unit

À droite et page de gauche, en bas:
Dessins pour le brevet n° 2343764
de la Dymaxion Deployment Unit

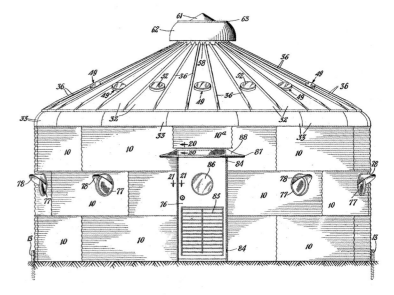

KONRAD WACHSMANN, WALTER GROPIUS

PACKAGED HOUSE SYSTEM

General Panel Corporation, Lincoln, Massachusetts, USA
1947–1952

Hand-drawn cover of a contemporary
documentation
Handgezeichnetes Titelblatt einer
zeitgenössischen Dokumentation
Couverture dessinée à la main d'un
document de l'époque

The General Panel Corporation was established by the German immigrants Konrad Wachsmann and Walter Gropius in 1941. They developed a system of building components for prefabricated wooden houses, which became known as the Packaged House System. According to company information, the prefabricated building panels made it possible for five untrained workers to erect a house in less than nine hours. The dimensions of the building elements were all adapted to fit the square grid on which the construction system was based. Hence, it was possible for all of the components, including the plumbing and electrical installations, to be produced in a factory.

The Packaged House System consisted of supporting wooden frames filled in with sheets of plywood and insulated with fiberglass. These sheets were connected to each other using special X-shaped wedge connectors developed by Wachsmann, which enabled the same type of building elements to be used both for the walls and the ceilings. This procedure made it possible to erect either single- or multi-story buildings. The façade was additionally clad in vertically arranged wooden boards. The windows, doors, fittings, electrical and sanitary installations were already integrated into the prefabricated building elements. Wachsmann developed a linear wedge system which made it possible to connect internal walls invisibly at the intersections.

Although the production facilities established in 1947 had already been shut down by 1952, due to the lack of demand, the construction and production principles continued to influence wooden construction in the United States.

Die General Panel Corporation wurde 1941 von den deutschen Emigranten Konrad Wachsmann und Walter Gropius gegründet. Sie entwickelten ein Konzept für Holzfertighäuser, das unter dem Namen „Packaged House System" bekannt wurde. Vorgefertigte Tafelbauelemente ermöglichten die Errichtung eines Hauses, das nach Angaben der Firma fünf ungelernte Arbeiter in weniger als neun Stunden aufbauen konnten. Die Größen der Bauelemente sind alle auf das quadratische Grundraster abgestimmt, das dem Bausystem zugrunde liegt. So konnten sämtliche Komponenten einschließlich der haustechnischen Elemente in einer Fabrik hergestellt werden.

Das Packaged House System bestand aus tragenden Holzrahmen, die mit leichten Sperrholzplatten ausgefacht und mit einer Glaswollefüllung isoliert wurden. Diese Tafeln waren durch vierteilige Standardknoten miteinander verbunden – eine neue Verbindungsmechanik, die von Wachsmann entwickelt worden war und die Montage gleichartiger Bauelemente sowohl als Wand- als auch als Deckenelemente ermöglichte. Mit diesem Verfahren ließen sich nach Belieben ein- oder mehrstöckige Gebäuden konstruieren. Die Fassade wurde zusätzlich mit einer senkrecht verlaufenden Holzverschalung versehen. Fenster, Türen, Beschläge sowie die Haustechnik waren in die vorgefertigten Bauteile bereits integriert. Für den Innenbereich entwickelte Wachsmann ein lineares Stecksystem, das ermöglichte, die Innenwände an den Kreuzungspunkten unsichtbar miteinander zu verbinden.

Auch wenn die 1947 errichtete Fabrikationsanlage ihren Betrieb aufgrund mangelnder Auslastung bereits 1952 einstellen musste, hatte das Konstruktions- und Herstellungsverfahren Einfluss auf die amerikanische Holzbauindustrie.

La General Panel Corporation fut fondée en 1941 par les émigrés allemands Konrad Wachsmann et Walter Gropius. Ils développèrent un concept de construction pour des maisons préfabriquées en bois qui fut connu sous le nom de Packaged House System. Les éléments préfabriqués sous forme de panneaux permettaient la construction d'une maison qui, selon les concepteurs, pouvait être montée en moins de neuf heures par cinq ouvriers non qualifiés. Les tailles des éléments de construction sont toutes adaptées à la trame carrée qui constitue la base du système de construction. Ainsi, tous ces composants, dont la domotique, pouvaient être fabriqués dans une usine.

Le Packaged House System était composé de structures de bois porteuses accueillant de légers panneaux de contreplaqué, isolés avec un remplissage de laine de verre. Ces panneaux étaient reliés entre eux par des nœuds standard en quatre parties, un nouveau mécanisme d'assemblage développé par Wachsmann qui permettait le montage d'éléments de construction similaires, ainsi que d'éléments de murs et de plafonds. Ce procédé offrait la possibilité de construire des bâtiments de un à plusieurs niveaux à volonté. La façade reçut un revêtement vertical de bois supplémentaire. Fenêtres, portes, ferrures et domotique étaient déjà intégrées aux éléments préfabriqués. Pour l'intérieur, Wachsmann développa un système d'emboîtement linéaire permettant un raccord invisible des parois aux intersections.

Même lorsque l'unité de fabrication créée en 1947 dut stopper son activité dès 1952 en raison du manque d'activité, les principes de construction et de fabrication avaient déjà exercé une influence certaine sur l'industrie américaine des constructions en bois.

Below: The lines of the grid indicate a module of 3 ft., 4 inches which constitutes the unit of measure upon which all of the parts are based.

Unten: Die Rasterlinien definieren Quadrate mit einer Kantenlänge von rund 1 m. Aus diesem Modul ergibt sich das Grundmaß für sämtliche Bauteile.

En bas: Les lignes de la grille délimitent un module d'environ 1 m qui constitue l'unité de mesure servant de base pour tous les éléments.

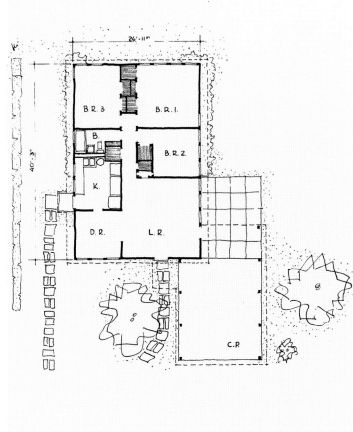

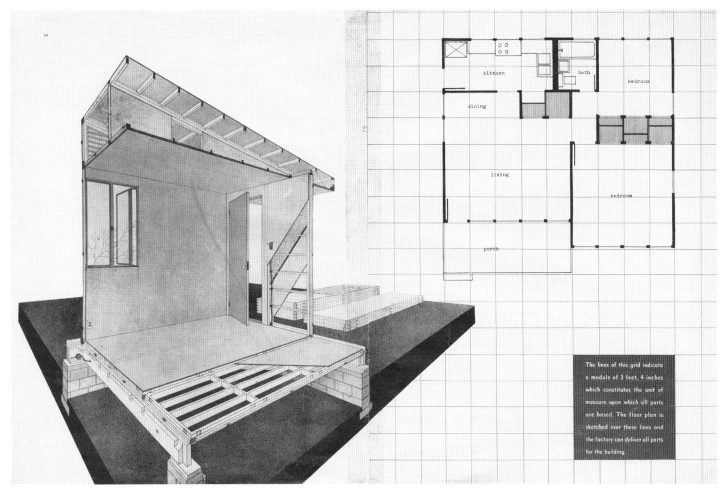

The lines of this grid indicate a module of 3 feet, 4 inches which constitutes the unit of measure upon which all parts are based. The floor plan is sketched over these lines and the factory can deliver all parts for the building.

Above and right page: Floor plan and perspective, one of many alternative designs

Oben und rechte Seite: Grundriss und Perspektive einer von vielen Entwurfsalternativen

Page de droite, en haut: Plan et perspective d'une des nombreuses versions du projet

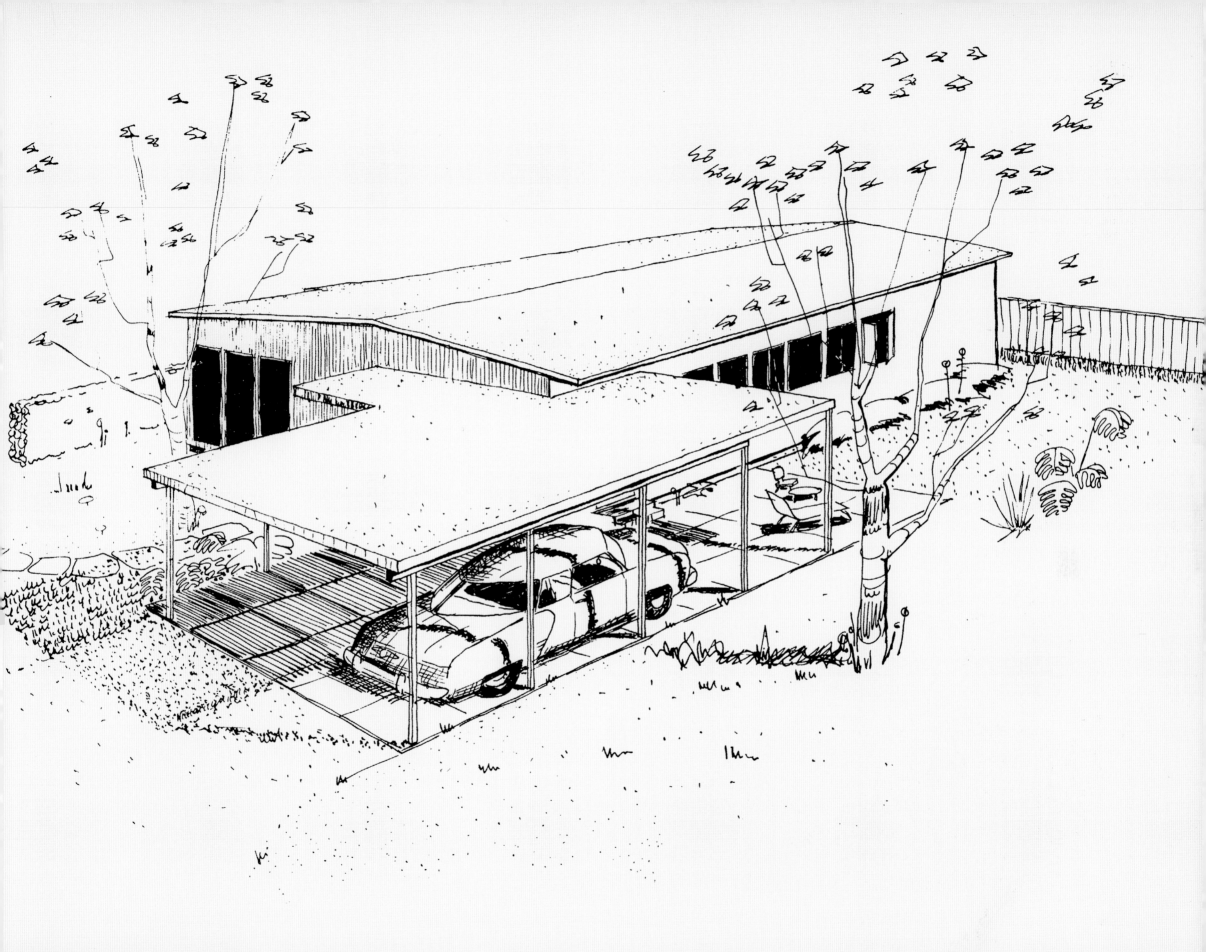

Plan of the factory layout
Planung der Fabrikeinrichtung
Plan de l'usine

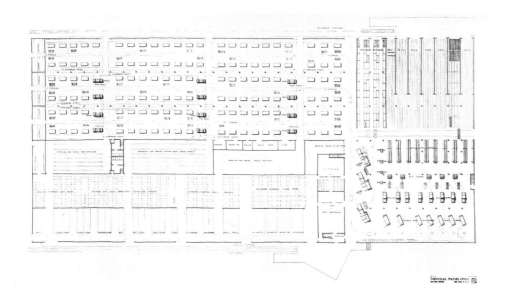

Photograph of a model
Modellfoto
Photo de maquette

Walter Gropius and Konrad Wachsmann
Walter Gropius und Konrad Wachsmann
Walter Gropius et Konrad Wachsmann

One truck transports all of the pre-fabricated parts for a single-family house to the building site, including all of the built-in furniture and the fixtures for the kitchen and bathroom.

Ein Lastwagen transportiert alle Fertigteile eines Einfamilienhauses einschließlich sämtlicher Einbaumöbel und der Küchen- und Badezimmereinrichtung zur Baustelle.

Un camion transporte tous les éléments de construction d'une maison unifamiliale – meubles encastrés et équipement de cuisine et de salle de bains compris – jusqu'au chantier.

Assembly at the building site
Montage auf der Baustelle
Montage sur le chantier

Production in the factory
Fertigung in der Fabrik
Fabrication à l'usine

Left and right page: The living room from two perspectives

Links und rechte Seite: Das Wohnzimmer aus zwei Blickrichtungen

À gauche et page de droite : Le salon vu de deux perspectives

Model of the connection between the wall elements

Modell des Anschlusses der Wandelemente

Maquette du raccord des éléments de murs

Opposite page: A molded plywood screen by Charles Eames separates the desk from the breakfast nook.

Rechte Seite: Ein Wandschirm aus Formschichtholz, von Charles Eames entworfen, trennt Arbeitsbereich und Frühstücksecke.

Page de droite : Un paravent en contreplaqué moulé conçu par Charles Eames sépare le bureau du coin petit déjeuner.

The location of the windows in the bedroom and bathroom, directly over the bed and the bathtub, may not have been popular with some clients.

Die Lage der Fenster im Schlaf- und Badezimmer direkt über dem Bett bzw. der Badewanne dürfte für viele Nutzer etwas problematisch gewesen sein.

L'emplacement des fenêtres de la chambre et de la salle de bains, à savoir au-dessus du lit et de la baignoire, posa sans doute problème à de nombreux utilisateurs.

DYMAXION HOUSE II

Beech Aircraft Company/Fuller Houses Inc., Wichita, Kansas, USA
1947

Right: Drawing of a patent for the Dymaxion house, submitted but never granted

Rechts: Zeichnung zum eingereichten, aber nie genehmigten Patent des Dymaxion-Hauses

À droite: Dessin du brevet déposé mais jamais accepté de la maison Dymaxion

Opposite page: Assembly of the prototype

Rechte Seite: Montage des Prototyps

Page de droite: Montage du prototype

In 1944 the irrepressible inventor Richard Buckminster Fuller was given another opportunity to realize the Dymaxion House that he had originally developed in 1927. His partner was now the Beech Aircraft Company in Wichita, Kansas, which was looking to diversify its product line, since the company's order books were no longer full. For a full two years, the directors of the company gave Fuller a free hand in the factory so that he could develop an aluminum house, which they were hoping to sell at a volume of fifty to sixty thousand per year and at a price of $6,500 (roughly the price of a luxury car). Beech and Fuller jointly founded Fuller Houses Inc. for this purpose.

The new version of the Dymaxion, whith a circular floor plan, was to be suspended slightly above the ground. The floor plate was to be held up by steel cables attached to a slender steel mast. The circular floor plan was intended to provide stability while simultaneously requiring the lowest possible volume of building material. The house measures 36 ft. in diameter and weighs 5,000 lbs. including the built-in furnishings.

The roof is a flat dome with a ventilator mounted in a cap on top in order to circulate the air within the house. The central mast contains all of the utility cables as well as the pipes for the kitchen and the two bathroom units, which were patented by Fuller in 1936 and designed to be highly water-efficient. Rainwater could also be collected from the roof.

The 1,000 sq.ft. of living space also offeres enough room for a vestibule, a living room, two bedrooms, a dining room, and a pantry adjacent to the

1944 bot sich für den unermüdlichen Erfinder Richard Buckminster Fuller eine Chance, sein 1927 entwickeltes Dymaxion-Haus endlich zu realisieren. Partner war diesmal der Flugzeugbauer Beech in Wichita, Kansas, dessen Auftragsbücher nicht mehr ausgelastet waren und der sich deshalb nach neuen Geschäftsfeldern umsah. Die Firmenchefs ließen Fuller für zwei Jahre freie Hand in ihrer Fabrik, um ein Aluminiumhaus zu entwickeln, von dem sie jährlich 50 bis 60000 Stück zu je 6500 $ (etwa der Preis eines Luxus-Autos) verkaufen wollten. Beech und Fuller gründeten eigens hierfür die Fuller Houses Inc.

Die neue Dymaxion-Version sollte auf rundem Grundriss nur knapp über dem Boden schweben. Die Bodenplatte ist mit Stahlseilen an einem schlanken stählernen Mast aufgehängt. Die runde Form sollte dem Gebäude Stabilität verleihen und zugleich möglichst wenig Material erfordern. Das Haus hat einen Durchmesser von knapp 11 m und wiegt 2200 kg – die Einbaumöbel inklusive.

Eine Haube bildet das Dach, obenauf sitzt ein Ventilator, der die Luft im Haus umwälzt. Im zentralen Mast laufen die Leitungen und die Installationsrohre zur Küche und den beiden Badezimmern, die nach einem 1936 von Fuller entwickelten und patentierten Verfahren besonders wassersparend arbeiten sollten. Über das Hausdach sollte Regenwasser gesammelt werden.

Auf 94 m² Wohnfläche finden außerdem Platz: eine Diele, ein Wohnzimmer, zwei Schlafzimmer, ein Esszimmer und eine Vorratskammer neben

En 1944, une nouvelle chance s'offrit à l'infatigable inventeur Richard Buckminster Fuller de réaliser enfin sa maison Dymaxion, développée en 1927. Cette fois, son partenaire était le constructeur d'avions Beech à Wichita, au Kansas. Son carnet de commande n'étant plus rempli, ce dernier cherchait à s'ouvrir à de nouveaux domaines d'activité. Pendant deux ans, les chefs d'entreprise laissèrent carte blanche à Fuller dans leur usine afin qu'il développe une maison d'aluminium dont il comptait vendre 50000 à 60000 exemplaires à 6500 $ pièce (environ le prix d'une voiture de luxe). Beech et Fuller fondèrent tout spécialement la Fuller Houses Inc. dans cette optique.

De plan circulaire, la nouvelle version de la maison Dymaxion devait légèrement flotter au-dessus du sol. Le radier est suspendu à un mince mât d'acier par des câbles en acier. La forme ronde devait donner de la stabilité au bâtiment tout en nécessitant un minimum de matériel. La maison fait tout juste 11 m de diamètre et pèse 2200 kg avec les meubles encastrés.

Le toit forme un capot sur lequel se trouve un ventilateur qui assure la circulation de l'air dans la maison. Les canalisations et les conduits se trouvant dans le mât central desservent la cuisine et les deux salles de bains, conçues selon un procédé permettant d'économiser l'eau que Fuller avait développé et breveté en 1936. L'eau de pluie devait être collectée par le toit de la maison.

Sur une surface habitable de 94 m² se trouvaient également un hall, une salle de séjour, deux chambres, une salle à manger ainsi qu'un cellier à côté

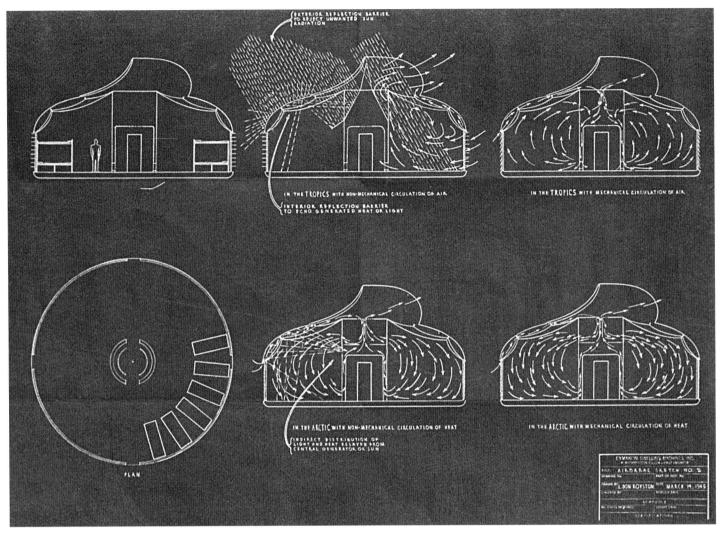

Plan illustrating the flow of
convection currents in the Dymaxion
House

Skizze der Luftzirkulation im
Dymaxion-Haus

Plan de la circulation de l'air dans la
maison Dymaxion

Opposite page: Assembly of the
prototype

Rechte Seite: Montage des Prototyps

Page de droite: Montage du
prototype

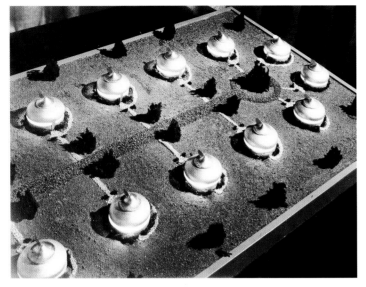

Conceptual model for a Dymaxion
House colony (left) and the interior
of a house (right)

Ideenmodelle für eine Dymaxion-
Haus-Siedlung (links) und die Inneneinrichtung (rechts)

Proposition de maquette pour un
lotissement de maisons Dymaxion
(à gauche) et pour leur aménagement
intérieur (à droite)

kitchen. Special features included folding doors and "o-volving shelves", storage cabinets that swing into the room at the press of a button. The wraparound panorama windows provided a perfect view in every direction. After two prototypes, with which Fuller was not satisfied himself, the Beech Aircraft Company decided to abandon the project. A question that was never clarified was how the project should be marketed, particularly since there was so much resistance against it by local builders and trade unions, which saw their members' livelihoods threatened by it. Fuller left Wichita in 1947—thus another of his projects was stranded halfway towards completion.

The entrepreneur William Graham bought the prototype and had a "hybrid version" attached to his house in Wichita. Graham and his family used the building for roughly thirty years, although some of Fuller's innovations, such as the ventilator on the roof, were never operated.

In 1991, the family donated the Dymaxion House and all of its related parts to the Henry Ford Museum in Dearborn, Michigan, where it was restored to its original condition in years of painstaking work.

der Küche. Besonderheiten sind die Falttüren und die „O-Volving shelves", per Knopfdruck in das Zimmer schwenkbare Stauschränke. Die umlaufenden Panoramafenster gewähren einen vorzüglichen Ausblick in alle Richtungen.

Nach zwei Prototypen, mit denen auch Fuller selbst nicht zufrieden war, entschied die Firma Beech, das Projekt aufzugeben. Vor allem blieb unklar, wie das Projekt vermarktet werden könnte, zumal lokale Bauunternehmen, die sich davon in ihrer Existenz bedroht sahen, zusammen mit den Baugewerkschaften dagegen Front machten. Fuller verließ Wichita 1947 – wieder einmal blieb ein Projekt auf halbem Wege stecken.

Der Unternehmer William Graham kaufte die Prototypen und ließ 1948 eine „Hybridversion" an sein Haus in Wichita anbauen. Graham und seine Familie nutzten den Bau etwa 30 Jahre lang, einige von Fullers Innovationen wie der Ventilator auf dem Dach wurden allerdings nie in Betrieb genommen.

1991 vermachten sie das Dymaxion-Haus und alle zugehörigen Teile dem Henry Ford Museum in Dearborn, Michigan, wo man in jahrelanger Kleinarbeit die Originalgestalt rekonstruierte.

de la cuisine. Les portes pliantes et les « O-Volving shelves », des placards pivotant dans la pièce d'une simple pression de bouton, étaient caractéristiques de cette maison. Les fenêtres panoramiques circulaires offrent une vue admirable dans toutes les directions.

Après deux prototypes dont Fuller n'était pas satisfait, l'entreprise Beech décida d'abandonner le projet. La façon dont le projet allait pouvoir être commercialisé était notamment floue, d'autant plus que les entreprises du bâtiment locales se sentant menacés dans leur existence, firent front contre ce projet avec les syndicats. Fuller quitta Wichita en 1947, laissant derrière lui un projet de plus inachevé.

L'entrepreneur William Graham acheta les prototypes et se fit construire une « version hybride » en 1948 à côté de sa maison à Wichita. Graham et sa famille utilisèrent le bâtiment pendant une trentaine d'années. Certaines innovations de Fuller, telles que le ventilateur du toit, ne furent toutefois jamais mises en service.

En 1991, ils léguèrent la maison Dymaxion ainsi que tous ses éléments au musée Henry Ford à Dearborn, dans le Michigan, où le modèle original fut méticuleusement reconstruit sur plusieurs années.

Below: The house on William
Graham's property, 1946

Unten: Das Haus auf dem Grundstück von William Graham, 1946

En bas: La maison sur le terrain
de William Graham, 1946

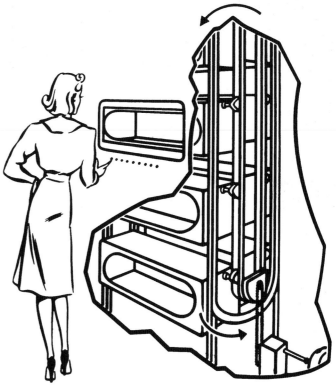

Sketch of the installation of the
rotating shelves based on the
paternoster principle

Skizze zum Einbau rotierender
Regale nach dem Paternoster-
Prinzip

Esquisse de l'installation d'étagères
pivotantes selon le principe de
l'ascenseur à marche continue

EDWARD LARRABEE BARNES, HENRY DREYFUSS

VULTEE HOUSE

Consolidated Vultee Aircraft Corporation, San Diego, California, USA
1947

Connection of walls with ground
plate
Verbindung von Wänden mit der
Bodenplatte
Assemblage des murs avec le radier

After the Second World War there were dozens of aircraft manufacturers in the United States with idle production facilities. At the same time, there was an enormous demand for new housing. Hence, it seemed to make perfect sense to use these dormant resources in order to develop and build prefabricated houses. One of these companies was the Consolidated Vultee Aircraft Company in California, which commissioned the industrial designer Henry Dreyfuss and the architect Edward Larrabee Barnes to develop two prototypes for a prefabricated house.
The Vultee House consisted of a series of factory-finished wall and roof elements. The building components had a stiff, honeycomb-like paper core with a thin sheet of aluminum on both sides. These panels were similar in structure to those used for the airplane bodies built by the workers in this same factory during the war. The sheet metal house consisted of 28 components. Since windows accounted for three quarters of the wall space, it seemed larger than the 800 sq.ft. it measured.
Excited by the innovative design, Reginald Fleet, who was the president of Southern California Houses, the company that marketed the house, moved into one of the two prototypes with his family in South Pasadena. It was his intention to demonstrate the advantages of a modern prefabricated home for potential buyers directly on site. Yet the Vultee House was still not a success; apparently people were not quite ready to live in a house that was reminiscent of an airplane.
Both prototypes were long considered to have been lost; however the Fleet Family's house in South Pasadena, mentioned above, was recently rediscovered and saved from demolition.

Kurz nach dem Ende des Zweiten Weltkrieges existierten in den USA Dutzende von Flugzeugfabriken, deren Fertigungsanlagen nicht mehr benötigt wurden. Gleichzeitig bestand großer Bedarf an neuem Wohnraum. Was also lag näher, als die ungenutzten Ressourcen für die Entwicklung und den Bau vorgefertigter Wohnhäuser zu nutzen? Einer dieser Flugzeughersteller war die Consolidated Vultee Aircraft Company in Kalifornien. Das Unternehmen beauftragte den Industriedesigner Henry Dreyfuss und den Architekten Edward Larrabee Barnes mit der Entwicklung zweier Prototypen eines Fertighauses.
Das Vultee-Haus wurde aus einer Reihe von fabrikgefertigten Wand- und Dachelementen zusammengesetzt. Die Bauteile hatten einen steifen, wabenförmigen Papierkern, der beidseitig mit dünnem Aluminiumblech belegt wurde. Diese Paneele ähnelten in ihrer Struktur den Flugzeugrümpfen, die von den Arbeitern während des Krieges in derselben Fabrik gefertigt worden waren. Das Blechhaus besteht aus 28 Komponenten. Da drei Viertel seiner Wandflächen mit Fensterflächen versehen sind, wirkt es größer, als es mit seinen 75 m² Grundfläche tatsächlich ist.
Begeistert von dem neuartigen Design, zog Reginald Fleet, der Präsident der Firma Southern California Houses, die das Haus vermarktete, mit seiner Familie in einen der beiden Prototypen in South Pasadena ein. Er wollte potenzielle Käufer direkt vor Ort empfangen, um ihnen die Vorzüge eines modernen Fertighauses aus erster Hand zu demonstrieren. Dennoch sollte dem Vultee-Haus kein Erfolg beschieden sein; möglicherweise war die Zeit noch nicht reif dafür, in einem Haus zu leben, das stark an ein Flugzeug erinnerte.
Beide Prototypen des Vultee galten lange als verschollen; unlängst wurde jedoch das oben erwähnte Haus in South Pasadena, in dem Familie Fleet gewohnt hatte, wiederentdeckt und vor dem Abriss bewahrt.

Peu de temps après la Deuxième Guerre mondiale, on trouvait aux États-Unis de nombreuses usines aéronautiques aux unités de production désaffectées. Le besoin de nouveaux logements étant alors considérable, quoi de plus logique que d'utiliser les ressources abandonnées pour développer et construire des maisons préfabriquées? L'une de ces entreprises était la Consolidated Vultee Aircraft Company en Californie, qui confia au designer industriel Henry Dreyfuss et à l'architecte Edward Larrabee Barnes le développement de deux prototypes d'une maison préfabriquée.
La maison Vultee était composée d'une série de modules préfabriqués de cloisons et de toiture. Les éléments de construction au noyau de papier rigide, en forme de nids d'abeilles, étaient recouverts sur les deux faces de minces feuilles d'aluminium. Par leur structure, ces panneaux ressemblaient aux fuselages d'avions fabriqués dans cette même usine pendant la guerre. La maison était composée de 28 éléments. Avec ses baies vitrées occupant les trois quarts de la surface murale, cette maison de tôle semblait plus grande que sa surface effective de 75 m².
Enthousiasmé par ce nouveau design, Reginald Fleet, président de la Southern California Houses, l'entreprise qui commercialisait la maison, emménagea avec sa famille dans l'un des deux prototypes à South Pasadena. Il espérait ainsi attirer directement sur site des acquéreurs potentiels en leur faisant la démonstration immédiate des avantages d'une maison préfabriquée moderne. Cependant, la maison Vultee ne connut pas le succès escompté, probablement parce que l'époque n'était pas encore assez avancée pour que l'on envisage de vivre dans une maison rappelant fortement un avion.
Les deux prototypes étaient portés disparus depuis longtemps lorsque la maison dans laquelle la famille Fleet avait vécu fut récemment retrouvée à South Pasadena et sauvée de la démolition.

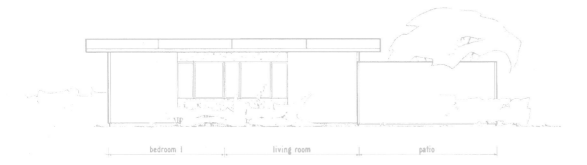

bedroom 1 | living room | patio

tools | patio | kitchen | bath | bedroom 2

Opposite page: The model house
in the factory

Rechte Seite: Das Musterhaus in
der Werkhalle

Page de droite: La maison-témoin
à l'usine

Elevations and plan

Ansichten und Grundriss

Élévations et plan

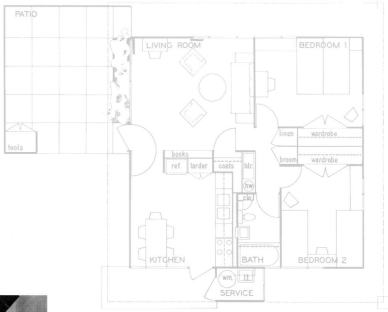

PATIO

LIVING ROOM

BEDROOM 1

tools

linen | wardrobe

books | broom | wardrobe

ref. | larder | coats | htr.

hw

clo.

KITCHEN

BATH

BEDROOM 2

w.m. | t.l.

SERVICE

Assembly of wall elements in the
factory

Montage der Wandelemente in der
Fabrik

Assemblage des éléments de murs
à l'usine

Opposite page and right: The interior of the model house erected in the factory

Linke Seite und rechts: Einrichtung des in der Werkhalle aufgebauten Musterhauses

Page de gauche et à droite: Aménagement de la maison-témoin montée à l'usine

LUSTRON HOMES

Lustron Corporation, Columbus, Ohio, USA
1948–1950

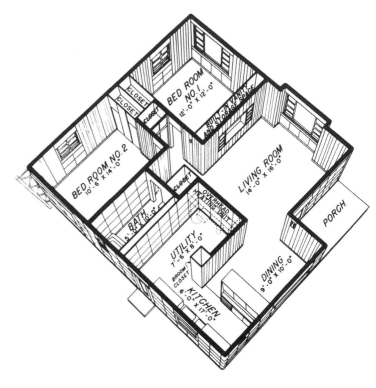

Opposite page: The many parts of a Lustron house in a promotional photo, 1949
Rechte Seite: Sämtliche Einzelteile eines Lustron-Hauses auf einem Werbefoto, 1949
Page de droite: Ensemble des composants d'une maison Lustron sur une photo publicitaire, 1949

After the Second World War, the United States government reacted to the housing shortage by granting generous loans to domestic builders. The intention was to promote the production of low-cost, quickly built, standardized houses. One of the builders was the Swedish-born inventor Carl Strandlund, who had already made a name for himself by producing prefabricated service stations. In 1947, he established the Lustron Corporation at a decommissioned airplane factory in Columbus, Ohio, in order to introduce a prefabricated house onto the market. Like Strandlund's service stations, the Lustron Houses consisted entirely of metal. The supporting structure was made of steel, the wall segments and roofing elements were made of sheet steel, and the façade consisted of extremely durable and easy-to-clean enameled sheet steel panels. The roof was made of enameled steel shingles.

Production of the Lustron houses in series began in 1948. The assembly of the roughly 3,000 parts, which weighed 12 t and were delivered on purpose-built flatbed trucks, took about eight days. Of the many versions available, the "Westchester" was the most common model, with roughly 1,000 sq.ft. of floor space. The façade panels were offered in four colors: maize yellow, dove gray, surf blue and desert tan. They were insulated with a thin layer of fiberglass between the wall elements. The built-in furnishings were also made of sheet metal. The color scheme was proposed by the interior decorator Herbert Ketchum, who had already made a name for himself by designing the interior of PanAm airplanes. The bathrooms and bedrooms were equipped with pocket doors. Pictures could be hung on the walls with magnets. The flooring laid down on the concrete foundation was usually marbleized dark brown linoleum.

Yet, the attraction of this new industrial product was apparently short-lived.

Nach dem Ende des Zweiten Weltkrieges reagierte die US-amerikanische Regierung auf die herrschende Wohnungsnot im Land mit der Vergabe großzügiger Kredite an einheimische Bauunternehmer. Vor allem die Produktion kostengünstiger und schnell zu errichtender standardisierter Häuser sollte angeregt werden. Einer dieser Bauunternehmer war der in Schweden geborene Erfinder Carl Strandlund, der sich mit der Produktion von vorgefertigten Tankstellen bereits einen Namen gemacht hatte. 1947 gründete er in einer stillgelegten Flugzeugfabrik in Columbus, Ohio, die Lustron Corporation, die ein vorgefertigtes Haus auf den Markt brachte. Wie schon die Tankstellen Strandlunds bestand auch das Lustron-Haus völlig aus Metall: Das Tragwerk war aus Stahl, die Wandsegmente und Deckenelemente waren aus Stahlblech und die Fassade bestand aus sehr widerstandsfähigen und leicht zu reinigenden Stahlblechtafeln, die mit einer Emailleschicht versehen waren. Das Dach war mit emaillierten Stahlschindeln gedeckt.

Ab 1948 wurden die Lustron-Häuser in Serie produziert. Der Aufbau der rund 3000 Teile, die 12 t wogen und auf einem eigens konstruierten Tieflader angeliefert wurden, dauerte etwa acht Tage. Es gab verschiedene Ausführungen, besonders verbreitet war das Modell „Westchester" mit einer Grundfläche von etwa 100 m². Die Fassadenpaneele wurden in vier Farben angeboten: maisgelb, taubengrau, surferblau und wüstenbraun; gedämmt wurde mit einer dünnen Fiberglaswolle zwischen den Wandelementen. Auch die Einbaumöbel waren in Stahlblech ausgeführt. Die Farbgebung stammte von dem Innenarchitekten Herbert Ketchum, der sich bereits mit der Ausstattung für die Flugzeuge von PanAm einen Namen gemacht hatte. Die Bade- und Schlafzimmer waren mit in der Wand laufenden Schiebetüren ausgestattet. Bilder ließen sich mit Magneten an der Wand

Après la Deuxième Guerre mondiale, le gouvernement américain réagit à la pénurie de logements régnant dans le pays par l'attribution de crédits généreux aux entreprises du bâtiment locales. Il s'agissait principalement de stimuler la production de maisons standardisées bon marché et rapides à monter. L'un des entrepreneurs concernés était l'inventeur suédois Carl Strandlund qui s'était déjà fait connaître avec la production de stations-services préfabriquées. En 1947, il fonda dans une usine aéronautique désaffectée à Columbus, dans l'Ohio, la Lustron Corporation qui commercialisa une maison préfabriquée. Tout comme les stations-services de Strandlund, la maison Lustron était intégralement en métal: l'ossature était en acier, les segments des parois et les éléments de plafond, en tôle d'acier, et la façade en panneaux de tôle d'acier émaillés très résistants et faciles d'entretien. Le toit était recouvert de bardeaux d'acier émaillés.

À partir de 1948, les maisons Lustron furent produites en série. Le montage des quelque 3000 éléments qui pesaient 12 t et étaient livrés sur une remorque spéciale, prenait environ huit jours. Il existait différents modèles. Avec sa surface d'environ 100 m², le modèle Westchester était particulièrement répandu. Les panneaux des façades étaient disponibles en quatre couleurs: jaune maïs, gris pigeon, bleu surfer et brun désert. L'isolation était assurée par une fine couche de laine de verre entre les éléments de murs. Les meubles encastrés étaient également en tôle d'acier. Les coloris étaient conçus par l'architecte d'intérieur Herbert Ketchum qui s'était fait connaître avec l'aménagement intérieur des avions de la PanAm. Les salles de bains et les chambres étaient pourvues de portes coulissantes qui disparaissaient dans la paroi. Les tableaux se fixaient au mur par des aimants. Les sols des fondations étaient généralement recouverts d'un linoléum brun foncé agrémenté de motifs marbrés.

Left: A Lustron delivery truck

Links: Transporter der Firma Lustron

À gauche: Camion de l'entreprise Lustron

Below: Carl Strandlund posing in front of a Lustron transporter decorated with a large ribbon

Unten: Carl Strandlund in Pose vor dem mit einer großen Geschenkschleife verzierten Lustron-Transporter

En dessous: Carl Strandlund posant devant le camion Lustron orné d'un grand ruban

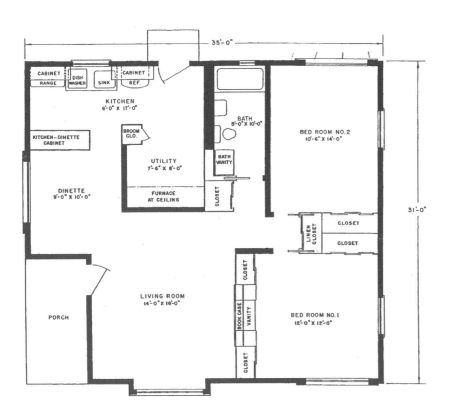

Left: Floor plan from the Lustron Home Erection Manual

Links: Grundriss aus der Bauanleitung für das Lustron Home

À gauche: Plan de la notice de montage pour la maison Lustron

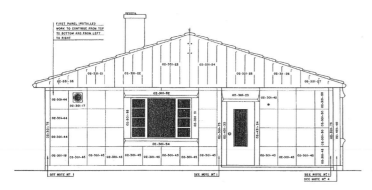

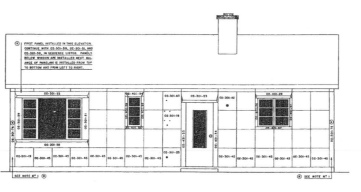

Elevations (above), the house under construction (right), and completed (far right)

Ansichten (oben), Gebäude während des Aufbaus (rechts) und in fertigem Zustand (ganz rechts)

Élévations (en haut), maison en construction (à droite) et terminée (tout à droite)

The number of orders began to decline as early as 1949, after it became clear that the prices ranging between $10,000 and $12,000 were up to 50% higher than originally advertised. Instead of producing 100 houses per day as planned, the daily output was generally only about twenty. *Time* magazine, in particular, derisively followed the rapid demise of the company and ridiculed the houses by comparing them to a "hot dog stand", while relishing in accounts of the company's losses and fuelling the public's skepticism by asking whether anyone really wanted to live in a steel house.

By 1950 the company was bankrupt, not least of all because of Strandlund's dubious business dealings. Particularly controversial was his deal with Joseph McCarthy, in the wake of which the senator wrote an article entitled "A Dollar's Worth of Housing for Every Dollar Spent" making a case for prefabricated housing in general and for the products of the Lustron Corporation in particular. Strandlund had paid the Republican senator, who later became known for his witch-hunts against purported Communists, the generous sum of $10,000 and financed his exorbitant wagers on horses. Of the roughly 2,500 Lustron Houses delivered to locations as far apart as Los Alamos and Alaska, roughly 1,800 still exist today, often lovingly cared for by owners who are aware of their history.

aufhängen. Die Böden des Betonfundaments waren meist mit einem dunkelbraunen Linoleum mit marmoriertem Muster ausgelegt.

Doch der Reiz des neuen Industrieprodukts verflog offenbar schnell. Schon 1949 brachen die Bestellungen ein, nachdem sich herausgestellt hatte, dass die Häuser mit einem Preis zwischen 10 000 $ und 12 000 $ um bis zu 50 % teurer ausfielen als angekündigt. So wurden statt der anvisierten 100 nur etwa 20 Häuser täglich produziert. Das „Time Magazine", das den raschen Niedergang des Unternehmens voller Häme begleitete und die Häuser als Würstchenbuden verspottete, bilanzierte genüsslich die auflaufenden Verluste und nährte die Skepsis des Publikums mit der süffisanten Frage, ob man denn wirklich in einem stählernen Haus leben wolle.

1950 war die Firma bankrott, nicht zuletzt auch wegen der dubiosen Geschäfte, in die Strandlund verstrickt war. Ruchbar wurde sein Deal mit Joseph McCarthy, in dessen Folge dieser in einem Artikel mit dem Titel „A Dollar's Worth of Housing for Every Dollar Spent" für Fertighäuser allgemein und insbesondere für jene der Firma Lustron warb. Dafür zahlte Strandlund dem später als Kommunistenjäger verschrienen republikanischen Senator ein nicht allzu bescheidenes Honorar von 10 000 $ und finanzierte ihm seine exorbitanten Ausgaben für Pferdewetten.

Von den rund 2 500 Lustron-Häusern, die zwischen Los Alamos und Alaska ausgeliefert wurden, existieren heute noch etwa 1 800, oft sehr liebevoll gepflegt von den um ihre Geschichte wissenden Besitzern.

Toutefois, l'attrait de ce nouveau produit industriel se dissipa apparemment très vite. Dès 1949, les commandes s'effondrèrent lorsque les maisons, vendues entre 10 000 $ et 12 000 $, s'avérèrent jusqu'à 50 % plus chères que le prix annoncé. Au lieu des cent unités quotidiennes prévues, seules vingt furent produites. Le *Time Magazine* accompagnait le déclin rapide de l'entreprise de ses commentaires hargneux et tournait les maisons en dérision en les assimilant à des stands de hot-dogs. Il fit le bilan de l'accumulation de ses pertes avec délectation et nourrit le scepticisme du public à son égard en demandant avec arrogance s'il était des personnes désireuses de vivre dans une maison d'acier.

En 1950, l'entreprise avait fait faillite, notamment en raison des affaires douteuses dans lesquelles Strandlund était impliqué. Son accord avec Joseph McCarthy fut ébruité, accord suite auquel ce dernier fit de la publicité pour les maisons préfabriquées en général, et pour celles de l'entreprise Lustron en particulier, dans un article intitulé *A Dollar's Worth of Housing for Every Dollar Spent*. Pour cet article, Strandlund avait versé à Joseph McCarthy – le sénateur républicain pourfendeur de communistes décrié par la suite – un honoraire peu modique de 10 000 $, et financé ses dépenses exorbitantes aux courses de chevaux.

Il reste aujourd'hui environ 1 800 maisons Lustron parmi les quelque 2 500 qui furent livrées entre Los Alamos et l'Alaska, souvent entretenues avec soin par des propriétaires au fait de leur histoire.

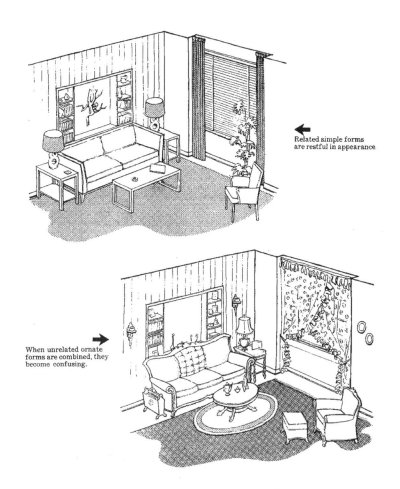

← Related simple forms
are restful in appearance.

When unrelated ornate →
forms are combined, they
become confusing.

In a brochure Lustron recommended
examples of modern interiors.

In einer Broschüre gab Lustron
Empfehlungen für eine passende,
moderne Einrichtung.

Dans une brochure, Lustron donnait
des conseils pour un aménagement
moderne et adapté.

Bedroom with a dressing table (left);
built-in cabinet between kitchen and
dining space (right)

Schlafzimmer mit Frisiertisch
(links); Einbauschrank zwischen
Küche und Essbereich (rechts)

Chambre avec coiffeuse (à gauche);
placard séparant cuisine et salle à
manger (à droite)

Lustron house utility room
Waschküche im Lustron-Haus
Buanderie de la maison Lustron

MAISON STANDARD MÉTROPOLE

Ateliers Jean Prouvé, Maxéville, France
1949–1952

Opposite page: The colony in
Meudon, France, 1949

Rechte Seite: Die Siedlung in
Meudon, Frankreich, 1949

Page de droite: Le lotissement à
Meudon, France, 1949

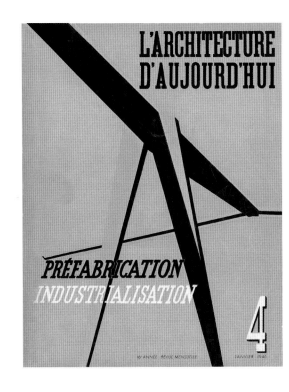

L'ARCHITECTURE D'AUJOURD'HUI

PRÉFABRICATION INDUSTRIALISATION

4

For Jean Prouvé it was only natural for things to be produced industrially, whether it was the furniture or the entire building. Having already designed simple wooden barracks for the military in 1939, he began to concentrate on the construction of residential structures in metal after the war. A common characteristic of his buildings was the use of central supports arranged in rows and rigidly joined to the ridge beam. In a 1946 design, these central supports resembled an upside down V, but he subsequently executed them at right angles, so that they could be more easily integrated into the interior design.

On the recommendation of Eugène Claudius-Petit, the French Minister for Reconstruction and Urban Development, Jean Prouvé and his workshops in Maxéville, near Nancy, were commissioned to design a prefabricated, lightweight, steel frame house that could be produced at low cost and assembled quickly and easily on site. After it became clear that the costs would overrun the proposed budget, the ministry distanced itself from the plan to purchase 25 of the "Maisons standards métropoles". After long negotiations, it was agreed that ten of the standard houses, and four additional houses of the "coque" type, would be erected in a park-like area in the Paris suburb of Meudon. Construction was overseen by the architects André Sive and Prouvé's brother Henri, who also designed some of the foundations on which the houses were set. Four of the standard houses built in Meudon had 26 x 26 ft. of floor space, the other six had 26 x 39 ft. The remaining 15 of the 25 standard houses prefabricated in Maxéville were later distributed throughout France; a few of them were even sent to Algeria.

Depending on the size of the house, the supporting structure consisted of

Industrielle Fertigung war für Jean Prouvé eine Selbstverständlichkeit, sei es für Möbel oder auch für Gebäude. Hatte er bereits 1939 für das Militär einfache Baracken aus Holz entworfen, so konzentrierte er sich nach dem Krieg auf Metallkonstruktionen im Wohnhausbau. Gemeinsames Merkmal seiner Gebäude war die Verwendung von Mittelstützen, die, in Reihe aufgestellt, durch einen Firstbalken biegesteif verbunden wurde. Im Entwurf von 1946 glichen diese Mittelstützen noch einem umgekehrten V, dann führte Prouvé sie rechtwinklig aus, um sie besser in die Einrichtung zu integrieren.

Auf Empfehlung des französischen Ministers für Wiederaufbau und Städtebau Eugène Claudius-Petit erhielten Jean Prouvé und seine Werkstätten in Maxéville bei Nancy den Auftrag, einen Fertighaustyp auf der Basis einer leichten Stahlkonstruktion zu entwerfen, der kostengünstig zu produzieren und vor Ort unkompliziert und schnell aufzubauen sein sollte. Nachdem sich herausgestellt hatte, dass die Kosten das anvisierte Budget übersteigen würden, rückte das Ministerium von seiner Zusage ab, die 25 Exemplare des Maison standard métropole abzunehmen. Nach längeren Verhandlungen einigte man sich darauf, zehn der Standard-Häuser und vier zusätzliche des Typs „Coque" auf einem Parkgelände im Pariser Vorort Meudon aufzustellen. Den Aufbau überwachten als Architekten André Sive und Prouvés Bruder Henri, der auch die Mauersockel für einige der Häuser entworfen hatte. Vier der in Meudon realisierten Standard-Häuser verfügten über eine Grundfläche von 8 x 8 m, die weiteren sechs maßen 8 x 12 m. Die restlichen 15 der 25 in Maxéville vorproduzierten Standard-Häuser wurden später über ganz Frankreich verteilt, einige wenige gelangten auch nach Algerien.

Pour Jean Prouvé, qu'il s'agisse de meubles ou de bâtiments, la fabrication industrielle tombait sous le sens. Après avoir conçu des baraquements en bois pour les militaires dès 1939, il se concentra après la guerre sur des constructions métalliques destinées à l'habitat. La caractéristique commune de ses bâtiments était l'utilisation de portiques axiaux lesquels, alignés, étaient reliés par une poutre faîtière rigide. Dans son projet de 1946, ils ressemblaient encore à un V inversé, puis Prouvé les façonna à angles droits afin de mieux les intégrer à l'installation.

Sur la recommandation du ministre français de la Reconstruction et de l'Urbanisme Eugène Claudius-Petit, Jean Prouvé et ses ateliers à Maxéville près de Nancy reçurent une commande officielle pour la réalisation d'un modèle de maison préfabriquée à ossature d'acier légère, de production bon marché et de montage simple et rapide. Lorsqu'il s'avéra que les coûts dépasseraient le budget prévu, le ministère abandonna le projet d'acquisition de 25 exemplaires de la Maison standard métropole. À l'issue de longues négociations, il fut convenu de monter dix maisons standard, et six du type « coque », dans un parc résidentiel à Meudon, en banlieue parisienne. Le montage fut supervisé par les architectes André Sive et Henri Prouvé, frère de Jean Prouvé. Ce dernier avait aussi conçu quelques-uns des soubassements. Quatre des maisons standard réalisées à Meudon avaient une superficie de 8 m x 8 m, six autres faisaient 8 m x 12 m. Sur les 25 maisons standard préfabriquées à Maxéville, les 15 restantes furent ultérieurement dispersées en France, quelques-unes prirent également la direction de l'Algérie.

En fonction de la taille de la maison, l'ossature était composée d'un ou de deux cadres de tôle pliée en acier ayant la forme d'un U retourné et inté-

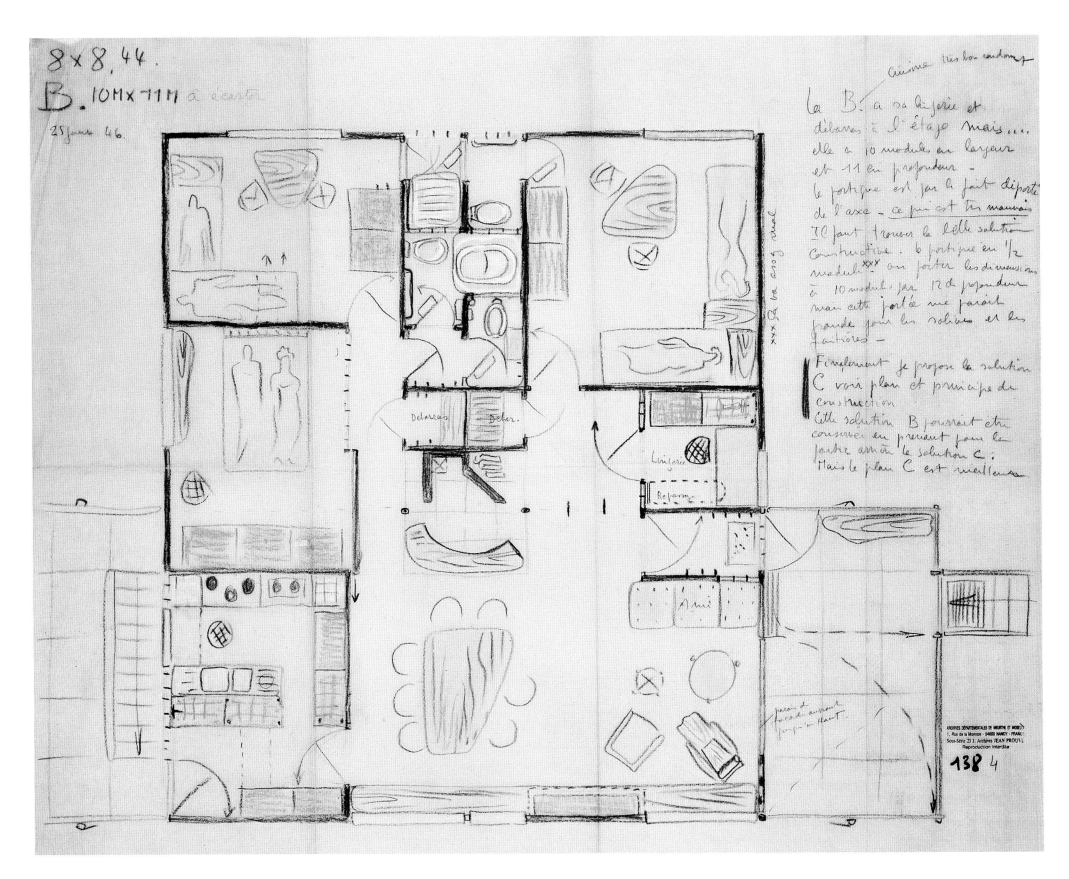

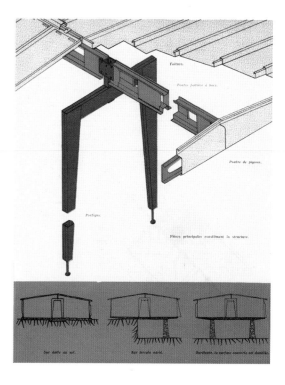

The Maison standard métropole at
the *Salon des arts ménagers*, 1950

Das Maison standard métropole auf
der Messe „Salon des arts ménagers",
1950

La Maison standard métropole au
Salon des arts ménagers, 1950

Assembly in Meudon, 1949

Montage in Meudon, 1949

Montage à Meudon, 1949

one or two frames made of folded sheet steel shaped like an upside-down
"U" with a groove into which the roof beam fit. This support system was a
refinement of the framing system that Prouvé had already designed during
the war, together with Pierre Jeanneret and Charlotte Perriand, for the
"Maison à portique" and also used for the "Maisons tropicales" exported
to Niamey, in Niger, and Brazzaville, in the Congo, in 1949.
The façade consisted of 3-ft. 3-in. panels of sheet aluminum. Doors and
windows were integrated as modules, and their arrangement could be
determined by the customer. Sheet steel segments connected the elements.
A filling of glass wool provided thermal insulation, with steel springs between the inner and outer walls to ensure stability. To this day, the
ensemble consisting of 14 houses in Meudon has been well preserved, and
many of the owners have lived in these lightweight metal icons for over
half a century.

Das Tragwerk bestand je nach Größe des Hauses aus einem oder zwei Rahmen aus gefalztem Stahlblech, die wie ein auf den Kopf gestelltes U aussa-
hen und den Firstbalken aufnahmen. Dieses Tragsystem war eine Weiterentwicklung der Rahmenkonstruktion vom Typ „Maison à portique", die
Prouvé bereits während des Krieges zusammen mit Pierre Jeanneret und
Charlotte Perriand ersonnen hatte und die 1949 auch bei den nach Niamey
in Niger und Brazzaville in Kongo exportierten „Maisons Tropicales" eingesetzt wurde.
Die Fassade setzte sich aus 1 m breiten Aluminiumblechpaneelen zusammen, Türen und Fenster waren in die Module integriert und konnten in ihrer Abfolge vom Kunden ausgewählt werden. Stahlblechprofile verbanden
die Elemente. Eine Glaswollfüllung sorgte für die Wärmedämmung, während Stahlfedern zwischen Innen- und Außenwänden die Stabilität garantierten. Bis heute hat sich die Wohnsiedlung der 14 Häuser in Meudon sehr
gut erhalten, manche der Besitzer bewohnen die Leichtmetall-Ikonen
schon seit über einem halben Jahrhundert.

grant le faîtage. Ce système porteur était un développement de la charpente du modèle Maison à portique imaginé par Prouvé avec Pierre Jeanneret
et Charlotte Perriand pendant la guerre, et utilisé sur les Maisons
Tropicales exportées en 1949 à Niamey au Niger et Brazzaville au Congo.
La façade était constituée de panneaux en feuille d'aluminium d'un mètre.
Les portes et les fenêtres étaient intégrées dans les modules et le client
pouvait choisir leur disposition. Des profils de tôle d'acier reliaient les éléments entre eux. Un remplissage en laine de verre assurait l'isolation thermique tandis que des ressorts d'acier entre les parois intérieures et extérieures garantissaient la stabilité. À ce jour, le lotissement des quatorze
maisons de Meudon est très bien conservé. Certains propriétaires habitent
ces icônes de métal léger depuis bientôt plus d'un demi-siècle.

The Maison standard métropole
in Meudon, France, 1949

Das Maison standard métropole
in Meudon, Frankreich, 1949

La Maison standard métropole
à Meudon, France, 1949

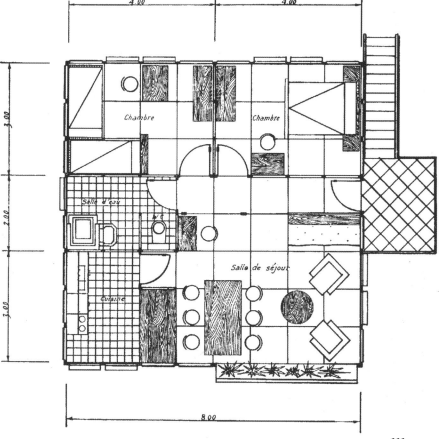

Plan of the prefabricated house
model Standard métropole

Grundriss des Fertighaustyps
Standard métropole

Plan de la maison préfabriquée
standard métropole

JEAN PROUVÉ

MAISON TROPICALE

Ateliers Jean Prouvé, Maxéville, France
1949–1951

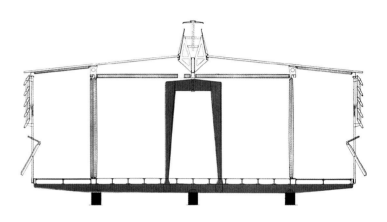

Right: The section shows the structure of the central support and the chimney-like ventilation opening in the roof.
Rechts: Der Schnitt zeigt die Mittelstützenkonstruktion und die kaminartige Lüftungsöffnung im Dach.
À droite: La coupe montre le portique axial et le trou d'aération du toit de type cheminée.

Opposite page: Trial assembly of a part of the building on the premises of the factory in Maxéville, 1949
Rechte Seite: Probeaufbau eines Teils des Gebäudes auf dem Werksgelände in Maxéville, 1949
Page de droite: Montage test d'une partie du bâtiment sur le site des ateliers à Maxéville, 1949

Prouvé's attempts to utilize the extensive production capacity of the plant he established after the Second World War in Maxéville by building prefabricated houses proved to be unexpectedly difficult. Hence, the request he received from Paul Herbé, who had been appointed as a town planner for Niger, must have been more than welcome. Herbé was interested in a house that was not only suited to the tropics but could also be transported by airplane. The first of these houses was intended for the director of the University of Niamey, and others were to follow—but, it never came to that. Prouvé's factory was only ever able to deliver two additional houses—to Brazzaville two years later, and these had already been revised.

Instead of standing on a flat ground plate, the houses in Brazzaville stood on stilts and were connected to each other by a bridge. They served as the office and residence of the director of the local office of the Bureau d'Information de l'Aluminium Français. The reason for putting the buildings up on stilts was the steep slope of the terrain along the street. Prouvé had considered various means of adapting the building to the climate: the inner core consists of various fixed and sliding aluminum walls with circular perforations; there is also a narrow wrap-around veranda, which is enclosed by a railing and adjustable blinds for solar protection. The roof also adheres to the two-layer principle; natural ventilation between the two layers is meant to reduce the heat from the tin roof in the sun. All of the load-bearing components were made of folded sheet steel; all of the others, particularly the roof, were made of sheet aluminum.

Unfortunately, there were never any subsequent orders, because the houses were simply too expensive. Yet the prototype houses, with their grid structure and obviously industrial character on open display, became prominent examples of successful modern architecture. All three of the houses have been preserved. In the meantime, they have been taken apart and restored, and one of them was sold by Christie's at an auction in 2007.

Prouvés Versuche, seine nach dem Zweiten Weltkrieg angelegten umfangreichen Fertigungsanlagen in Maxéville mit dem Bau von Fertighäusern auszulasten, erwiesen sich als unerwartet schwierig. Da mußte ihm eine Anfrage von Paul Herbé, dem Planungsbevollmächtigten für Niger, hochwillkommen erscheinen. Dieser wünschte ein tropengerechtes Wohnhaus, das per Flugzeug transportiert werden konnte. Ein erstes war für den Rektor der Universität von Niamey gedacht, weitere sollten folgen. Doch dazu kam es nicht. Prouvés Fabrik konnte lediglich zwei Jahre später noch zwei weitere Häuser nach Brazzaville liefern, die dem ersten Bau allenfalls ähnelten.

Statt auf einer flachen Bodenplatte standen die Häuser in Brazzaville auf Stelzen und waren durch einen Steg verbunden. Sie dienten als Büro und Wohnung des Direktors der lokalen Vertretung des „Bureau d'Information de l'Aluminium Français". Grund für die aufgeständerte Bauweise war das neben der Straße stark abfallende Gelände. Prouvé hatte sich verschiedene Maßnahmen überlegt, um seinen Bau dem Klima anzupassen: Der innere Kern ist von teils festen, teils verschiebbaren Aluminiumwänden mit runden Bullaugenlöchern gebildet; ihn umgibt ein schmaler Steg, der wiederum vom Geländer und verstellbaren Sonnenschutzlamellen begrenzt ist. Auch das Dach folgt der Idee von zwei Schichten; natürliche Ventilation zwischen diesen sollte eine Aufheizung des Blechdachs in der Sonne verringern. Alle tragenden Teile waren aus gebogenem Stahlblech gebaut, alle anderen, besonders das Dach, hingegen aus Aluminiumblech.

Leider kam es damals zu keinen weiteren Bestellungen, da die Häuser einfach zu teuer waren. Doch die ausgeführten Musterhäuser wurden mit ihrer offen gezeigten Rasterbauweise und der unverschleierten Industrialität ihrer Fertigung zu herausragenden Beispielen geglückter, moderner Architektur. Alle drei Häuser sind erhalten, wurden inzwischen abgebaut und restauriert, eines davon wurde 2007 im Auktionshaus Christie's verkauft.

Contre toute attente, les tentatives de Prouvé d'exploiter les vastes capacités de production développées après la Deuxième Guerre mondiale dans ses ateliers de Maxéville en construisant des maisons préfabriquées se révélèrent difficiles. C'est pourquoi la demande de Paul Herbé, le responsable de la planification du Niger, ne pouvait mieux tomber. Ce dernier souhaitait une maison d'habitation adaptée aux tropiques, pouvant être transportée par avion. Une première maison était destinée au recteur de l'université de Niamey, d'autres devaient suivre. Cela ne fut toutefois pas le cas. L'usine de Prouvé ne parvint à livrer deux autres maisons à Brazzaville que deux ans plus tard, modèles qui avaient d'ailleurs été remaniés.

Au lieu de reposer sur un radier, les maisons étaient posées sur des pilotis. Elles servaient de bureau et d'appartement au directeur de l'antenne locale du Bureau d'Information de l'Aluminium Français. La construction était en hauteur en raison du terrain très en pente se trouvant à côté de la rue. Prouvé avait réfléchi à plusieurs solutions afin d'adapter son bâtiment au climat: son centre est constitué de parois d'aluminium soit fixes soit coulissantes dotées de hublots ronds. Une étroite passerelle en fait le tour, limitée à son tour par des rampes et des pare-soleil réglables. Le toit reprend également cette idée de double couche: la ventilation intermédiaire devait limiter l'échauffement du toit en tôle lié au soleil. Tous les éléments porteurs étaient en tôle d'acier, tandis que les autres étaient en tôle d'aluminium.

Les maisons s'étant avérées trop chères, il n'y eut hélas pas d'autre commande. Avec leur type de construction à trame ouverte et le caractère industriel apparent de leur fabrication, les maisons-témoins devinrent réalisées d'éminents spécimens d'une architecture moderne réussie. Les trois maisons sont conservées, même si elles ont été démontées et restaurées entre temps. L'une d'elle a même fait l'objet d'une vente aux enchères en 2007 chez Christie's.

Below: Floor plan, elevation and section of both houses in Brazzaville

Unten: Grundriss, Ansicht und Schnitt der beiden Häuser in Brazzaville

En dessous: Plan, élévation et coupe des deux maisons à Brazzaville

Right: Unloading building parts from the plane in Niamey, Niger, 1949

Rechts: Entladung von Gebäudeteilen aus dem Flugzeug in Niamey, Niger, 1949

À droite: Déchargement des éléments de construction de l'avion à Niamey, Niger, 1949

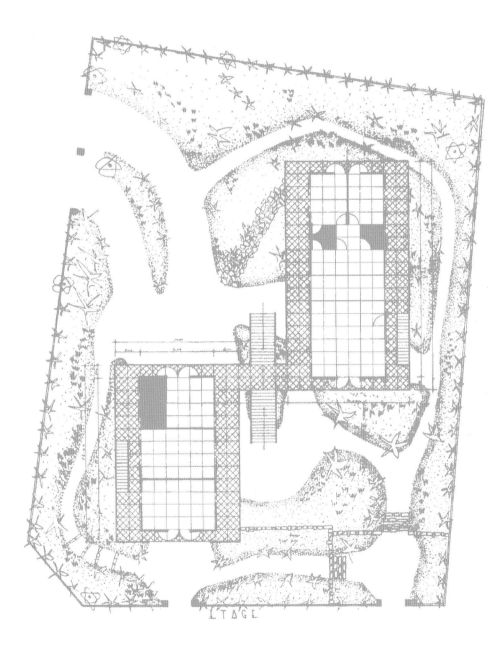

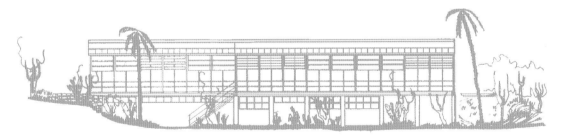

MAISON "T" A USAGE DE BUREAUX

ELEVATION OUEST

COUPE

Above right: Assembly of the house on a concrete ground plate in Niamey, Niger, 1949

Oben rechts: Montage des Hauses in Niamey, Niger auf einer Betonbodenplatte, 1949

En haut à droite: Montage de la maison à Niamey, Niger, sur un radier en béton, 1949

Below right: Construction of the houses in Brazzaville on stilts

Unten rechts: Aufbau der Häuser in Brazzaville auf Stelzen

En bas à droite: Construction des maisons sur pilotis à Brazzaville

LE BUREAU D'INFORMATION DE BRAZZAVILLE

Le Bureau d'Information de Brazzaville a été officiellement inauguré le 3 décembre 1951 par M. Jean Dupin, président du Conseil d'Administration de L'Aluminium Français, entouré de MM. Marcel Pubellier, directeur de la Cégédur, Roger Voisard, directeur de Studal, et Jacques Piget, directeur de ce bureau africain. A cette manifestation assistaient les personnalités les plus marquantes de l'A. E. F. On notait la présence de MM. Bordier, chef de cabinet de M. Chauvet, Haut-Commissaire de la République; Mestre, représentant le Gouverneur Cédile; Cabou, directeur général des Affaires Économiques; Puech, directeur général des Douanes, ainsi que la plupart des autorités militaires et des dirigeants des affaires industrielles, commerciales, bancaires, etc.

Cette réception ayant eu lieu à la tombée de la nuit, il a été impossible de recevoir les personnalités du Congo belge par suite des horaires des vedettes traversant le fleuve. A leur intention, une deuxième réception a été organisée le mercredi 5 décembre à laquelle une quarantaine de personnes de tous les milieux assistaient.

La présentation du nouveau Bureau d'Information de L'Aluminium Fran-

58

115

CARL KOCH

TECHBUILT HOUSE

Techbuilt, Inc., Cambridge, Massachusetts, USA
1954–1967

Right: Cover of Carl Koch's 1958
book *At Home with Tomorrow*
Rechts: Umschlag von Carl Kochs
1958 erschienenem Buch „At Home
with Tomorrow"
À droite: Couverture du livre de Carl
Koch paru en 1958, *At Home with
Tomorrow*

Carl Koch was one of the first architects in America to be influenced by
European Modernism. While still at Harvard, where he was taught by
Walter Gropius and Marcel Breuer, among others, he was inspired by the
idea of the Bauhaus and worked in the office of the Functionalist architect
Sven Markelius from 1940 to 1941 in Stockholm. In the post-war period,
Koch became convinced that the housing shortage could be alleviated by
the construction of prefabricated houses that could be easily assembled
and disassembled. In 1948 he created the box-like Acorn House, his first
prefabricated house, on which *Life* magazine reported extensively, but this
did not ensure financial success.

The prefabricated house developed in 1952 by Techbuilt, Inc. was an entirely different case: Koch placed less emphasis on the formal austerity of
the Bauhaus and more on a pleasant exterior, to which the deeply overhanging eaves of the pitched roof, inspired by Japanese architecture, made
a considerable contribution. It was presumably the first prefabricated house
to be marketed on television. Millions saw the broadcast in February 1954
in which the assembly of a Techbuilt kit was minutely demonstrated. After
the broadcast the company was swamped with orders.

Koch soon established a franchise system with offices throughout the
country. On Eastern Long Island alone, more than 50 Techbuilt Houses
were erected in the early 1960s. The houses had between 570 and 775 sq.ft.
of floor space, and even the least expensive version cost less than $20,000.
The building components were delivered on a truck and could be easily assembled in just a few days. The pre-assembled wall panels, insulated with
fiberglass, pre-cut beams, windows, and the sliding doors, were all assembled on the basis of a simple post-and-beam structure.

Roughly 100 of the 500 Techbuilts delivered within the United States are
still standing.

Der Amerikaner Carl Koch gehörte zu den ersten Architekten in der Neuen
Welt, die die Einflüsse der europäischen Moderne aufnahmen. Während
seines Harvard-Studiums, u.a. bei Walter Gropius und Marcel Breuer, hatte
er sich vom Bauhausgedanken inspirieren lassen und war von 1940 bis
1941 im Büro des Funktionalisten Sven Markelius in Stockholm tätig
gewesen. In der Nachkriegszeit gelangte Koch zur Überzeugung, dass der
Wohnungsnot durch die Errichtung vorgefertigter und demontierbarer
Häuser begegnet werden könne. 1948 schuf er mit dem kistenförmigen
Acorn House sein erstes Fertighaus, das zwar ausführlich vom Life-Maga-
zin besprochen wurde, sich aber dennoch als wirtschaftlicher Flop erwies.
Ganz anders lief es bei seinem 1952 für die Firma Techbuilt entwickelten
Fertighaus: Hier nahm Koch die formale Strenge des Bauhauses zugunsten
eines gefälligeren Erscheinungsbildes zurück, wozu nicht zuletzt das weit
überstehende, an japanische Vorbilder erinnernde Satteldach beitrug. Es
war vermutlich das erste Fertighaus, das im Fernsehen vermarktet wurde.
Millionen sahen im Februar 1954 die Sendung, in der seine Montage ausführlich präsentiert wurde. Die Firma Techbuilt wurde nach der Ausstrah-
lung von Aufträgen überschwemmt.

In Windeseile etablierte Koch ein Franchise-System mit Büros im ganzen
Land. Allein auf Eastern Long Island wurden in den frühen 1960er Jahren
mehr als 50 Techbuilt-Häuser errichtet. Die Häuser waren zwischen 53 und
72 m² groß und kosteten selbst in der teuersten Variante weniger als
20 000 $. Die Bauteile wurden auf einem LKW ausgeliefert und konnten
problemlos innerhalb weniger Tage aufgebaut werden. Die vormontierten,
mit Fiberglas isolierten Wandpaneele, zugeschnittene Balken, Fenster und
Glasschiebetüren wurden auf Basis einer einfachen Pfosten- und Träger-
konstruktion zusammengesetzt.

Von den ungefähr 500 in den USA ausgelieferten Techbuilts existieren bis
heute noch rund 100.

L'Américain Carl Koch fait partie des premiers architectes à avoir été in-
fluencés par le modernisme européen. Pendant ses études à Harvard
auprès de Walter Gropius et Marcel Breuer entre autres, il s'était imprégné
des idées du Bauhaus. Entre 1940 et 1941, il avait exercé dans l'agence du
fonctionnaliste Sven Markelius à Stockholm. Après la guerre, Koch avait
acquis la certitude que la crise du logement pouvait être résolue par la
construction de maisons préfabriquées et démontables. En 1948, il conçut
l'Acorn House de forme cubique, sa première maison préfabriquée qui, bien
que faisant l'objet d'une recension détaillée dans le magazine *Life*, s'avéra
un échec commercial.

Il en fut tout autrement avec la maison préfabriquée développée pour l'entreprise Techbuilt en 1952: Koch reprit là l'austérité formelle du Bauhaus au
profit d'un aspect plus plaisant, auquel contribua grandement son toit largement saillant rappelant les toits japonais en bâtière. Ce fut probablement
la première maison préfabriquée commercialisée à l'aide de la télévision.
En février 1954, des millions de téléspectateurs virent le reportage détaillé
de son montage. Suite à cette diffusion, l'entreprise Techbuilt fut submer-
gée de commandes.

Koch lança rapidement un système de franchise avec des bureaux dans
tout le pays. Plus de 50 maisons Techbuilt furent construites sur la seule
partie est de Long Island au début des années soixante. La surface des maisons était comprise entre 53 m² et 72 m² et elles coûtaient – même dans leur
version la plus chère –, moins de 20 000 $. Les éléments de construction
étaient livrés par camion et pouvaient facilement être assemblés en quelques jours. Les panneaux de parois prémontés, à isolation en fibre de verre,
les poutres taillées sur mesure, les fenêtres et les portes vitrées coulissantes étaient montés sur une simple ossature poteaux-poutres. Il ne reste
aujourd'hui plus qu'une centaine de maisons parmi les 500 Techbuilt
livrées aux États-Unis.

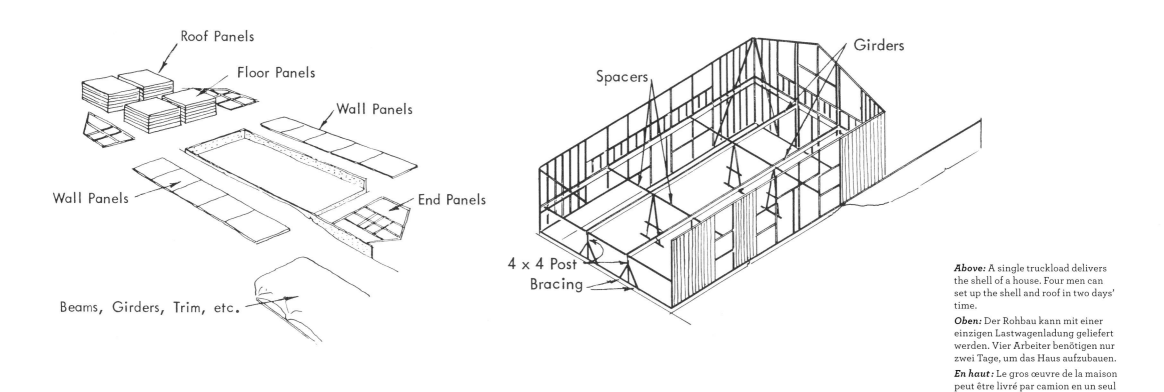

Roof Panels

Floor Panels

Wall Panels

Wall Panels

End Panels

Beams, Girders, Trim, etc.

Spacers

Girders

4 × 4 Post Bracing

Above: A single truckload delivers the shell of a house. Four men can set up the shell and roof in two days' time.

Oben: Der Rohbau kann mit einer einzigen Lastwagenladung geliefert werden. Vier Arbeiter benötigen nur zwei Tage, um das Haus aufzubauen.

En haut: Le gros œuvre de la maison peut être livré par camion en un seul chargement. Deux jours suffisent à quatre hommes pour monter la maison.

Right: Unlike most houses built in the United States, the ground floor of Techbuilt Houses was slightly below ground level.

Rechts: Anders als bei der üblichen Bauweise in Amerika wurde beim Techbuilt das Erdgeschoss leicht in den Boden versenkt.

À droite: Contrairement aux types de construction habituels en Amérique, le rez-de-chaussée de la maison Techbuilt était légèrement enfoncé dans le sol.

Below left: Interior view
Unten links: Innenansicht
En bas à gauche: Vue intérieure

Right: Floor plan
Rechts: Grundriss
À droite: Plan

Below right: The Techbuilt Cottage was a simpler, one-story addition to the program.
Unten rechts: Das Techbuilt Cottage ergänzte das Programm um ein einfacheres, einstöckiges Gebäude.
En bas à droite: Le Techbuilt Cottage venait compléter le programme avec un bâtiment simple, d'un étage.

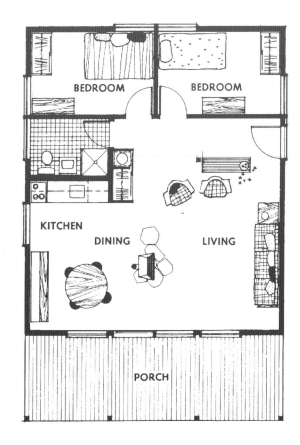

ERDMAN PREFAB NO. 1

Marshall Erdman and Associates, Inc., (ME&A), Madison, Wisconsin, USA
1956–1961

Opposite page: Catherine and William Cass House, "The Crimson Beech" on Staten Island, New York, 1959

Rechte Seite: Das Haus von Catherine und Willam Cass, „The Crimson Beech", in Staten Island, New York, 1959

Page de droite: La maison de Catherine et William Cass, «The Crimson Beech» à Staten Island, New York, 1959

Right: Perspective drawing
Rechts: Perspektivische Zeichnung
À droite: Dessin en perspective

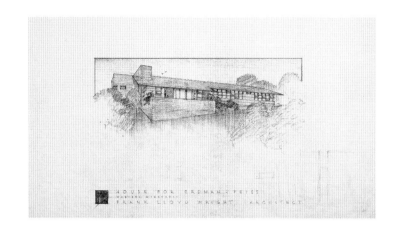

This was not the first collaboration between Frank Lloyd Wright and Marshall Erdman. Wright had already put this master builder of Lithuanian extraction in charge of executing his designs for the First Unitarian Society Church in Madison, Wisconsin, between 1949 and 1951. Hence, after Erdman had established a company to build prefabricated houses in 1951, Wright saw an opportunity to resume their successful collaboration in what he recognized as the important field of prefabricated residential construction in 1954. However, it was 1956 before he submitted the plans for his three prefab versions of the Usonian Houses that he had developed for the American middle class in the 1930s. The first Prefab No. 1 was built that same year, and this new type of prefabricated house was presented in a cover story by *House & Home* magazine.

The Prefab No. 1, however, can only be partially seen as a prefabricated house, since it is a combination of prefabricated parts and brickwork. The house is laid out as an elongated "L". It is divided into a sleeping area under the pitched roof on the long side and a carport under a flat roof on its short side. These two segments, which are made of prefabricated parts, are connected to each other by a brick-built living area with a kitchen and a fireplace. The Prefab No. 1 is a one-story building and, depending on its configuration, provides between 1,860 and 2,400 sq.ft. of floor space. The façades of the prefabricated parts are clad in cream-colored Masonite panels and decorated with strips of American redwood, emphasizing the horizontal orientation of the building. The house looks closed from the front, while wide windows in the back open up to the garden. The roof is covered with terneplate, rolled iron coated with a tin-lead alloy. The furnishings were also designed by Wright. Nearly all of the built-in elements are made of mahogany. Before Wright began his work, he asked the

Es war nicht das erste Mal, dass Frank Lloyd Wright und Marshall Erdman zusammenarbeiteten. In den Jahren 1949 bis 1951 hatte der Baumeister litauischer Herkunft nach Wrights Entwürfen den Kirchenbau der First Unitarian Society in Madison/Wisconsin realisiert. Nachdem Erdman 1951 eine Firma für Fertighäuser gegründet hatte, sah Wright 1954 die Gelegenheit gekommen, die erfolgreiche Zusammenarbeit wieder aufzunehmen und sich ein weiteres Mal auf dem von ihm als wichtig erkannten Gebiet des Fertighausbaus zu engagieren. Doch erst 1956 legte er die Pläne für drei Varianten des Prefab vor, ein Fertighaus im Stil der Usonia-Häuser, die der Architekt in den 1930er Jahren für die amerikanische Mittelschicht entwickelt hatte. Noch im gleichen Jahr wurde der neue Fertighaustyp von der Zeitschrift „House & Home" im Rahmen einer Coverstory vorgestellt und darüber hinaus das erste Prefab No. 1 gebaut.

Das Prefab No. 1 ist allerdings nur bedingt als Fertighaus anzusprechen, ist es doch eine Kombination aus vorgefertigten Teilen und Mauerwerk. Der Grundriss des Hauses beschreibt ein langgestrecktes L. Es gliedert sich in einen Schlaftrakt unter einem Satteldach an der Langseite des L und einen Carport unter einem Flachdach an der Kurzseite des L. Diese beiden Trakte aus vorgefertigten Teilen sind miteinander durch einen gemauerten Wohntrakt mit Küche und Kamin verbunden. Das Prefab No. 1 ist eingeschossig und je nach Ausstattung zwischen 173 m² und 223 m² groß.

Die Fassaden der vorfabrizierten Gebäudeteile sind mit cremefarbenen Masonit-Holzfaserplatten und regelmäßig gesetzten Zierlatten aus amerikanischem Rotholz verkleidet, die die Horizontalität des Gebäudekörpers betonen. Auf der Eingangsseite wirkt das Haus abgeschlossen, zum Garten hin öffnet es sich jedoch durch eine breite Fensterfront. Das Dach ist mit

Ce projet n'était pas la première collaboration de Frank Lloyd Wright et Marshall Erdman. De 1949 à 1951, le maître d'œuvre d'origine lituanienne avait réalisé la construction de l'église de la First Unitarian Society à Madison, dans le Wisconsin, sur les plans de Wright. Après qu'Erdman eut créé son entreprise de construction de maisons préfabriquées en 1951, Wright vit en 1954 l'opportunité de renouveler cette collaboration fructueuse et de s'engager de nouveau dans le domaine de la construction de maisons préfabriquées qu'il considérait comme majeur. Mais ce n'est qu'en 1956 qu'il produisit les plans de trois versions de la Prefab, une maison standardisée dans le style des maisons Usonia développées par l'architecte dans les années trente pour les classes moyennes américaines. La même année, le nouveau modèle de maison préfabriquée fit la une du magazine *House & Home* et la Prefab No. 1 fut construite.

La Prefab No. 1 ne peut toutefois être citée comme maison préfabriquée que sous réserve, car elle combine éléments préfabriqués et maçonnerie. Le plan de la maison décrit un long L, qui se répartit en une aile pour les chambres sous un toit en pente de son côté longitudinal, et en un abri pour voiture sous un toit plat du côté étroit du L. Ces deux ailes constituées d'éléments préfabriqués sont reliées entre elles par une aile d'habitation en maçonnerie avec cuisine et cheminée. La Prefab No. 1 est une maison à un étage et a une surface comprise entre 173 m² et 223 m² selon l'agencement choisi.

Les façades de ses ailes préfabriquées présentent un parement de panneaux de fibres de bois de couleur crème et de lattes décoratives en sapin rouge du Nord, dont la disposition régulière souligne l'horizontalité du corps de bâtiment. Du côté de l'entrée, la maison semble fermée alors qu'elle s'ouvre du côté du jardin par une façade dotée de nombreuses fenêtres.

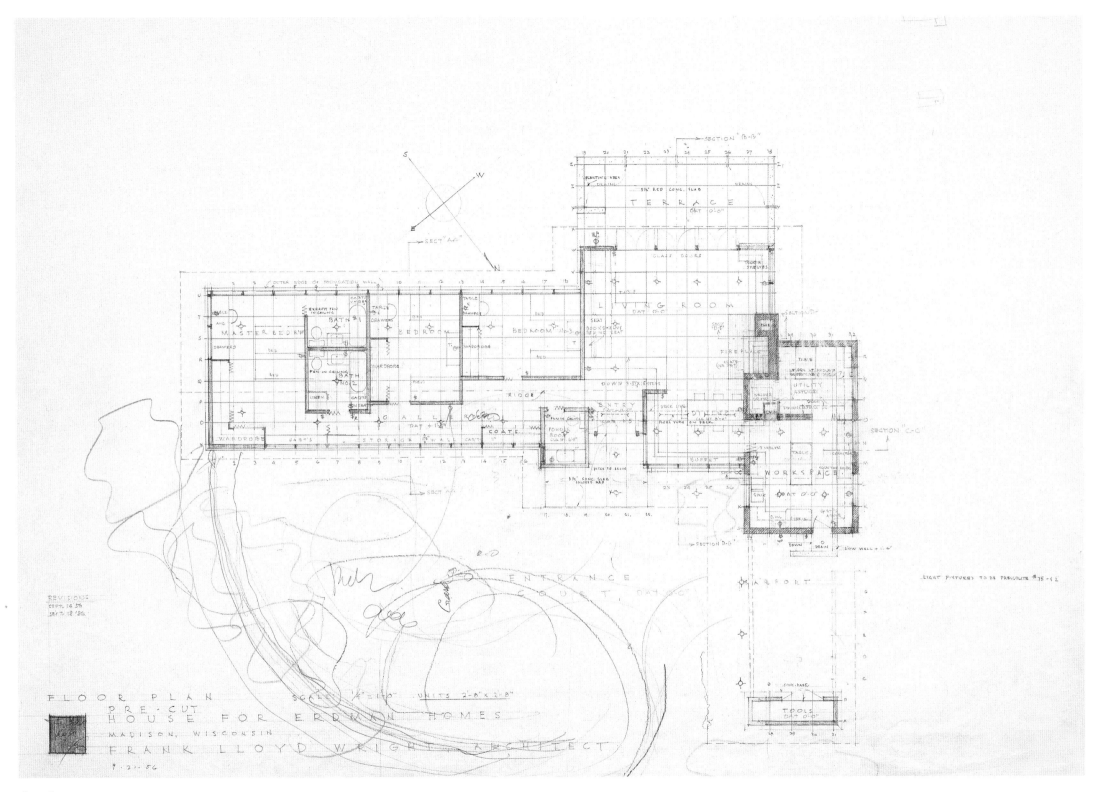

Floor plan
Grundriss
Plan

Cass House, street view
Haus Cass, Straßenansicht
Maison Cass, vue de la rue

clients to submit a topographical map and photos of the lot in order to gain a better understanding of the building site. He also insisted on inspecting the houses after they were completed.

It is obvious that with this level of individual involvement, similar to what would be expected in conventional building practice, only eleven prefabs were ever built. Two of them, however, proved to be surprisingly mobile: in 1985 one was moved over a distance of 40 miles from its original location in Madison to Beaver Dam, Wisconsin, the other one was moved over a distance of 525 miles from the Greater Chicago area to a location in Pennsylvania in 2007, where it is now used as a guest house.

Ternblech belegt, einem mit einer Zinn-Blei-Legierung überzogenen Eisenblech. Auch die Inneneinrichtung war von Wright entworfen. Nahezu alle Einbauten wurden in Mahagoni ausgeführt. Um sich ein genaues Bild von den Gegebenheiten zu verschaffen, erbat Wright im Vorfeld von den Bauherren eine topografische Karte sowie Fotos vom Baugelände. Er ließ es sich außerdem nicht nehmen, die Häuser nach ihrer Fertigstellung zu begutachten.

Es lag auf der Hand, dass bei einer derart individuellen Umsetzung, die an konventionelle Bauweise grenzte, nur insgesamt elf Prefabs errichtet wurden. Immerhin aber haben zwei dieser Häuser eine erstaunliche Mobilität an den Tag gelegt: Während das eine 1985 von seinem ursprünglichen Standort Madison um rund 70 km nach Beaver Dam versetzt wurde, zog das andere 2007 aus dem Großraum Chicago an einen rund 850 km entfernten Ort in Pennsylvania um, wo es heute als Gästehaus dient.

Le toit est recouvert d'une tôle de fer terne revêtue d'un alliage plomb-étain. Wright était également à l'origine de l'ameublement intérieur. Presque tous les meubles encastrés furent réalisés en acajou. Afin de se faire une idée précise de la réalité, Wright s'était fait remettre au préalable une carte topographique ainsi que des photos du terrain à construire par les maîtres d'ouvrage. Par ailleurs, il tenait à expertiser personnellement les maisons une fois achevées.

Vu le caractère individuel de cette réalisation, à la limite du type de construction conventionnel, il est bien naturel que seules onze Prefabs aient vu le jour. Toujours est-il que deux de ces maisons ont fait preuve d'une étonnante mobilité : alors que l'une d'elles a été déplacée de Madison vers Beaver Dam, à plus de 70 km de son site originel, en 1985, une autre, sise dans l'agglomération de Chicago, s'est vue transposée de 850 km vers un site éloigné en Pennsylvanie, où elle fait aujourd'hui office de maison d'hôtes.

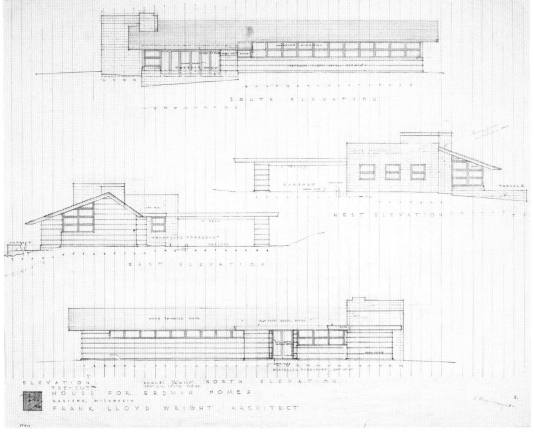

Above: Elevations
Oben: Ansichten
En haut: Élévations

Opposite page: Interior of the Cass House
Rechte Seite: Innenansicht des Cass Hauses
Page de droite: Vue intérieure de la maison Cass

Left: Cass House, garden front
Links: Haus Cass, Blick auf die Gartenseite
À gauche: Maison Cass, façade donnant sur le jardin

MAISON ALBA

Ateliers Jean Prouvé, Maxéville, France
1956–1962

Seynave House in Beauvallon,
France, 1962

Haus Seynave in Beauvallon,
Frankreich, 1962

Maison Seynave à Beauvallon,
France, 1962

The 'seed' from which the single-family house called Alba (*Aluminium-béton armé*) developed was the prefabricated small bathroom unit that Jean Prouvé built in 1935 for the Aero Club in the French town of Buc. In his workshops in Maxéville, he collaborated with his employee Maurice Silvy in further developing the Alba single-family house, which contained a "monobloc"—a prefabricated kitchenette, bathroom and toilet—at its core, which simultaneously served as a supporting element in the construction of the house. This monobloc was made of reinforced concrete and set down on a foundation trough of in-situ concrete.

A modified version of the Maison Alba, with a simplified floor plan and monobloc made of metal, was built within the context of a charitable program: Abbé Pierre of Paris, who had dedicated his life to fighting homelessness, approached Prouvé in 1955, asking him to develop a system for building low-cost single families houses. On February 21, 1956, a model of the Alba was erected in the middle of Paris, on the banks of the Seine, in a spectacular publicity event witnessed by numerous onlookers. On only 560 sq.ft. of floor space the Alba boasted two bedrooms and a multifunctional living room, which one entered directly through the front door. However, the innovative model was never produced in series since the building authorities refused to grant approval of the central sanitary unit in the middle of the living room.

However, between 1961 and 1962 Prouvé erected two more of the Alba houses. Working with the architect Neil Hutchinson, he constructed the

Der ‚Keim' für den Einfamilienhaustyp Alba (Aluminium-béton armé) war eine vorgefertigte Nasszelle, die Jean Prouvé bereits 1935 für sein Gebäude für den Aero-Club in Buc im Département Yvelines konstruiert hatte. In seinen Werkstätten in Maxéville entwickelte er 1950 zusammen mit seinem Mitarbeiter Maurice Silvy das Einfamilienhaus Alba, das als konstruktiven Kern einen „Monobloc" – eine vorgefertigte Funktionszelle mit Kochnische, Bad und WC – enthielt, der zugleich als tragendes Element der Hauskonstruktion diente. Dieser Monobloc war aus Stahlbeton gefertigt und wurde auf eine Fundamentwanne aus Ortbeton aufgesetzt.

Zum Einsatz kam das Maison Alba in modifizierter Form (der Grundriss war hier vereinfacht und der Monobloc aus Metall) im Rahmen einer karitativen Aktion: Der Pariser Abbé Pierre, der sich die Bekämpfung der Obdachlosigkeit auf die Fahnen geschrieben hatte, war 1955 an Prouvé mit der Bitte herangetreten, ein System für ihn zu entwickeln, mit dem sich kostengünstige Einfamilienhäuser herstellen ließen. Ein Exemplar des Alba wurde am 21. Februar 1956 im Rahmen einer spektakulären Werbeaktion vor einer Menge Schaulustiger an der Seine, mitten in Paris, aufgestellt. Es hatte eine Grundfläche von nur 52 m² und verfügte über zwei Schlafzimmer sowie einen multifunktionalen Wohnraum, den man direkt durch die Eingangstür des Hauses betrat. Das innovative Modell ging dennoch nicht in Serie, da die Baubehörde gerade wegen des inmitten des Wohnzimmers stehenden Sanitärkerns ihre Zustimmung versagte.

Zwischen 1961 und 1962 errichtete Prouvé dennoch zwei weitere Häuser

Le type de maison individuelle Alba (Aluminium Béton Armé) tire son origine d'une petite salle d'eau préfabriquée que Jean Prouvé avait fait fabriquer pour son bâtiment du Club d'aviation à Buc en 1935, dans le département des Yvelines. En 1950, il développa avec son collaborateur Maurice Silvy la maison individuelle Alba dans ses ateliers de Maxéville, dont le noyau structurel était un «monobloc», une cellule fonctionnelle préfabriquée comportant le coin cuisine, la salle de bains et les toilettes, et faisant également fonction d'élément porteur de la construction. Ce monobloc fabriqué en béton armé fut disposé sur une cuve de fondation en béton coulé sur place.

La maison Alba fut utilisée pour la première fois sous une forme modifiée (le plan était ici simplifié et le monobloc de métal) dans le cadre d'une action caritative: engagé dans la lutte pour les sans-abri, l'abbé Pierre avait demandé à Jean Prouvé en 1955 de concevoir un système permettant la construction de maisons individuelles économiques. Un exemplaire de la maison Alba fut monté le 21 février 1956 en plein cœur de Paris lors d'un événement promotionnel spectaculaire se déroulant devant une foule de badauds près de la Seine. D'une surface de 52 m², elle comportait deux chambres ainsi qu'un séjour multifonctionnel auquel on accédait directement depuis la porte d'entrée. Toutefois, ce modèle innovant ne fut pas produit en série: les pouvoirs publics du bâtiment refusèrent de donner leur accord en raison de l'emplacement du bloc sanitaire au centre du salon.

Entre 1961 et 1962, Prouvé construisit malgré tout deux autres maisons

Seynave House, terrace view (opposite page), conceptual sketch (below), floor plan (right)

Haus Seynave, Ansicht der Terrasse (linke Seite), Entwurfsskizze (unten), Grundriss (rechts)

Maison Seynave, vue sur la terrasse (page de gauche), dessin d'étude (ci-dessous), plan (à droite)

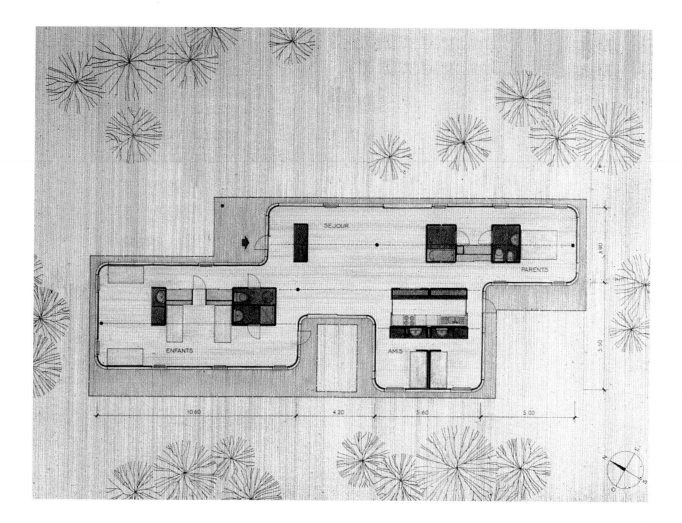

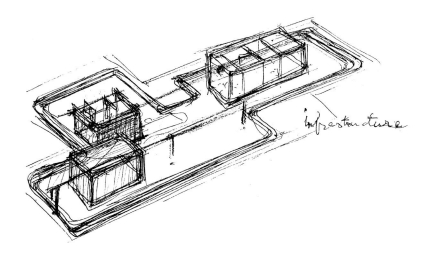

holiday home "Seynave" in Beauvallon for a paper manufacturer from Lorraine. Horizontal support beams bearing the ceiling load rest on a number of concrete cores that contain parts of the kitchen, the toilet, and storage space. Slender red steel pipes provide additional stability, while the façade and the remaining interior walls were executed in sheets of laminated wood. In 1962 Prouvé built the other Alba in Saint-Dié, together with the architects Baumann and Remondino, as a home for his daughter Françoise and her husband Pierre Gauthier. Here, however, unlike the holiday home in Beauvallon, both the inside and the outside of the two-layer wall structures were clad in corrugated aluminum panels and thermally insulated with polystyrene.

des Alba-Typs. Für einen lothringischen Papierfabrikanten realisierte er zusammen mit dem Architekten Neil Hutchinson das Ferienhaus Seynave in Beauvallon. Auf den verschiedenen Betonkernen im Inneren, die Küche, WC und Stauräume bergen, lagern horizontale Tragbalken, so dass die Kerne die Deckenlast aufnehmen. Für zusätzliche Stabilität sorgen filigrane, rot gestrichene Stahlrohrstützen, während die Fassade und die restlichen Innenwände mit Sichtholzplatten ausgeführt waren. Das andere Alba realisierte Prouvé 1962 mit den Architekten Baumann und Remondino in Saint-Dié als Wohnhaus für seine Tochter Françoise und deren Mann Pierre Gauthier. Anders als noch beim Feriendomizil in Beauvallon waren bei der zweischaligen Wandkonstruktion sowohl die Innenseite als auch die Fassade mit geriffelten Aluminiumblechplatten verkleidet und mit Polystyrol wärmegedämmt.

Alba. Avec l'architecte Neil Hutchinson, il réalisa la villa de vacances Seynave à Beauvallon pour un industriel lorrain de la papeterie. Ici, les poutres porteuses horizontales sont posées sur les différents noyaux de béton de l'intérieur qui abritent les parties de la cuisine, des toilettes et des rangements, de sorte que ces noyaux supportent la charge du plafond. De minces poteaux en acier peints en rouge assurent une stabilité supplémentaire. Le revêtement de la façade et des cloisons est en contreplaqué. L'autre maison Alba réalisée par Prouvé en 1962 à Saint-Dié avec les architectes Baumann et Remondino était une maison d'habitation pour sa fille Françoise et son mari Pierre Gauthier. À la différence de la villa de vacances de Beauvallon, les panneaux sandwichs des parois intérieures, comme des façades, avaient pour revêtement extérieur de la tôle d'aluminium striée et du polyester expansé pour isolant.

Seynave House in Beauvallon,
France, 1962

Haus Seynave in Beauvallon,
Frankreich, 1962

Maison Seynave à Beauvallon,
France, 1962

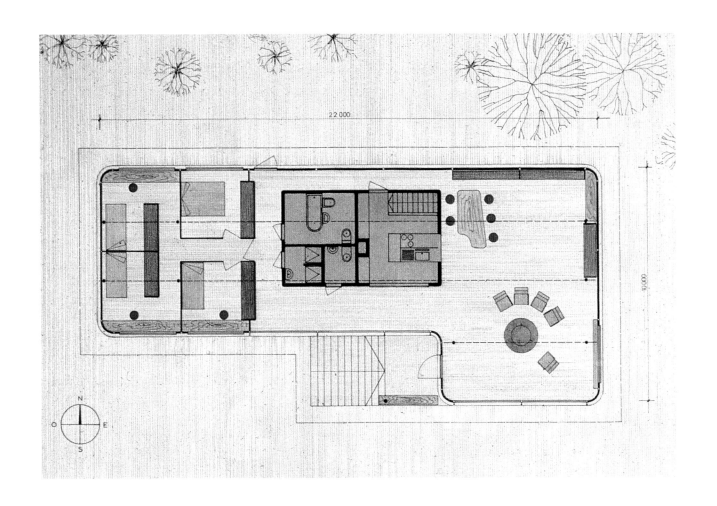

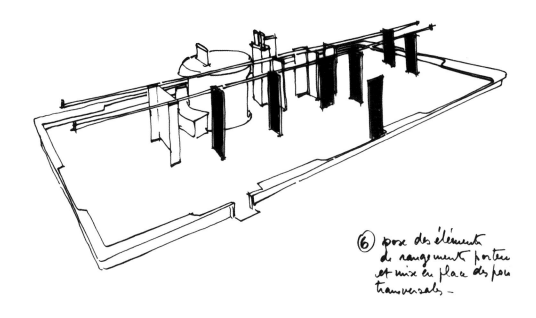

⑥ pose des éléments
de rangement porteur
et mise en place des pou
transversales –

Gauthier House, Saint-Dié, France,
1962, overall view (below left) and
plan (opposite page above)

Haus Gauthier, Saint-Dié, Frankreich, 1962, Gesamtansicht (unten
links) und Grundriss (linke Seite
oben)

Maison Gauthier, Saint-Dié, France,
1962, vue d'ensemble (en bas à
gauche) et plan (page de gauche en
haut)

House for Abbé Pierre on the banks
of the Seine in Paris, France, 1956,
overall view (right), conceptual
sketch (opposite page below right)

Haus für den Abbé Pierre am Seine-
ufer in Paris, Frankreich, 1956, Gesamtansicht (rechts), Entwurfsskizze
(linke Seite unten rechts)

Maison pour l'abbé Pierre sur les
quais de Seine à Paris, France, 1956,
vue d'ensemble (à droite), dessin
d'étude (page de gauche en bas à
droite)

PRE-BUILT HOUSE

U.S. Department of Housing, Washington, D.C., USA
1957

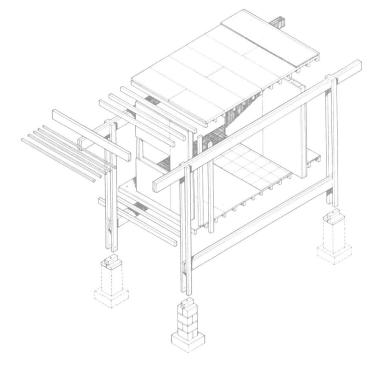

Opposite page: Pre-Built House No. 5, manufactured in Camden, Maine, 1957

Rechte Seite: Pre-Built-Haus Nr. 5, hergestellt in Camden, Maine, 1957

Page de droite: Pre-Built House n° 5, fabriquée à Camden, Maine, 1957

Right: Isometric drawing showing bent construction

Rechts: Isometrie der „Bent Construction"

À droite: Dessin isométrique montrant la *Bent construction*

Norman Cherner (1920–1987) was a famous furniture designer; his best-known design is the Plycraft Cherner Armchair, a softly curving chair made of plywood, which he introduced in 1958. The prominent role that chairs came to play within Cherner's oeuvre is reflected in the name of the company his two sons established in 1999 in order to market their father's products: The Cherner Chair Company. Yet Cherner also designed tables, storage units, textiles, glassware, lamps—and houses. In the 1950s, he spent an extended period concentrating on prefabricated housing, publishing his thoughts and designs in several books. *Fabricating Houses from Component Parts* was published in 1957 and presents, as the fifth of fifteen designs, the "Bent House", commissioned by the U.S. Department of Housing. After having been shown at an exhibition in Vienna, the house was erected in Ridgefield, Connecticut, where it served Cherner as a residence and workplace. Technical literature today refers to it as "Cherner's Pre-Built".

It is a one-story flat roofed building on stilts, with a floor plan determined by the construction method: "Bent Construction" uses a number of wooden frames consisting of two supports, ceiling and roof beams, which are connected to each other by wall elements. Hence the walls are not load-bearing. The house, mounted on pillars, rests on foundation pads. The "bents" were produced in a factory in a variety of shapes. Cherner's own pre-built house consists of six bents, each 16 ft. in length, which are assembled with an axial distance of eight ft. Hence, the house is 5 x 8 = 40 ft. long and 16 ft.

Norman Cherner (1920–1987) war ein berühmter Möbeldesigner; sein bekanntester Entwurf ist der Plycraft Cherner Armchair: ein weich gekurvter Sperrholz-Sessel, den er 1958 vorstellte. Welch prominente Stellung gerade Sitzmöbel in Cherners Werk einnehmen, zeigt der Name der Firma, die seine beiden Söhne 1999 gründeten, um Produkte des Vaters wieder zu vertreiben: The Cherner Chair Company. Cherner entwarf aber auch Tische, Schränke, Textilien, Glaswaren, Lampen – und Häuser. In den 1950er Jahren beschäftigte er sich eine Zeit lang intensiv mit dem Fertighausbau, seine Überlegungen und Modellentwürfe veröffentlichte er in mehreren Büchern. „Fabricating Houses from Component Parts" erschien 1957 und stellte als fünftes von 15 Entwürfen ein „Bent House" vor, das vom US-amerikanischen Wohnungsbauministerium (U.S. Department of Housing) in Auftrag gegeben worden war. Nachdem es auf einer Ausstellung in Wien gezeigt worden war, wurde es in Ridgefield, Connecticut, aufgebaut, wo es Cherner als Wohnhaus und Arbeitsstätte diente. In der Literatur kennt man es heute als „Cherner's Pre-Built".

Es handelt sich um einen eingeschossigen aufgeständerten Flachdachbau, dessen Raumplan sich aus der Konstruktion ableitet: Bei der „Bent Construction" werden mehrere Holzrahmen aus zwei Stützen, Boden- und Dachbalken aufgestellt und durch Wandelemente miteinander verbunden, die Wände sind also nicht-tragend. Das auf diese Stützen aufgeständerte Haus ruht auf Punktfundamenten. Die „Bents" wurden in der Fabrik hergestellt und sind von ganz unterschiedlicher Form. Cherners eigenes

La réalisation la plus connue du fameux designer de meubles Norman Cherner (1920-1987) est le *Plycraft Cherner Armchair*, un fauteuil en contreplaqué moulé qu'il présenta en 1958. The Cherner Chair Company, nom de l'entreprise fondée par ses deux fils en 1999 afin de commercialiser de nouveau les réalisations de leur père, illustre l'importance que prennent les sièges dans l'œuvre de Cherner. Elle compte toutefois aussi des tables, des armoires, des tissus, de la verrerie, des lampes, ainsi que des maisons. En effet, dans les années cinquante, il se consacra un temps à la construction de maisons préfabriquées et publia ses réflexions ainsi que ses plans dans divers ouvrages. Publié en 1957, « Fabricating Houses from Component Parts » présentait en cinquième position parmi quinze projets une « Bent House », maison commandée par le ministère américain du logement. Après avoir été exposée à Vienne, elle fut montée à Ridgefield, dans le Connecticut, où elle fit office de logement et d'atelier pour Cherner. Dans la littérature, elle est aujourd'hui connue sous le nom de « Cherner's Pre-Built ».

C'est un bâtiment surélevé de plain-pied à toit plat, dont le plan dans l'espace découle de la structure : dans le cas de la « Bent Construction », plusieurs ossatures de bois composées de deux poteaux, de solives de plancher et d'entraits sont montées et reliées par des panneaux de murs. Les murs ne sont donc pas porteurs. La maison est surélevée sur ces poteaux qui reposent sur des semelles de fondation isolées. Les *Bents* peuvent être fabriqués en usine et revêtir des formes très diverses. La propre Pre-Built House de

Woodlands House, Ramapo, New
York, 1948

Woodlands House, Ramapo, New
York, 1948

Woodlands House, Ramapo, New
York, 1948

| Multiple Bents | Porch & Overhang | Multiple Bent | Cantilever Wall Bent |
| Shed Roof Bent | Pitched Roof Bent | Trussed Bent | Butterfly Roof Bent |

Above: Diagram showing different
types of bent construction

Oben: Die Zeichnung der „Bent
Construction" zeigt verschiedene
Haustypen.

En haut: Diagramme de la *Bent
construction* présentant différents
types de maisons

Opposite page: Woodlands House,
interior

Rechte Seite: Woodlands House,
Innenansicht

Page de droite: Woodlands House,
intérieur

wide. The middle section of the house, accessible by an outdoor stairway, contains the hallway, bathroom, and the kitchen unit, jutting out of the living room. The square living and dining area is located to the right of the entrance, the two bedrooms are to the left. The house has 7-ft. ceilings, with the floor 3 ft. above the ground.

The "Girder House" is another one of the structures presented by Cherner. Here, two or more beams installed in parallel are borne by supports and connected to each other by rafters. Non-load-bearing walls, glass façades, or wide sliding doors can be hung from the beams across the entire length of the house.

Pre-Built-Haus besteht aus sechs 4,88 m (16 Fuß) langen Bents, die mit jeweils 2,44 m (8 Fuß) Achsabstand aufgestellt wurden. Das Haus misst somit in der Länge etwa 12 m (5 x 8 = 40 Fuß) und in seiner Breite rund 5 m (16 Fuß). In seinem Mittelteil, dem eine Außentreppe vorgesetzt ist, sind die Diele, das Badezimmer und die aus dem Wohnzimmer herausgerückte Küchenzeile untergebracht. Auf der vom Eingang her gesehenen rechten Seite liegt das quadratische Wohn- und Esszimmer, im linken Teil befinden sich die zwei Schlafzimmer. Die Raumhöhe im Haus beträgt 2,13 m (7 Fuß), der Fußboden des Raumes liegt ca. 90 cm (3 Fuß) über dem Erdboden.

Eine weitere von Cherner vorgestellte Konstruktion ist das „Girder House" („Tragbalkenhaus"), bei dem zwei oder mehr parallel („wie Bahnschienen") liegende Balken von Stützen getragen und durch Dachsparren miteinander verbunden werden. Von den Tragbalken können in ganzer Länge nicht-tragende Wände, Glasfronten oder weite Schiebetüren abgehängt werden.

Cherner est composée de six *Bents* de 4,88 m (16 pieds) de long montés avec un entraxe respectif de 2,44 m (8 pieds). La maison mesure donc environ 12 m (5 x 8 = 40 pieds) de long et presque 5 m (16 pieds) de large. Dotée d'un escalier extérieur, la partie centrale abrite le hall, la salle de bains, ainsi que la cuisine intégrée qui fait une avancée dans la salle de séjour. Sur le côté droit à partir de l'entrée se trouvent la salle de séjour-salon de plan carré et, à gauche, les deux chambres. À l'intérieur, la hauteur sous plafond est de 2,13 m (7 pieds), le plancher se trouve à environ 0,90 m (3 pieds) au-dessus du sol.

Cherner a également présenté une autre construction, la « Girder House » dans laquelle au moins deux poutres parallèles (« telles des rails ») sont soutenues par des poteaux et reliées entre elles par des chevrons. Des cloisons non porteuses, des baies vitrées ou de grandes portes coulissantes peuvent être suspendues à ces poutres porteuses.

Fredric Bensen Summer Residence,
Saltaire, Fire Island, New York, 1958.
Exterior photo, section, plan and
axonometric drawing

Sommerhaus von Fredric Bensen,
Saltaire, Fire Island, New York, 1958.
Teilansicht von außen, Schnitt,
Grundriss und Axonometrie

Maison de campagne de Fredric
Bensen, Saltaire, Fire Island, New
York, 1958. Photo d'extérieur, coupe,
plan et axonométrie

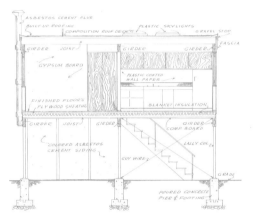

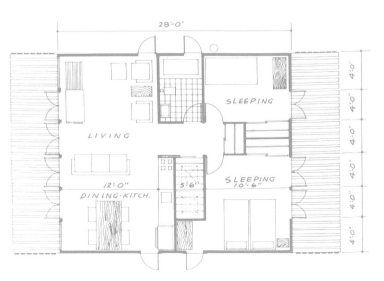

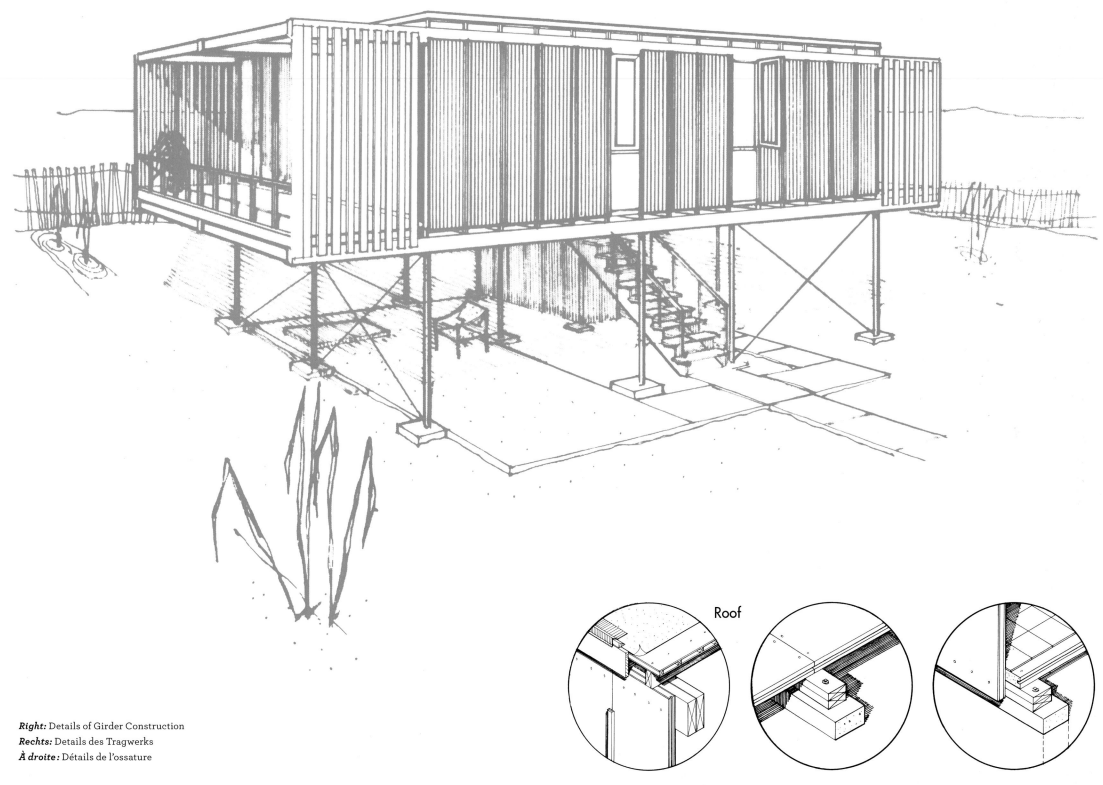

Roof

Right: Details of Girder Construction
Rechts: Details des Tragwerks
À droite: Détails de l'ossature

AARNO RUUSUVUORI

MARIHOUSE

**Marikylä Corporation, Bökars, Finland
1966**

The model house, 1963
Das Musterhaus, 1963
La maison-modèle, 1963

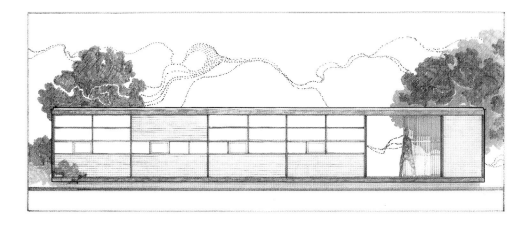

When the visionary textile designer Armi Ratia and her husband Viljo established the Marimekko company in 1951, it could hardly have been anticipated that just a few years later the small textile manufacturer would become a label for which there would be a great demand throughout the world. After Jacqueline Kennedy bought seven of their dresses in 1960, Marimekko shops were opened in the United States, Europe, Japan, and Australia. In 1962 the couple began to cooperate with the architect Aarno Ruusuvuori, known for the modernity and asceticism of his designs, who took charge of designing the Marimekko shops. However, the Ratias were not only interested in printing and selling textiles, but also in creating a new lifestyle. In 1963 Ruusuvuori was commissioned by Marimekko to design a model development for 3,500 inhabitants, including company staff, near Porvoo, a country town 31 miles east of Helsinki. In order to produce the prefabricated houses that were foreseen for this project, Ruusuvuori established the Marikylä Corporation that same year.

The building components of the model house were produced in Bökars near Porvoo, the headquarters of the Marimekko company. Contemporary color photographs, made for advertising purposes, show a wood-clad one-story residential box full of colorful interiors in the middle of a forest of birch and pine trees. The 520 sq.ft. block was assembled on site out of four prefabricated room units: one contained the bedroom, another the bathroom and kitchen, two others contained the living room. Brightly visible in the large windows of this "blue submarine" (a title bestowed upon it by the

Als die visionäre Textildesignerin Armi Ratia und ihr Mann Viljo 1951 ihre Firma Marimekko gründeten, war kaum zu ahnen, dass aus der kleinen Stoffmanufaktur binnen weniger Jahre ein Label werden sollte, das auf der ganzen Welt gefragt war. Nachdem Jacqueline Kennedy 1960 sieben Kleider dieser Marke gekauft hatte, wurden in den USA, Europa, Japan und Australien eigene Marimekko-Shops eröffnet. Seit 1962 arbeiteten die beiden mit dem für die Modernität und Askese seiner Entwürfe bekannten Architekten Aarno Ruusuvuori zusammen, der die Gestaltung der Marimekko-Geschäfte übernahm. Doch die Ratias wollten nicht nur Stoffe bedrucken und verkaufen, sondern auch einen neuen Lebensstil kreieren. 1963 erhielt Ruusuvuori den Auftrag, für Marimekko in der Nähe von Porvoo, einem Landstädtchen 50 km östlich von Helsinki, eine Modellsiedlung für 3 500 Einwohner zu entwerfen, in der u.a. auch die Angestellten der Firma wohnen sollten. Um die hierfür vorgesehenen Fertighäuser zu produzieren, gründete Ruusuvuori noch im selben Jahr die Marikylä Corporation.

Die Baukomponenten des Musterhauses wurden in Bökars vorgefertigt, dem Stammsitz der Firma Marimekko in der Nähe von Porvoo. Zeitgenössische Farbfotografien, die zu Werbezwecken gemacht wurden, zeigen eine holzverkleidete eingeschossige Wohnbox voller farbenfroher Interieurs, der inmitten von Birken- und Kiefernwäldern steht. Zusammengesetzt wurde die 48 m² große Box aus vier vorgefertigten Raumeinheiten vor Ort: Die erste enthielt das Schlafzimmer, die zweite Badezimmer und Küche, die

Lorsque la créatrice de textile visionnaire Armi Ratia et son mari Viljo créèrent leur entreprise Marimekko en 1951, nul ne pensait que la petite fabrique de tissus allait devenir une marque de renom international en l'espace de quelques années. Après que Jacqueline Kennedy eut acheté sept robes de la marque en 1960, des boutiques Marimekko ouvrirent leurs portes aux États-Unis, en Europe, au Japon et en Australie. Depuis 1962, ils travaillaient avec l'architecte Aarno Ruusuvuori connu pour la modernité et la sobriété de ses projets, qui se chargea alors de la décoration intérieure des magasins Marimekko. Mais l'impression et la vente de tissus ne suffisaient pas aux Ratia qui souhaitaient également créer un nouveau style de vie. En 1963, Ruusuvuori fut chargé de réaliser un petit village près de Porvoo, à 50 km à l'est d'Helsinki, un lotissement-témoin pour 3 500 habitants où devaient vivre entre autres les salariés de l'entreprise. Afin de pouvoir produire les maisons préfabriquées prévues pour le village, Ruusuvuori créa la Marikylä Corporation la même année.

Les éléments de construction de la maison-témoin furent produits à Bökars, siège de l'entreprise Marimekko près de Porvoo. Des photographies d'époque prises pour la promotion du projet montrent un parallélépipède rectangle à revêtement de bois à un niveau, à l'intérieur vivement coloré, qui se dresse au milieu d'une forêt de bouleaux et de pins. Cette boîte de 48 m² fut montée sur place à partir de quatre unités préfabriquées : la première contenait la chambre, la deuxième, la salle de bains et la cuisine, la troisième et la quatrième, la salle de séjour. Des rideaux en tissus natu-

Elevation, floor plan and axonometric
drawing
Ansicht, Grundriss und Axonometrie
Élévation, plan et axonométrie

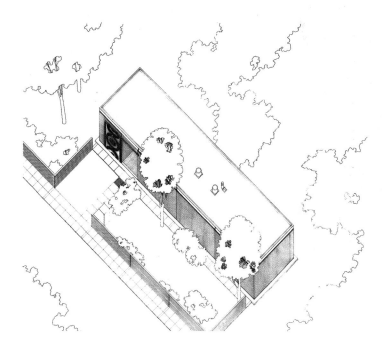

contemporary press) were curtains of natural materials in patterns designed for the company by Marimekko's head designer Maija Isola.
The press reacted enthusiastically, celebrating Marimekko's project as a departure into new architectural territory. But all of the enthusiasm was to no avail. The very first inhabitants—of all people Armi and Viljo's son and his family—found the living quarters too cramped. The failure of this residential utopia was ultimately due to the cost, and even more so to the reluctance of the company's employees to live in an isolated development deep in the woods.

dritte und vierte das Wohnzimmer. Aus den großen Fenstereinschnitten des „blauen Unterseebootes" (so titelte die zeitgenössische Presse) leuchteten aus natürlichen Materialien hergestellte Gardinen in Mustern, die von Maija Isola, der Chef-Designerin von Marimekko, entworfen worden waren. Die Presse war begeistert und feierte Marimekkos Projekt als Aufbruch in architektonisches Neuland. Doch aller Enthusiasmus half nichts. Schon die ersten Bewohner, Armis Sohn Ristomatti mit seiner Familie, empfanden das Wohnen in diesem Gebäude als äußerst beengt. Die Wohnutopie scheiterte schließlich an den Kosten, mehr noch aber am Unwillen der Firmenangestellten, in einer Siedlung fernab in der Einsamkeit des Waldes zu wohnen.

rels aux motifs conçus par Maija Isola, la designer en chef de Marimekko, étincelaient à travers les grandes ouvertures vitrées du «sous-marin bleu» (qualificatif donné alors par la presse).
La presse s'enthousiasma pour le projet de Marimekko et le célébra comme une percée vers des contrées architectoniques inexplorées. Tout cet enthousiasme ne servit pourtant à rien. Les premiers habitants, Ristomatti – le fils même de la famille Ratia – et sa famille, s'y trouvèrent trop à l'étroit. Finalement, l'utopie de logement échoua devant les coûts, mais bien plus encore devant le mécontentement des employés de l'entreprise de devoir habiter un lotissement dans l'isolement de la forêt.

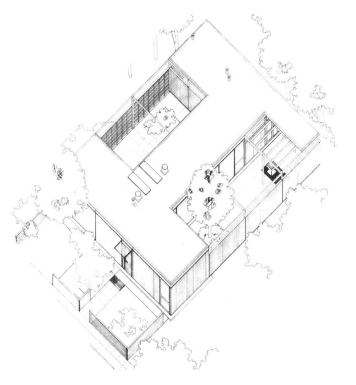

Planned, but never realized, version with more floor space

Geplante, aber nicht verwirklichte Variante mit größerer Wohnfläche

Variante avec surface habitable plus grande, prévue mais non réalisée

Opposite page: Aarno Ruusuvuori designed a sauna for Marimekko intended for the international market, but—like the Marihouse Project—it never went into serial production.

Rechte Seite: Prototyp der von Aarno Ruusuvuori für Marimekko entwickelten Sauna, die für den internationalen Markt bestimmt war, aber ebenso wie das Marihouse-Projekt nicht in Serie ging.

Page de droite: Prototype du sauna conçu par Aarno Ruusuvuori pour Marimekko et destiné au marché international, mais qui, comme la Marihouse, ne fut pas fabriqué en série.

Left: The kitchen in the Marihouse
Links: Die Küche im Marihouse
À gauche: La cuisine de la Marihouse

BULLE SIX COQUES

Bati-Plastique, Chantiers Dubigeon, Nantes, France
1967–1970

Opposite page: In 1971 the Bulle
Six Coques was presented at the
International Plastics Exhibition
(IKA) in Lüdenscheid, Germany,
under the name "Orion".
Rechte Seite: Das Bulle Six Coques
1971 unter dem Namen „Orion" auf
der Kunststoff-Ausstellung IKA in
Lüdenscheid
Page de droite: La Bulle six coques
est présentée sous le nom Orion lors
de l'Exposition internationale de la
maison en plastique (IKA) de 1971
à Lüdenscheid, en Allemagne.

Right: Advertising for the holiday
village owned by the Elf oil company
in the French Pyrenean town of
Gripp
Rechts: Werbung für das Feriendorf
des Mineralölkonzerns Elf im
französischen Pyrenäen-Ort Gripp
À droite: Publicité pour le village de
vacances du groupe pétrolier Elf à
Gripp, dans les Pyrénées françaises

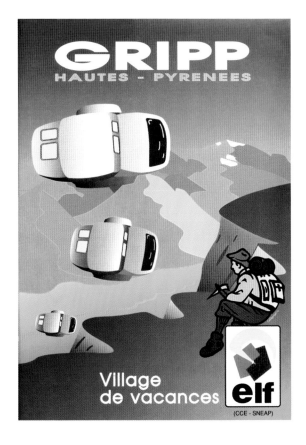

The excellent tensile characteristics of fiber-reinforced plastics have been familiar to us since the 1940s, due to their use in airplane, automobile, and boat construction. However, it took until the 1960s for a number of architects to discover plastic as a building material. Fiber-reinforced plastic resins are very lightweight and therefore perfectly suited for use in lightweight supporting structures spanning broad distances, as well as for houses that are to be transported. In 1964, the French architect and city planner Jean Maneval (1923–1986) designed a mini-weekend house measuring only 390 sq.ft. Twenty of these houses were erected in Gripp, in the Campan region of the Département Hautes-Pyrénées, in 1967. There they formed an experimental vacation village.

As the name indicates, the house "Bulle six coques" ("bubble made of six shells") consists of six "shells" (coques) made of polyester and grouped in the shape of a star around a central element (bulle = bubble). They are screwed to each other as well as to the steel skeleton that supports the floor. The house floats on a support just over 3 ft. above the ground. Every shell is roughly 6 ½ ft. wide, the diameter of the building is roughly 22 ½ ft., and the ceiling height is just over 8 ft. There are two basic models, which can be freely combined with each other: shells with full length windows at the front, or shells with a completely closed front but with one or two small

Seit den 1940er Jahren kennt man aus dem Flugzeug-, dem Automobil- und dem Bootsbau die hervorragenden statischen Eigenschaften von faserverstärkten Kunststoffen. Doch erst in den 1960er Jahren wurde Kunststoff von zahlreichen Architekten als Baustoff entdeckt. Faserverstärkte Kunststoffe sind sehr leicht und daher bestens geeignet für leichte Tragwerke über große Spannweiten, aber auch für Häuser, die transportiert werden sollen. 1964 entwarf der französische Architekt und Stadtplaner Jean Maneval (1923–1986) ein nur 36 m² großes Mini-Ferienhaus, von dem 1967 20 Stück in Gripp (Gemeinde Campan) im Département Hautes-Pyrénées aufgestellt wurden – sie bildeten dort ein experimentelles Feriendorf.

Das Haus Bulle six coques („Blase aus sechs Schalen") besteht, wie der Name sagt, aus sechs „Schalen" (coques) aus Polyester, die sternförmig um eine Mitte (bulle = Blase) gruppiert sind. Sie sind miteinander sowie mit einem Stahlskelett, das den Boden trägt, verschraubt. Das Haus schwebt auf einer Stütze knapp 1 m über dem Boden. Jede Muschel ist etwa 2 m breit, der Durchmesser des Hauses beträgt 6,90 m, die Raumhöhe 2,50 m. Es gibt zwei unterschiedliche Grundtypen, die frei kombinierbar sind: Muscheln mit einem vom Boden bis zur Decke reichenden Fenster in der Stirnseite und Muscheln mit geschlossener Stirnseite und einem oder zwei kleinen

Les excellentes propriétés statiques des matières plastiques renforcées de fibres utilisées dans la construction aéronautique, automobile et navale sont connues depuis les années quarante. Mais ce n'est que dans les années soixante que de nombreux architectes découvrent le plastique comme matériau de construction. Les matières plastiques renforcées de fibres sont très légères et, par conséquent, idéales pour des ossatures légères au-dessus de grandes travées, mais aussi pour des maisons destinées à être transportées. En 1964, l'architecte et urbaniste français Jean Maneval (1923–1986) conçut une «minimaison» de vacances dont la surface se limitait à 36 m² et dont 20 unités furent montées à Gripp (commune de Campan) dans le département des Hautes-Pyrénées en 1967. Elles donnèrent lieu à un village de vacances expérimental.

Comme son nom l'indique, la maison Bulle six coques est composée de six coques en polyester regroupées autour du cœur (la bulle) à la façon d'une étoile. Elles sont vissées entre elles et à une charpente métallique qui supporte le plancher. La maison flotte sur un poteau à près d'un mètre du sol. Chaque coque fait environ 2 m de large. Le diamètre de la maison est de 6,90 m, la hauteur sous plafond de 2,50 m. Il existe deux modèles de base différents pouvant être combinés librement : des coques à une fenêtre allant du sol au plafond sur la façade, et des coques à façade fermée percée

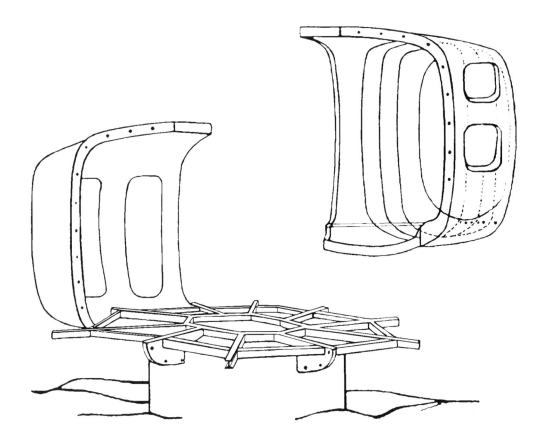

Cross section perspective
Schnittperspektive
Vue en coupe

windows on the narrow side. The entrance to the house is reached over an outdoor stairway leading to a door on the narrow side of the shell.
The water and power supply lines run through a shaft in the support column. Consequently, Maneval installed the kitchen unit, and the toilet and shower unit in the middle of the house, separated from each other by walls. The remainder of the space could be used as dining, living, or sleeping areas. The storage units at the center of the house and the other furniture were executed in wood and metal, according to designs by Maneval.
The house went into production in series in 1968. It was available in three colors, white, green, and chestnut brown. The six shells, each weighing 463 lbs., were delivered by truck. Only a very few of the houses were ever sold—the figures range between 30 and 100—before production was discontinued in 1970. The holiday complex in Gripp was dismantled in 1998, but some of the houses were preserved.

Fenstern an einer Schmalseite. Der Eingang ins Haus führt über eine Freitreppe durch die Schmalseite einer Muschel.
Die Wasser- und Stromleitungen laufen durch den Schaft der Stütze. Daher platzierte Maneval die Küchenzeile, die Toilette und die Duschkabine, durch Wände voneinander getrennt, in der Mitte des Hauses. Der übrige Grundriss kann individuell gestaltet und als Ess-, Wohn- oder Schlafbereich genutzt werden. Die Wandschränke im Zentrum des Hauses und die anderen Möbel sind nach Entwürfen von Maneval aus Holz und Metall gefertigt.
Das Haus ging 1968 in Serie: Zur Wahl standen die drei Farb-Versionen weiß, grün und kastanienbraun. Die sechs Muscheln, die jeweils 210 kg wiegen, wurden per LKW angeliefert. Es wurden jedoch nur wenige Häuser verkauft – die Zahlen schwanken zwischen 30 und 100 –, ehe man 1970 die Produktion wieder einstellte. Die Feriensiedlung in Gripp wurde 1998 abgebaut, einige Häuser sind jedoch noch erhalten.

d'une ou de deux petites fenêtres sur un côté. L'entrée dans la maison s'effectue par le côté étroit d'une coque via un escalier indépendant.
Les conduites d'eau et les câbles électriques passent par le fût du poteau, raison pour laquelle Maneval disposa la cuisine intégrée, les toilettes et la cabine de douche – autant d'éléments séparés les uns des autres par des parois – au centre de la maison. Le plan restant pouvait être aménagé individuellement et être utilisé comme coin salle à manger, salon ou repos.
Les placards du centre de la maison, ainsi que les autres meubles, furent réalisés en bois et métal selon les plans de Maneval.
En 1968, la maison fut fabriquée en série en trois couleurs au choix : blanc, vert et marron. Les six coques, qui pesaient chacune 210 kg, étaient livrées par camion. Cependant, peu de maisons furent vendues. On estime entre 30 et 100 leur nombre avant l'arrêt de la production en 1970. Le village de vacances de Gripp fut démonté en 1998. Il reste toutefois encore quelques maisons.

Assembly and interior of the model
house, 1967

Aufbau und Einrichtung des
Musterhauses, 1967

Montage et aménagement d'une
maison-témoin, 1967

Section and plan (below)

Schnitt und Grundriss (unten)

Coupe et plan (ci-dessous)

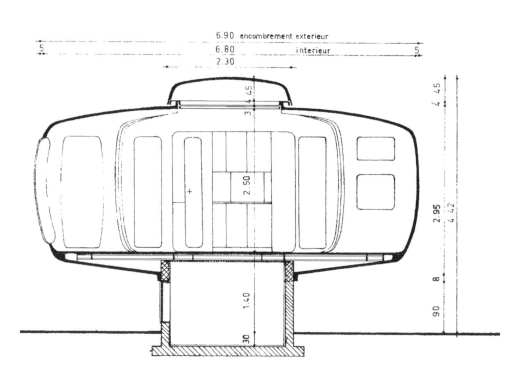

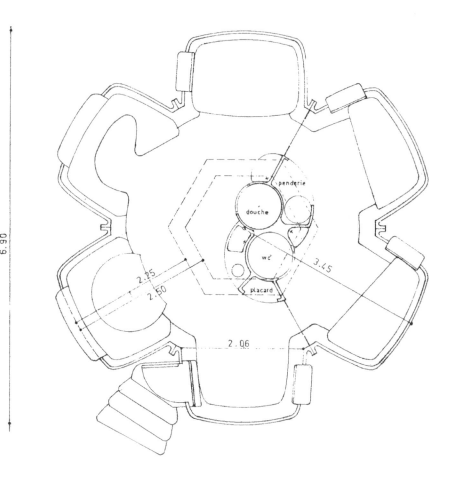

The Elf oil company's holiday
village in Gripp

Das Feriendorf des Mineralölkonzerns Elf in Gripp

Le village de vacances du groupe
pétrolier Elf à Gripp

Below: Plan and section of the
Minibulle (Bulle trois coques)

Unten: Grundriss und Schnitt des
Minibulle (Bulle trois coques)

En dessous: Plan et coupe de la
Minibulle (Bulle trois coques)

Opposite Page: Invasion from outer
space: the Bulle Six Coques at the
International Plastics Exhibition in
Lüdenscheid, Germany, in 1971. Matti
Suuronen's Futuro can be seen on the
left and the space capsule-like Rondo
house by Casoni & Casoni on the
right.

Rechte Seite: Invasion der Außer-
irdischen: Das Bulle Six Coques 1971
auf der Kunststoff-Ausstellung in
Lüdenscheid, Deutschland. Links im
Bild sind das Futuro von Matti
Suuronen sowie im Hintergrund das
raumkapselartige Haus Rondo von
Casoni & Casoni zu erkennen.

Page de droite: Une invasion extra-
terrestre: La Bulle six coques à
l'Exposition internationale de la
maison en plastique de 1971 à
Lüdenscheid, en Allemagne. À
gauche sur la photo, on reconnaît la
Futuro de Matti Suuronen, ainsi que
la maison Rondo en forme de capsule
spatiale de Casoni & Casoni.

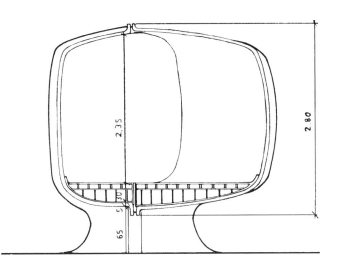

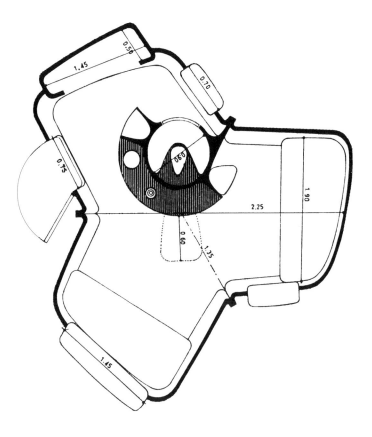

RISOM HOUSE

Stanmar, Inc., Wayland, Massachusetts, USA
1967

In contrast to the standard version, the house has been extended and opened up in the front by means of extensive glazing.

Gegenüber der Standardversion wurde das Haus verlängert und an den Stirnseiten durch großzügige Verglasung geöffnet.

Par rapport à la version standard, la maison fut rallongée et dotée de grandes baies vitrées sur les façades.

In 1967, the Risoms decided to build a vacation home on Block Island, just off the coast of Rhode Island. In order to save money and time, Risom chose a prefabricated wooden house built by Stanmar Inc., a company from Wayland, Massachusetts, but altered a few details in the plans. After a two-month building period—according to the building company an earlier completion date was delayed by heavy fog—the Risoms were able to take possession of their "custom made prefab". Up until this point, this is a relatively unspectacular story. Yet this house became famous for three reasons: one is that Jens Risom, who was born in Copenhagen in 1916 and had been living in or near New York since 1938, was already a famous designer. Secondly, this inspired *Life* magazine to publish a photo essay on the Risoms' house in 1967, and, thirdly, the house really is very special. The frontal view printed in *Life* is quite spectacular. Surrounded on two sides by a wooden terrace built on stilts, both the house and terrace seem to be floating over the green grass of the island—an effect that is amplified by the open flight of stairs. Its form is as simple as possible: one story with a pitched roof. Through the gable end of the house, which is fully glazed from top to bottom, there is a view of the living room with a comfortable sitting area, a dining table, an open kitchen, and the son's loft up on a gallery at the back. The rich green of the surroundings shimmers through a window at the back. Two additional bedrooms and bathrooms, which cannot be seen, are located at the rear on the ground floor, under the loft. A highly dramatic, 20-ft. wall extending all the way up to the peak of the roof is made of wooden boards stained gray; it provides a counterpoint to all this

Im Jahr 1967 beschloss das Ehepaar Risom, sich auf Block Island vor der Küste Rhode Islands ein Ferienhaus zu bauen. Risom entschied sich aus Kosten- und Zeitgründen für ein hölzernes Fertighaus der Firma Stanmar aus Wayland, Massachusetts, dessen Plan er in einigen Punkten abänderte. Nach zwei Monaten Bauzeit – wegen starken Nebels, sonst wäre es, so der Bauunternehmer, viel schneller gegangen – konnten die Risoms ihr „custom made prefab" in Besitz nehmen. So weit, so unspektakulär. Dass das Haus dennoch berühmt wurde, hat drei Gründe: Zum einen war und ist Jens Risom, geboren 1916 in Kopenhagen und seit 1938 in oder bei New York wohnend, ein berühmter Designer. Zum zweiten veröffentlichte das Magazin „Life" aus diesem Grund 1967 eine große Fotostory über Risoms Haus. Und drittens ist es in der Tat etwas Besonderes. Geradezu spektakulär ist die in „Life" abgedruckte Frontalansicht. Auf zwei Seiten von einer Holzterrasse auf Stützen umgeben, scheint das Haus mitsamt der Terrasse über dem grünen Inselboden zu schweben – ein Effekt, der durch die hölzerne Freitreppe noch verstärkt wird. Es zeigt die schlichtest mögliche Form: eingeschossig mit Satteldach. Durch die komplett verglaste Stirnseite geht der Blick in den Wohnraum, der die ganze Breite und Höhe des Hauses einnimmt. Man sieht die gemütliche Sitzecke, den Esstisch, die offene Küche und im hinteren Teil auf einer Zwischendecke das Loft der Söhne. Durch die rückwärtigen Fenster schimmert das satte Grün der Umgebung. Zwei weitere Schlaf- und Badezimmer liegen, dem Blick entzogen, unter dem Loft im hinteren Teil des Erdgeschosses. Einen Kontrapunkt zu dieser Transparenz bildet die geradezu dramatisch

En 1967, le couple Risom décide de construire une maison de vacances sur Block Island, en face de la côte de Rhode Island. Pour des raisons de temps et de coût, Risom opte pour une maison de vacances en bois de l'entreprise Stanmar de Wayland, Massachusetts, dont il modifie le plan en quelques points. Après deux mois de construction en raison du brouillard – ce sans quoi cela serait allé bien plus vite d'après le constructeur –, les Risom peuvent prendre possession de leur « custom made prefab ». Jusque-là, rien de spectaculaire. Trois raisons expliquent pourtant la raison du succès remporté par la maison : premièrement, Jens Risom, né en 1916 à Copenhague et résidant depuis 1938 entre New York et ses alentours, est un designer de renom de longue date. Deuxièmement, cette même raison mènera le magazine *Life* à publier en 1967 un grand photo-reportage sur la maison des Risom. Et troisièmement, elle est bel et bien exceptionnelle. La vue de la façade publiée par *Life* est tout simplement spectaculaire. Avec sa terrasse en bois sur deux côtés qui repose sur des piliers, la maison semble flotter au-dessus du sol vert de l'île, un effet encore renforcé par le perron de bois. La forme qu'elle revêt est des plus sobres : un simple niveau coiffé d'un toit en pente. La façade complètement vitrée offre une vue sur le séjour qui occupe toute la largeur et la hauteur de la maison. On distingue le confortable coin salon, la table à manger, la cuisine ouverte et, dans la partie arrière, le loft des fils sur une mezzanine. Dérobées aux regards, deux chambres et deux salles de bains supplémentaires se trouvent en dessous du loft, à l'arrière du rez-de-chaussée. Contrastant avec cette transparence par son parement de panneaux de bois gris foncé, le mur imposant de

Whether viewed from inside the living room, or from the surrounding landscape, pictures of both the completed house, and the house while under construction, show the glazed gable to be the frame of a distinctly dramatic feature.

Ebenso wie im fertigen Haus scheint bei den Fotos vom Aufbau der verglaste Giebel Rahmen einer dramatischen Inszenierung zu sein, vom Wohnraum oder der Landschaft – je nach Blickrichtung.

Que ce soit sur les photos de la maison terminée ou en construction, le pignon vitré semble être le cadre d'une mise en scène spectaculaire, vue du séjour ou de l'extérieur, selon la direction du regard.

Kitchen, dining room, and living room area
Küche, Ess- und Wohnbereich
Cuisine, coin salle à manger et coin salon

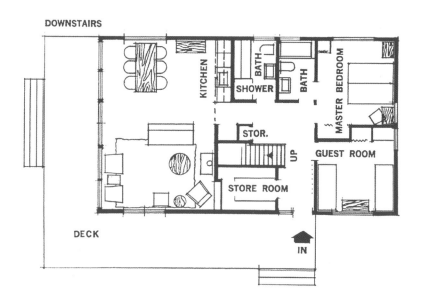

DOWNSTAIRS

KITCHEN
BATH
SHOWER
BATH
MASTER BEDROOM
STOR.
UP
GUEST ROOM
STORE ROOM

DECK

IN

transparency and a backdrop for the chimney pipe from the wood-burning stove. The walls on either side of the living area are the same color—while the wood of the floors and on the underside of the roof has been left naturally light.

The view from the house is no less spectacular; it overlooks a lighthouse and the ocean. Seen from the back, however, the house is far less exciting: here its origin in a catalogue is more obvious—narrow windows in between vertical wooden siding on the outside. The walls, which were partially prefabricated in a factory, are anchored to the concrete foundation using massive bolts to keep the house safe during storms. The roof is covered with wooden shingles. The overall floor space of the house is 24 x 42 ft., the greater part of which (16 x 24 ft.) is taken up by the living room.

6,10 m (20 Fuß) hoch bis zum Dachfirst aufragende Wand aus dunkelgrau gebeizten Holzbrettern, die den Abzug des Kamins hinterfängt. Auch die Seitenwände des Wohnraums zeigen diesen Farbton, während das Holz des Bodens und des Dachstuhls hell belassen ist.

Nicht minder spektakulär ist der Blick aus dem Haus hinaus in Richtung Leuchtturm und Ozean. Die Rückansicht dagegen ist weit weniger aufregend: Hier offenbart das Haus Risom seinen Ursprung aus dem Katalog – mit kleinen Fenstern zwischen den vertikal verlegten Schalungsbrettern der Außenwände. Die teilweise in der Fabrik vorgefertigten Wände sind mit massiven Bolzen im Betonfundament verankert, um das Haus sturmsicher zu machen. Das Dach ist mit Holzschindeln gedeckt. Die Grundfläche des Hauses misst in der Länge 12,80 m (42 Fuß), von denen 4,88 m (16 Fuß) auf das Wohnzimmer entfallen, in der Breite 7,31 m (24 Fuß).

6,10 m (20 pieds) se dresse de toute sa hauteur jusqu'à l'arête du toit, encadrant le conduit de la cheminée. Les murs latéraux du salon présentent également cette teinte, alors que le bois du plancher et la charpente du toit sont laissés de couleur claire.

Non moins spectaculaire : la vue depuis la maison en direction du phare et de la mer. En revanche, la vue arrière présente moins d'attrait. La maison Risom dévoile là son origine de maison de catalogue, avec ses petites fenêtres entre les panneaux de coffrage verticaux des murs extérieurs. Les murs partiellement préfabriqués en usine sont solidement fixés aux fondations de béton à l'aide de goujons massifs, afin de sécuriser la maison contre les risques de tempête. Le toit est recouvert de bardeaux de bois. La surface de la maison est de 12,80 m (42 pieds) de longueur, dont 4,88 m (16 pieds) reviennent au salon, et 7,31 m (24 pieds) de largeur.

FUTURO

Oy Polykem AB, Helsinki, Finland
1968–1978

Opposite page: The Futuro in
Philadelphia, Pennsylvania, 1970

Rechte Seite: Das Futuro in
Philadelphia, Pennsylvania, 1970

Page de droite: La Futuro à
Philadelphie, Pennsylvanie, 1970

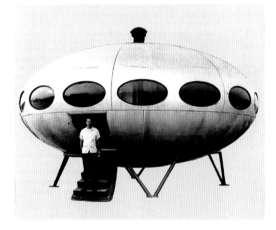

WHERE ARE THE LITTLE GREEN MEN?

It was a simple ski house that the Finnish architect Matti Suuronen was asked to design for a friend in 1965. It was supposed to be easy to build in difficult terrain and quick to heat. What ultimately resulted was an icon of the belief in progress predominant in the age of space travel during the late 1960s; it attracted worldwide attention, for its creator had made a ski house that looked more like a UFO: an ellipsoid on four legs. The structure was made of fiberglass reinforced polyester. The architect had already gained experience building with plastic while fulfilling a commission to design a plastic dome for the top of a grain silo. The solution he adopted also made it possible for the capsule to be transported by helicopter, since it weighed relatively little.

The prototype he presented on the grounds of the Polykem company in 1968 measured over 26 ft. in diameter and 11 ft. 6 in. in height. Even in cold weather, the barely 540 sq.ft. of space in the capsule could be brought up to a comfortable indoor temperature within half an hour, thanks to its electric heating and polyurethane insulation. The most fascinating pieces of furniture were the pull-out lounge chairs, which were grouped around the fireplace in the middle. However, the price of $12,000 was exorbitant at the time.

After tremendous success in London at the Finnfocus Export Fair in October 1968, Polykem Ltd. decided to start producing the house in series. Within a short time, over 400 enquiries had been received from foreign companies interested in procuring production rights; licenses were granted in 25 countries. The Futuro House came on a truck in the form of 16 curved, fiberglass reinforced composite shells, which were screwed together on site and set onto a foundation ring. An even more effective

Es war eine schlichte Skihütte, die der finnische Architekt Matti Suuronen 1965 für einen Freund entwarf. Sie sollte auch in unwegsamem Gelände einfach zu konstruieren und schnell zu beheizen sein. Was dabei herauskam, war eine der Ikonen der fortschrittsgläubigen Raumfahrtära der Endsechziger-Jahre und erregte weltweite Aufmerksamkeit. Denn ihr Schöpfer hatte der Hütte das Aussehen eines UFOs verliehen: ein auf Stützen gestelltes Ellipsoid, ovale Fenster und eine integrierte Treppe. Die Konstruktion bestand aus glasfaserverstärktem Polyester. Konstruktive Erfahrungen mit diesem Kunststoff hatte der Architekt bereits 1964 im Rahmen des Auftrags, eine Kunststoffkuppel für ein Getreidesilo zu entwerfen, sammeln können. Diese Lösung machte es möglich, dass die Kapsel aufgrund ihres verhältnismäßig geringen Eigengewichts auch mit dem Helikopter transportiert werden konnte.

Der 1968 auf dem Gelände der Firma Polykem vorgestellte Prototyp hatte einen Durchmesser von 8 m und eine Höhe von 3,5 m. Selbst bei kaltem Wetter ließ sich die knapp 50 m² große Kapsel dank elektrischer Heizung und Polyurethan-Isolation innerhalb einer halben Stunde auf angenehme Innentemperaturen bringen. Faszinierendstes Einrichtungselement waren die ausziehbaren Liegesessel, die sich um einen Kamin in der Mitte gruppierten. Der Preis von umgerechnet rund 12 000 $ war für damalige Verhältnisse exorbitant hoch.

Nach dem einschlagenden Erfolg auf der Finnfocus-Exportmesse im Oktober 1968 in London entschied sich die finnische Firma Polykem zur Aufnahme der Serienproduktion. Binnen kurzer Zeit lagen über 400 Anfragen von ausländischen Firmen vor, die sich die Herstellungsrechte sichern wollten; Lizenzen gingen in 25 Länder. Das Futuro-Haus kam in 16 gekrümmten,

En 1965, l'architecte finnois Matti Suuronen dut concevoir un simple chalet de ski pour un ami. Il devait être facile à construire – même sur terrain escarpé – et rapide à chauffer. Il en résulta une des icônes de l'ère de la navigation spatiale de la fin des années soixante, confiante dans le progrès. Elle capta l'attention internationale en raison de l'apparence de soucoupe volante que lui avait donnée son créateur, une forme ellipsoïdale reposant sur des supports, des fenêtres ovales et un escalier intégré. La structure était en polyester renforcé de fibres de verre. En 1964, l'architecte s'était déjà essayé à une construction avec ce matériau dans le cadre de la commande d'une coupole en matière plastique pour un silo à céréales. En raison de son poids relativement faible, cette solution permettait également de transporter la capsule par hélicoptère.

Le prototype présenté en 1968 sur le site de l'entreprise Polykem avait un diamètre de 8 m et une hauteur de 3,5 m. Même par grand froid, grâce au chauffage électrique et à l'isolation en polyuréthane, les 50 m² de la capsule atteignaient une température ambiante agréable en une demi-heure. L'élément mobilier le plus fascinant étaient les fauteuils-couchettes dépliants disposés autour de la cheminée centrale. Par rapport au niveau de vie de l'époque, le prix de 12 000 $ était exorbitant.

Suite au succès fulgurant remporté lors du salon Finnfocus Export à Londres en octobre 1968, l'entreprise finlandaise Polykem. décida d'en lancer la production en série. En peu de temps, elle reçut plus de 400 demandes d'entreprises étrangères qui voulaient s'assurer les droits de fabrication. 25 pays obtinrent des licences. La maison Futuro était livrée par camion, sous la forme de 16 coques composites arrondies, renforcées de fibres de verre, puis était montée sur site et posée sur un anneau de fondations. Le

A Futuro being delivered to its final location by a Swedish airforce helicopter in 1969.

Dieses Futuro wird 1969 mit einem Helikopter der schwedischen Luftwaffe an seinen Standort gebracht.

Cette Futuro est acheminée vers son emplacement par un hélicoptère de l'armée de l'air suédoise en 1969.

Opposite page: The Futuro at the 1971 International Plastics Exhibition (IKA 71) in Lüdenscheid, Germany. The Rondo house by Casoni & Casoni can be seen on the right.

Linke Seite: Das Futuro 1971 auf der Internationalen Kunststoff-Ausstellung IKA 71 in Lüdenscheid. Rechts im Bild ist das Haus Rondo von Casoni & Casoni zu erkennen.

Page de gauche: La Futuro à l'Exposition internationale de la maison en plastique de 1971 à Lüdenscheid (IKA 71), en Allemagne. À droite sur la photo, on reconnaît la maison Rondo de Casoni & Casoni.

advertising measure proved to be the option of having the complete Futuro delivered by helicopter.
In the 1970s, the photographer and advertising guru Charles Wilp had a Futuro erected on the roof of his own house in Düsseldorf, where he received guests like Andy Warhol and Christo, who also later wrapped the plastic ellipsoid during one of his art actions. The Futuro with the serial number 13 was purchased by the GDR and installed in the Cultural Park in the Berlin district of Treptow in 1969. The 'space capsule' soon became an attraction there, although some people suspected that it was a Stasi monitoring station. In fact, it only served as an information center and as a radio studio from which music was broadcast throughout the park. In the meantime it has been sold and removed from the now neglected park. It has since been transported to a nearby site on the banks of the Spree River. Between 1968 and 1978, 20 Futuros were built in Finland alone. Worldwide the number of existing capsules is estimated at about 60.

glasfaserverstärkten Verbundschalen auf einem LKW und wurde vor Ort verschraubt und auf einen Fundamentring gesetzt. Weit werbewirksamer war jedoch die Möglichkeit, sich das fertige Futuro per Helikopter anliefern zu lassen.
In den 1970er Jahren empfing der Fotograf und Werbeguru Charles Wilp in seinem auf dem Dach des eigenen Hauses in Düsseldorf aufgestellten Futuro Gäste wie Andy Warhol oder Christo. Letzterer sollte das Kunststoff-Ellipsoid im Rahmen einer Kunstaktion später auch verpacken. Eines der Futuros, mit der Seriennummer 13, wurde von der DDR erworben und 1969 im Kulturpark in Berlin-Treptow aufgestellt. Dort avancierte die ,Raumkapsel' alsbald zu einer der Attraktionen, von einigen wurde sie allerdings argwöhnisch als mögliche Stasi-Abhöranlage betrachtet. Tatsächlich diente sie nur als Informationszentrale und als Funkstudio, von dem aus der Park mit Musik beschallt werden konnte. Unlängst wurde sie verkauft und aus der mittlerweile verwahrlosten Anlage auf ein nahegelegenes Grundstück umgesetzt.
Zwischen 1968 und 1978 wurden allein in Finnland etwa 20 Futuros gebaut; weltweit wird die Zahl der noch existierenden Kapseln auf etwa 60 Exemplare geschätzt.

must demeurait cependant la possibilité de se faire livrer le modèle monté par hélicoptère.
Dans les années soixante-dix, le photographe et grand publicitaire Charles Wilp recevait des invités dans sa Futuro posée sur le toit de sa maison à Düsseldorf, tels qu'Andy Warhol ou Christo, lequel enveloppa plus tard l'ellipsoïde de plastique dans le cadre d'une action artistique. Une des Futuro, la numéro de série 13, fut achetée par la RDA et installée en 1969 dans le premier parc d'attractions de Berlin-Treptow. En tant que « capsule de l'espace », elle devint immédiatement l'une des attractions. D'aucuns la soupçonnèrent toutefois d'abriter une éventuelle table d'écoute de la Stasi. Elle servait dans les faits de centre d'informations et d'émetteur radio d'où était diffusée la musique du parc. Elle a été récemment vendue et déplacée du terrain à l'abandon où elle se trouvait vers un terrain près de la Spree. Entre 1968 et 1978, pas moins de 20 Futuro furent construites en Finlande. On estime à 60 le nombre d'exemplaires existant encore à l'échelle planétaire.

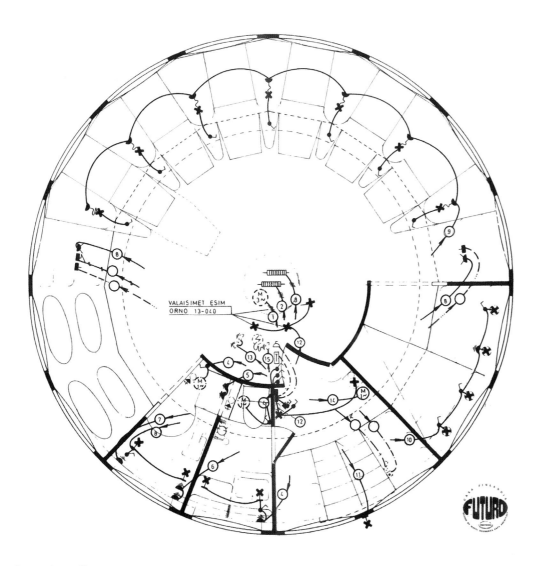

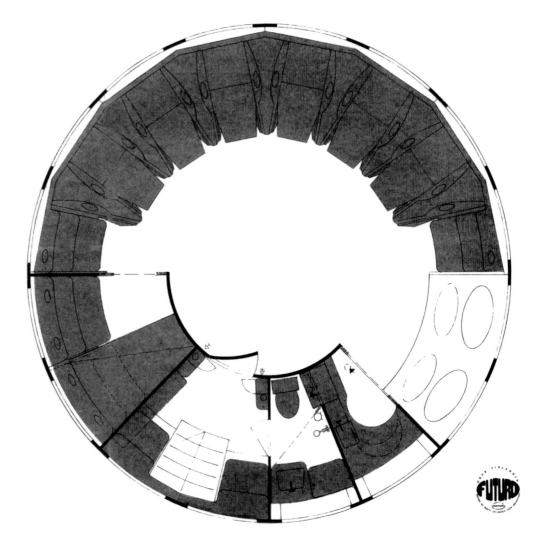

Plans with installation instructions
Grundrisse mit Installationsangaben
Plans avec indications pour l'installation

Opposite page: The permanently installed seating does not allow for any changes.

Rechte Seite: Die fest eingebauten Sitzgelegenheiten gestatteten keine Veränderungen.

Page de droite: Les sièges fixés n'autorisaient aucune autre disposition.

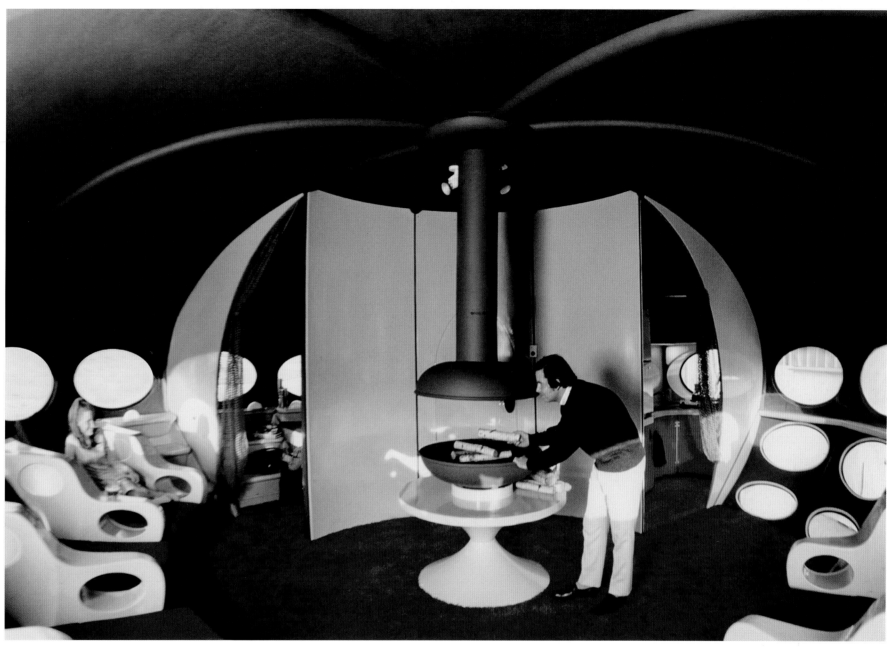

The advertising photo shows the fireplace and, in the background, niches for the kitchen (right) and a double bed (left).

Das Werbefoto zeigt die zentrale Feuerstelle und im Hintergrund die Nischen für die Küche (rechts) und ein Doppelbett (links).

La photo publicitaire montre le foyer central et, en arrière-plan, les alcôves pour la cuisine (à droite) et un lit à deux places (à gauche).

Opposite page: One of C.G. Hagström's fashion photos for Vuokko

Linke Seite: Eines von C.G. Hagströms Modefotos für Vuokko

Page de gauche: L'une des photos de mode de C.G. Hagström pour Vuokko

KUNSTSTOFFHAUS FG2000

Wolfgang Feierbach Kunststofftechnik, Altenstadt, Germany
1968–1970

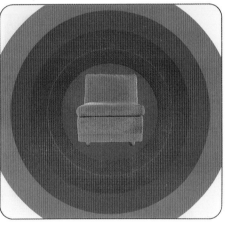

A brochure for fiberglass furniture,
Feierbach's main product

Prospekt für Fiberglasmöbel,
Hauptprodukt der Firma Feierbach

Brochure pour meubles en fibre
de verre, produit principal de
l'entreprise Feierbach

Wolfgang Feierbach was always fascinated by plastics. After training as a model builder, he passed his examination as a master craftsman at the age of 24, then went into business for himself. He began to design not only switchboxes, protective hoods and similar money-bringing items, but also plastic furniture. And since fiberglass reinforced polyester resin, or fiberglass, has tremendous tensile strength, he asked himself whether he could build an entire house out of the material—a house in which he and his family could feel at home.

Feierbach was already considering the possibility of production in series when he decided not to build the house in one piece, but out of individual elements instead. Since there is always a danger of the fiberglass parts warping during the production process, he designed the supporting wall elements with a slight curvature from the outset. In a number of experiments he determined the thickness and the length of the roof elements. In one test he left a truck parked on prototypes for the elements which he had laid across saw-horse-like supports—it had no effect on them. Thus, Feierbach was finally convinced that his concept would work.

On July 18, 1968 at 7 o'clock in the morning, ten of Feierbach's employees began under the watchful eyes of numerous journalists to assemble 13 roof and 26 wall elements, including six with windows: two wall elements and one roof element were put in place on the reinforced concrete roof of the Feierbach office building and screwed together—without using a crane or hoists, but instead only hydraulic lifts. The windows were fitted into the

Kunststoff faszinierte Wolfgang Feierbach schon immer. Der gelernte Modellbauer machte sich nach der Meisterprüfung mit 24 Jahren selbständig und begann, neben Schaltkästen, Schutzhauben und ähnlichen Dingen, die das Geld einbrachten, Kunststoffmöbel zu bauen. Und da glasfaserverstärktes Polyesterharz, kurz Fiberglas genannt, enorm belastungsfähig ist, fragte er sich, ob man daraus nicht ein ganzes Haus bauen könnte – ein Haus, in dem er sich mit seiner Familie wohl fühlen würde.

Feierbach dachte bereits an eine mögliche Serienproduktion, als er sich entschloss, sein Haus nicht aus einem Stück, sondern aus einzelnen Elementen aufzubauen. Da die Gefahr bestand, dass sich gerade Fiberglas-Teile bei der Herstellung verziehen, entwarf er die tragenden Wandelemente von vornherein mit leichter Krümmung. In verschiedenen Experimenten bestimmte er Dicke und Länge der Dachelemente. So ließ er eine Nacht lang einen LKW auf den aufgebockten Probe-Elementen stehen – es machte ihnen nichts aus. Schließlich war sich Feierbach sicher, dass sein Konzept funktionieren würde.

So begannen am 18. Juli 1968 um 7 Uhr morgens zehn Mitarbeiter der Firma Feierbach, unter Beobachtung zahlreicher Journalisten, auf dem Stahlbetondach des Feierbachschen Bürogebäudes 13 Dach- und 26 Wandelemente, davon sechs mit Fenstern, zusammenzusetzen: Je ein Dachelement wurde mit zwei Wandelementen verschraubt – alles ohne Kran und Hebezeug, nur mit Hilfe hydraulischer Böcke. Die Fensterfronten an den Stirnseiten wurden mit Fenstern geschlossen, und um 17 Uhr stand er

Les matières plastiques avaient toujours fasciné Wolfgang Feierbach. Suite à son examen de maîtrise clôturant sa formation de modéliste, il se mit à son compte à 24 ans et commença à construire des meubles en plastique en parallèle des boîtiers de commande, capots et autres objets analogues qui lui rapportaient de l'argent. Comme la résine de polyester renforcé de fibres de verre – dite fibre de verre – présente une résistance très élevée, il se demanda s'il ne serait pas possible de s'en servir pour construire une maison, une maison dans laquelle il se sentirait bien avec sa famille.

Feierbach avait déjà à l'esprit une éventuelle production en série lorsqu'il décida de réaliser sa maison non pas d'un seul tenant, mais à partir d'éléments individuels. Il détermina l'épaisseur et la longueur des éléments de toiture suite à diverses expérimentations. Ainsi, il laissa un camion reposer une nuit entière sur les éléments à tester surélevés, mais cela ne les affecta nullement. En fin de compte, Feierbach eut la certitude que son concept était viable.

À 7 h du matin, le 18 juillet 1968, dix collaborateurs de l'entreprise Feierbach commencèrent le montage des 13 éléments de toiture et 26 éléments de murs – dont six avec fenêtres – sous le regard attentif de nombreux journalistes. Deux éléments de murs et un élément de toiture furent positionnés à leur place sur le toit de béton et d'acier du bâtiment de bureaux de Feierbach et vissés, sans avoir recours à une quelconque grue ou engin de levage, avec la seule aide de vérins hydrauliques. Les façades de fenêtres des côtés furent fermées avec des fenêtres et, à 17 h, le gros œuvre

The lightweight wall elements could be set into their foundations by four workmen.

Die leichten Wandelemente konnten von nur vier Monteuren in ihre Fundamente gehoben werden.

Quatre installateurs suffisaient pour hisser les légers éléments de murs sur leurs fondations.

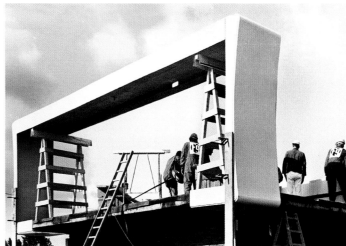

Lamination of a roof element

Laminieren eines Dachelements

Pelliculage d'un élément de toiture

Like the house itself, the roof elements were installed without lifting equipment.

Ebenso wie das Haus selbst wurden auch die Dachelemente ohne Hebezeuge montiert.

Tout comme la maison elle-même, les éléments de toiture furent montés sans l'aide d'engin de levage.

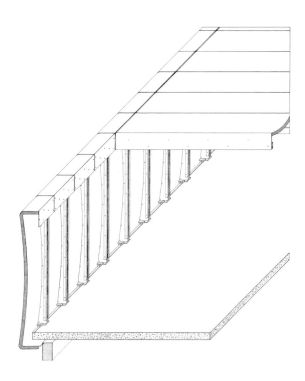

front and back façades and by around five o'clock the shell of the largest plastic house ever built was completed. The wall and ceiling elements that opened up to the interior were clad with upholstered plywood. In order to provide insulation, the thin walls were constructed in two layers with a core of insulating hard plastic foam.

The layout is divided into two parts: one combines the living, dining, and cooking areas; the other, at the back, holds the master bedroom, children's room and bathroom, separated either by closets or by folding textile doors. The interior was decorated according to original designs, using some of the company's own custom products. A control panel is found at the heart of the house's technical installations, located between the living and sleeping areas. It includes a digital clock, weather station, thermostat to regulate the room temperature, and switches to operate the lighting, motorized curtains, awning, and small side windows. Over the course of a year, hundreds of visitors viewed the model house, then Feierbach moved in with his family of five. In 1979 they moved into a new plastic house; while the original model house is still standing without ever having to be repaired. It is still used as an office.

fertig da: der Rohbau des bis dahin größten je gebauten Kunststoffhauses. Die nach innen offenen Wand- und Deckenelemente wurden mit Spanplatten verschlossen, die gepolstert und mit Wohndekor-Stoffen überzogen waren. Zur Isolierung waren die dünnen Wände doppelschalig mit einem isolierenden Kunststoff-Hartschaum-Kern ausgeführt.

Der Grundriss war zweigeteilt: Der eine Hausteil verband Wohn-, Ess- und Kochbereich, der rückwärtige Teil Elternschlafzimmer, Kinderzimmer und Badezimmer, abgetrennt jeweils durch Schränke oder textile Falttüren. Die Innengestaltung erfolgte nach eigenen Entwürfen und zum Teil in eigener Fertigung. Technisches Herz des Hauses war die zwischen Wohn- und Schlafbereich platzierte elektrische Schalttafel mit Digitaluhr, Wetterstation, Raumthermostat und Schalter für die Beleuchtung, die elektrisch bewegbaren Gardinen, die Markisen und die kleinen Seitenfenster. Ein Jahr lang wurde das Musterhaus täglich von Hunderten Besuchern besichtigt, dann zog Feierbach mit seiner fünfköpfigen Familie ein. 1979 zogen sie in ein neues Kunststoffhaus um; das erste Musterhaus aber steht bis heute, ohne dass es je repariert werden musste, und wird als Büro genutzt.

de la plus grande maison en plastique jamais construite était terminé. Les éléments de murs et de plafonds donnant sur l'intérieur furent parés de panneaux d'aggloméré capitonnés et recouverts de tissus d'ameublement. Les doubles parois minces étaient isolées par un cœur en mousse rigide de polyuréthanne.

Le plan était en deux parties: la première reliait les coins salon, salle à manger et cuisine, et la partie arrière la chambre des parents, la chambre des enfants et la salle de bains, séparées par des placards ou des portes pliantes en tissu. Placé entre les coins salon et repos, le cœur technique de la maison était concentré en un tableau de commande regroupant horloge numérique, station météorologique, thermostat de température ambiante et interrupteur pour l'éclairage, les rideaux électriques, les stores et les petites fenêtres latérales. Pendant un an, des centaines de visiteurs visitèrent la maison-témoin chaque jour, puis Feierbach y emménagea avec les quatre autres membres de sa famille. En 1979, ils emménagèrent dans une nouvelle maison en plastique. La première existe toujours, sans avoir jamais eu à subir de réparations. Elle sert aujourd'hui de bureau.

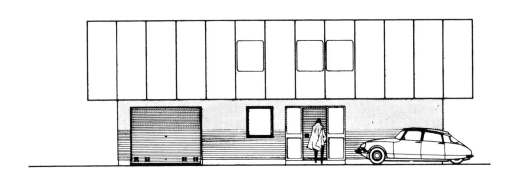

NORDANSICHT

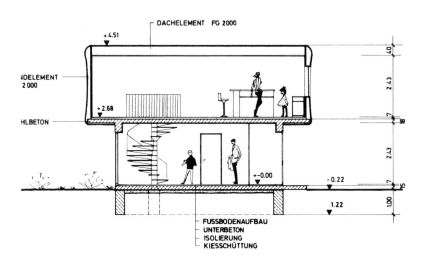

SCHNITT A-A

The above ground foundation was built in a conventional manner and served as a substitute for a cellar and a garage.

Das Sockelgeschoss entstand in konventioneller Bauweise und ersetzte Kellerräume und Garage.

L'étage de soubassement avait été construit de manière traditionnelle et remplaçait les caves et le garage.

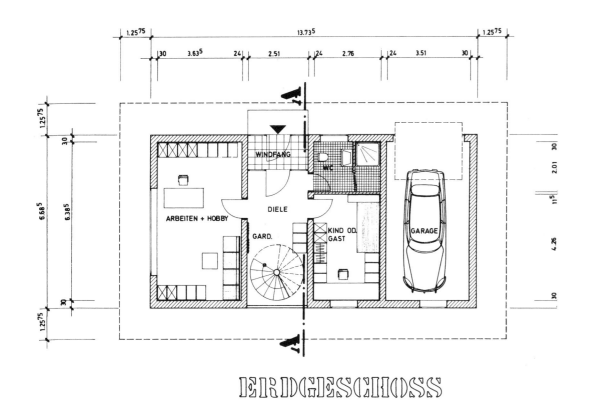

ERDGESCHOSS

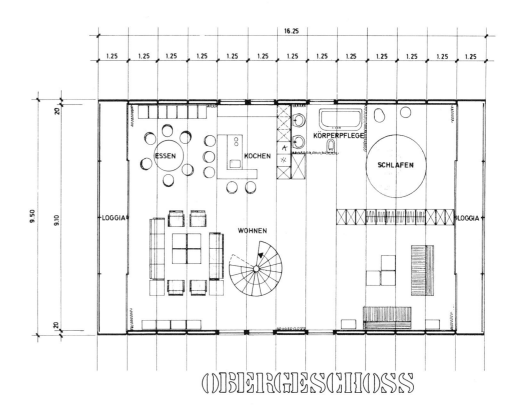

OBERGESCHOSS

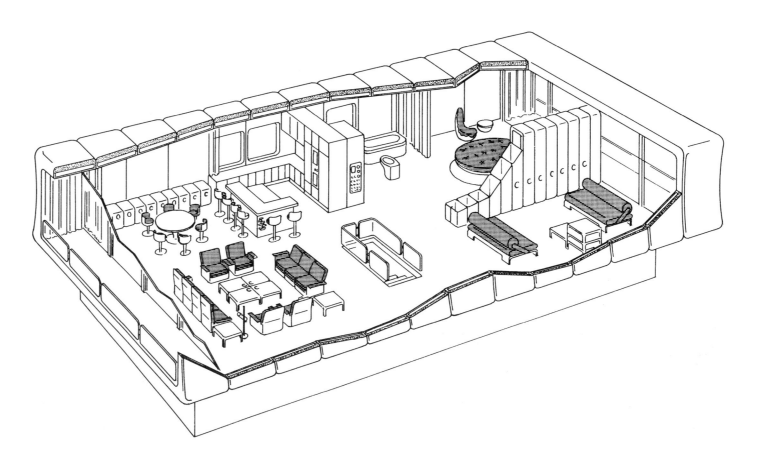

The isometric drawing shows the interior of a room divided only by furniture.

Die Isometrie zeigt den lediglich durch Möbel unterteilten Innenraum.

L'isométrie montre l'espace intérieur uniquement divisé par des meubles.

The fiberglass furniture and ceiling decorated with colorful shag carpeting determined the character of the interior. The walls were upholstered.

Der Charakter des Innenraums wird durch die Fiberglasmöbel und die Decke aus farbigen, hängenden Fäden bestimmt. Die Wände sind stoffbespannt.

Le caractère de l'espace intérieur est marqué par les meubles en fibre de verre et le plafond recouvert de moquette à poils longs colorés. Les murs sont recouverts de tissus.

The bar in the living area (below left), the bathroom (below right) and the bedroom with a round, free-standing bed (opposite page)

Bar im Wohnbereich (links unten), Badezimmer (rechts unten) und Schlafzimmer mit rundem frei-stehenden Bett (rechte Seite)

Bar dans l'espace séjour (ci-dessous à gauche), salle de bains (ci-dessous à droite) et chambre avec lit rond sur pied (à droite)

HEINRICH BERNHARD HELLMUTH

FERTIGHAUS TANJA

**Schneckenburger & Co., Rottenburg am Neckar, Germany
1970–2009**

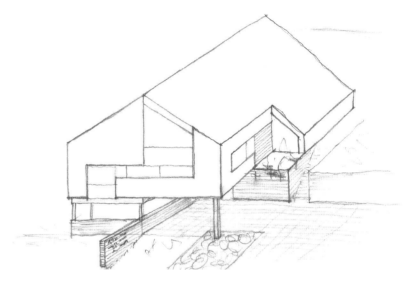

The open side of the house facing the garden differs considerably from the closed side facing the driveway.

Die offene Gartenseite des Hauses unterscheidet sich deutlich von der eher verschlossenen Seite zur Auffahrt hin.

La façade ouverte de la maison donnant sur le jardin contraste avec la façade plutôt fermée du côté de l'allée.

The homes designed by Heinrich Bernhard Hellmuth and built by Schneckenburger & Co. of the Swabian town of Rottenburg provide proof that a freelance architect committed to design excellence can work effectively with a prefabricated housing builder who is forced to take economic constraints into consideration. Hellmuth produced the first designs for prefabricated houses in the early 1960s; the collaboration ended in 2009 when Schneckenburger closed the company due to his age. The house model was named after Hellmuth's older daughter Tanja and developed in 1970; over 40 of these houses were built. A subsequent smaller model was named after his younger daughter Katja.

Hellmuth developed the prototype as his own home in the town of Bieringen. He established his architectural office on the ground floor, which receives natural light from one side due to its location on a slope. The "studio house" has a number of different faces. The floor plan describes nearly a perfect square, with one exciting variation: the living area extends beyond the limits of the otherwise compact layout. When the house is approached from the valley, it seems compact and enclosed under a slightly asymmetrical pitched roof. Seen from the slope behind the house, the entire back opens up to the garden; the roof also extends down over the living room. Hence, the dark line of the slate-clad edge of the roof leads from the ground up over the peak to the other side, where it doubles back to underline the balcony; the white brick chimney makes for an effective vertical counterpoint.

The house encompasses a total of 1,800 sq.ft. of living space on two floors. On the ground floor, there is a living room and a children's area: the two

Dass ein freier Architekt mit Gestaltungswillen und eine ökonomischen Zwängen unterworfene Fertighausfirma durchaus eine langjährige, glückliche Symbiose eingehen können, beweisen die Häuser, die die Firma Schneckenburger aus dem schwäbischen Rottenburg nach Entwürfen von Heinrich Bernhard Hellmuth gebaut hat. Anfang der 1960er Jahre lieferte Hellmuth die ersten Fertighaus-Entwürfe; die Zusammenarbeit endete 2009 mit der Schließung der Firma Schneckenburger aus Altersgründen des Inhabers. Zum Erfolgsmodell mit über 40 realisierten Bauten wurde vor allem das Haus Tanja, das Hellmuth 1970 entwickelte. Er benannte es nach seiner älteren Tochter, das später folgende kleinere Modell trug den Namen der jüngeren Tochter Katja.

Der Prototyp entstand als Hellmuths eigenes Wohnhaus in Bieringen. Im Untergeschoss, das durch die Hanglage zur einen Seite hin natürlich belichtet wird, richtete er sein Architekturbüro ein.

Das „Atelierhaus" ist ein Bau mit verschiedenen Gesichtern. Der Grundriss ist fast quadratisch, jedoch spannungsvoll verunklart durch das Herausrücken des Wohnraumes aus der kompakten Grundform. Zum Tal hin, von wo aus man das Haus erreicht, zeigt es sich kompakt und geschlossen unter dem leicht asymmetrischen Satteldach. Zum Hang hin, auf der Gartenseite, öffnet es sich in größerer Breite; hier ist das Dach über dem Wohnzimmer weit nach unten gezogen. Die schieferbesetzte, dunkle Dachkante führt hier vom Boden aus hinüber zur anderen Seite und setzt sich im Balkon fort; der weiß aufgemauerte Schornstein bildet einen wirkungsvollen vertikalen Gegenakzent.

Das Haus umfasst auf zwei Geschossen eine Wohnfläche von 170 m². Im

Les maisons bâties par la société Schneckenburger de la ville souabe de Rottenburg sur les plans de Heinrich Bernhard Hellmuth sont la preuve qu'un architecte indépendant, désireux d'exprimer sa créativité, et une entreprise spécialisée en maisons préfabriquées soumise à des contraintes économiques peuvent jouir de relations professionnelles durables et harmonieuses. C'est au début des années soixante qu'Hellmuth livra ses premiers plans de maisons préfabriquées. La collaboration prit fin en 2009 avec la fermeture de l'entreprise Schneckenburger en raison du grand âge de son propriétaire. Parmi plus de 40 constructions, la maison Tanja de 1970 fut le modèle le plus vendu réalisé par Hellmuth. Il la nomma ainsi d'après le nom de sa fille aînée, tandis que le petit modèle projeté ultérieurement prit le nom de leur plus jeune fille Katja.

Le prototype vit le jour comme maison d'habitation privée d'Hellmuth à Bieringen. Il y installa son bureau d'architecture au rez-de-chaussée, niveau naturellement éclairé d'un côté en raison de l'inclinaison du terrain.

La « maison atelier » est un bâtiment présentant plusieurs facettes. Son plan de forme quasiment carrée, altérée par l'avancée de la salle de séjour au-delà de cette forme de base compacte, sort de l'ordinaire. Du côté de la vallée par lequel on atteint la maison, elle apparaît massive et fermée sous son toit en pente légèrement asymétrique. Du côté du jardin donnant sur la pente, elle s'ouvre sur une grande partie de sa largeur. Ici, le toit au-dessus de la salle de séjour descend très bas. La sombre bordure du toit d'ardoise part du sol jusqu'au côté opposé et se poursuit sur le balcon. La cheminée blanche constitue un contraste vertical saisissant.

La maison comporte une surface habitable de 170 m² sur deux étages. Les

The gallery with the master bedroom is reached from the spacious living room, while the children's rooms form a separate area on the ground floor.

Vom großzügigen Wohnraum erreicht man die Empore mit Eltern-schlafzimmer, während die Kinder-zimmer im Erdgeschoss einen eigenen, abgetrennten Bereich bilden.

On atteint la galerie où se trouve la chambre des parents à partir du spacieux séjour, tandis que les chambres des enfants forment un espace indépendant au rez-de-chaussée.

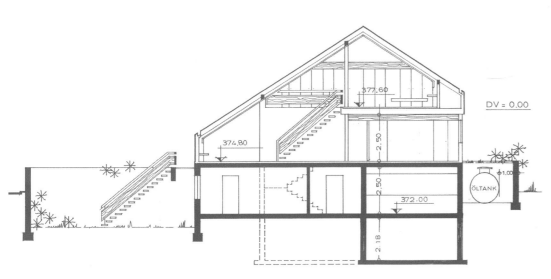

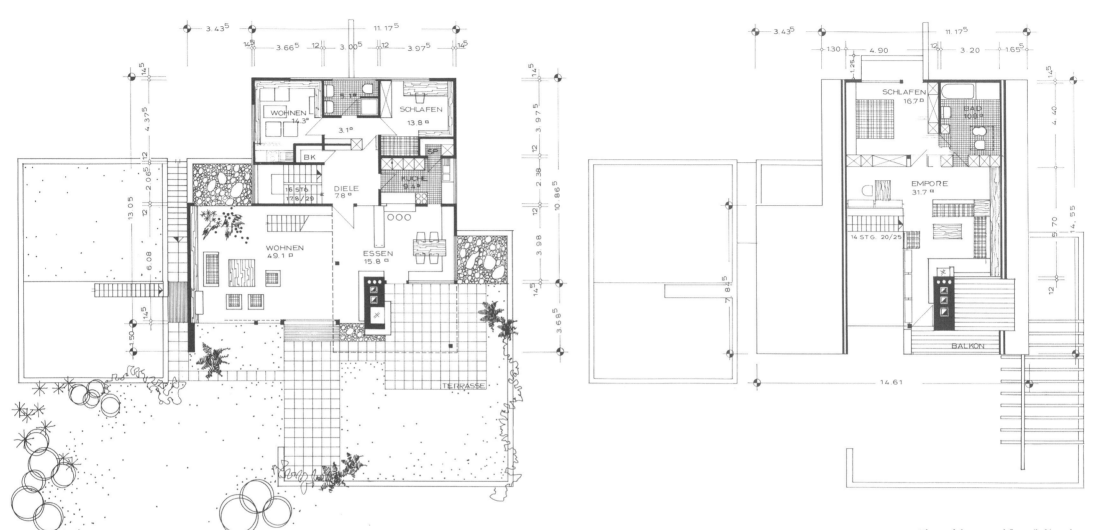

Plans of the ground floor (left) and
the upper level (right)

Grundrisse von Erdgeschoss (links)
und Dachgeschoss (rechts)

Plans du rez-de-chaussée (à gauche)
et du niveau supérieur (à droite)

children's rooms and a bathroom overlook the valley. The hallway with
stairs to the lower level serves as a buffer zone—also against possible noise
from the children's rooms—between the nearly 430-sq.ft. "Grand Room"
under the slanted roof and the dining room, which is connected to the
kitchen via a "breakfast bar". The roofed terrace with an open fireplace is
located in front of the dining room. On the upper floor there is a "quiet
zone" that includes the master bedroom, bathroom, and a large gallery,
which also has an open fireplace and is reached from the living room via a
straight flight of stairs. The interior rooms prominently feature wooden
paneling.
The house is built as a wooden structure. Schneckenburger offered Tanja
models in different variations, including with different roofs, with or without a cellar, and with or without a recessed balcony.

Erdgeschoss sind die Wohnräume und der Kinderbereich untergebracht:
Zum Tal hin liegen die zwei Kinderzimmer und ein Bad. Die Diele mit der
Treppe ins Untergeschoss dient als Pufferzone – auch akustisch gegen
möglichen Lärm aus den Kinderzimmern – zur fast 40 m² großen „Wohn-
halle" unter dem Schrägdach und dem Esszimmer, das durch eine „Früh-
stücksbar" mit der Küche verbunden ist. Vor dem Essraum liegt die
überdachte Terrasse mit dem offenen Kamin. Im Obergeschoss befindet
sich die „Ruhezone" der Eltern mit Schlafzimmer, Bad und einer großen
„Empore", ebenfalls mit offenem Kamin, die man aus dem Wohnzimmer
über eine geradläufige Treppe erreicht. Die Innenräume sind durch Holzverkleidung geprägt.
Das Haus ist in einer Holzverbundkonstruktion erstellt. Schneckenburger
bot das Haus Tanja in verschiedenen Variationen an, u.a. mit verschiedenen Dachformen, mit oder ohne Keller, mit oder ohne Loggia-Anbau.

pièces à vivre et le coin enfants se trouvent au rez-de-chaussée : deux
chambres pour enfants et une salle de bains donnent sur la vallée. Le hall
avec l'escalier menant au sous-sol sert de zone tampon – également sur le
plan acoustique contre le bruit éventuel provenant des chambres d'enfants
– entre le grand «hall à vivre» d'environ 40 m² se trouvant sous le toit en
pente, et la salle à manger reliée à la cuisine par un «bar à petit déjeuner».
Équipée d'une cheminée ouverte, la terrasse couverte donne devant la salle
à manger. À l'étage se trouve la «zone de repos» des parents avec leur
chambre, une salle de bains, et une grande «galerie», également dotée d'une
cheminée ouverte que l'on peut atteindre à partir du salon par un escalier
droit. Les pièces intérieures se caractérisent par un revêtement de bois.
La maison a une structure mixte en bois. Schneckenburger a proposé la
maison Tanja en divers modèles, dont une version avec diverses formes de
toit, avec ou sans cave, avec ou sans loggia.

A variety of materials in the house (left to right): wood paneling on the slanted ceiling in the bedroom, laminated cabinet doors in the kitchen, a carpet clad wall in the entryway, and tile in the bathroom

Materialvielfalt im Haus (v.l.n.r.): holzverkleidete Dachschräge im Schlafzimmer, Laminatfronten in der Küche, teppichbelegte Wand im Eingangsbereich, Fliesen im Bad

Diversité des matériaux utilisés dans la maison (de gauche à droite) : pente du toit lambrissée de bois dans la chambre, portes de placards stratifiées dans la cuisine, mur tapissé dans l'entrée et carrelage dans la salle de bains

Elevations

Ansichten

Élévations

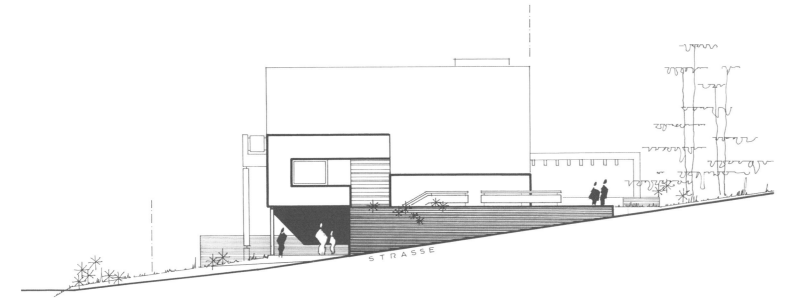

STRASSE

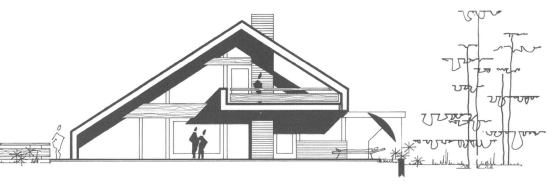

VENTURO

Oy Polykem AB, Helsinki, Finland
1971

Brochure and advertising photo
from 1971
Prospekt und Werbefoto von 1971
Brochure et photo publicitaire de
1971

In Polykem's brochure for its Casa Finlandia prefabricated house program, Suuronen's famous Futuro by no means stood alone. The CF Futuro, often called the UFO, was flanked by the FF-12 plastic tunnel for commercial car washes, the CF-100/200 shell roof for restaurants or railway stations, the smaller CF-10 and CF-16 for kiosks, as well as the Venturo CF-45 for leisure homes or smaller branch offices. The model numbers also indicate the floor space in square meters. Once it became obvious that the Futuro would not be a commercial success, marketing efforts concentrated on the Venturo. The name Venturo is programmatic: an Italian word, it can be translated as "next" or "coming". In contrast to the Futuro, which suggested a radical departure into a distant future in space, the Venturo still appeared to be a contemporary house, designed to be at home on the planet earth. This was reflected not least of all in the fact that it was possible to furnish the house in a conventional manner; unlike the Futuro, it even allowed the inhabitants to bring their own furniture with them. Thus, the transformation from the aesthetics of futuristic space travel to trendy Modernism was complete, and this expanded the options for use considerably. One brochure shows the house being used by fashionably dressed vacationers in Marimekko outfits. Plans for the house, in addition to its use as a leisure home, included combining multiple units to form larger ensembles.

The Venturo is not made entirely of plastic: there are aluminum supports within the rounded shell. The Venturo, which could be assembled on site from just a few parts, weighed only four tons, hence it could be erected on very simple foundations. The house consisted of three modules, which could be delivered on two trucks. The two-layer fiberglass structure had 2-in. foam panels installed as insulation. The production of thousands of the Venturo houses was planned, but ultimately only 19 of them ever left the plant, and half of those came to be used as service stations.

In einem Prospekt für das Fertighausprogramm „Casa Finlandia" von Polykem stand Suuronens bekanntes Futuro nicht allein. Es gab auch noch neben dem "CF Futuro" genannten „UFO" den Kunststofftunnel FF-12 für Waschanlagen, das Schalendach CF-100/200 für Restaurants oder Bahnhöfe, die kleineren CF-10 und CF-16 für Kioske sowie das Venturo CF-45 für Wochenendhäuser (leisure homes) oder kleinere Geschäftsfilialen. Bei den Zahlen handelte es sich um Hinweise auf die Grundfläche in Quadratmetern. Nachdem das Futuro sich kommerziell als relativer Mißerfolg herausgestellt hatte, konzentrierten sich alle Marketinganstrengungen auf das Venturo.

Der Name „Venturo" ist programmatisch: Aus dem Italienischen abgeleitet, lässt er sich mit „das Nächste" übersetzen. Im Gegensatz zum Futuro, das den radikalen Aufbruch in eine ferne Zukunft im All suggerierte, blieb das Venturo ein zeitgenössisches Heim, konzipiert für den Heimatplaneten Erde. Dies schlug sich nicht zuletzt darin nieder, dass eine konventionelle Ausstattung möglich war; anders als beim Futuro konnten die Bewohner hier ihre eigenen Möbel mitbringen. So hatte sich der Wandel von einer futuristischen Raumfahrtästhetik hin zu einer trendigen Moderne vollzogen, was die Nutzungsmöglichkeiten beträchtlich erweiterte. Ein Prospekt zeigte modisch gekleidete Urlauber im Marimekko-Outfit. Neben Wochenendhäusern waren jedoch auch Kombinationen von Hauseinheiten zu größeren Ensembles vorgesehen.

Das Venturo ist kein reiner Kunststoffbau: In der abgerundeten Hülle stecken Aluminiumträger. Das geringe Gewicht von nur vier Tonnen des aus wenigen Teilen vor Ort aufstellbaren Venturo ließ einfachste Fundierung zu. Das Haus bestand aus drei Modulen, die auf zwei Lastwagen angeliefert werden konnten. Als Isolierung waren 5 cm dicke Schaumplatten in die doppelschalige Fiberglaskonstruktion eingebracht. Tausende der Venturo-Häuser sollten produziert werden, aber im Endeffekt verließen wohl nur 19 Stück die Fertigungsanlagen, davon sollte fast jedes zweite als Tankstellenhäuschen Verwendung finden.

Dans un dépliant sur le programme de la maison préfabriquée Casa Finlandia de Polykem, la fameuse Futuro de Suuronen n'était pas la seule présentée. On y trouvait également, à côté de l'extra-terrestre CF Futuro, le tunnel en plastique FF-12 pour stations de lavage, la toiture en coque CF-100/200 pour restaurants ou gares, les petits CF-10 et CF-16 pour les kiosques, ainsi que la Venturo CF-45 pour des maisons de week-end ou pour des petites filiales commerciales. Les chiffres indiquaient la superficie en mètres carrés. Après l'échec commercial relatif de Futuro, les efforts marketing se concentrèrent sur Venturo.

En soi, le nom de Venturo est programmatique : venant de l'italien, il se traduit par « le prochain ». Contrairement à la Futuro qui suggère un départ radical dans l'espace dans un futur éloigné, la Venturo est un chez-soi contemporain, conçu pour la planète terre. Ceci se manifestait notamment dans la possibilité de la meubler de manière conventionnelle : à la différence de la Futuro, les habitants pouvaient y apporter leurs propres meubles. Ainsi s'était réalisée la mutation d'une esthétique spatiale futuriste vers une modernité tendance, élargissant l'éventail des possibilités de façon considérable. Un dépliant montrait des vacanciers habillés à la dernière mode en costume Marimekko. Parallèlement aux maisons de week-end, des combinaisons d'unités d'habitation formant de plus grands ensembles étaient également prévues.

La Venturo n'est pas une construction uniquement en plastique : des piliers d'aluminium se trouvent sous son enveloppe arrondie. Son faible poids se limitait à quatre tonnes et elle était composée de peu d'éléments, assemblables sur site, permettant des fondations élémentaires. La maison était composée de trois modules qui pouvaient être transportés par deux camions. Des panneaux en matière plastique de 5 cm d'épaisseur étaient intégrés à la structure de fibre de verre à paroi double. Il était prévu de produire des milliers de maisons Venturo, mais, en fin de compte, seuls 19 exemplaires sortirent du site de production, dont une sur deux furent utilisées comme abri de station-service.

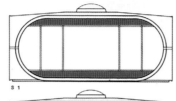

The "Venturo" is a modular, easily transportable building system, having excellent insulation, low weight and designed for minimum assembly on site.
It is built of high quality materials in order to ensure maximum weathering properties for use in arctic as well as tropical climates and is almost maintenance free.
Being of low weight and factory preassembled, the Venturo means very low erection and foundation costs, where heavy equipment can be avoided.
The basic unit (fig. 1) is usually delivered to the site on a truck with trailer in two major sections, a and b, one containing the bathroom/kitchenette, the other with the centre sections (c) packed inside.
For easy transportation all sections are 2,3 m (appr. 7' 6'') wide; length 6,9 m (appr. 23 ft). Then basic unit (fig. 1) is when assembled, 6,9 m x 6,9 m (23 x 23 ft), giving a floor area of appr. 45 sq. m. (509 sq.ft.). This basic unit can be enlarged by adding extra centre sections; to make still larger buildings two or more basic units are linked. In this way an unlimited variation of buildings in size and plans can be formulated.

The height of the preassembled sections (a and b) is appr. 290 cm (9.1/2 ft), inside height of room 240 cm (appr. 8 ft).
The roof and corner sections are large double skin mouldings of fibreglass with off-white gel-coated exterior surface as standard, with a 2'' polyurethane foam insulation.
The floor is an insulated composite beam construction of marine grade plywood and wood with all facia parts showing, covered with fibreglass mouldings.
The facades, available as standard in several colors and designs as per fig. 2, consist of prefabricated anodized aluminium framing with insulated prepainted aluminium exterior panels in various attractive colors.
Glazing may be either insulated glass or single or double sheet glazing.

Design and Engineering
The structural calculation is made by Mr. Matti Sihvonen, Civil Eng. RIL.
Design loads 180 kg/sq.m. (36 lbs/sq.ft) snowload and windload 100 kg/sq.m. (21 lbs/sq.m), (W = 40 m/sec., appr. 80 mph).
Designer of the house is Mr. Matti Suuronen, Arch. SAFA.
The design is registered in most Patent offices throughout the world.

Manufacturer
The Venturo is manufactured and developed by Oy Polykem Ab, Finland, and manufactured under license in several countries by local manufacturers.

Assembly and site preparations
The preassembled sections, delivered to the site by a truck with trailer, are, depending on ground conditions, installed on a flat surface or on 16 small piers. The basic unit weighs appr. 4 tons.
Electricity, water and waste-line are hooked up under the floor. Where electricity, water or sewerage are not obtainable prophane gas and/or gasoline motor driven generators can be used. For sewage septic tanks may be used. Please specify local conditions for further advice on nonstandard deliveries.
Kindly make your color choice for the facades among the below standard colors.

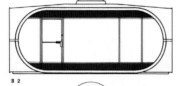

S 1

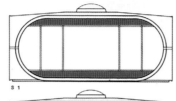

S 2

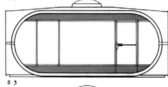

S 3

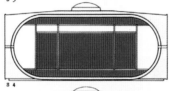

S 4

S 5

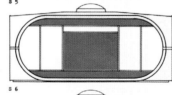

S 6

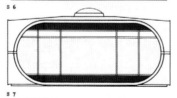

S 7

| COLOR Y | COLOR Z | COLOR B | COLOR O |

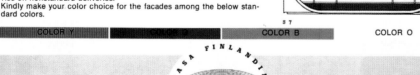

oy POLYKEM ab
ETELÄINEN RAUTATIEKATU 10 A
00100 HELSINKI 10
FINLAND

PRINTED IN FINLAND BY KIVIRANTA

Brochure and advertising photo from 1971

Prospekt und Werbefoto von 1971

Brochure et photo publicitaire de 1971

In contrast to the Futuro, the
Venturo was intended to appeal to a
somewhat more traditional clientele.

Anders als das Futuro sollte das
Venturo die etwas traditionellere
Kundschaft ansprechen.

Contrairement à la Futuro, la Venturo
devait attirer une clientèle un peu
plus traditionnelle.

The historical photos depict the house in such a clever way that it appears surprisingly spacious despite its modest footprint of 484 sq.ft.

Die historischen Fotos inszenieren das Gebäude so geschickt, dass es trotz seiner bescheidenen Grundmaße von 45 m² großzügig wirkt.

Les photos historiques présentent le bâtiment si adroitement qu'il semble étonnamment spacieux malgré ses modestes 45 m².

MANFRED ADAMS

HUF FACHWERKHAUS 2000

Huf Haus GmbH & Co. KG, Hartenfels, Germany
1972–

Opposite page: Clients can choose to have the houses delivered with white or dark wood.

Rechte Seite: Je nach Wunsch werden die Häuser mit weißem oder dunklem Holz geliefert.

Page de droite: Les maisons peuvent être livrées en bois blanc ou foncé, au choix.

Right: Initially, a version with a flat roof was also offered.

Rechts: In der Anfangszeit wurde auch eine Flachdachvariante angeboten.

À droite: Au début, un modèle à toit plat était également proposé.

The founding of the company dates back to a carpentry shop established by Johann Huf in the village of Krümmel in the Westerwald in 1912. A year later, the workshop had already moved to the nearby town of Hartenfels, where the company still has its headquarters. After the Second World War, Johann's son Franz Huf expanded the company's operations beyond the region. Huf made its first appearance in an international context after being commissioned by Sep Ruf and Egon Eiermann to do the woodwork for the Arabian and German pavilions at the Brussels World's Fair in 1958. In 1972, Manfred Adams, a student of Sep Ruf's, designed the Huf Fachwerkhaus 2000. It marked the cornerstone of a new orientation for the company: the fundamentals of the design developed by Adams in this context are still applied to every Huf model today.

Wood and glass are the decisive materials in a Huf Haus, which is built as an open wooden skeleton structure with characteristically deep eaves and an amply overhanging pitched roof. The half-timbered structure made of laminated wood has floor-to-ceiling glazing; the remainder of the façade consists of thermally insulated stuccoed composite panels. The floor plan is spacious; on the ground floor there is an open kitchen with a bar and a dining and living area; the upper floor features a gallery, the master bedroom, two children's rooms, and two bathrooms.

Since 1996, the grandsons Georg Huf and Thomas Huf have been in charge

Die Anfänge des Unternehmens gehen auf eine Zimmerei zurück, die Johann Huf 1912 im Westerwalddorf Krümmel gründete. Bereits im Jahr darauf zog der Betrieb in das nahegelegene Hartenfels um, wo die Firma noch heute ihren Sitz hat. Nach dem Zweiten Weltkrieg baute der Sohn Franz Huf den Betrieb zu einem überregionalen Unternehmen aus. Schon 1958 betrat die Firma Huf internationales Parkett, nachdem sie von Sep Ruf und Egon Eiermann den Auftrag erhalten hatte, die Holzarbeiten des arabischen und des deutschen Pavillons auf der Brüsseler Weltausstellung zu übernehmen. 1972 entwarf Manfred Adams, ein Schüler von Sep Ruf, für das Unternehmen das Huf Fachwerkhaus 2000. Damit war das Fundament für die Neuausrichtung des Unternehmens gelegt: Die Entwurfsgrundsätze, die Adams hierbei entwickelte, werden bis heute bei allen Huf-Modellen angewandt.

Holz und Glas sind die bestimmenden Materialien für den offenen Holzskelettbau des Huf-Hauses mit seiner charakteristisch tief heruntergezogenen Traufe und den weiten Satteldachüberständen. Die Leimholz-Fachwerkkonstruktion ist bodentief verglast, die Fassade besteht aus strukturverputzten Wärmedämmverbundplatten. Das Raumprogramm ist großzügig: Im Erdgeschoss finden sich eine offene Küche, eine Bar und der Ess- und Wohnbereich, im Obergeschoss eine Galerie, das Elternschlafzimmer, zwei Kinderzimmer und zwei Bäder.

Seit 1996 leiten die Enkel Georg Huf und Thomas Huf das Unternehmen

Les débuts de l'entreprise remontent à une menuiserie que Johann Huf avait créée en 1912 au village Krümmel dans le Westerwald. Dès l'année suivante, elle déménagea un peu plus loin, à Hartenfels, où l'entreprise possède encore aujourd'hui son siège. Après la Deuxième Guerre mondiale, le fils Franz Huf étend l'activité de l'entreprise à l'échelle nationale. Dès 1958, l'entreprise s'impose sur la scène internationale lorsque Sep Ruf et Egon Eiermann sont chargés de réaliser la charpenterie des pavillons arabe et allemand de l'Exposition internationale de Bruxelles. En 1972, Manfred Adams, élève de Sep Ruf, projette la maison à colombage Huf 2000 pour l'entreprise. Dès lors, les principes de conception que Manfred Adams avait développés ici ont été repris pour tous les modèles Huf.

Bois et verre sont les matériaux déterminants de l'ossature en bois ouverte de la maison Huf, avec ses profonds débords de toit caractéristiques et son toit en bâtière faisant saillie. Cette construction à colombage en bois lamellé-collé est vitrée jusqu'au sol. Sa façade se compose de panneaux d'isolation thermique composites crépis. L'intérieur est spacieux: au rez-de-chaussée se trouvent une cuisine américaine, un bar, la salle à manger-séjour; à l'étage, un couloir, la chambre des parents, deux chambres d'enfants et deux salles de bains.

Depuis 1996, les neveux Georg Huf et Thomas Huf dirigent l'entreprise qui est désormais présente sur la scène internationale. Jusqu'à aujourd'hui, les

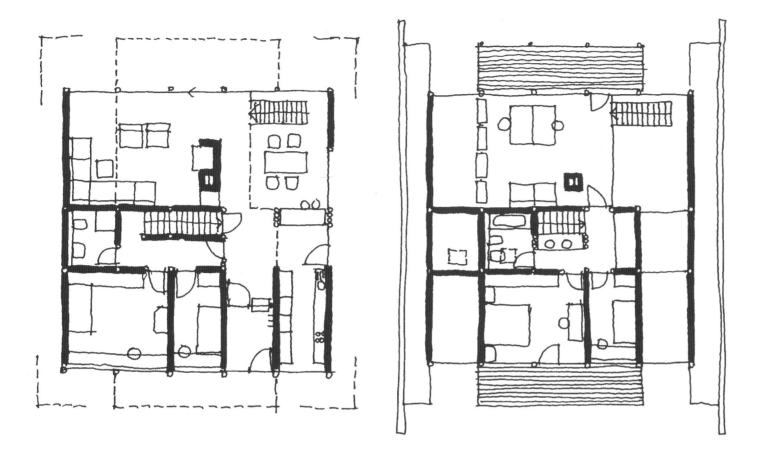

of the company, which in the meantime operates globally. These prefabricated houses from the Westerwald have already been delivered to England, France, Austria, and Switzerland. There has even been interest in the houses in China, where an electronics company recently ordered five Huf houses for a small residential development.

The company has limited the export of its houses to 200 per year, of which roughly fifty are delivered to England. The English customers gladly travel to Hartenfels in order to view the model houses and make their selections from hundreds of carpets and all sorts of flooring at the Huf showrooms. In the meantime, there is even a "Huf Haus Owners' Group" in England, the members of which share information concerning their experience with this German product. At roughly 1 million euros, a Huf Haus is hardly one of the cheapest prefabricated houses on the market, but they do set new standards, particularly in terms of their energy balance.

Seit 1996 leiten die Enkel Georg Huf und Thomas Huf das Unternehmen, das nunmehr global präsent ist. Bisher wurden die Fertighäuser aus dem Westerwald bereits nach England, Frankreich, Österreich und die Schweiz geliefert. Doch jüngst wurde man auch in China auf die Marke aufmerksam, wo ein Elektrokonzern fünf Huf-Häuser für einen kleinen Wohnpark bestellte.

Das Unternehmen hat seinen Export auf 200 Häuser pro Jahr begrenzt, von denen mittlerweile rund 50 nach England gehen. Die Briten reisen gern nach Hartenfels, um die dortigen Musterhäuser zu besichtigen und in den Schauräumen von Huf aus Hunderten von Teppichen und allen möglichen Parkettvarianten zu wählen. Inzwischen hat sich auf der Insel sogar eine „Huf Haus Owners Group" gegründet, deren Mitglieder sich über ihre Erfahrungen mit dem deutschen Produkt austauschen. Mit rund einer Million Euro ist das Huf-Haus nicht gerade eines der billigsten Fertighäuser auf dem Markt, dafür aber setzen die Modelle vor allem auch in der Energiebilanz Maßstäbe.

maisons préfabriquées du Westerwald étaient livrées en Angleterre, en France, en Autriche et en Suisse. Mais depuis peu, la marque a également gagné en notoriété en Chine où un groupe d'électrotechnique a passé commande de cinq maisons Huf pour une petite zone résidentielle. L'entreprise a limité ses exportations à 200 maisons par an, dont cinquante à destination de l'Angleterre. Les Britanniques se rendent volontiers à Hartenfels afin d'y visiter les maisons-témoins exposées sur place et de choisir parmi les centaines de tapis et de modèles de parquets dans les salles d'exposition de Huf. Il existe même désormais un *Huf Haus Owners' Group* (Groupe de propriétaires de maison Huf) sur l'île, dont les membres discutent de leurs expériences avec leur construction allemande. Vendue 1 million d'euros, la maison Huf ne fait pas partie des maisons préfabriquées les plus économiques du marché. En revanche, elle constitue surtout une référence en matière d'économie d'énergie.

FRANK HUSTER, PETER HÜBNER

TBS TROPICAL BUILDING SYSTEM

Staudenmayer Bauproduktion, Salach, Germany
1976–1977

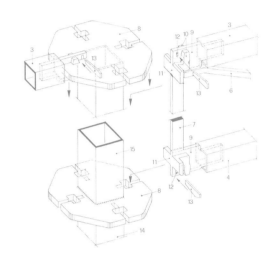

Right: Detail of the hub between the supports illustrates the principle of the interlocking joints.
Rechts: Das Knotendetail der Stützen-/Träger-Verbindung zeigt das Prinzip der Steckverbindungen.
À droite: Le détail du raccordement entre les poteaux et les poutres illustre le principe d'assemblage mécanique.

Like Jean Prouvé's Maisons Tropicales, the tropical building system (TBS) developed by Frank Huster and Peter Hübner was intended to provide an effective solution to a number of building tasks in countries with tropical heat. The components of this system for buildings with one or more stories for a variety of uses were required to withstand extreme weather conditions, be as extensively prefabricated as possible, easy to transport, and able to be assembled by untrained workers in a short time. The finished building had to provide protection against outdoor temperatures often in excess of 50° C (122° F) while being cooled by refrigeration units—it was basically a refrigerator under a beach umbrella.

Hollow steel sections are used to support the structure, their dimensions can be adapted to the tensile requirements. Solid caps attached to the ends of these sections contain the bores and threads for connecting the support grid in which prefabricated reinforced concrete elements are laid to form the floor slabs. The components that fill in the walls and the vaulting of the sunroof are made of fiberglass-reinforced polyester; the wall elements were paneled with plasterboard on the inside. The sanitary facilities are made of prefabricated polyester elements.

In 1976, the first two prototypes were erected in Saudi Arabia. An additional experimental building was created as Frank Huster's home in the Swabian town of Neckartenzlingen. By the end of 1977, twelve TBS health centers were finally built at the ten airports that existed in Saudi Arabia at the time in order to provide care for the airport personnel and airline passengers.

Das Tropenbausystem (tropical building system = TBS) wurde von Frank Huster und Peter Hübner – ähnlich den Maisons Tropicales von Jean Prouvé – mit dem Ziel entwickelt, in Ländern mit tropisch heißem Klima verschiedene Bauaufgaben effektiv lösen zu können. Die Bestandteile des für unterschiedliche Nutzungen in ein- und mehrgeschossiger Bauweise ausgelegten Systems mussten extremen Witterungsbedingungen standhalten, möglichst weitgehend vorgefertigt, leicht transportierbar und von ungelernten Arbeitern in kurzer Zeit zu errichten sein. Das fertige Gebäude sollte Schutz vor der oft über 50° C hohen Außentemperatur bieten und zudem mit Kühlaggregaten klimatisiert sein. Im Grunde war es ein Kühlschrank unter einem Sonnenschirm.

Die Stützen der Konstruktion bestehen aus Stahlhohlprofilen, die je nach statischen Erfordernissen dimensioniert werden können. Stützen und Träger des Tragrostes werden lediglich über gesteckte Knotenpunkte verbunden und durch Keile gesichert. In die Felder des Tragrostes werden Stahlbetonfertigteile eingelegt, die die Geschossdecke bilden. Die selbsttragenden Wandbauteile und die Halbtonnen des Sonnendaches sind aus glasfaserverstärktem Polyester hergestellt, die Wandelemente sind innen mit Gipskartonplatten beplankt. Die Sanitärzellen wurden aus vorgefertigten Polyester-Elementen zusammengefügt.

1976 wurden die ersten beiden Prototypen in Saudi-Arabien errichtet. Ein weiterer Versuchsbau entstand als Frank Husters Wohnhaus im schwäbischen Neckartenzlingen. Schließlich wurden bis Ende 1977 auf den damals zehn saudi-arabischen Flughäfen zwölf TBS-Healthcenter zur Versorgung des Flughafenpersonals und der Fluggäste aufgebaut.

Tout comme les Maisons Tropicales de Jean Prouvé, le système de construction tropical (tropical building system = TBS) a été conçu par Frank Huster et Peter Hübner dans le but de trouver des solutions efficaces pour différents types de constructions dans les pays à climat tropical. Les composantes de ce système de construction d'un à plusieurs étages conçu pour des utilisations variées devaient résister à des conditions climatiques extrêmes, être en majeure partie préfabriquées, faciles à transporter et à monter par des ouvriers non qualifiés, le tout en peu de temps. Le bâtiment monté devait offrir une protection contre les hautes températures dépassant souvent les 50° C et, dans ces régions, être climatisé à l'aide de groupes frigorifiques. Autrement dit, un réfrigérateur sous un parasol.

Les poteaux de la construction sont constitués de profils creux en acier pouvant être redimensionnés en fonction des exigences statiques. Les poteaux et poutres de la charpente sont simplement reliés par des points de jonction encastrés et sécurisés par des clavettes. Des éléments préfabriqués de béton armé sont insérés dans les cavités de la charpente pour constituer le plafond de l'étage. Les éléments muraux autoporteurs et les demi-voûtes de la marquise sont en polyester renforcé de fibres de verre. À l'intérieur, le revêtement des éléments de parois est constitué de panneaux de plâtre. Le bloc sanitaire est réalisé avec des éléments préfabriqués en polyester.

En 1976, les deux premiers prototypes furent édifiés en Arabie Saoudite. Une autre maison expérimentale devint la maison d'habitation de Frank Huster à Neckartenzlingen, en Souabe. Finalement, sur les 10 aéroports que comptait alors l'Arabie Saoudite, 12 centres de santé TBS destinés aux soins du personnel de l'aéroport et des voyageurs virent le jour jusqu'à fin 1977.

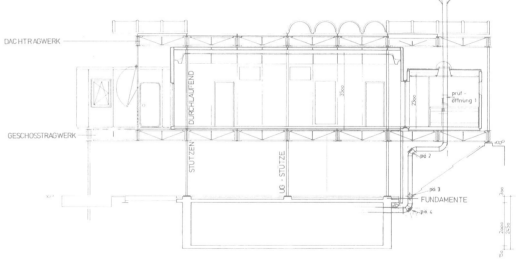

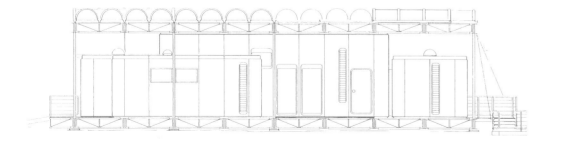

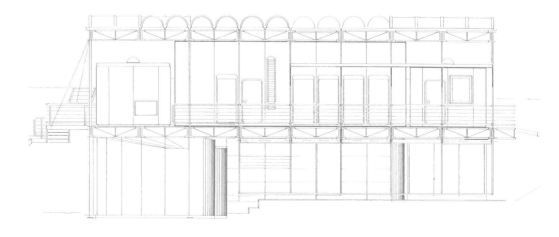

The solar protection roof on steel girders and the building system for the space created using fiberglass reinforced plastic panels are two separate elements.

Das Schattendach auf Stahlträgern und das raumbildende Bausystem aus GFK-Platten bilden zwei getrennte Einheiten.

Le toit de protection solaire sur poteaux d'acier et le système constructif à cloisonnage en panneaux renforcés de fibre de verre constituent deux unités séparées.

197

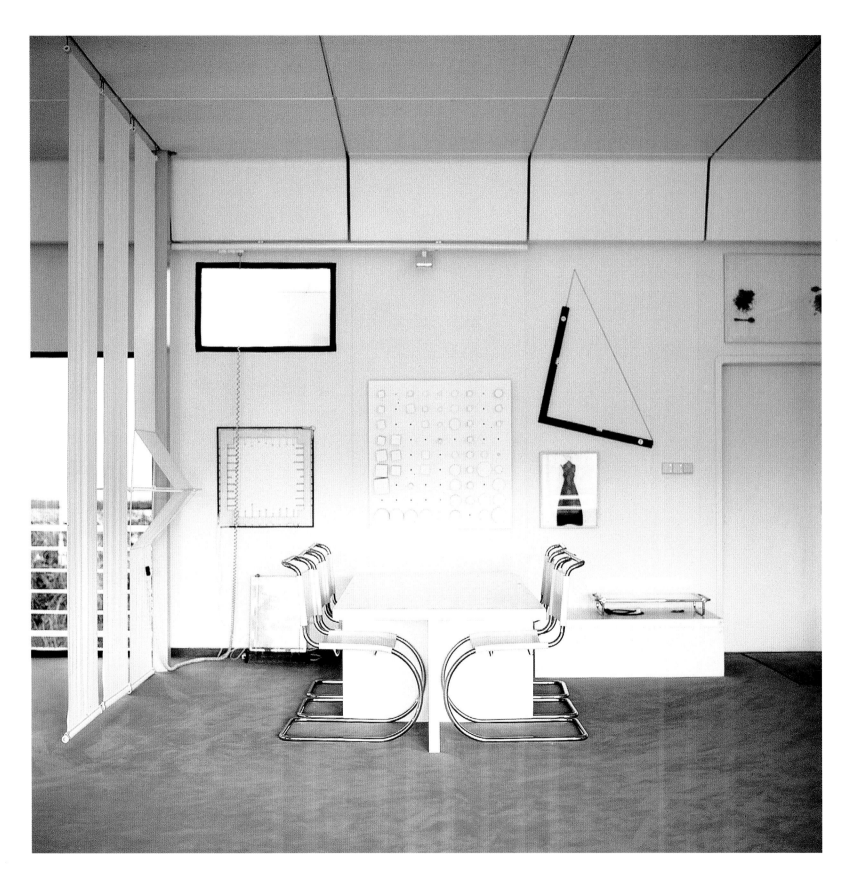

The structural separation of the ceiling and wall elements is visually emphasized by the extended edges of the ceiling elements.

Die konstruktive Trennung von Decken- und Wandelementen wird durch die herabgezogenen Randelemente visualisiert.

La séparation structurelle des éléments de plafond et de murs est soulignée visuellement par le prolongement des bords des éléments de plafond.

Floor plans of the lower level (left)
and the upper level (right)

Grundrisse von Untergeschoss
(links) und Obergeschoss (rechts)

Plans du rez-de-chaussée (à gauche)
et du niveau supérieur (à droite)

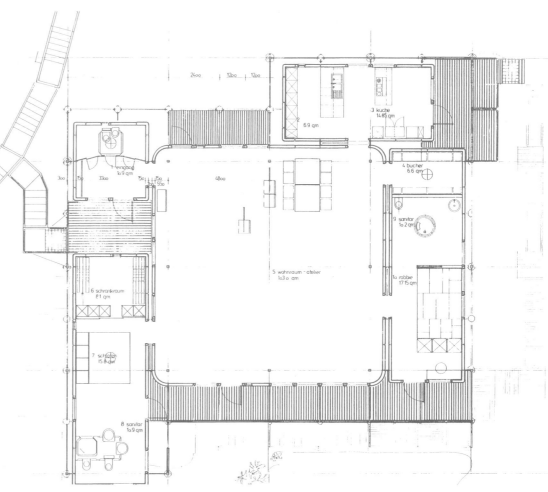

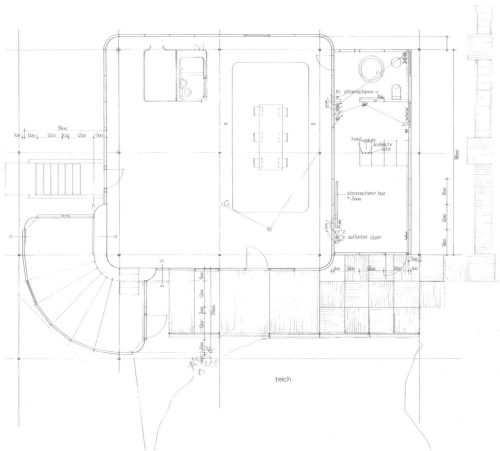

KÁRI THOMSEN, OLE VANGGAARD

EASY DOMES

Easy Domes Ltd., Tórshavn, Faroe Islands, Denmark
1992–

Easy Domes can be built to stand alone or combined within larger units, as in this photograph of a model (right).

Die Easy Domes können einzeln, aber auch zu größeren Einheiten kombiniert aufgebaut werden, wie das Modellfoto (rechts) zeigt.

Les Easy Domes peuvent être assemblées pour être isolées ou intégrées à de larges unités, comme le montre la photo de la maquette (à droite).

Kári Thomsen is presumably the first architect from the Faroe Islands to have his houses slated for construction on the Persian Gulf. The Easy Domes, which he developed along with the Danish engineer Ole Vanggaard, are to be built as a holiday complex in Abu Dhabi.
The first Easy Dome has been standing in Tórshavn, the capital of the Faroe Islands, since 1992: the Greenland Society's House of Culture, with 1,080 sq.ft. of floor space. In subsequent years a number of additional Easy Domes were built on this group of islands, which belong to Denmark. After a number of holiday homes with 269 sq.ft. of floor space had successfully withstood the harsh climate of the North Atlantic for several years, Easy Domes began to be exported throughout the world. They are built in a factory in Denmark.
The Easy Dome is somewhat more angular than a football, but built in the same manner: it is a "truncated icosahedron", a regular polygon consisting of pentagonal and hexagonal faces. This form is optimal in terms of volume, weight, materials used and usable floor space. The polygonal houses from the Faroe Islands are built on foundations of concrete or wood and consist of 21 pinewood elements covered with plywood, 21 plywood or plasterboard elements for the interior cladding and three elements for the (main) entrance, in addition to thermo energy windows, interior walls and floors. The assembly can be completed by two to three workers in one day without a crane. The sections are bolted together and the edges are sealed with asphalt paper or rubber.
The holiday homes on the Faroe Islands were also additionally insulated in a traditional manner with a 6-in. layer of peat. The living area is in the lower part of the house with a bedroom for two people up above. In 2008 the first residential building of this type was erected in Denmark. With ceilings of over 16 ft., it is a spacious, two-story, low energy house.

Kári Thomsen ist vermutlich der erste färöische Architekt, dessen Häuser bald auch am Persischen Golf stehen werden. Die von ihm und dem dänischen Ingenieur Ole Vanggaard entwickelten Easy Domes sollen in einer Ferienhaus-Anlage in Abu Dhabi aufgebaut werden.
Der erste Easy Dome steht seit 1992 in der färöische Hauptstadt Tórshavn: das 100 m² große Kulturhaus der Grönländischen Gesellschaft. In den folgenden Jahren wurden einige weitere Easy Domes auf der zu Dänemark gehörenden Inselgruppe errichtet. Nachdem auch einige 25 m² große Ferienhäuser dieses Typs jahrelang den harschen klimatischen Bedingungen im Nordatlantik erfolgreich getrotzt haben, sollen die Easy Domes nun in alle Welt exportiert werden. Gebaut werden sie in einer Fabrik in Dänemark.
Der Easy Dome ist zwar eckiger als ein Fußball, aber auf gleiche Weise konstruiert: Es handelt sich um einen „abgestumpften Icosaeder", ein aus Fünf- und Sechsecken zusammengesetztes regelmäßiges Vieleck. Diese Form ist optimal, was Volumen, Gewicht, Materialaufwand und Nutzfläche angeht. Die färöischen Vieleck-Häuser werden auf einem Beton- oder Holzfundament errichtet und bestehen aus 21 Sperrholzplatten in einem Kiefernholzrahmen, 21 Sperrholz- oder Gipsplatten für die Innenverkleidung und drei Elementen für den (Haupt-)Eingang, außerdem Thermoenergie-Fenstern, Innenwänden und Böden. Der Aufbau kann durch zwei oder drei Arbeiter an einem Tag und ohne Kran bewältigt werden. Die Platten werden durch Metallbolzen miteinander verbunden, die Ecken mit Asphaltpapier oder Gummi versiegelt.
Die Ferienhäuser auf den Färöer-Inseln wurden zusätzlich auf traditionelle Art mit einer 15 cm dicken Torfschicht isoliert. Sie haben ein Wohnzimmer unten und ein Schlafzimmer für zwei Personen im oberen Teil des Hauses. Im Jahr 2008 wurde das erste Wohnhaus in Dänemark errichtet: ein mit 5 m Raumhöhe sehr großzügiges zweigeschossiges Niedrigenergie-Haus.

Kári Thomsen est sans doute le premier architecte féroïen dont les maisons se dresseront bientôt également dans le golfe Persique. En effet, les Easy Domes qu'il a développées en collaboration avec l'ingénieur danois Ole Vanggaard devraient être montées dans un parc de maisons de vacances à Abou Dhabi.
La première Easy Dome se trouve depuis 1992 dans la capitale des îles Féroé, Tórshavn : sur 100 m², elle abrite la grande maison de la culture de la société groenlandaise. Les années qui ont suivi, quelques autres Easy Domes ont été édifiées sur l'archipel danois. Après avoir affronté les rudes conditions climatiques de l'Atlantique Nord du haut de leurs 25 m² pendant des années, quelques maisons de vacances de ce type ont prouvé que les Easy Domes sont désormais prêtes à être exportées à l'international.
L'Easy Dome est un « icosaèdre tronqué », un polygone régulier composé de pentagones et d'hexagones. Cette forme est optimum pour ce qui concerne le volume, le poids, le matériel utilisé et la surface exploitable. Les maisons polygonales des îles Féroé sont bâties sur des fondations de béton ou de bois et sont constituées de 21 panneaux de contreplaqué sur un cadre en bois de pin, 21 panneaux de contreplaqué ou de plâtre pour le revêtement intérieur, trois éléments pour l'entrée principale, ainsi que des fenêtres thermiques, des parois intérieures et des planchers. Le montage peut être effectué sans l'aide d'une grue par deux ou trois ouvriers en une journée. Les panneaux sont fixés entre eux par des goujons métalliques, les angles vitrifiés avec du papier goudronné ou du caoutchouc.
Les maisons de vacances des îles Féroé ont été en outre isolées selon une méthode traditionnelle avec une couche de tourbe de 15 cm d'épaisseur. Le salon se trouve au rez-de-chaussée et la chambre à coucher pour deux personnes à l'étage de la maison. En 2008, la première maison d'habitation a été construite au Danemark : une maison spacieuse à deux étages, aux pièces de 5 m de hauteur sous plafond, à basse consommation d'énergie.

Construction of the house
on a concrete foundation

Aufbau des Hauses auf einem
Betonfundament

Assemblage de la maison
sur des fondations de béton

Section and floor plans of a house in Denmark with a living room, kitchen and bath on the lower and two bedrooms on the upper level

Schnitt und Grundrisse des Wohnhauses in Dänemark mit Wohnzimmer, Küche und Bad im Unter- und zwei Schlafzimmern im Obergeschoss

Coupe et plan d'une maison d'habitation au Danemark avec salle de séjour, cuisine et salle de bains au rez-de-chaussée et deux chambres à l'étage supérieur

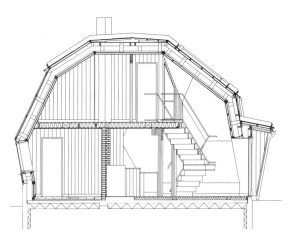

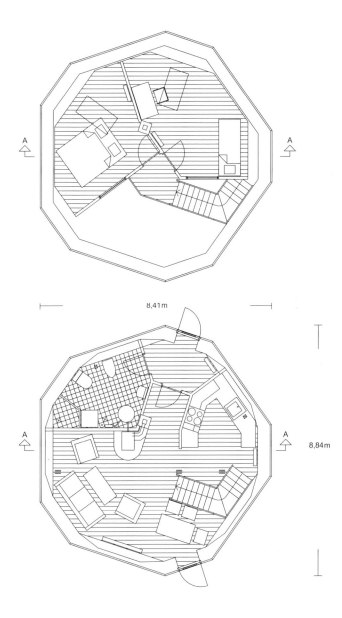

8,41m

8,84m

FURNITURE HOUSE

Lake Yamanaka, Yamanashi, Japan
1995–

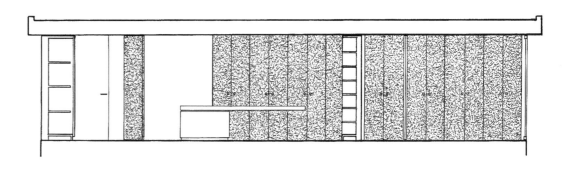

The walls either consist of furniture elements or are completely glazed.

Die Wände sind konsequent entweder aus Möbelelementen gebildet oder komplett verglast.

Les murs se composent de meubles, ou sont complètements vitrés.

The Furniture House that Shigeru Ban erected in the Japanese city of Yamanakako (Yamanashi prefecture) in 1995 is informed by the architect's experience with earthquakes. In an earthquake, furniture kills people when it falls on them, but it also saves people by supporting collapsed roofs. "So I thought, if furniture is strong enough to kill or save people, why not just make a house out of furniture?"

The Furniture House is constructed entirely of floor-to-ceiling closets and bookshelves that serve both as built-in furniture and as supporting walls. Each of the shelving units, which measure 8 ft. in height and either 18 or 27 in. in depth, weighs roughly 174 lbs. and can be easily assembled by a single person. These modules, which are prefabricated in a furniture factory, are aligned at the building site to form walls, that are connected by means of a wooden beam at the top and then horizontally reinforced with sheets of plywood.

Shigeru Ban's approach to design thrives not least of all from the fact that once he has discovered a system, he always continues to develop upon it. Thus, he built two other Furniture Houses in Japan: a larger one, in 1996, and one made of steel, two years later. For a fourth version, built in China, he discovered a type of indigenous plywood made of woven strips of bamboo, which is usually used for form boards when pouring concrete. The most recent house by the Japanese architect based on prefabricated shelving units is the Sagaponac House, a villa that consists entirely of closets that was built on Long Island in 2006. In designing its floor plan he drew upon to the "Landhaus in Backstein" (Brick Country House) designed by Mies van der Rohe (1924), but never built.

Im Furniture House, das Shigeru Ban 1995 im japanischen Yamanakako (in der Präfektur Yamanashi) errichtete, haben Erfahrungen, die der Architekt mit Erdbeben machte, ihren Niederschlag gefunden. Bei einem Erdbeben würden Leute mitunter von umstürzenden Möbelstücken erschlagen, erklärt der Architekt, andere hingegen würden durch Möbel gerettet, etwa wenn diese vor einstürzenden Dächern schützten. „So dachte ich: Wenn Möbel stark genug sind, um Menschen zu töten oder zu schützen, dann sollte man doch aus ihnen auch ein ganzes Haus bauen können."

Die Konstruktion des Furniture-Hauses besteht aus einem System von deckenhohen Wandschränken und Bücherregalen, die sowohl als Einbaumöbel als auch als tragende Wände fungieren. Jede einzelne der 2,40 m hohen und 0,45 bzw. 0,69 cm tiefen Regaleinheiten wiegt ungefähr 79 kg und kann beim Aufbau leicht von einer einzelnen Person bewältigt werden. Diese in einer Möbelfabrik vorgefertigten Module werden auf der Baustelle zu Wänden aufgereiht, durch einen Holzträger auf der Oberseite verbunden und mit Sperrholzplatten horizontal ausgesteift.

Shigeru Bans Entwurfspraxis lebt nicht zuletzt davon, dass er einmal erfundene Systeme immer weiter entwickelt. So baute er in Japan zwei weitere Furniture Houses: 1996 ein zweites, größeres, dann zwei Jahre später ein weiteres, diesmal jedoch aus Stahl gefertigtes. Für eine vierte Version in China verwendete er ein landestypisches Sperrholz aus miteinander verwobenen Bambusstreifen, das normalerweise für die Verschalung von Beton verwendet wird. Als bisher letztes Haus auf der Basis vorgefertigter Regaleinheiten realisierte der japanische Architekt 2006 auf Long Island das Sagaponac House, eine wahre Schrankwandvilla, für deren Grundriss er auf das nie gebaute „Landhaus in Backstein" von Mies van der Rohe (1924) zurückgriff.

Les expériences de séismes de l'architecte se reflètent dans la Furniture House que Shigeru Ban a bâti en 1995 à Yamanakako (préfecture de Yamanashi) au Japon. «Lors d'un tremblement de terre, il arrive que des personnes soient écrasées par des meubles qui basculent», explique-t-il, «alors que d'autres sont justement sauvées par les meubles qui retiennent un toit qui s'effondre. Si un meuble est assez fort pour tuer ou protéger des gens, il doit alors être possible de construire une maison entière à partir de meubles.»

La structure de la Furniture House repose sur un système de placards et de rayonnages de livres toute hauteur faisant à la fois fonction de meubles encastrés et de murs porteurs. Chaque unité de 2,40 m de hauteur, 0,45 cm ou 0,69 cm de profondeur, pèse environ 79 kg. Une personne seule peut facilement venir à bout du montage. Ces modules préfabriqués dans une usine de meubles sont alignés sur le chantier pour former les murs, reliés en leur sommet par des poutres en bois, et renforcés horizontalement par des plaques de contreplaqué.

La pratique de la conception de Shigeru Ban repose notamment sur le développement continu des systèmes qu'il a inventés. Ainsi, il a construit deux autres Furniture House au Japon : une en 1996, plus grande, puis, deux ans plus tard, une autre, en acier cette fois. Pour une quatrième version en Chine, il a utilisé un contreplaqué typique du pays, constitué de bandes de bambou entremêlées, habituellement utilisé pour le coffrage du béton. Sur Long Island, l'architecte japonais a bâti en 2006 la Sagaponac House, dernière maison réalisée jusqu'à ce jour sur la base d'unités d'étagères préfabriquées. Pour le plan de cette véritable «villa placard», il s'est inspiré de la Landhaus in Backstein (maison de campagne en briques) jamais construite de Mies van der Rohe (1924).

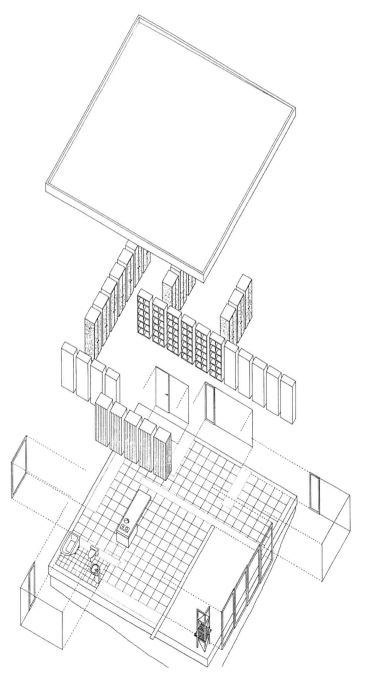

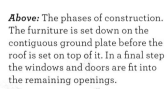

Above: The phases of construction.
The furniture is set down on the
contiguous ground plate before the
roof is set on top of it. In a final step
the windows and doors are fit into
the remaining openings.

Oben: Die Phasen des Aufbaus:
Auf eine durchgehende Bodenplatte
werden die Möbel gestellt und darauf
das Dach gelegt. Am Schluss werden
Fenster und Türen in die verbleiben-
den Öffnungen gesetzt.

En haut: Les étapes du montage :
les meubles sont positionnés sur un
radier continu, puis le toit est placé
dessus. Les fenêtres et les portes
sont posées en dernier lieu dans les
ouvertures restantes.

Mount Fuji is visible at a distance from the terrace; later, Ban's paper house was built on the slope below.

Von der Terrasse aus ist in der Ferne der Berg Fuji zu sehen; später entstand am Hang weiter unten Bans Papierhaus.

Depuis la terrasse, on voit le mont Fuji au loin; plus tard, la maison de papier de Ban fut bâtie en contrebas.

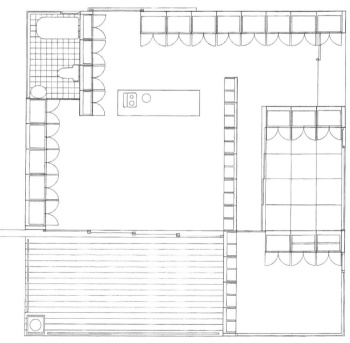

THOMAS SCHNYDER

LIVING BOX

Architeam 4, Basel, Switzerland
1996–

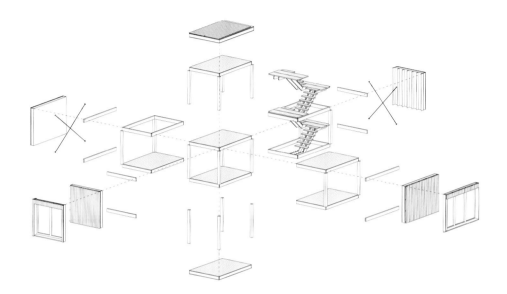

Opposite page: The Living Box
Wolken in Küblis, Switzerland, 2003
Rechte Seite: Living Box Wolken
in Küblis, Schweiz, 2003
Page de droite : Living Box Wolken
à Küblis, Suisse, 2003

The idea of making "as much living space as possible" out of the least amount of material was seminal for the development of the "Living Box", a prefabricated house designed in 1993 by Thomas Schnyder from the Basel architectural office "Architeam 4" for RUWA, a company based in Küblis that specializes in wooden construction; it is an idea he continuously refines, applying the design principles Le Corbusier formulated in his "five points of new architecture" in 1926. The external and internal walls are non-load-bearing. Thus, the floor plans and façades can be freely designed. Pad footings or cellars serve as foundations. Most of the Living Boxes also have a flat roof and ribbon windows.

Schnyder was also inspired by the social Utopian designs of Soviet Constructivists like Moisei Ginzburg. The Living Box is most notable for the fact that it makes it possible to realize smaller living units that can be expanded at will. The basic structure of the Living Box is a supporting skeleton made of prefabricated wooden supports and wood-concrete-composite ceilings on a grid of 8 ft. by 12 ft. = 93 sq.ft. Three pairs of steel cross struts per story provide structural reinforcement. The supporting skeleton can be expanded in every direction. The system is only limited in terms of height, to three stories. This ensures the greatest possible degree of flexibility with regard to its use. Correspondingly, it is possible to install, and later move, internal walls of wood or glass—by one's self.

Living Boxes are "direct gain houses", which require only a thirtieth of the heating energy of a conventional house in locations with good solar radiation. This is made possible, for one, by the fact that the houses open up towards the south, while the other façades remain for the most part closed:

Aus möglichst wenig Material möglichst viel Wohnraum zu machen, dieser Gedanke leitete Thomas Schnyder vom Basler Büro „Architeam 4" bei der Entwicklung der „Living Box", einem Fertighaus, das er 1993 für die Holzbaufirma RUWA in Küblis entwickelte und seitdem stetig verfeinerte. Schnyder wandte dabei gestalterische Grundsätze an, die Le Corbusier 1926 als „fünf Punkte einer neuen Architektur" formuliert hatte. Außen- und Innenwände sind nicht tragend ausgebildet. Somit können die Grundrisse und Fassaden frei gestaltet werden. Als Fundament dienen Punktfundamente oder ein Kellergeschoss. Die meisten Living Boxes haben darüber hinaus ein Flachdach und Fensterbänder.

Inspiriert wurde Schnyder zudem von den sozialutopischen Entwürfen sowjetischer Konstruktivisten wie Moisej Ginsburg. Die Living Box zeichnet sich durch die Möglichkeit aus, kleine Wohneinheiten zu realisieren, die sich beliebig erweitern lassen. Grundstruktur der Living Box ist ein Tragskelett aus vorgefertigten hölzernen Stützen und Holz-Beton-Verbunddecken mit einem Raster von 2,48 m x 3,68 m = 8,64 m². Statisch ausgesteift wird es über drei Stahlspannkreuze pro Geschoss. Das Tragskelett ist in jede Richtung erweiterbar. Nur in der Höhe ist das System auf drei Geschosse beschränkt. Somit ist eine größtmögliche Flexibilität im Hinblick auf die Nutzung gewährleistet. Dementsprechend können bei der Living Box Holz- oder Glasinnenwände beliebig platziert und später auch wieder versetzt werden – und das eigenhändig.

Living Boxes sind „Direktgewinnhäuser", die an guten Sonnenlagen mit einem Dreißigstel der Heizenergie eines konventionellen Hauses auskommen. Möglich wird das zum einen dadurch, dass sich die Häuser nach

Générer le plus d'espace d'habitation possible à partir du minimum de matériau : telle était l'idée de Thomas Schnyder de l'agence de Bâle Architeam 4 lors de la conception de la Living Box, une maison préfabriquée qu'il avait développée pour l'entreprise de constructions en bois RUWA à Küblis en 1993, et qu'il n'a cessé d'améliorer depuis. Pour ce projet, Schnyder mit en pratique de manière cohérente les principes architecturaux que Le Corbusier avait formulés en 1926 dans ses « cinq points de l'architecture moderne ». Les murs intérieurs et extérieurs ne sont pas porteurs, permettant des plans et des façades libres. Les fondations sont des fondations sur semelles ou un sous-sol. La plupart des Living Box présentent en outre un toit plat et des fenêtres en bandeaux.

Schnyder fut par ailleurs inspiré par les projets d'utopie sociale du constructiviste soviétique Moisei Ginzbourg. La Living Box se distingue par la possibilité qu'elle offre de réaliser des petites unités d'habitation, extensibles à souhait. La structure de base de la Living Box est une ossature porteuse constituée de supports en bois préfabriqués et de dalles mixtes bois-béton d'une trame de 2,48 m x 3,68 m = 8,64 m². Trois contrefiches d'acier en croix par niveau en renforcent la stabilité. L'ossature porteuse est extensible dans chaque direction. Ce n'est qu'en hauteur que le système se limite à trois niveaux, garantissant par là même la plus grande flexibilité d'utilisation possible. Par conséquent, dans la Living Box, les parois de bois ou de verre peuvent être positionnées librement, puis de nouveau déplacées, et cela sans aucune aide.

Les Living Box sont des « maisons à rendement direct » qui, lorsqu'elles jouissent d'un bon ensoleillement, peuvent consommer un trentième de

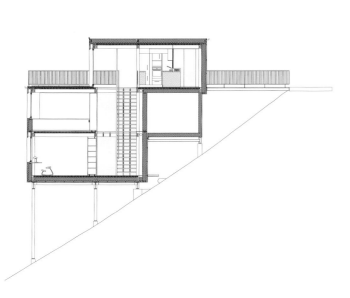

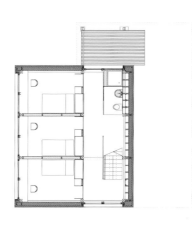

Section and floor plans of the Living
Box in Küblis, interior views

Schnitt und Grundrisse der Living
Box in Küblis, Innenansichten

Coupe et plans de la Living Box
à Küblis, vues intérieures

The Living Box Flüeler in Luzein, Switzerland, features an additional pitched roof.

Die Living Box Flüeler in Luzein, Schweiz, zeichnet sich durch ein zusätzliches Satteldach aus.

La Living Box Flüeler à Luzein, en Suisse, se distingue par un toit en pente additionnel.

solar radiation is stored in the solid wood-concrete-composite ceilings and gradually dispersed into the ambient air. In addition, the building's skin is airtight and highly insulated by using cellulose from recycled paper and special glass. The ventilation system with heat recovery equipment prevents energy from being exhausted from the building. Residual energy from the exhaust system, solar collectors, and mini heat pumps are used to heat water for domestic use. Solar panels can further reduce energy consumption.

The upgradable installation concept is also innovative: along one of the façades there is a zone for plumbing and utilities; it can be expanded incrementally or used as a closet or a bookcase.

Süden hin öffnen, während die anderen Fassaden weitgehend geschlossen bleiben; die einströmende Sonnenenergie wird in den massiven Holz-Betonverbund-Decken gespeichert und zeitversetzt an die Raumluft abgegeben. Zum andern ist die Gebäudehülle mit Zellulose aus Recyclingpapier und Spezialgläsern hochwärmegedämmt und luftdicht ausgeführt. Die Lüftungsanlage mit Wärmerückgewinnung vermindert das Ablüften von Energie. Über die Restenergie der Hausabluft, Sonnenkollektoren oder Kleinstwärmepumpen wird das Nutzwasser erwärmt. Fotovoltaikzellen können den Energieverbrauch weiter reduzieren.

Wegweisend neu ist das nachrüstbare Installationskonzept: Entlang einer der Fassaden ist eine Zone für Haustechnik vorgesehen, die schrittweise ausgebaut oder aber als Schrank oder Bücherregal genutzt werden kann.

l'énergie de chauffage nécessaire à une maison conventionnelle. Pour cela, les maisons doivent s'ouvrir vers le sud, tandis que leurs autres façades doivent rester en grande partie fermées. L'énergie solaire entrante est emmagasinée dans les dalles mixtes bois-béton et rediffusée dans l'air ambiant en différé. De plus, l'enveloppe du bâtiment à base de cellulose de papier recyclé et de verres spéciaux garantit une étanchéité totale, ainsi qu'une haute isolation thermique. Le système de ventilation à récupération de chaleur réduit la déperdition d'énergie. L'eau de traitement est chauffée par les résidus d'énergie d'air d'extraction, des collecteurs solaires ou des pompes à chaleur miniatures. Les cellules photoélectriques peuvent également contribuer à réduire la consommation d'énergie.

Le système de plomberie modulable est innovant : une zone pour les installations techniques est prévue le long d'une des façades, qui pourra être peu à peu aménagée ou utilisée comme placard ou bibliothèque.

OSKAR LEO KAUFMANN, JOHANNES KAUFMANN

SU-SI

KFN Kaufmann Product GmbH, Dornbirn, Austria
1998–

The first Su-Si had only 452 sq.ft. of floor space, yet still seemed spacious.

Das erste Su-Si hatte eine Wohnfläche von 42 m² und wirkt trotzdem großzügig.

Malgré sa surface habitable ne dépassant pas 42 m², la première Su-Si semblait spacieuse.

The Kaufmanns are a family from the Vorarlberg region that has been involved in carpentry for generations. The son of this dynasty, the architect Oskar Leo Kaufmann, established the company KFN Products along with his cousin, the carpenter Johannes Kaufmann. Just a year later, they were already enjoying tremendous success: a prefabricated house that he had originally designed for his sister Susanne became a big seller. In each of the following two years, roughly twenty of these houses were sold under the name SU-SI house (in honor of the sister). The house was low in cost: very few of the buyers paid more than €80,000 for their building kits. The components are delivered by truck and the house can be erected on site within a few days. The sanitary fixtures and heating are preinstalled. The SU-SI can even be built on stilts in order to create a carport; otherwise the box rests on a concrete foundation.
The flat-roofed house is supported by a post-and-beam structure. On the long side, which features floor-to-ceiling glazing, the supporting structure simultaneously serves as a continuous shelving unit. The entire structure consists of wood, the ceiling and floors are made of solid spruce, and the walls of laminated wooden panels. Other materials can be also be selected for the outer skin, the interior cladding, and the floors.
The standard house, which is 10 ft. high, can be delivered in various sizes with lengths ranging from 10 to 13 ft. and widths from 33 to 46 ft., resulting in 323 to 538 sq.ft. of living space.

Die Kaufmanns sind eine Vorarlberger Familie, die seit Generationen im Zimmermannsgeschäft tätig ist. Ein Spross dieser Dynastie, der Architekt Oskar Leo Kaufmann, gründete 1996 mit seinem Cousin, dem Zimmermann Johannes Kaufmann, die Firma KFN Product. Nur ein Jahr später bereits gelang ihm der große Coup: Ein Fertighaus, das er ursprünglich für seine Schwester Susanne entworfen hatte, wurde ein Verkaufsschlager. Unter dem Namen SU-SI-Haus (eine Hommage an die Schwester) wurde es in den darauffolgenden beiden Jahren rund zwanzigmal verkauft. Das Haus war erschwinglich: Kaum einer der Käufer musste für die Baukomponenten und deren Aufbau mehr als 80 000 € zahlen.
Die Komponenten werden per LKW angeliefert und das Haus kann vor Ort binnen weniger Tage errichtet werden. Sanitärbereich und Heizung sind bereits vorinstalliert. Um Unterstellplatz, beispielsweise für ein Auto, zu schaffen, kann das SU-SI sogar aufgeständert werden, ansonsten ruht die Box auf einem Betonfundament.
Das Flachdach-Haus ist eine Pfosten-Riegel-Konstruktion. An der durchgehend verglasten Längsseite ist die Konstruktion dabei als durchgehendes Regalsystem ausgebildet. Der Aufbau ist komplett in Holz ausgeführt, Decke und Boden sind aus massiver Fichte, die Wände aus Schichtholzplatten – es können aber auch andere Oberflächenmaterialien für die Außenhülle, die Innenverkleidung und die Bodenbeläge gewählt werden. Das standardisierte Haus ist bei einer Höhe von 3 m in verschiedenen Größen mit einer Länge von 10 bis 14 m und einer Breite von 3 bis 4 m lieferbar und verfügt über eine Nutzfläche von 30 bis 50 m².

Les Kaufmann sont issus d'une famille de charpentiers de tradition, originaire du Vorarlberg. Descendant de cette dynastie, l'architecte Oskar Leo Kaufmann fonda l'entreprise KFN Products avec son cousin, le charpentier Johannes Kaufmann, en 1996. À peine un an plus tard, il réussît un coup retentissant : la maison préfabriquée qu'il avait conçue initialement pour sa sœur Susanne fut un véritable succès commercial. Sous le nom de SU-SI-Haus (en hommage à sa sœur), une vingtaine d'exemplaires furent vendus les deux années suivantes. Très abordable, l'achat des composants, montage compris, ne dépassait pas les 80 000 €.
Les composants sont livrés par camion et la maison peut être montée sur site en quelques jours. Les sanitaires et le chauffage sont pré-installés. Pour créer un espace abritant un véhicule par exemple, la maison SU-SI peut même être surélevée. Autrement, la boîte repose sur des fondations de béton.
Cette maison à toit plat est une construction poteaux-poutres. Sur le côté longitudinal vitré, la structure présente un système d'étagères en continu. L'ossature est intégralement en bois, le plafond et le plancher sont en épicéa massif, les murs en panneaux de contreplaqué. Il est cependant possible de choisir d'autres matériaux pour l'enveloppe extérieure, le revêtement intérieur et les revêtements des planchers.
La maison standardisée est disponible dans différentes tailles, avec une hauteur de 3 m, une longueur de 3 m à 4 m et une largeur de 10 m à 14 m. Sa surface utile va de 30 m² à 50 m².

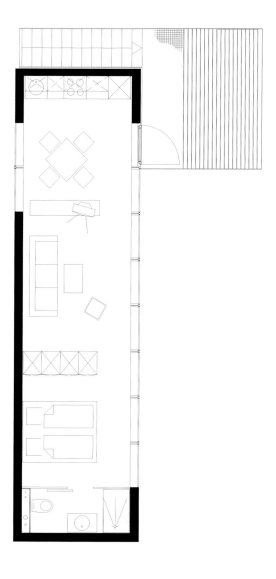

The bar-shaped structure is
delineated on either of the
narrow sides by the kitchen
and the bathroom.

Der Gebäuderiegel wird an
den Schmalseiten jeweils durch
Küche und Sanitärteil begrenzt.

Cette construction en forme
de barre est délimitée à ses
extrémités par la cuisine et
les sanitaires.

SMALLHOUSE/ WEBERHAUS OPTION

WeberHaus GmbH & Co. KG, Rheinau-Linx, Germany
1999–

The photograph of the model (right)
shows the back of the house, the
photograph of the house (opposite
page) shows the completed front.

Das Modellbild (rechts) zeigt die
Rückseite des Hauses, die Fotografie
(rechte Seite) des ausgeführten Baus
die Vorderseite.

La photo de la maquette (à droite)
montre l'arrière de la maison, la
photo (page de droite) de la
construction terminée, la façade
avant.

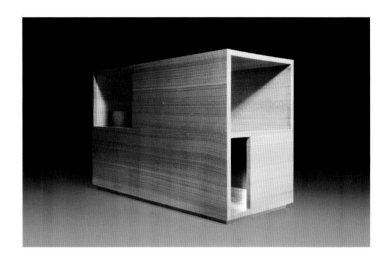

The Swiss architectural group Bauart, centered around Marco Ryter, has specialized in solutions involving wooden construction since 1987, when the company was established, and built various municipal facilities in Switzerland such as schools and kindergartens. The architects were also seeking to develop a prefabricated house out of wood that, despite a relatively limited floor space of roughly 750 sq.ft., would overshadow many larger conventional single-family houses in its spaciousness and elegance. Bauart presented the smallhouse in 1999 for the first time, it was built as a modular wooden structure.

The two-story residential cube has a footprint of 38 x 15 ft. and no corridors; each of the floors is divided only by either the open kitchen or the bathroom. Thus, four rooms—or, more precisely, functional areas—are created in a rather matter-of-fact manner; there are no other internal divisions. Yet the houses do not seem confined, not least of all due to the open stairs and large windows, which can fill the entire back wall of the one or the other floor, thereby providing plenty of natural light. The smallhouse does not present itself as a hermetic box, but rather as a flowing continuum.

In the meantime, the prototype presented in 1999 has been developed further in conjunction with the German company WeberHaus. Under the

Die Schweizer Architektengruppe Bauart um Marco Ryter hat sich seit ihrer Gründung 1987 auf die Holzbauweise spezialisiert und verschiedene städtische Einrichtungen wie Schulen oder Kindergärten in der Schweiz gebaut. Aus diesem Material ein Fertighaus zu entwickeln, das trotz seiner verhältnismäßig geringen Wohnfläche von rund 70 m² ein Maß an räumlicher Großzügigkeit und Eleganz bietet, die so manches herkömmliche größere Einfamilienhaus in den Schatten stellt – dies war das Ziel, das dem Architekturbüro vorschwebte. 1999 stellte Bauart erstmals das smallhouse vor, das in Holzmodulbauweise gefertigt war.

Der zweigeschossige Wohnkubus des smallhouse verzichtet auf einer Grundfläche von ca. 11 x 4,50 m auf Flure und unterteilt Erd- sowie Obergeschoss lediglich durch eine offene Küche und das Bad. So entstehen geradezu beiläufig vier Räume oder vielmehr nutzungsvariable Bereiche, denn auf weitere Unterteilungen wurde im Inneren verzichtet. Nicht zuletzt dank der offenen Treppe und der großen Fensterflächen, welche die gesamte Stirnseite einer Etage einnehmen können und den Innenraum mit viel Licht versorgen, verliert sich jeder Eindruck von Beengtheit. Das smallhouse präsentiert sich nicht als hermetische Kiste, sondern als fließendes Kontinuum.

Depuis sa création en 1987 autour de Marco Ryter, le groupe d'architectes Bauart s'est consacré à la construction en bois et a bâti divers établissements municipaux en Suisse, tels que des écoles et des jardins d'enfants. Le bureau d'architectes s'était fixé comme objectif de concevoir une maison préfabriquée en bois qui, malgré sa surface habitable relativement réduite de 70 m², parvienne à offrir un espace vaste et élégant qui surpasse de nombreuses maisons particulières traditionnelles plus spacieuses. En 1999, Bauart présenta sa smallhouse pour la première fois, une maison réalisée selon le principe de construction modulaire en bois.

Avec sa surface de 11 m x 4,5 m, la smallhouse, un cube d'habitation de deux étages, renonce aux couloirs. Les niveaux sont uniquement subdivisés par la cuisine américaine et la salle de bains. On obtient pour ainsi dire quatre pièces, ou plutôt espaces fonctionnels modulables, l'espace intérieur n'étant pas davantage subdivisé. L'escalier ouvert et les grandes surfaces vitrées pouvant occuper toute la façade d'un étage, et fournissant ainsi une grande luminosité à l'espace intérieur, ôtent toute sensation d'exiguïté. La smallhouse ne se présente pas comme une boîte hermétique, mais comme un espace en continu.

Entre-temps, le prototype présenté en 1999 a été perfectionné et

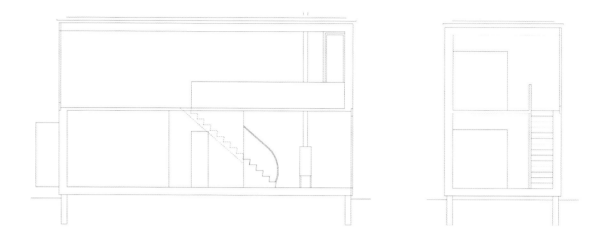

The appearance of the interior can be varied by using different materials for the floor, walls, and ceilings.

Die Erscheinung der Räume kann durch wechselnde Oberflächen an Boden, Wand und Decke variiert werden.

L'apparence de l'intérieur peut être modifiée par le choix de divers matériaux de revêtement pour les planchers, les murs et les plafonds.

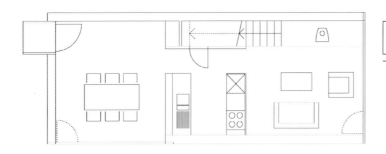
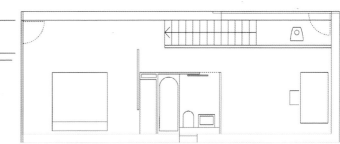

name "WeberHaus Option" it has since been introduced onto the market. The prefabricated elements are assembled on a floor slab cast on site. The flat-roofed house, with its neutral, reduced design vocabulary, is suited for use in the most diverse locations: as an extension of an already existing building, as a residential unit for one or two people, as a holiday home, or as a studio. Fully equipped bathrooms (with bathtubs) are offered, as well as fireplaces. It is possible to arrange a number of cubes alongside each other; the modular concept also allows for floor plans in the form of an "L" or a "U".

Mittlerweile wurde der 1999 vorgestellte Prototyp gemeinsam mit dem deutschen Hersteller WeberHaus unter dem Namen „WeberHaus Option" weiterentwickelt und auf den Markt gebracht. Die vorgefertigten Elemente werden vor Ort über der gegossenen Bodenplatte aufgebaut. Einzusetzen ist das Flachdachhaus, dessen reduziert-neutrale Formensprache die Verwendung an unterschiedlichen Standorten erlaubt, als Erweiterung eines schon bestehenden Gebäudes, als Wohnhaus für eine oder auch für zwei Personen, aber auch als Ferienunterkunft oder Atelier. Angeboten werden ein voll ausgestattetes Bad samt Badewanne sowie ein Kaminofen. Durch die modulare Konzeption können mehrere Quader in Reihe aneinandergesetzt, aber auch Grundrissvarianten in L- oder U-Form realisiert werden.

commercialisé en collaboration avec le fabricant allemand WeberHaus sous le nom de WeberHaus Option. Les éléments préfabriqués sont assemblés sur le radier coulé sur le sol. Il ne reste plus qu'à investir la maison à toit plat dont le langage formel neutre et le petit format permettent de s'intégrer à divers sites : comme extension d'un bâtiment existant, maison d'habitation pour une ou deux personnes, mais aussi comme résidence de vacances ou comme atelier. Une salle de bains tout équipée, baignoire comprise, et une cheminée à foyer fermé sont proposées. Grâce à la conception modulaire, plusieurs volumes peuvent venir se juxtaposer les uns aux autres. Des variantes de plans en L ou en U sont également réalisables.

LV HOME

Rocio Romero LLC, St. Louis, Missouri, USA
2000–

LV Homes in Perryville, Missouri
(right) and Elliott, Maine (opposite
page)
LV Homes in Perryville, Missouri
(rechts) und Elliott, Maine (rechte
Seite)
LV Homes à Perryville, Missouri
(à droite) et Elliott, Maine (page
de droite)

The Chilean-American architect and Berkeley graduate Rocio Romero originally designed the LV prefabricated house as a weekend house for her parents to use in Laguna Verde, a small town south of Valparaiso in Chile, hence the name. It offered a little over 1,000 sq. ft of living space and was built directly on a hill overlooking the Pacific Coast. The view of the ocean and the landscape was intended to be part of the living experience. Low cost, weather resistance, and energy efficiency were the most important considerations informing the design.

The weekend house then became the prototype for the LV Home, which is a wood and metal frame structure on concrete supports. The outer skin consists mainly of corrugated sheet zinc aluminum, aluminum, and laminated glass, while the interiors are executed in laminated wood. Romero also designed furniture made of rust-free steel and a built-in kitchen for the house. With its elongated floor plan and 9-ft. ceilings, the house contains a living room, two bathrooms, two bedrooms, and a kitchen area. On one side there are sliding glass doors that can be opened completely, thus making for a nearly seamless transition between the living area and the surrounding landscape.

All of the LV Series prefabricated homes have a standard width of approx. 25 ft., but they vary in size due to differences in the length; the smallest, the LVM, is approx. 25 ft. long and the largest, the LVL, is approx. 59 ft. 6 in. long. The standard siding on the LV Series Home is galvanized steel coated with silver metallic Kynar 500. LV Homes are available starting at roughly $37,000. However, with expenditures for construction and the interior finish, the total reaches an average $138,000 to $224,000. The standardized panel building kit is produced in a factory in Perryville, Missouri, which is roughly an hour away from St. Louis. Since the completion of the prototype in 2000, Romero has introduced her LV onto the market in various sizes and versions suited for mass production.

Das LV-Fertighaus hatte die chilenisch-US-amerikanische Architektin und Berkeley-Absolventin Rocio Romero ursprünglich als Wochenendhaus für ihre Eltern im chilenischen Laguna Verde (daher auch der Name), einer Kleinstadt südlich von Valparaiso, entworfen. Es bot etwas über 100 m² Wohnfläche und wurde direkt an der Pazifikküste auf einem Hügel errichtet. Der Ausblick auf das Meer und die Landschaft sollte Teil des Wohnerlebens werden. Niedrige Kosten, Wetterbeständigkeit und Energieeffizienz waren die Leitmaximen des Entwurfs.

Das Wochenendhaus avancierte zum Prototyp des LV Home. Es ist eine Rahmenkonstruktion aus Holz und Metall auf Betonstützen. Die Außenhülle besteht hauptsächlich aus gewelltem Zinkaluminiumblech, Aluminium und Verbundglas, während die Interieurs in Schichtholz ausgeführt sind. Dazu gestaltete Romero Möbel aus rostfreiem Stahl und eine Einbauküche. Bei einem langgestreckten Grundriss und 2,75 m hohen Decken umfasst das Haus einen Wohnraum, zwei Badezimmer, zwei Schlafzimmer und einen Küchenbereich und öffnet sich zu einer Seite mit einer komplett verglasten Wand aus Schiebetüren, dank derer der Wohnraum fast übergangslos mit der Umgebung verschmilzt.

Alle Fertighäuser der LV-Serie haben eine Standardbreite von 7,53 m, unterscheiden sich aber in der Länge: Das kleinste Modell (LVM) ist 7,53 m lang, das größte (LVL) 17,85 m. Als Standardverkleidung kommen silbrig glänzende verzinkte Stahlplatten mit Polyvinylidenfluorid-Beschichtung (Kynar 500) zum Einsatz. Die LV Homes gibt es ab etwa 37 000 $. Mit den Aufwendungen für Aufbau und Interieurs kommen Kosten von durchschnittlich 138 000 $ bis 224 000 $ zusammen. Der standardisierte Paneel-Bausatz wird in einer Fabrik in Perryville, Missouri, hergestellt, das etwa eine Stunde von St. Louis entfernt ist. Seit Fertigstellung des Prototyps im Jahr 2000 hat Romero ihr LV massenfertigungstauglich in verschiedenen Größen und Ausführungen auf den Markt gebracht.

La première maison préfabriquée LV conçue par Rocio Romero, l'architecte américano-chilienne diplômée de l'université de Berkeley, était une résidence secondaire pour ses parents au Chili, à Laguna Verde – d'où le nom –, une petite ville au sud de Valparaiso. D'une surface habitable supérieure à 100 m2, elle fut directement édifiée sur une colline de la côte pacifique : la vue sur la mer et la campagne devaient être parties intégrantes du concept de vie en ce lieu. Coûts bas, résistance aux intempéries et efficacité énergétique, tels étaient les mots d'ordre du projet.

Cette maison de week-end fut promue prototype de la LV Home. Sa construction à ossature de bois et métal repose sur des poteaux en béton. Son enveloppe extérieure est principalement constituée de tôles ondulées en alliage d'aluminium-zinc, d'aluminium et de verre feuilleté, tandis que l'intérieur est en bois contreplaqué. En outre, Romero conçut des meubles en acier inoxydable ainsi qu'une cuisine intégrée. Avec un plan tout en longueur et un plafond de 2,75 m de hauteur, la maison abrite un salon, deux salles de bains, deux chambres et un espace cuisine, et s'ouvre sur un côté par une baie vitrée à portes coulissantes, permettant à l'espace d'habitation de se fondre quasiment sans transition avec l'environnement.

Toutes les maisons préfabriquées de la série LV ont une largeur standard de 7,53 m, mais se distinguent par leur longueur : le plus petit modèle (LVM) fait 7,53 m de long, le plus grand (LVL) 17,85 m. Le revêtement standard utilisé est constitué de plaques d'acier galvanisées couleur argentée et brillante, recouvertes d'une résine PVDF Kynar 500® (polyfluorure de vinylidène). Les LV Homes se vendent à partir de 37 000 $. Avec les frais de montage et d'aménagement, les coûts s'élèvent en moyenne entre 138 000 $ et 224 000 $. Le kit de panneaux standardisé est fabriqué dans une usine de Perryville, dans le Missouri, à environ une heure de Saint Louis. Depuis la fabrication du prototype en 2000, Romero a commercialisé sa maison LV en diverses tailles et modèles variés, qui se prêtent à une production en série.

Above right: Plan of a house built with a cellar

Oben rechts: Grundriss bei unterkellerter Bauweise

En haut à droite: Plan de maison avec cave

Below right: Plan of a house built on one level

Unten rechts: Grundriss bei eingeschossiger Bauweise

En bas à droite: Plan de maison de plain-pied

A narrow band of windows on the
side opposite the terrace facilitates
cross-ventilation.

Schmale Fensterbänder auf der der
Terrasse gegenüber gelegenen Seite
gestatten eine Querlüftung.

Un étroit bandeau de fenêtres du
côté opposé à la terrasse favorise
une ventilation transversale.

GLIDEHOUSE

Blu Homes, Inc., Waltham, Massachusetts, USA
2003–

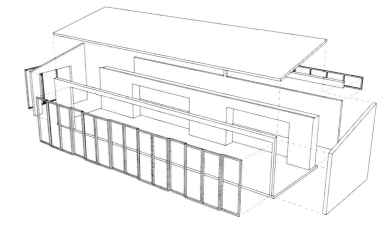

Right: Drawing of elements
pre-installed in the factory
Rechts: Schema der im Werk
vormontierten Elemente
À droite: Schéma des éléments
préassemblés à l'usine

After six months of fruitlessly searching for an affordable single-family home, Michelle Kaufmann lost her patience. The architect, a former employee in Frank O. Gehry's office, decided to build the home she envisioned for herself: a modern house, based on principles of sustainability, at the lowest possible cost. During the design process, friends and colleagues already began asking her if she could also build them one.

Hence, Michelle Kaufmann established her own office, mkd, in 2002. While designing her own home, she also created a model for the first of her houses to be built in series, the Glidehouse, which was an immediate success. In the meantime, six additional models have been added. They come completely assembled and are set down on a solid foundation on site. Smaller houses are built as a single module, larger houses consist of a number of modules, which are joined together on site. They are delivered by truck, and this limits their size: as a rule they are 15 ½ ft. wide and just as tall. The reference costs are $250 to $300 per square foot (incl. transport and assembly.

Kaufmann sees her "pre-designed" houses explicitly as "products" that are available in different versions. In addition to the houses produced in series, Kaufmann and her team are also willing to develop individual designs, which are then built in a factory.

With their clear lines, Kaufmann's houses stand in the tradition of classic

Nach sechs Monaten vergeblicher Suche nach einem erschwinglichen Eigenheim hatte Michelle Kaufmann genug. Die Architektin, eine ehemalige Mitarbeiterin im Büro von Frank O. Gehry, entschloss sich, das Domizil, das ihr vorschwebte, selbst zu bauen: ein an den Prinzipien der Nachhaltigkeit orientiertes und in seinen Formen modernes Haus zu möglichst geringen Kosten. Noch während des Entwerfens fragten Freunde und Kollegen sie: Kannst Du uns nicht auch eines bauen?

So gründete Michelle Kaufmann 2002 ihr eigenes Büro „mkd". Mit ihrem eigenen Wohnhaus schuf sie zugleich ihr erstes Serienhaus-Modell: das Glidehouse, das auf Anhieb ein Erfolg war. Sechs weitere Modelle sind mittlerweile hinzugekommen, die alle bereits vorgefertigt und vor Ort auf ein festes Fundament gesetzt werden. Kleinere Häuser werden als ein Modul gefertigt, größere bestehen aus mehreren Modulen, die vor Ort zusammengefügt werden. Sie werden per LKW angeliefert, und das beschränkt ihre Größe: Sie sind in der Regel 4,72 m (15,5 Fuß) breit und exakt ebenso hoch. Richtwert für die Kosten sind 250 bis 300 $ pro Quadratfuß (2700 bis 3230 $/m²) – inkl. Transport und Aufbau.

Kaufmann versteht ihre „vor-entworfenen" Häuser explizit als „Produkte", die in verschiedenen Ausführungsvarianten angeboten werden. Daneben bieten Kaufmann und ihr Team neben den Serienhäusern die Entwicklung individueller Entwürfe an, die dann ebenfalls in der Fabrik gebaut werden.

Après six mois de vaines recherches pour trouver une maison individuelle abordable, Michelle Kaufmann en eut assez. L'architecte, ancienne collaboratrice de l'agence de Frank O. Gehry, décida de construire elle-même le logement auquel elle aspirait: une maison aux formes modernes, s'inspirant des principes du développement durable, à un coût minimum. Mais alors qu'elle n'en était encore qu'au stade de la conception, ses amis et collègues lui demandaient déjà si elle pourrait aussi leur en construire une.

C'est ainsi que Michelle Kaufmann fonda sa propre agence «mkd» en 2002. En même temps que sa propre maison d'habitation, elle créa son premier modèle de maison préfabriquée: la Glidehouse, qui fut d'emblée un succès. Entre-temps, six autres modèles s'y sont rajoutés, tous préfabriqués puis destinés à être posés sur site sur des fondations en dur. Les plus petites maisons constituent un module unique, tandis que les plus grandes se composent de plusieurs, assemblés sur site. Leur transport par camion limite leur taille: ils font généralement 4,72 m (15,5 pieds) de large pour une hauteur identique. La valeur indicative du prix au pied carré se situe entre 250 $ et 300 $ (2700 $/m² à 3230 $/m³), transport et montage inclus. Kaufmann considère clairement ses maisons «pré-conçues» comme des «produits» déclinés en divers modèles. Parallèlement à leurs maisons préfabriquées, Kaufmann et son équipe proposent de développer des projets individuels qui sont ensuite également fabriqués en usine.

The mono-pitched roofs arranged opposite each other define the external and internal spaces.

Das Prinzip der gegeneinander versetzten Pultdachelemente definiert Außen- und Innenräume

Le principe des éléments de toit en appentis disposés à l'opposé définit les espaces extérieur et intérieur.

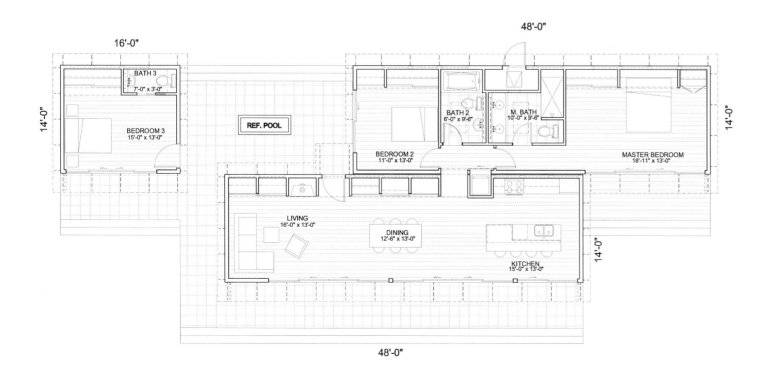

48'-0"

16'-0"

14'-0"

BATH 3
7'-0" x 3'-0"

BEDROOM 3
15'-0" x 13'-0"

REF. POOL

BATH 2
6'-0" x 9'-6"

M. BATH
10'-0" x 9'-6"

BEDROOM 2
11'-0" x 13'-0"

MASTER BEDROOM
18'-11" x 13'-0"

14'-0"

LIVING
16'-0" x 13'-0"

DINING
12'-6" x 13'-0"

KITCHEN
15'-0" x 13'-0"

14'-0"

48'-0"

Opposite page: The external sliding solar protection elements prevent the interior from becoming too hot.

Rechte Seite: Durch außen ange-brachte, verschiebbare Schattierungs-elemente wird eine Aufheizung des Innenraums verhindert.

Page de droite: Les éléments coulissants de protection solaire extérieurs préviennent l'échauffement de l'espace intérieur.

The Glidehouse G3 contains three bedrooms on 1568 sq.ft. of floor space.

Das Glidehouse G3 verfügt über drei Schlafzimmer auf einer Grundfläche von 146 m².

La Glidehouse G3 comporte trois chambres pour une surface habitable de 146 m².

Modernism. They are also energy efficient and made of sustainable materials. There are two versions, one for the snowy regions in the north, and the other one for the milder climate of California. Large glass windows with sliding doors open the house up towards the south, the other external walls are made of weatherproof COR-TEN steel. The roofs are covered with heat resistant galvanized sheet-metal and allow for the easy installation of photo-voltaic cells.

The architect describes the inclusion of a large wall of cabinets with abundant storage space as a design characteristic—meant to ensure that the living space remains free of clutter.

The Glidehouse, Michelle Kaufmann's first and to date most successful model, is available in five different sizes: they range from the 672-sq.ft. "studio" (with a separate bedroom and bathroom) to the large Glidehouse, with a courtyard and an H-shaped floor plan made up of four modules totaling 2,240 sq.ft. of floor space. The center of this house is a large living and dining area with a kitchen. The four bedrooms and three bathrooms, as well as a "library", are in the wings.

Die Kaufmann'schen Häuser stehen mit ihren klaren Formen in der Tradition der klassischen Moderne, sind energieeffizient und aus nachhaltigen Materialien gebaut. Es gibt sie in zwei Versionen, die eine für die Schneeregionen des Nordens, die andere für das milde Klima Kaliforniens. Große Glaswände mit Schiebetüren öffnen das Haus nach Süden hin, die übrigen Außenwände sind aus witterungsbeständigem Cor-ten®-Stahl. Die Dächer sind mit wärmebeständigem Galvalume®-Blech belegt, Photovoltaik-Zellen können problemlos aufmontiert werden.

Als ein Charakteristikum ihrer Entwürfe stellen die Architekten heraus, dass es in allen Häusern eine große Schrankwand gibt, in der man viel verstauen kann – damit der Wohnraum möglichst frei von herumliegendem Kram bleibt.

Das Glidehouse, Michelle Kaufmanns erstes und bis heute erfolgreichstes Modell, wird in fünf Größen angeboten: Sie reichen vom 62 m² messenden „Studio" (mit separiertem Schlafzimmer und Badezimmer) bis zum aus vier Modulen H-förmig zusammengesetzten, 208 m² großen „Glidehouse with courtyard", das im Zentrum über einen großen Wohn- und Essraum mit Küche und in den Flügeln über vier Schlaf-, drei Badezimmer und eine „Bibliothek" verfügt.

Avec leurs formes claires, les maisons de Kaufmann s'inscrivent dans la tradition du modernisme classique. Caractérisées par leur haute efficacité énergétique, elles sont construites avec des matériaux durables et existent en deux versions : l'une pour les régions enneigées du nord, l'autre pour le doux climat californien. De grandes baies vitrées à portes coulissantes ouvrent la maison en direction du sud, tandis que les autres murs extérieurs sont en acier Corten®, résistant à la corrosion atmosphérique. Les toits sont recouverts de tôle d'acier Galvalume® thermorésistante. Des cellules photovoltaïques peuvent y être montées sans problème.

Les architectes soulignent la présence caractéristique d'un grand placard intégré dans toutes ses maisons, offrant une grande capacité de rangement qui permet de débarrasser au maximum la salle de séjour.

La Glidehouse, le premier modèle de Michelle Kaufmann et, à ce jour, celui qui a remporté le plus grand succès, est proposée en cinq tailles, allant de studios de 62 m² (avec chambre à coucher et salle de bains séparées) à la grande « Glidehouse with courtyard » en forme de H, formée de quatre modules assemblés et faisant 208 m². Cette dernière accueille en son centre une grande salle à manger-salon avec cuisine et, dans les ailes, quatre chambres, trois salles de bains et une bibliothèque.

WEEHOUSE

Alchemy LLC, St. Paul, Minnesota, USA
2003–

The weeHouses designed by Alchemy Architects prove that it is possible to do a lot with a small space. The architectural office, founded by Geoffrey Warner in 1992, originally designed a small vacation home for the violinist Stephanie Arade in 1992. The wood and steel structure was completely assembled in a factory and then installed on Lake Pepin, Wisconsin, in 2003. The 336-sq.ft. house, which is indeed "wee", was photogenically located on a slope, where it attracted considerable attention from architectural journals and brought the "workshop of Alchemists" numerous subsequent commissions. This marked the birth of the prefabricated house line called weeHouses. In the meantime, the architects have already built over forty prefabricated houses in the United States and Canada, most of them as vacation homes. "People are more inclined to experiment in this sector and, besides, they want everything to be built very fast", says Geoffrey Warner. The basic weeHouse module is a 14-ft.-wide and 8-ft.-high box, which is available in three lengths: 26 ft. (for either the one-room "studio" or the "weeHouse small" with a separate bathroom), 48 ft. and 58 ft. The "weeHouse large" measures 812 sq.ft. and has a living and dining area with a kitchen unit, two bedrooms, and a bathroom. By stacking the basic modules, or by placing them alongside each other, five other variations can be created—including a two-story, 1372 sq.ft. "tall pair large", which has a living and dining room with a kitchen area, along with a bedroom and a bathroom, on the ground floor, as well as two bedrooms, a bathroom and a roof terrace on the upper floor.

Once the client has decided upon the size, he has only a limited number of alternatives with regard to the foundation, roof, external walls, and interior design. Hence, all of the "weeHouses" that have been built to date clearly reveal the same handwriting: clean, simple lines, and high quality materials. They are also quite reasonably priced: the reference price is currently \$125 per square foot. The houses are completely built in the factory and then delivered by truck either as a single module or in two parts, depending on the size, and then installed on the site.

Dass man aus wenig Raum viel machen kann, demonstrieren die weeHouses der Alchemy Architects. Für die Geigerin Stephanie Arado entwarf das Büro, das 1989 von Geoffrey C. Warner gegründet wurde, 2003 ein kleines Ferienhaus, das als Holz- und Stahlkonstruktion komplett in der Fabrikhalle gebaut und dann am Lake Pepin, Wisconsin, aufgestellt wurde. Das mit 31 m² in der Tat „winzige" Haus („wee" heißt im Englischen winzig), fotogen in Hanglage gesetzt, erregte viel Aufmerksamkeit in der Fachpresse und bescherte den „Alchemisten" zahlreiche Folgeaufträge. So entstand die Fertighaus-Produktlinie weeHouses. Über vierzig Fertighäuser hat das Büro inzwischen in den USA und Kanada gebaut, überwiegend Ferienhäuser. „Da experimentieren die Leute eher, und außerdem soll alles schnell gehen", sagt Geoffrey Warner.

Grundmodul des weeHouse ist eine 4,27 m (14 Fuß) breite Kiste, die 2,44 m (8 Fuß) hoch ist und in drei Längen angeboten wird: 7,9 m (26 Fuß; als „Studio" mit nur einem Raum oder als „weeHouse Small" mit separatem Badezimmer), 14,6 m (48 Fuß) und 17,7 m (58 Fuß). 75 m² misst dieses „weeHouse Large", das ein Wohn- und Esszimmer mit Küchenzeile, zwei Schlafzimmer und ein Badezimmer umfasst. Durch Stapeln oder Aneinanderfügen des Grundmoduls entstehen fünf weitere Varianten – bis hin zum zweigeschossigen, 127 m² großen „Tall Pair large", das unten Wohn-Esszimmer mit Küchenbereich, Schlafzimmer und Bad, im Obergeschoss zwei Schlafzimmer, ein Bad sowie eine Dachterrasse bietet.

Hat sich der Bauherr für eine Größe entschieden, so stehen ihm, was Fundament, Dach, Außenwände und Inneneinrichtung angeht, nur wenige Alternativen zur Wahl. Für die Außenwandgestaltung sind sogar nur zwei Wahlmöglichkeiten vorgesehen: Container oder Corncrib. Alle realisierten weeHouses zeigen deshalb die gleiche Handschrift: klare, einfache Formen und hochwertige Materialien. Und sie sind in der Tat preiswert: Der Richtwert liegt bei 125 \$ pro Quadratfuß (ca. 1345 \$/m³). Die Häuser werden komplett in der Fabrik gebaut und dann – je nach Größe in einem oder zwei Modulen – per LKW zum Bauplatz transportiert und aufgestellt.

Les weeHouses des Alchemy Architects sont la preuve qu'il est possible de faire beaucoup à partir de peu d'espace. En 2003, l'agence créée en 1992 par Geoffrey Warner conçut un petit maison de vacances pour la violoniste Stephanie Arado. Intégralement construite en usine, la construction de bois et d'acier fut ensuite installée à Lake Pepin, Wisconsin. Avec ses 31 m², cette maison photogénique effectivement minuscule (du terme « wee » en anglais), érigée sur un terrain en pente, attira beaucoup l'attention de la presse spécialisée et voulut aux « alchimistes » de nombreuses commandes subséquentes. C'est ainsi que la gamme de maisons préfabriquées weeHouses vit le jour. Depuis, l'agence a construit plus de quarante maisons préfabriquées aux États-Unis et au Canada, en majorité des maisons de vacances. D'après Geoffrey Warner : « Les gens sont plus enclins à expérimente dans ce domaine, et en plus, il faut que ça aille vite. »

Le module de base de la weeHouse est une caisse de 4,27 m (14 pieds) de large et 2,44 m (8 pieds) de haut, proposée en trois longueurs : 7,9 m (26 pieds ; comme « Studio » avec une seule pièce ou comme la « weeHouse Small » avec salle des bains séparée), 14,6 m (48 pieds) et 17,7 m (58 pieds). La « weeHouse Large » mesure 75 m² et comprend une salle de séjour-salle à manger avec cuisine intégrée, deux chambres et une salle de bains. Il est possible d'obtenir cinq autres variantes en empilant ou juxtaposant le module de base, pouvant aller jusqu'à la spacieuse version de 127 m², la « Tall Pair large » de deux étages, qui accueille une salle de séjour-salle à manger avec cuisine intégrée, chambre et salle de bains, ainsi qu'un toit en terrasse.

Une fois que le maître d'ouvrage a opté pour une taille, son choix concernant les fondations, le toit, les murs extérieurs et la décoration intérieure s'avère assez restreint. Toutes les weeHouses réalisées portent par conséquent clairement la même griffe, à savoir des formes claires et simples, avec des matériaux de grande qualité. Elles sont effectivement bon marché : la valeur indicative se situe à 125 \$ le pied carré. Les maisons sont intégralement construites à l'usine – en un ou deux modules selon la taille choisie – puis transportées par camion sur le terrain à bâtir et montées.

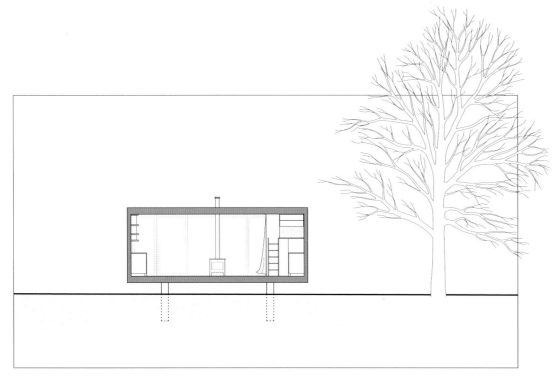

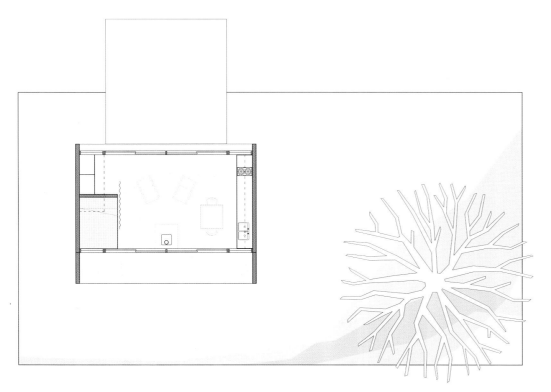

The prototype of the weeHouse in Pepin, Wisconsin, 2003. The exterior is clad in cementitious siding painted with an oxidizing paint. The interior is completely wrapped in Douglas fir. Section and plan (left) show the simpler layout.

Der Prototyp des weeHouse in Pepin, Wisconsin, 2003. Die Außenflächen haben eine zementgebundene Verkleidung und einen oxydierenden Anstrich. Die Innenverkleidung besteht gänzlich aus Douglasfichte. Schnitt und Grundriss (links) zeigen die einfache innere Organisation.

Prototype de la weeHouse à Pepin, Wisconsin, 2003. L'extérieur a un revêtement lié au ciment et un enduit résistant à la corrosion. Le revêtement intérieur est intégralement en sapin de Douglas. La coupe et le plan (à gauche) illustrent le simple agencement intérieur.

1 X

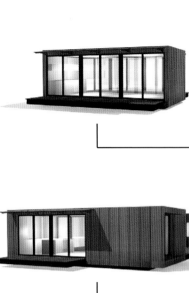

2 X

2 X

3 X

4 X

A weeHouse in Marfa, Texas, outside
of a small artists' colony in West
Texas

WeeHouse in Marfa, Texas, in der
Nähe einer kleinen Künstlerkolonie
in West-Texas

WeeHouse à Marfa, Texas, près d'une
petite colonie d'artistes à West Texas

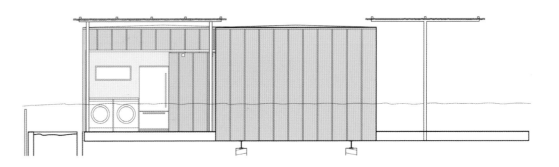

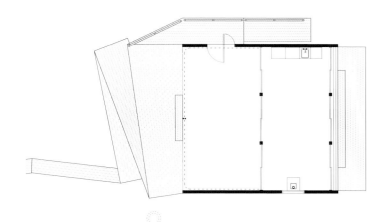

N
0   10'
3m

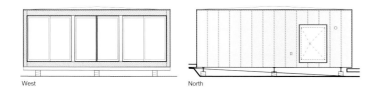

West   North

A weeHouse in Burlington,
Wisconsin, a 28 x 28 ft., two-module
house with an open porch, blue and
yellow container siding, ipe floors,
and eucalyptus cabinets

WeeHouse in Burlington, Wisconsin:
Ein quadratisches Haus von 8,5 m
Kantenlänge, bestehend aus zwei
Baueinheiten mit einem offenen Vor-
dach und blauen und gelben
Container-Seitenwänden. Die Böden
sind aus Ipe-Holz und die Schränke
aus Eukalyptus-Holz.

WeeHouse à Burlington, Wisconsin:
maison carrée de 8,5 m de côté,
composée de deux modules, avec un
avant-toit ouvert et des murs latéraux
de container maritime bleu et jaune.
Les planchers sont en ipé et les placards en bois d'eucalyptus.

A weeHouse in Honesdale, Pennsylvania, with three bedrooms on a total of 2,200 sq.ft. of floor space. This retreat home consists of a larger main unit accommodating most daily activities and a smaller sleeping tower. Both units are connected by an elevated patio bridge component.

WeeHouse in Honesdale, Pennsylvania, mit drei Schlafzimmern und 204 m² Wohnfläche. Dieses Wochenend-Haus besteht aus einer größeren Haupteinheit für verschiedene Aktivitäten und einem kleineren Schlafturm. Die beiden Einheiten sind durch eine Brücke über den Innenhof miteinander verbunden.

Weehouse à Honesdale, en Pennsylvanie, avec trois chambres et 204 m² de surface habitable. Cette maison de week-end consiste en une grande unité principale destinée à diverses activités et en une petite tour pour le repos. Les deux unités sont reliées par un pont passant au-dessus de la cour intérieure.

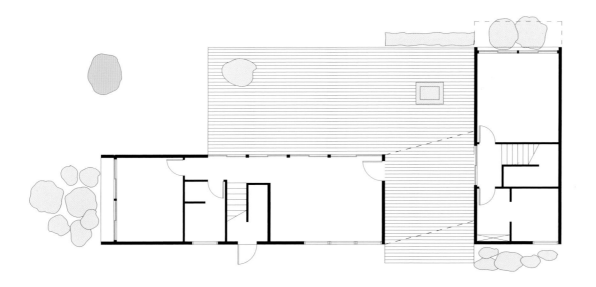

RESOLUTION: 4 ARCHITECTURE

MODERN MODULAR

New York, New York, USA
2003–

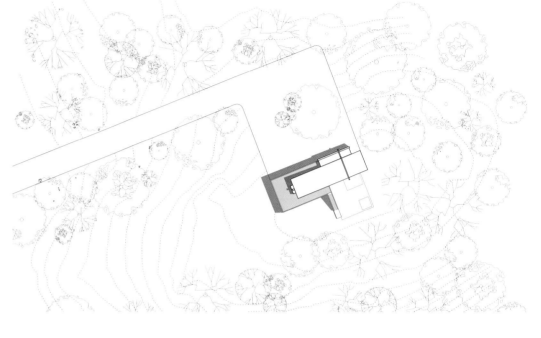

A team of New York architects, Joseph Tanney and Robert Luntz, established Resolution: 4 Architecture in 1990. The office developed factory finished modules on the basis of wood frame construction. By applying this principle, which the two architects call "Modern Modular", it is possible to build prefabricated houses with diverse floor plans and sizes and respond to individual client wishes on the most diverse building sites. The company offers 20 different models. The prefabricated modules are produced by different companies and delivered to the building site by truck.

In 2003 the office won the prestigious competition staged by *Dwell* magazine for their modern modular principle. In the meantime, a number of houses have been built according to the modern modular principle, including the "Dwell Home" and the "Mountain Retreat". The houses are produced and equipped according to state-of-the-art ecological criteria. They have a solar power system, geothermal heating and cooling, aluminum clad low energy windows and doors, and much more.

The Dwell Home (which is named for the magazine that awarded the prize) was produced by Carolina Building Solutions, a prefabricated housing company in Pittsboro, North Carolina. The five modules arranged as a two-story structure consists of two interlocking rectangular volumes that provide 2,042 sq.ft. of living space. The living, dining and kitchen area is located on the ground floor and opens onto the spacious deck. The private part of the house, with three bedrooms and two bathrooms, is located in the rectangular volume that stands at a right angle.

The Mountain Retreat, which was built in 2005 by the prefabricated housing company Apex Homes, is somewhat smaller with its 1,800 sq.ft. of floor space. A large part of the building's volume rests on slender concrete columns. Thus, a carport is created on the ground level in addition to a

Resolution: 4 Architecture wurde durch das New Yorker Architektenteam Joseph Tanney und Robert Luntz 1990 gegründet. Das Büro hat auf der Basis einer Holzrahmenkonstruktion fabrikgefertigte Module entwickelt. Nach diesem Prinzip, das die beiden Architekten „Modern Modular" nennen, lassen sich Fertighäuser in unterschiedlichen Grundrissen und Größen realisieren, was ein individuelles Eingehen auf Kundenwünsche und eine Realisierung auf unterschiedlichsten Baugründen ermöglicht. Die Firma bietet allein 20 verschiedene Modelle an. Die Fertigbaumodule werden von verschiedenen Firmen hergestellt und per LKW an den Bauplatz geliefert.

2003 gewann das Büro mit dem Modern-Modular-Prinzip den aufsehenerregenden Wettbewerb des Architektur- und Wohnmagazins „Dwell". Inzwischen wurden mehrere Häuser nach dem Modern-Modular-Prinzip realisiert, darunter auch das „Dwell Home" und das „Mountain Retreat". Die Häuser sind nach neuesten ökologischen Kriterien hergestellt und eingerichtet. Sie verfügen über eine Solaranlage, geothermische Heizung und Kühlung, aluminiumverkleidete Niedrigenergiefenster und –türen und vieles mehr.

Das Dwell Home (das seinen Namen zu Ehren des preisverleihenden Magazins erhielt) wurde 2004 durch den Fertighaushersteller Carolina Building Solutions in Pittsboro im Staat North Carolina ausgeführt. Es ist eine zweistöckige Anlage, die über 190 m² Wohnfläche verfügt und aus zwei rechtwinklig ineinandergesteckten Riegeln gebildet ist. Der Wohn-, Ess- und Küchenbereich befindet sich im Erdgeschoss und kann zur großen Veranda hin geöffnet werden. Im sich darüber quer dazu erstreckenden Riegel befindet sich der private Teil des Hauses mit drei Schlafzimmern und zwei Badezimmern.

Resolution: 4 Architecture a été fondé par le duo d'architectes new-yorkais Joseph Tanney et Robert Luntz en 1990. Sur la base d'une ossature bois, le bureau a développé des modules préfabriqués. Selon ce principe – que les deux architectes ont baptisé « Modern Modular » – il est possible de réaliser des maisons préfabriquées de tailles et de plans variés, permettant par la même de répondre aux souhaits des clients et de construire sur un large éventail de terrains à bâtir. L'entreprise ne propose pas moins de 20 modèles différents. Les modules de construction préfabriqués sont produits par diverses entreprises et livrés sur le site de construction par camion.

Avec son principe de Modern Modular, le bureau remporta le concours très en vue du magazine d'architecture et d'habitat *Dwell* en 2003. Entre-temps, plusieurs maisons ont été réalisées selon ce principe, dont la Dwell Home et la Mountain Retreat. Les maisons sont produites et aménagées conformément aux tous derniers critères écologiques. Elles disposent d'un capteur solaire, d'un chauffage et d'un système de refroidissement géothermique, de fenêtres et de portes à économie d'énergie, et bien plus encore.

La Dwell Home (nom donné en l'honneur du magazine lui ayant attribué le prix) fut réalisée en 2004 par le fabricant de maisons préfabriquées Carolina Building Solutions à Pittsboro dans l'État de Caroline du Nord. C'est un bâtiment de deux étages, de plus de 190 m² de surface, composé de deux barres rectangulaires imbriquées l'une dans l'autre. Les coins salon, salle à manger et cuisine se trouvent au rez-de-chaussée et peuvent s'ouvrir sur la grande véranda. La barre s'étendant perpendiculairement au-dessus abrite la partie privée de la maison, avec trois chambres et deux salles de bains.

Construite en 2005 par le fabricant de maisons préfabriquées Apex Homes, avec ses 167 m² de surface habitable, la Mountain Retreat est un peu plus

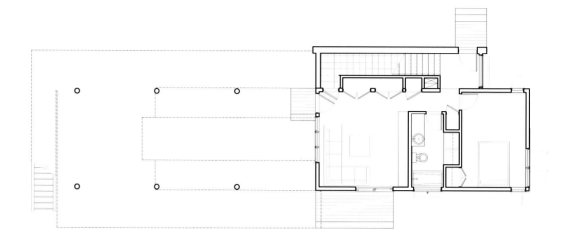

The Mountain Retreat in Kerhonkson, New York, 2005, follows the basic principle of the Lifted bar and the 2-story bar. Floor plans of the ground floor (above) and the upper floor (below).

Das Mountain Retreat in Kerhonkson, New York, 2005, folgt dem Grundtypus Lifted bar (aufgeständerter Riegel) und 2-story bar (zweistöckiger Riegel). Grundrisse von Erdgeschoss (oben) und Obergeschoss (unten)

La Mountain Retreat à Kerhonkson, New York, 2005, reprend le principe de base de la « Lifted bar » (barre surélevée) et de la « 2-story bar » (barre de deux étages). Plans du rez-de-chaussée (en haut) et du niveau supérieur (en bas)

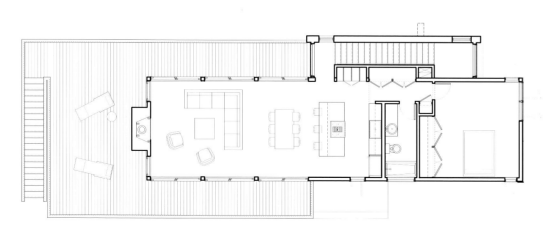

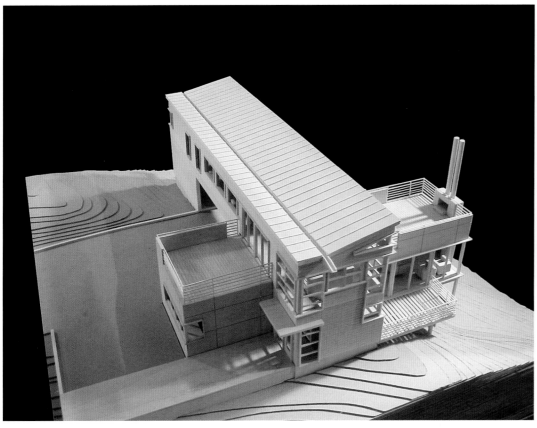

In the case of the Dwell Home in Pittsboro in Chatham County, North Carolina (above, photographs of a model) the building elements are combined in a different manner than in the Mountain Retreat (left page). The roof also has a different pitch, yet is still the characteristic butterfly style.

Beim Dwell Home in Pittsboro in Chatham County, North Carolina (Modellfotos oben) sind die Bauelemente anders zusammengefügt als beim Mountain Retreat (linke Seite). Auch das Dach ist anders geneigt, behält aber seine charakteristische Schmetterlingsform.

Pour la Dwell Home à Pittsboro dans le comté de Chatham, en Caroline du Nord (photos de maquette en haut), les éléments de construction sont agencés différemment que pour la Mountain Retreat (page de gauche). Même le toit a une pente différente, même s'il garde toujours la forme caractéristique d'un toit-papillon.

separately accessed residential unit. The actual residential levels are located above it, creating the impression of a tree house suspended in the crowns of the surrounding trees. The loft-like living space contains the kitchen and dining area and is surrounded by a cedar veranda on all three of its nearly fully glazed sides. The gray exterior of the cubic stairway stands in contrast to the horizontal lines of the cedar-clad façade. Inside, this alternation between light and dark is repeated in the interplay between the whitewashed bamboo floors and the dark countertops in the kitchen and the bathroom. A special feature of the design is the butterfly roof, the slant of which is echoed by trapezoidal windows just underneath it, which provide additional light. The architects even designed waterspouts that channel rainwater off the roof in decorative cascades.

Das Mountain Retreat, das 2005 durch den Fertighaushersteller Apex Homes ausgeführt wurde, ist mit 167 m² Wohnfläche etwas kleiner ausgefallen. Ein großer Teil des Baukörpers ruht auf schlanken Betonpfeilern. So entsteht auf Erdgeschossebene neben einer separat erschlossenen Wohnung noch ein Carportbereich. Die eigentliche Wohnebene befindet sich darüber und hat die Anmutung eines in den Baumkronen schwebenden Baumhauses. Der loftartige Wohnraum enthält auch Küche und Essbereich und ist auf seinen drei großflächig verglasten Seiten von einer Veranda aus Zedernholz umgeben. Das graue Äußere des kubischen Treppenhauses bildet einen Kontrast zu der horizontal verlaufenden Zedernholzfassade. Im Inneren wiederholt sich dieses Hell-Dunkel-Spiel im Wechselspiel der gekalkten Bambusböden zu den dunklen Arbeitsflächen, mit denen die Küchen- und Badezimmermöbel ausgestattet wurden. Besonderes Gestaltungselement ist das Schmetterlingsdach, unter dessen beiden Firsten trapezförmige Fenster die Schrägen nachvollziehen und für zusätzliches Licht sorgen. Selbst an Wasserspeier wurde gedacht, die das ablaufende Regenwasser in dekorativen Kaskaden ableiten.

petite. Le corps de bâtiment repose en grande partie sur de minces piliers de béton et forme un auvent de protection pour voitures jouxtant un appartement séparé s'ouvrant au niveau du rez-de-chaussée. Le niveau du séjour se trouve au-dessus et ressemble à une cabane flottant sur la cime des arbres. L'espace séjour de type loft regroupe la cuisine et la salle à manger et est flanqué d'une terrasse en bois de cèdre sur laquelle donnent les trois côtés dotés de grandes baies vitrées. L'extérieur gris de la cage d'escalier cubique tranche avec les panneaux de bois horizontaux de la façade en cèdre. À l'intérieur, ce jeu d'opposition clair-sombre est repris par le contraste des planchers en bambou enduits à la chaux et des plans de travail sombres recouvrant le mobilier de la cuisine et de la salle de bains. Le toit papillon constitue un élément architectonique particulier, sous les deux faîtes duquel des fenêtres trapézoïdes suivent les plans inclinés et fournissent un éclairage supplémentaire. Même la gargouille fut conçue de façon à évacuer l'eau de pluie en une cascade esthétique.

The original Dwell Home was the winning design of the Dwell Home Design Invitational. Sixteen architecture firms from the US and abroad were selected to submit design entries.

Der Prototyp des Dwell Home gewann den Ersten Preis für Design beim Ideenwettbewerb des Magazins „Dwell". Sechzehn Firmen aus dem In- und Ausland waren eingeladen, Entwürfe einzureichen.

Le prototype de la Dwell Home a gagné le premier prix du design du magazine Dwell. Seize bureaux d'architectes avaient été invités aux États-Unis et à l'international à présenter leurs projets.

FLATPAK HOUSE

Lazor Office LLC, Minneapolis, Minnesota, USA
2004–

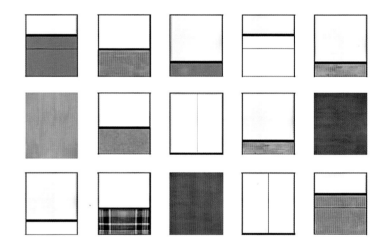

Opposite page: FlatPak house
in Woodstock, New York

Rechte Seite: FlatPak-Haus in
Woodstock, New York

Page de droite: Maison FlatPak
à Woodstock, New York

The reviews of the first FlatPak house in Minneapolis were euphoric. *Newsweek* described the FlatPak system as "the first revolution in American housing in decades." *Dwell* wrote, "FlatPak just might be the project that revolutionizes the prefab industry."
What made the system developed by Charlie Lazor and his Lazor Office so special was the flexibility it afforded builders. Every FlatPak house is developed on the basis of 8-ft.-wide wall elements, which can be combined at will. The step-by-step instructions on the Internet promise, "Every 8', you, along with your FlatPak designer make a decision: all glass, no glass, some glass, high glass, low glass, frosted glass, glass that opens, glass that doesn't." Wall elements made of wood, glass, concrete and stone are available. A FlatPak house can be up to four stories high and, on steep slopes, it can be built on stilts. The design calls for a roof at a slight angle. In arranging the rooms, the builder can choose one of a number of standard floor plans or design an individual floor plan within a 2-ft. grid. In designing the interior, the builder can choose from a variety of fittings offered by FlatPak. They can also be freely combined and installed. It doesn't matter whether you choose one, two, three, or four bathrooms.
The individual parts are produced in a factory in Wisconsin, delivered by

Die Kritiken über das erste FlatPak-Haus in Minneapolis waren euphorisch. „Newsweek" bezeichnete das FlatPak-System als „die erste Revolution im amerikanischen Hausbau seit Jahrzehnten", das Magazin „Dwell" schrieb: „FlatPak könnte das Projekt sein, das die Fertighausindustrie revolutioniert."
Das Besondere an dem von Charlie Lazor und seinem Lazor Office entwickelten System ist die Flexibilität, die es den Bauherren gewährt. Jedes FlatPak-Haus ist aus 1,44 m (8 Fuß) breiten, ein Geschoss hohen Wandelementen entwickelt, die beliebig kombiniert werden können. Die Schritt-für-Schritt-Anleitung im Internet verspricht: „Alle acht Fuß fällen Sie, gemeinsam mit Ihrem FlatPak-Designer, eine Entscheidung: nur Glas, kein Glas, etwas Glas, ein hohes Fenster, ein niedriges Fenster, Milchglas; ein Fenster, das man öffnen kann; ein Fenster, das man nicht öffnen kann." Zur Wahl stehen Wandelemente aus Holz, Glas, Beton und Stein. Bis zu vier Geschosse kann ein FlatPak-Haus hoch sein, in Hanglagen kann es auf Stelzen gestellt werden. Als Dach ist eine leichte Schräge vorgesehen. Bei der Anlage der Räume kann der Bauherr einen von mehreren Standard-Grundrissen wählen oder seinen ganz eigenen Grundriss entwerfen: innerhalb eines Rasters von 61 cm (2 Fuß). Bei der Innenausstattung kann der

La réaction des critiques face à la première maison FlatPak de Minneapolis fut euphorique. *Newsweek* qualifia le système FlatPak de «première révolution dans l'habitat américain depuis des décennies», et le magazine *Dwell* écrivit: «FlatPak pourrait bien être le projet qui révolutionnera l'industrie du préfabriqué.»
La particularité du système développé par Charlie Lazor et son agence Lazor Office est la flexibilité qu'elle garantit aux maîtres d'ouvrage. Chaque maison FlatPak est composée d'éléments muraux modulables à volonté de 1,44 m (8 pieds) de large et de la hauteur d'un niveau. Le mode d'emploi pas à pas trouvé sur Internet promet: «Tous les huit pieds, vous prenez une décision avec votre designer FlatPak: uniquement du verre, pas de verre, un peu de verre, une fenêtre haute, une fenêtre basse, du verre dépoli, une fenêtre que l'on peut ouvrir, une fenêtre que l'on ne peut pas ouvrir.» Le choix entre des éléments de murs en bois, verre, béton et pierre est proposé. Une maison FlatPak peut avoir jusqu'à quatre étages, être montée sur pilotis sur terrain en pente. Un toit légèrement incliné est prévu. En ce qui concerne la disposition des pièces, le maître d'ouvrage peut choisir entre divers plans au sol standard ou inventer son propre plan dans la limite d'une trame de 61 cm (2 pieds). Pour l'aménagement intérieur, il

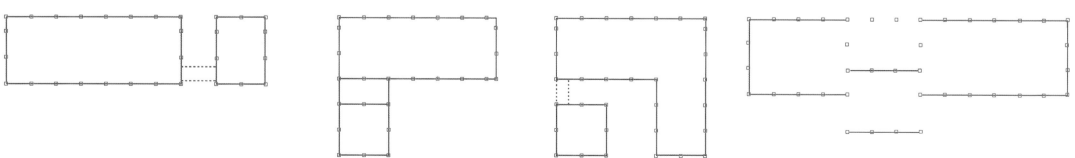

The prototype in Minneapolis, Minnesota (photos above and left page), design variations (below)

Der Prototyp in Minneapolis, Minnesota (oben und linke Seite), Entwurfsvarianten (unten)

Le prototype à Minneapolis, Minnesota (photos ci-dessus et page de gauche), variantes du projet (ci-dessous)

truck, boat, or helicopter, and assembled within a few days by a FlatPak fulfillment team. The prices depend upon the materials chosen and can be expected to range between $200 and $300 per square foot.

The man behind the idea, Charlie Lazor, studied architecture at Yale University, then opened an office for furniture design with two partners. He established the Lazor Office in 2003, in order to design architecture and consumer products. He built the first FlatPak house for his family in Minneapolis in 2004.

Bauherr die verschiedenen Einrichtungselemente, die FlatPak anbietet, ebenfalls frei kombinieren und platzieren. Ein, zwei, drei oder vier Badezimmer – kein Problem!

Die einzelnen Teile werden in einer Fabrik in Wisconsin hergestellt, per LKW, Boot oder Hubschrauber geliefert und innerhalb weniger Tage von einer FlatPak-Crew aufgebaut. Der Preis hängt von den gewählten Materialien ab, man sollte mit 200 bis 300 $ pro Quadratfuß (2150 bis 3200 $/m²) rechnen.

Der Mann hinter der Idee ist Charlie Lazor, der an der Yale University Architektur studierte, dann mit zwei Partnern ein Möbeldesignbüro eröffnete und 2003 das „Lazor Office" gründete, um neben Designprodukten auch Architektur zu entwerfen. Das erste FlatPak-Haus baute er 2004 in Minneapolis für sich und seine Familie.

peut combiner et disposer librement les différents éléments d'équipement que FlatPak propose : une, deux, trois, voire quatre salles de bains, aucun problème à cela !

Les différents éléments sont fabriqués dans une usine du Wisconsin, acheminés par camion, bateau ou hélicoptère et montés en quelques jours par une équipe FlatPak. Le prix dépend des matériaux choisis. Il faut compter entre 200 $ et 300 $ le pied carré (2150 $/m² à 3200 $/m²).

L'homme à l'origine de ce concept est Charlie Lazor, ancien étudiant d'architecture de la Yale University qui a ouvert son agence de design de meubles avec deux partenaires, et fondé le « Lazor Office » en 2003 afin de se consacrer également à la création architecturale, parallèlement aux produits design. Il a bâti la première maison FlatPak pour lui et sa famille à Minneapolis en 2004.

FlatPak houses in the Catskill Mountains, New York (exterior), in Woodstock, New York (living room) and Aspen, Colorado (bathroom)

FlatPak-Häuser in den Catskill Mountains, New York (Außenansicht), in Woodstock, New York (Wohnbereich) und in Aspen, Colorado (Badezimmer)

Maisons FlatPak dans les Catskill Mountains, New York (extérieur), à Woodstock, New York (séjour) et à Aspen, Colorado (salle de bains)

ROTORHAUS

Hanse-Haus GmbH, Oberleichtersbach, Germany
2004

The round window with its virtual mullions repeats the rotory motif of the floor plan.

Im Rundfenster wiederholt sich das Grundrissmotiv des Rotors als scheinbare Sprossenteilung.

Le motif du plan du rotor est repris sur la fenêtre ronde par des meneaux apparents.

Luigi Colani is always good for a surprise. On the occasion of the 75th anniversary of Hanse Haus, he created something very special: a compact prefabricated house on a floor plan measuring only 20 ft. x 20 ft., which nevertheless seems spacious. A fully functional model of this "residential study for the future" has been on exhibition at the Hanse Haus Visitors' Center in Oberleichtersbach, south of the city of Fulda, since 2004.

The goal in designing the house was to create maximum living space on the basis of minimum dimensions. Colani succeed in doing so by installing a sort of rotating stage in one of the corners, an innovation he refers to as a "rotor". It contains three different "functional areas": "sleeping", "cooking", and "bathing". When a button is pressed, the specially developed, silent "RotActions Module" is set in motion, turning the desired functional area towards the living space, thus making it a spacious kitchen, bedroom, or equally spacious bathroom. Each of the cells in the rotor measures 32 sq.ft., the living space itself measures 215 sq.ft., it is augmented by a small hallway, a toilet, and a built-in closet.

The model house is shaped like a simple box, but nevertheless seems just as dynamic as it does "organic" (Colani) due to the slight curve of the external walls and its rounded openings for the windows and the door. From the living room there is a clear view of the garden and terrace through floor-to-ceiling windows that include a sliding door. The interior is also dominated by the soft lines so typical of Colani. The building's outer shell is constructed in a manner that allows it to be stacked, if necessary. Like all of the Hanse Houses, the Rotor House is based on a wooden frame, which is glued together instead of being nailed. The interior is clad entirely in white plastic.

Luigi Colani ist immer für eine Überraschung gut. Zum 75. Firmenjubiläum der Firma Hanse-Haus entwarf er etwas ganz Besonderes: ein kompaktes Fertighaus, das auf einer Fläche von nur 6 x 6 m dennoch großzügige Räume bietet. Ein voll funktionsfähiges Modell dieser „Wohnstudie der Zukunft" kann man seit 2004 im Hanse-Haus-Wohnpark in Oberleichtersbach südlich von Fulda besichtigen.

Maximale Wohnfläche bei minimalem Außenmaß war das Ziel des Entwurfs, und das erreicht Colani mit Hilfe einer Art Drehbühne in einer Raumecke, von Colani selbst „Rotor" genannt. Sie enthält die „Funktionsbereiche" „Schlafen", „Kochen" und „Bad". Per Knopfdruck und mit Hilfe eines eigens entwickelten, lautlosen „RotActions"-Moduls wird der gewünschte Bereich in die Öffnung zum Wohnraum gedreht, der dadurch mal zur großzügigen Küche, mal zum ebenso großzügigen Badezimmer wird. Jeweils 3 m² messen die Zellen des Rotors, der Wohnraum selbst ist 20 m² groß. Dazu kommen ein kleiner Flur, die Toilette und ein Einbauschrank.

Das Musterhaus hat eine schlichte Kastenform, die durch die leichte Rundung der Außenwände und die Rundformen der eingeschnittenen Fenster und der Eingangstür gleichermaßen dynamisch wie „organisch" (Colani) wirkt. Vom Wohnraum öffnet sich durch eine große Glasfront mit Schiebetür der Blick auf Garten und Terrasse. Auch im Inneren finden sich überall die Colani-typischen weichen Formen. Der Baukörper ist so konstruiert, dass er sich gegebenenfalls stapeln lässt. Wie alle Hanse-Häuser ist auch das Rotorhaus eine Holzrahmen-Konstruktion, die nicht genagelt, sondern verleimt ist. Das Innere ist mit Kunststoff ganz in Weiß ausgekleidet.

Luigi Colani nous réserve toujours des surprises. À l'occasion du 75ᵉ anniversaire de l'entreprise Hanse-Haus, lui conçut un projet très particulier : une maison préfabriquée compacte offrant des pièces spacieuses en dépit de sa surface se limitant à 6 m x 6 m. On peut visiter une maison-témoin prête à l'usage de cette « étude d'habitat du futur » depuis 2004 dans le parc d'habitations de la Hanse-Haus à Oberleichtersbach, au sud de Fulda.

Une surface habitable maximale pour une dimension extérieure minimale : tel était l'objectif visé par Colani, qu'il parvint à atteindre en intégrant une sorte de plateau tournant dans l'angle d'une pièce, ledit « Rotor ». Cette surface comprend les « zones fonctionnelles » – couchage, cuisine et lavage. D'une simple pression sur un bouton, et par l'intermédiaire d'un module silencieux dit « RotActions » développé spécialement, la zone souhaitée apparaît dans l'ouverture s'ouvrant sur la salle de séjour, la transformant ainsi soit en une cuisine spacieuse, soit en une salle de bains tout aussi imposante. Chaque cellule du Rotor mesure 3 m² ; quant à la salle de séjour, elle fait 20 m². À cela s'ajoutent un petit vestibule, les toilettes, ainsi qu'un placard encastré. La maison-témoin a une simple forme de bloc qui, par le léger arrondi des murs extérieurs, des embrasures des fenêtres et de la porte d'entrée, confèrent un effet tant dynamique qu'« organique » (Colani) à l'ensemble. Depuis la salle de séjour, le regard donne sur le jardin et la terrasse à travers une grande baie vitrée à porte coulissante. L'intérieur est également empreint des douces formes caractéristiques de Colani. Le corps de bâtiment est construit de sorte à être éventuellement empilé. Comme toutes les maisons Hanse, la Rotorhaus est également une construction à ossature de bois, non pas clouée, mais encollée. L'intérieur présente un revêtement de plastique immaculé.

Right: Luigi Colani at the
presentation of the prototype
Rechts: Luigi Colani bei der
Präsenation des Prototyps
À droite : Luigi Colani lors de
la présentation du prototype

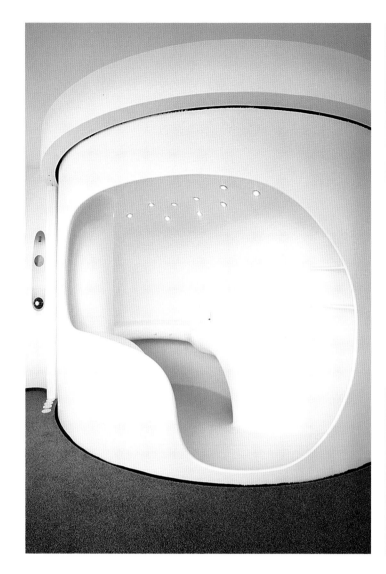

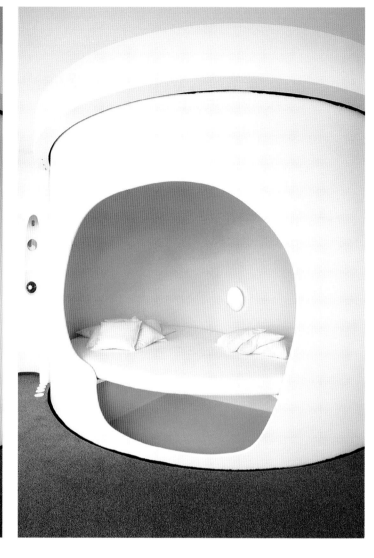

Size and shape of the rotor opening varies with its uses: The "bedroom" broadly resembles the cave-shape

Die Öffnung zum Rotor variiert mit der Nutzung: Das „Schlafzimmer" nähert sich der Höhlenform am meisten.

L'ouverture du rotor varie en fonction de son utilisation : la « chambre » ressemble le plus à une grotte.

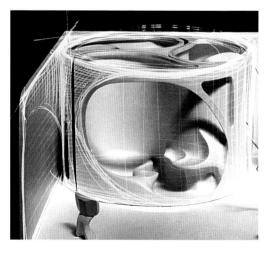

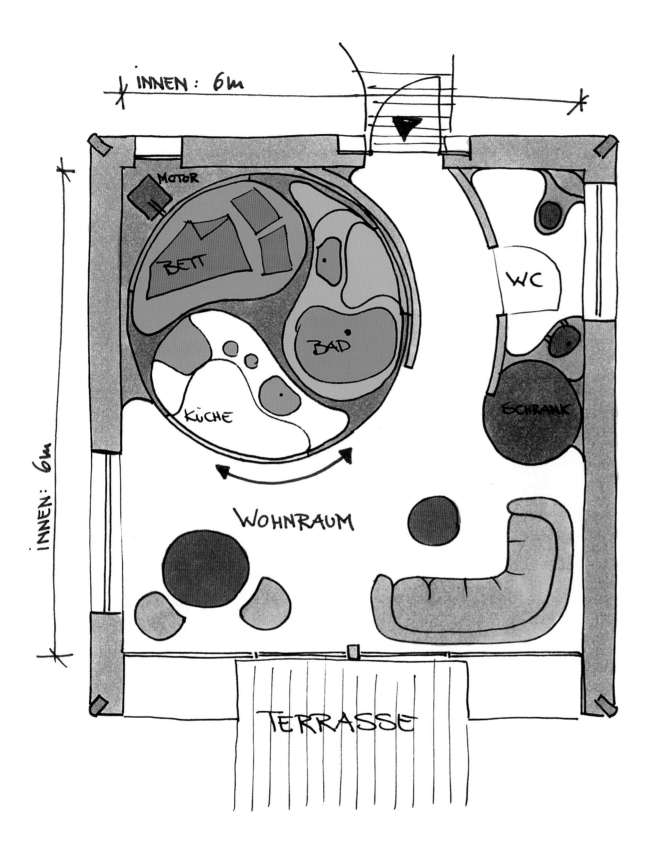

INNEN: 6m

INNEN: 6m

MOTOR

BETT

BAD

KÜCHE

WC

SCHRANK

WOHNRAUM

TERRASSE

Despite its small size, the little house has a hallway from which the toilet is accessed.

Trotz seiner geringen Größe verfügt das Häuschen über einen Flur, von dem aus die Toilette zugänglich ist.

Malgré sa taille réduite, la petite maison comporte une entrée d'où l'on accède aux toilettes.

ESPACE MOBILE

Meiberger Holzbau, Lofer, Austria
2004–2009

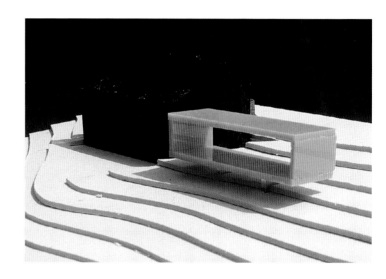

This concept displays the frame with a completely glazed front.

Das Modell zeigt die Konzeption des Rahmens, dessen Vorderseite voll verglast ist.

La maquette montre la structure dont la façade est totalement vitrée.

Imagine being required to move to a different city for a year for professional reasons and then subsequently taking the following year off in order to spend it in the mountains or near the ocean. How comfortable it would be, if it were possible to take your own house with you! There is a solution in cases like this: Espace mobile—the house you can take with you. You only need to buy a house once and then rent or buy a new piece of land whenever you need a place to put it.

The Espace mobile is a module that is produced in a factory, delivered by truck, and set down on the site by crane. The interior of the 53-ft.-long, 15-ft.-wide and 10-ft.-high cube can be divided flexibly and thus used for a variety of purposes: as an independent residence, as an extension to an existing house, as a temporary office, for example on a building site, as a classroom, an information stand, or a café. Once it has fulfilled its purpose, a crane and truck can come to transport it to another location. The building site that is left behind can then be used for a different purpose.

The Espace mobile is a wooden structure that adheres to low-energy standards. The model house, complete with its façade, windows, doors, flooring, plumbing, electrical installations and an open fireplace, was prefabricated within twelve days and made ready for occupancy on site within two—including all of the connections to public utilities. By 2009 it was available as a module in four different lengths at prices of between € 80,000 and € 140,000. The model house cost € 95,000.

It is bright inside due to a large glazed wall on one of the long sides. The

Stellen Sie sich vor, Sie müssen beruflich für ein Jahr in eine andere Stadt ziehen. Und danach wollen Sie sich endlich mal eine Auszeit nehmen und ein Jahr im Gebirge oder am Meer verbringen. Wie wäre es doch schön, man könnte mit dem eigenen Haus umziehen! Da gibt es eine Lösung: Espace mobile – das Haus zum Mitnehmen. Sie kaufen sich einmal ein Haus und mieten oder kaufen sich später nur immer wieder ein neues Stück Land, auf dem Sie es aufstellen lassen.

Das Espace mobile ist ein in der Fabrik vorgefertigtes Modul, das mit dem LKW angeliefert und per Kran auf seinen Standort gesetzt wird. Der 16 m lange, 4,50 m breite und 3 m hohe Kubus lässt sich innen flexibel unterteilen und ermöglicht daher vielfältige Nutzungen: als eigenständiges Wohnhaus, als Erweiterung eines bestehenden Hauses, als temporäres Büro etwa auf einer Baustelle oder auch als Klassenraum, als Inforaum oder als Café. Hat es seinen Zweck erfüllt, kommen Kran und LKW und bringen es woanders hin. Der zurückbleibende Baugrund kann nun anderweitig genutzt werden.

Das Espace mobile ist ein Holzbau in Niedrigenergiehaus-Standard. Das Modellhaus wurde mit Fassade, Fenster, Türen, Böden, Wasser-, Elektro- und Sanitär-Installationen und dem offenen Kamin binnen zwölf Tagen vorgefertigt und in zwei Tagen vor Ort bezugsfähig montiert, inklusive der Anschlüsse an die Ver- und Entsorgungsnetze. Als Modul wurde es bis 2009 in vier unterschiedlichen Längen angeboten, zu Preisen zwischen 80 000 und 140 000 €. Das Modellhaus kostete 95 000 €.

Imaginez-vous devoir partir une année dans une autre ville pour des raisons professionnelles. Après quoi vous souhaiteriez faire une pause et passer un an à la montagne ou à la mer. Ne serait-ce pas formidable de pouvoir déménager avec sa propre maison? Une solution existe : Espace mobile, la maison à emporter. Vous achetez une bonne fois pour toutes une maison et n'avez plus qu'à louer ou acheter ensuite un nouveau terrain sur lequel vous pouvez la faire monter.

L'Espace mobile est un module préfabriqué en usine destiné à être livré par camion et déposé sur son emplacement à l'aide d'une grue. L'intérieur de ce cube de 16 m de long, 4,50 m de large et 3 m de haut est facile à subdiviser, offrant ainsi de nombreuses utilisations possibles : comme maison d'habitation, comme extension d'une maison, comme bureau temporaire sur un chantier voire comme salle de classe, lieu d'information ou café. Une fois sa fonction remplie, grue et camion viennent la chercher pour l'acheminer ailleurs. Le terrain peut alors être utilisé à d'autres fins.

L'Espace mobile est une construction de bois aux normes des maisons à basse consommation d'énergie. La maison-témoin a été préfabriquée en 12 jours avec façade, fenêtres, portes, planchers, raccords d'eau et installations électriques et sanitaires, ainsi qu'une cheminée ouverte puis montée en deux jours sur site, raccordements et réseaux d'alimentation et d'évacuation inclus. Jusqu'en 2009, le module était décliné en quatre longueurs, à des prix allant de 80 000 à 140 000 €. La maison-témoin coûtait quant à elle 95 000 €.

The structure, up on stilts, can only be accessed via a bridge.

Der aufgeständerte Bau ist nur über eine Brücke zugänglich.

Surélevée sur pilotis, le bâtiment est uniquement accessible par un pont.

model house, located on a slope, can be reached over a catwalk. Painted red, with a terrace in front, it makes a very attractive impression. As a result of its subdued unadorned design, it is predestined to fit into a wide variety of environments.

This "mobile space" was developed by Simon Speigner and his office sps-architekten in Thalgau near Salzburg. Ultimately, it was never produced in series, and its purported mobility has yet to be put to the test. The model house developed for the Punto ese Project Development Company in Mondsee, Austria, is not only the sole example to date, it is also still in its original location.

Das Innere ist aufgrund der großen Glasfront an einer Längsseite sehr gut belichtet. In leichter Hanglage, zu erreichen über einen Steg, mit einer vorgesetzten Terrasse und dem roten Anstrich wirkt das Modellhaus auch optisch gelungen. Durch seine reduzierte schnörkellose Form ist es prädestiniert, in ganz unterschiedlichen Umgebungen aufgestellt zu werden. Entwickelt wurde der „mobile Raum" von Simon Speigner und seinem Büro sps-architekten in Thalgau bei Salzburg. Er sollte jedoch nicht in Serie gehen. Seine angepriesene Mobilität ist bisher nicht erprobt worden. Denn das für die Firma Punto ese Projektentwicklung GmbH in Mondsee in Österreich realisierte Modellhaus blieb nicht nur das einzige Exemplar, sondern es steht noch immer am gleichen Platz.

En raison de la grande baie vitrée se trouvant sur l'un des côtés longitudinaux, l'intérieur est très lumineux. Avec sa terrasse frontale et sa couleur rouge, cette maison située sur une pente douce à laquelle on accède par un chemin, est également du plus bel effet. Sa forme réduite dénuée d'ornementation la prédispose à s'adapter aux environnements les plus divers. L'Espace mobile a été développé par Simon Speigner et son bureau sps-Architekten à Thalgau près de Salzbourg. Il n'était toutefois pas destiné à une fabrication en série. Sa mobilité vantée n'a jusque-là pas été éprouvée. Car la maison-témoin réalisée par l'entreprise Punto ese Projektentwicklung GmbH à Mondsee en Autriche est non seulement l'unique exemplaire construit, mais il n'a en outre jamais quitté son emplacement.

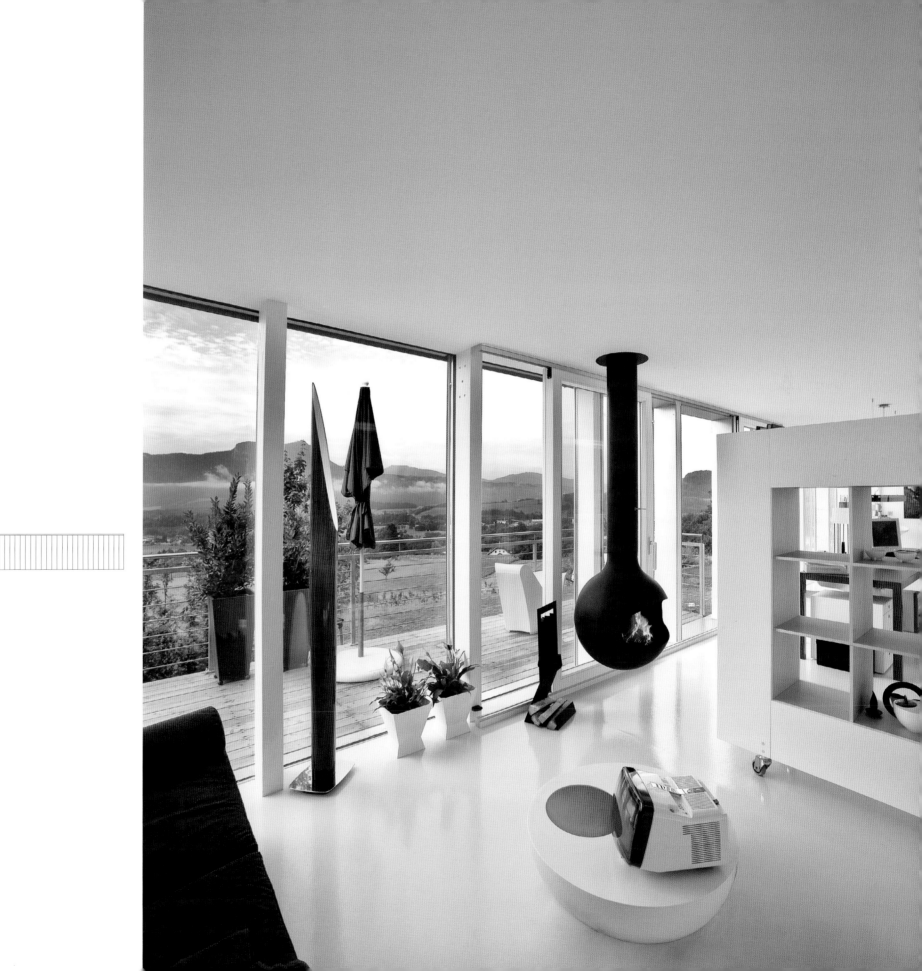

MUJI HOUSE

MUJI.net Co., Ltd., Tokyo, Japan
2004–

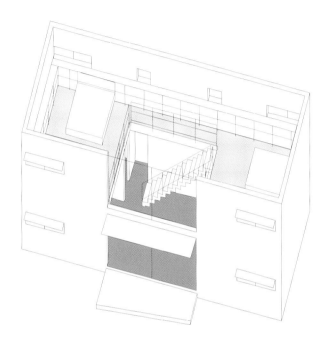

The axonometric drawing and the interior view illustrate the concept of a large, open interior.

Axonometrie wie Innenansicht zeigen das Konzept des großen, offenen Inenraums.

L'axonométrie et la vue intérieure illustrent le concept d'un intérieur spacieux et ouvert.

Kazuhiko Namba's Muji House is the first of two prefabricated houses developed by the architect in cooperation with the Japanese multistore Muji. The company had been previously known for its spectrum of products ranging from office articles to home furnishings through to a line of fashions.

Namba, who specializes in modular buildings, designed a simple residential cube with an open floor plan on the basis of reinforced concrete slab; it is particularly well suited to fit into dense urban contexts. While there is a small courtyard in front of the entry area on the street side of the house, the back of the extensively glazed house, clad in galvanized steel panels, faces a small garden area. Inside, a U-shaped gallery which provides space for sleeping and working, overlooks the two-story living and kitchen area.

With its various storage areas and a floor plan corresponding exactly to the furniture available at the store, the Muji Kit for $185,000, which is only available in Japan, is basically just the logical receptacle for the company's wide spectrum of products, ranging from their own soap dispenser to their own bed frame. The label is continuing to expand its involvement in the prefab segment: recently, Kengo Kuma designed two additional prefabricated house models for Muji.

Kazuhiko Nambas Muji-Haus ist das erste von zwei Fertighäusern, das von Architekten in Zusammenarbeit mit der japanischen Lifestyle-Kette Muji entwickelt worden ist. Das Unternehmen war bis zu diesem Zeitpunkt für seine Produktpalette von Büroartikeln über Einrichtungsgegenstände bis hin zu einer Modelinie bekannt.

Der auf modulare Bauten spezialisierte Namba hat auf der Basis einer Stahlbetonplatte einen einfachen, mit galvanisierten Stahlblechen verkleideten Wohnquader mit offenem Grundriss entworfen, der sich besonders dafür eignet, in beengte urbane Kontexte eingepasst zu werden. Während zur Straße hin dem Eingangsbereich ein kleiner Hof vorgelagert ist, öffnet sich das Haus großzügig verglast nach hinten zu einer kleinen Gartenparzelle. Innen erhebt sich über dem zweigeschossigen Wohn- und Küchenbereich eine U-förmige Galerie, in der der Schlaf- oder Arbeitsbereich untergebracht werden kann.

Mit seinen diversen Stauräumen und einem exakt auf die im eigenen Geschäft erhältlichen Möbel abgestimmten Grundriss ist das rund 185 000 $ teure, nur in Japan erhältliche Muji-System im Grunde die logische Ergänzung der unternehmenseigenen, alle Lebensbereiche abdeckenden Produktpalette von Haushalts- und Konsumwaren aller Art: vom Seifenspender bis zum Bettgestell. Muji hat sein Engagement auf dem Prefab-Sektor inzwischen noch ausgeweitet: Kengo Kuma hat vor kurzem zwei weitere Fertighaus-Modelle für die Handelskette entworfen.

La maison Muji de Kazuhiko Namba est la première de deux maisons préfabriquées développées par des architectes en collaboration avec la chaîne de magasin lifestyle japonais Muji. Jusque-là, l'entreprise était connue pour sa gamme de produits allant des articles de bureau à sa collection de mode, en passant par les objets d'équipement.

Spécialisé dans les constructions modulaires, Namba a conçu, sur la base d'une dalle de béton armé, un simple parallélépipède rectangle d'habitation à revêtement de tôle d'acier galvanisé à plan ouvert, idéal pour l'environnement exigu des villes. Du côté de la rue, l'entrée donne sur une petite cour. La maison s'ouvre à l'arrière par une grande baie vitrée sur une petite parcelle de jardin. À l'intérieur, au-dessus des deux niveaux accueillant l'espace séjour et la cuisine, se trouve une galerie en forme de U pouvant abriter la chambre ou le bureau.

Avec ses divers espaces de rangement et un plan précisément adapté aux meubles disponibles en magasin, le kit Muji – uniquement en vente au Japon au prix de 185 000 $ – constitue le complément logique de la gamme d'objets de la vie de tous les jours propre à l'entreprise, du distributeur de savon au cadre de lit. La marque poursuit son engagement dans le secteur du préfabriqué: récemment, Kengo Kuma a projeté deux nouveaux modèles de maisons préfabriquées pour Muji.

Plans of the ground floor (left) and
upper level (opposite page)

Grundrisse des Erdgeschosses
(links) und Obergeschosses (rechte
Seite)

Plans du rez-de-chaussée (à gauche)
et du niveau supérieur (page de
droite)

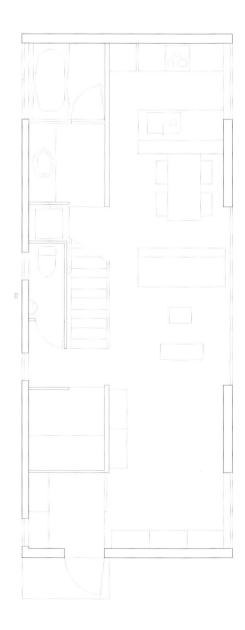

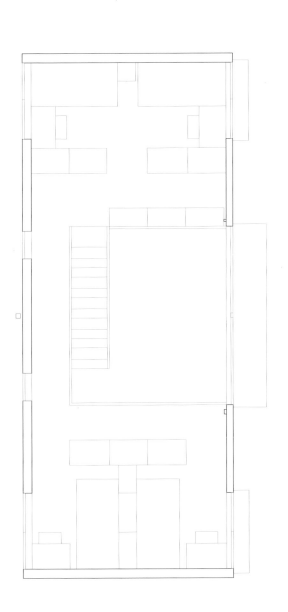

The open front of the house on a crowded building site (left) and with an extension of the roof over the balcony and the terrace (opposite page)

Die offene Front des Hauses auf einem beengten Grundstück (links) und mit einer Erweiterung des Daches über Balkon und Terrasse (rechte Seite)

La façade avant de la maison donnant sur un étroit terrain (à gauche) et avec une extension du toit au-delà du balcon et de la terrasse (page de droite)

Photovoltanic modules (Option)

Shelter 1 : Roof

Laminated timber frame

Plywood slab (Floor)

Shelter 2 : Wall

RC basement slab (Foundation)

Shelter 3 : Openings

HORDEN CHERRY LEE ARCHITECTS
HAACK + HÖPFNER . ARCHITEKTEN

MICRO-COMPACT HOME

micro compact home production gmbh, Uttendorf, Austria
2005–

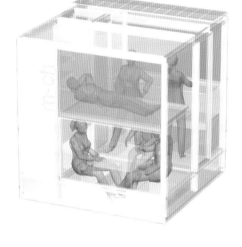

Munich, world famous as an Eldorado among bier lovers, is not exactly a paradise for students in search of housing. There is not enough and it is expensive. It was against this background that architecture students were called upon to develop a spatial concept for a minimal residential cell within the context of a seminar. It resulted in the design of a cubic micro house called "i-home", and it was so remarkable that it was even featured in national media.

Now sponsors were eager to support the idea, including the mobile telephone company O2. After the cube was further developed by the architectural office Haack + Höpfner, in cooperation with Richard Horden, and then named micro-compact home (m-ch), the first seven were erected in the "O2 Village", within the students' village in the Munich district of Freimann, at the beginning of the winter semester 2005. There they not only attracted attention, but also great recognition: the Federation of German Architects awarded the m-ch its prize for residential construction in 2006. In 2007 it had the honor of being presented within the context of the MoMA exhibition *Home Delivery: Fabricating the Modern Dwelling* as a commissioned project.

This residential cube measuring nearly 8 ft. 9 in. on the edges, and with only 76 sq.ft. of floor space, features cutting-edge technology and combines all of the functional areas of a conventional house by making use of the full height of the room. The wooden skeleton structure is clad on the outside in flat anodized aluminum panels and on the inside in PVC. The flooring material is based on an epoxy compound, and the windows are double-glazed. In order to achieve good thermal performance, a special vacuum insulation was chosen. The unit, which costs between €25,000 and €35,000 and produced by Gatterbauer in Austria, weighs 2.2 tons and can be delivered by truck or even on a trailer pulled by a car. Not a square inch of the m-ch is wasted space. After stepping into the

München ist nicht gerade ein elysisches Gefilde für wohnungssuchende Studenten. Unterkünfte sind knapp und teuer. Vor diesem Hintergrund wurde 2001 Architekturstudenten im Rahmen eines Entwurfsseminars die Aufgabe gestellt, das Raumkonzept einer minimierten Wohnraumzelle zu entwickeln. Das Ergebnis war der Entwurf eines würfelförmigen Mikro-Hauses namens „i-home", und der war so bemerkenswert, dass sogar die überregionale Presse darüber berichtete.

Nun wurden auch Sponsoren für die Idee begeistert, darunter der Mobilfunkanbieter O2. Nachdem der Würfel vom Architekturbüro Haack + Höpfner in Gemeinschaftsarbeit mit Richard Horden weiterentwickelt und micro-compact home (m-ch) getauft worden war, wurden die ersten sieben Exemplare zu Beginn des Wintersemesters 2005 im „O2 Village" auf dem Gelände des Studentendorfs in München-Freimann aufgestellt. Dort wurde ihnen nicht nur Aufmerksamkeit, sondern auch höchste Anerkennung zuteil: Vom Bund Deutscher Architekten wurde dem m-ch der Preis 2006 in der Kategorie Wohnungsbau zuerkannt. Und 2007 wurde ihm die Ehre zuteil, auf der Moma-Ausstellung „Home Delivery: Fabricating the Modern Dwelling" als Auftragsprojekt präsentiert zu werden.

Der Wohnwürfel von 2,66 m Kantenlänge und einer Grundfläche von nur 7 m² enthält die neuesten technischen Errungenschaften, und unter voller Ausnutzung der Raumhöhe vereinigt er alle Funktionsbereiche eines konventionellen Hauses. Die Konstruktion basiert auf einem Holzskelett, das außen mit flachen, eloxierten Aluminiumpaneelen und innen mit PVC verkleidet ist. Der Bodenbelag ist auf Epoxidbasis hergestellt, die Fenster sind doppelt verglast. Um eine gute Dämmung zu erreichen, wurde eine spezielle Vakuumisolierung gewählt. Die Einheit, die zwischen 25 000 € und 35 000 € kostet und in Österreich von der Firma Gatterbauer hergestellt wird, wiegt 2,2 Tonnen und kann per LKW und sogar auf einem PKW-Anhänger geliefert werden.

Munich, ville mondialement célébrée comme l'Eldorado des amateurs de bière, n'est pas exactement ce que l'on pourrait appeler un paradis pour les étudiants à la recherche d'appartements. Les logements y sont rares et chers. Au vu de cette situation, dans le cadre d'un cours sur la conception de projet, des étudiants en architecture reçurent pour mission en 2001 de développer un concept pour une cellule d'habitation minimaliste. Il en résulta le projet d'une micro-maison de forme cubique appelée « i-home », dont il fut également question dans la presse nationale.

Ce concept enthousiasma aussi des sponsors, dont l'opérateur de téléphonie mobile O2. Après la transformation du cube par le bureau d'architecture Haack + Höpfner, en collaboration avec Richard Horden, et le baptême de la micro-compact home (m-ch), les sept premiers exemplaires furent installés au début du semestre d'hiver 2005 au O2 Village sur le terrain du village étudiant de Munich-Freimann. Outre la grande attention dont ils firent l'objet, ils gagnèrent une grande reconnaissance. Dans la catégorie Construction de logements, la m-ch reçut le prix 2006 de la Fédération des architectes allemands. En 2007, ils eurent l'honneur d'être présentés dans le cadre de l'exposition du MoMA « Home Delivery: Fabricating the Modern Dwelling » comme projet de commande.

Ce cube d'habitation de 2,66 m de côté et d'une surface de seulement 7 m² concentre les toutes dernières avancées techniques, ainsi que toutes les zones fonctionnelles d'une maison conventionnelle, et tire totalement profit de la hauteur sous plafond. La structure repose sur une ossature de bois recouverte de panneaux d'aluminium anodisé plats à l'extérieur et de PVC à l'intérieur. Le revêtement du plancher est fabriqué avec de l'époxy, les fenêtres sont à double vitrage. Pour une bonne isolation, le choix s'est porté sur une isolation sous vide spéciale. L'unité fabriquée par l'entreprise Gatterbauer en Autriche coûte entre 25 000 € et 35 000 €. Elle pèse 2,2 t et peut être livrée par camion, voire même sur une remorque de voiture.

The low-energy model m-ch is
powered by electricity provided by
86 sq.ft. of photovoltaic panels and a
small vertical axis wind turbine on
the roof.

Das Niedrigenergie-Modell des m-ch
wird elektrisch betrieben, die Stromversorgung wird durch 8 m² Solarzellen und einen kleinen Windgenerator
mit vertikaler Achse auf dem Dach
gewährleistet.

Le modèle m-ch à basse
consommation d'énergie est alimenté
par l'électricité produite par 8 m² de
cellules photovoltaïques et une petite
éolienne à axe vertical sur le toit.

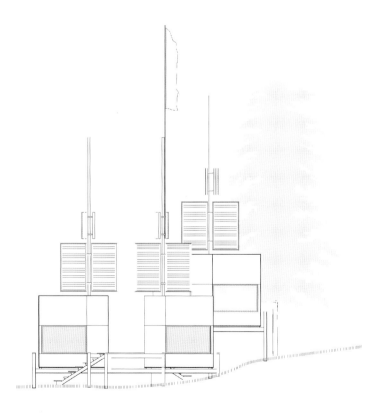

house through the first sliding door, the visitor finds himself in an entryway that also serves as a shower, the doormat is in the shower basin. One only needs to turn to the right to reach the toilet. The actual living space is entered by going through a second sliding door, on the right is a kitchen unit with the most modern appliances, on the left is a bed suited for a student who has no desire to make one—it simply folds up against the wall. The house includes other features to make studying easier: people who get great ideas in their sleep can slip right down from their beds and capture their inspiring thoughts on paper or type them into a computer at the desk located next to it—thus gliding from the sphere of dreams into sphere of work. The micro house, despite its small size, strictly separates the sleeping and living areas. However, in order to ensure that this cell for students does not seem too much like a monk's cell, the bed is big enough for two; there is also enough room, and places to sit at the desk, to allow time to be spent with friends over chips and beer—and if things escalate to a Bacchanal, the seat can be turned into a guest bed. In order to prevent attacks of claustrophobia, the residential cube has big windows that connect the interior with the exterior.

Kein Quadratzentimeter wurde bei dem m-ch vergeudet. Man betritt das Haus durch die erste Schiebetür, gelangt in den Vorraum und steht damit im Duschbecken, das gleichzeitig als Schuhabstreifer dient. Dort muss man sich nur nach rechts wenden und sich niederlassen – schon sitzt man auf dem Stillen Örtchen. Durch die zweite Schiebetür gelangt man in den eigentlichen Wohnraum: rechts eine Kücheneinheit mit modernsten Geräten, links das studentenfreundliche „Kein-Bock-auf-Aufräumen-Bett", das hochgeklappt werden kann. Ohnehin ist das Haus dem Studium ausgesprochen förderlich: Wem es der Herr im Schlafe gibt, der muss sich nur vom Bett vor den darunter befindlichen Arbeitstisch fallen lassen und kann seine Inspirationen zu Papier bzw. zu Notebook bringen – und ist dabei auch räumlich aus der Sphäre des Traumes in die der Arbeit hinübergeglitten. Denn so klein es auch ist, im Mikro-Haus lassen sich Schafen und Wohnen strikt voneinander trennen. Damit andererseits aus der Studenten- keine Mönchsklause wird, bietet das Bett Platz für zwei; außerdem ist um den Arbeitstisch noch genügend Platz und Sitzgelegenheit vorhanden, um sich mit ein paar Freunden bei Bier und Chips zu vergnügen – und sollte die Angelegenheit als bacchantisches Gelage enden, kann die Sitzgelegenheit zum Gästebett umfunktioniert werden. Um klaustrophobischen Attacken vorzubeugen, verfügt der Wohnwürfel über große Fenster, die den Innenraum mit dem Außen verbinden.

Dans la m-ch, pas un centimètre carré n'a été négligé. On rentre dans la maison par une première porte coulissante, arrive dans une entrée et se retrouve alors dans la cabine de douche qui sert aussi de rangement pour les chaussures. De là, il suffit de se tourner vers la droite pour s'installer directement au petit coin. Passée la deuxième porte coulissante, on arrive dans le véritable séjour avec, à droite, une petite cuisine équipée avec les appareils les plus modernes et, à gauche, adapté aux étudiants, le lit «qui peut bien rester encore défait» que l'on peut relever. La maison reste toutefois vraiment propice à l'étude: lorsque le cœur lui en dit, l'étudiant peut se laisser tomber de son lit vers son bureau situé juste en dessous, et coucher son inspiration sur le papier ou dans son portable, en ayant simplement glissé du royaume des rêves vers celui du travail. Car aussi petite soit-elle, la micro-maison sépare distinctement les fonctions dormir et habiter. Et comme ce n'est pas une cellule monastique, le lit offre deux places et le bureau est assez spacieux et doté d'un canapé pour accueillir quelques amis autour d'une bière et d'un plat de chips. Au cas où cela dégénèrerait en beuverie, le canapé peut être transformé en lit d'amis. Afin de prévenir les crises de claustrophobie, le cube d'habitation jouit d'une grande fenêtre qui fait le lien entre l'espace intérieur et extérieur.

Views of the student village at
Munich-Freimann

Ansichten des Studentendorfes in
München-Freimann

Vue du village étudiant à Munich-
Freimann.

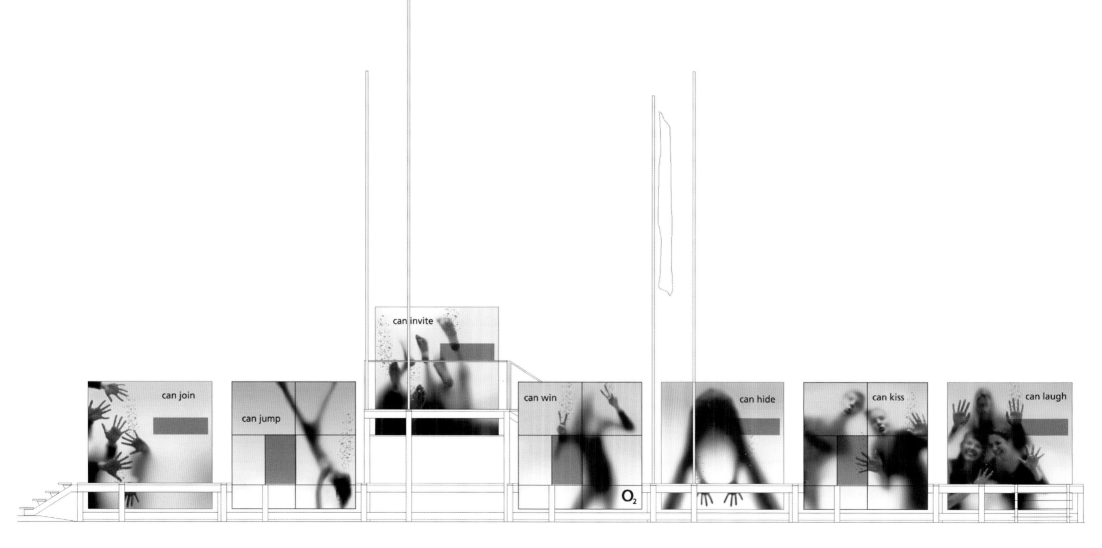

Left: A cube being delivered
by a building crane
Links: Anlieferung eines Würfels
mit einem Baukran
À gauche: Livraison d'un cube
par une grue de chantier

Right: Latitudinal and cross section
Rechts: Längs- und Querschnitt
À droite: Coupe longitudinale et
transversale

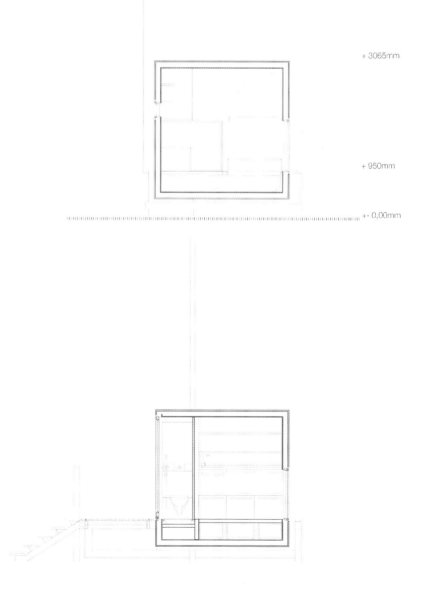

+ 3065mm

+ 950mm

+– 0,00mm

An inhabited student cube
Der bewohnte Studentenwürfel
Un cube étudiant habité

BLACK BARN

Pinc House AB, Stockholm, Sweden
2005–

With its distinctive pitched-roof
and elongated design, Black Barn is
a modern adaptation of the Viking
longhouse.

Mit seinem charakteristischen
Giebeldach und der langgestreckten
Konzeption ist das „Black Barn" eine
moderne Adaption der Langhäuser
aus der Wikingerzeit.

Avec son toit à pignon
caractéristique et sa forme allongée,
la Black Barn est une adaptation
moderne des longères du temps des
Vikings.

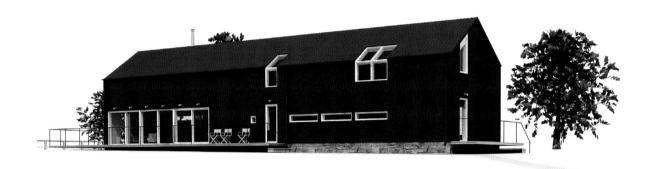

Pinc House of Stockholm ranks among the architectural offices noteworthy for having brought prefabricated houses onto the market that combine quality design with high standards in terms of building ecology and energy efficiency. In cooperation with the Ittur Group, the office offers three prefabricated houses in four different sizes. The most recent model was introduced in 2005, for which Pinc House won the prestigious Red Dot Design Award that same year.

With its black-tarred wooden roof, elongated central space, and visible interior roof beams, the Black Barn, designed by Maria Rutensköld, Johan Lionell and Jan Rutensköld, is a modern interpretation of the indigenous long house which has a tradition dating back to the Vikings. Unlike traditional longhouses, the black-washed pine mass of the building's exterior is perforated by numerous windows. Inside, black and white are the predominant colors.

The largest of the four Black Barn models has nearly 2,600 sq.ft. of floor space and a loft-like, open floor plan, with two bathrooms and two bedrooms on the ground floor, while a master suite and a large multifunctional space, along with a sauna and a laundry, are on the top floor.

There is also a version of the Black Barn for terraced housing developments. Each of the houses has its own garage. The open living area is on the lower level, but has a high ceiling that extends its height to that of the upper level. The bedrooms are on the upper level.

Zu den Architektenbüros, die Fertighäuser auf den Markt gebracht haben, bei denen sich Entwurfsqualität mit hohen baubiologischen und energietechnischen Maßstäben verbindet, gehört das Stockholmer Pinc House. Zusammen mit der Ittur Group bietet das Büro drei verschiedene Fertighäuser in jeweils vier unterschiedlichen Größen an. Das jüngste der drei Modelle ist das 2005 auf den Markt gebrachte Black Barn, mit dem Pinc House noch im selben Jahr den prestigeträchtigen Red Dot Design Award gewann.

Mit seinem schwarz geteerten Holzdach, dem langgestreckten Zentralraum und den innen sichtbar verlaufenden Dachbalken ist das von Maria Rutensköld, Johan Lionell und Jan Rutensköld entworfene Black Barn eine moderne Adaption des germanischen Langhauses, das auf Traditionen der Wikingerzeit zurückgeht. Anders als traditionelle Langhäuser verfügt der mit schwarz lasiertem Kiefernholz verkleidete Baukörper jedoch über zahlreiche Fensteröffnungen. Im Gebäudeinneren dominieren die Farben Schwarz und Weiß.

Das größte der vier Black-Barn-Modelle hat einen loftartig sich öffnenden Grundriss von 240 m² und verfügt im Erdgeschoss über zwei Bäder und zwei Schlafzimmer, während sich im Obergeschoss eine Mastersuite, ein großer, multifunktional nutzbarer Raum, eine Sauna und eine Wäschekammer befinden.

Es gibt auch eine Variante des Black Barn als Reihenhausanlage. Jedes der Reihenhäuser enthält eine Garage. Im unteren Stockwerk liegt der offen gestaltete Wohnbereich, der sich über einen Luftraum in das obere Stockwerk erstreckt. Dort befinden sich die Schlafzimmer.

Le cabinet Pinc House de Stockholm compte parmi les bureaux d'architectes ayant mis sur le marché des maisons préfabriquées alliant qualité du concept et normes de construction biologique et de technologie énergétique élevées. En collaboration avec l'Ittur Group, Pinc House propose trois maisons préfabriquées différentes, disponibles chacune en quatre tailles. Le modèle le plus récent est la Black Barn, commercialisée en 2005, avec laquelle Pinc House a gagné le prestigieux Red Dot Design Award la même année.

Avec son toit en bois recouvert de goudron, sa longue pièce centrale et les entraits visibles à l'intérieur, la Black Barn conçue par Maria Rutensköld, Johan Lionell et Jan Rutensköld est une adaptation moderne de la longère germanique, traditionnelle depuis l'ère des Vikings. Mais à la différence des longères traditionnelles, ce bâtiment au revêtement de pin enduit de lasure noire comporte de nombreuses ouvertures. L'intérieur est dominé par des tons noir et blanc.

Le plus grand des quatre modèles de la Black Barn se caractérise par un plan ouvert de type loft de 240 m² et accueille deux salles de bains et deux chambres au rez-de-chaussée, tandis que l'étage abrite une suite de maître, une grande pièce multifonction, un sauna et une buanderie.

Il existe également une variante de la Black Barn comme maison en enfilade. Chacune de ces maisons comporte un garage. L'étage inférieur accueille une partie séjour ouverte qui s'élève jusqu'à l'étage supérieur où se trouvent les chambres.

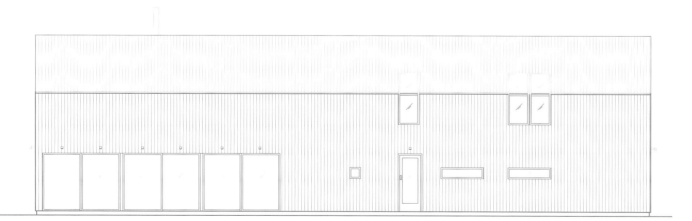
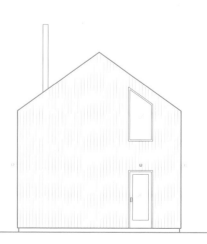

The sculptural mass of the black-washed wood exterior contrasts with the lightness of its interior, which features walls and pine floors painted white.

Die massiv erscheinenden, schwarz lasierten Holzaußenflächen bilden einen starken Kontrast zu der Leichtigkeit des Innenraumes mit Wänden und Fußböden aus weiß-gestrichenem Kiefernholz.

L'apparence massive du revêtement extérieur enduit de lasure noire contraste avec la légèreté de l'intérieur et de ses murs et planchers en bois de pin peints en blanc.

Bathrooms on the ground floor (left)
and on the upper level (right)

Badezimmer im Erdgeschoss (links)
und Obergeschoss (rechts)

Salle de bains au rez-de-chaussée
(à gauche) et à l'étage supérieur
(à droite)

Floor plans of the ground floor (left)
and the upper level (right)

Grundrisse von Erdgeschoss (links)
und Obergeschoss (rechts)

Plans du rez-de-chaussée (à gauche)
et de l'étage supérieur (à droite)

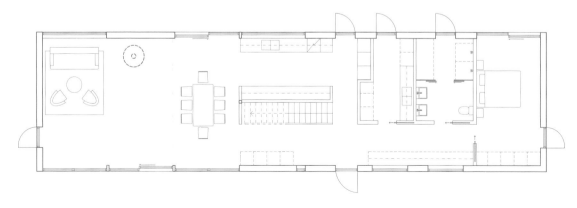

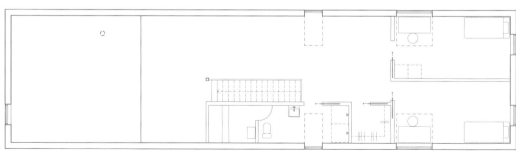

ERIC BIGOT

ZENKAYA

ZenKaya Ecohomes, Pretoria, South Africa
2005–

"Imagine a place where your soul is at peace. This place already exists. ZenKaya, for your peace of mind." It is no coincidence that Eric Bigot called his architectural office ZenKaya: this Japanese-South African linguistic creation means "Zen house". His ecohomes are very straightforward in terms of form and function, low in cost, built, delivered, and installed within a few weeks. They are also easy to purchase: since Bigot argues that the purchase of a house should be no more complicated than the purchase of an car. This French architect, who has worked in New York, Japan and many African countries, now lives in South Africa.

ZenKaya houses are available in various sizes "from S to XL". They are completely prefabricated and delivered to the building site by truck. Thus, their width is standardized at 11 ft.; the ceiling height is 8 ft. They vary only in terms of their length: the smallest version, the "ZenKaya Studio" is 20 ft. in length (67 sq. ft.) and has an all-purpose space—a kitchenette if desired—and a separate bathroom. The largest model is the 60-ft. "ZenKaya two bedrooms" with a living room, dining room, kitchen, two bedrooms, and a bathroom (610 sq. ft.).

The ZenKaya House earned the praise of architectural critics as a result of its both simple and dynamic appearance: the ceiling and floor are connected on one end of the house, forming a continuous band of white that encompasses it like a U flipped over on one side. The main façade is determined by the internal division of space: the façade in front of the bathroom is paneled in wood, while the façade in front of the main room is not only fully glazed, but can also be completely opened, letting the outside in. A veranda is located on the other end of the house and enclosed within its cubic

„Stellen Sie sich ein Haus vor, in dem Ihre Seele zur Ruhe kommt. Dieses Haus gibt es bereits. ZenKaya – für Ihren Seelenfrieden." Es ist kein Zufall, dass Eric Bigot sein Architekturbüro ZenKaya genannt hat: Zen-Haus bedeutet diese japanisch-südafrikanische Sprachkombination. Und tatsächlich sind seine „Öko-Häuser" klar in Form und Funktion, sie sind preiswert, werden binnen weniger Wochen gebaut, geliefert und aufgestellt – und sie sind einfach in der Anschaffung: Denn der Kauf eines Hauses, fordert Bigot, sollte nicht aufwendiger sein als der eines Autos. Der französische Architekt hat in New York, Japan und verschiedenen afrikanischen Staaten gearbeitet und lebt derzeit in Südafrika.

ZenKaya-Häuser gibt es in verschiedenen Größen „von S bis XL". Sie werden komplett vorgefertigt und per LKW an den Bauplatz gebracht. Deshalb ist ihre Breite standardisiert auf 3,40 m; die Raumhöhe beträgt 2,40 m. Sie unterscheiden sich allein in der Länge: Die kleinste Variante ist das „ZenKaya Studio", das auf 6 m Länge (20,4 m²) einen Allzweckraum – auf Wunsch mit Kochzeile – und ein separates Badezimmer aufweist. Größtes Modell ist das rund 18 m lange „ZenKaya Two Bedrooms" mit Wohn-/Esszimmer und Küche, zwei Schlafzimmern und einem Bad (56,7 m²).

Was dem ZenKaya-Haus viel Lob der Architekturkritik eingebracht hat, ist sein ebenso schlichtes wie dynamisches Erscheinungsbild: Decke und Boden sind an einer Schmalseite zu einem durchgängigen weißen Band verbunden, das wie ein auf die Seite gekipptes weißes U das Haus umfängt. Die Schauseite zeigt deutlich die innere Raumeinteilung: Die Außenwand des Badezimmers ist hier fensterlos mit Holz verkleidet; die Wand des Hauptraumes ist komplett in Glas aufgelöst und lässt sich vollständig

«Imaginez une maison où votre âme trouverait la tranquillité. Une telle maison existe bel et bien. ZenKaya – pour votre paix intérieure.» Ce n'est pas un hasard si Eric Bigot a dénommé son agence d'architecture «ZenKaya»: cette association linguistique japonaise et sud-africaine signifie «maison zen». Et ses maisons écologiques sont effectivement dotées d'une forme et d'une fonction simples, sont bon marché, peuvent être construites, livrées et posées en quelques semaines. De plus, leur acquisition est facile, car l'achat d'une maison ne doit pas être plus complexe que celui d'une voiture. Telle est l'exigence de Bigot, architecte français ayant travaillé à New York, au Japon et dans divers pays d'Afrique, et résidant actuellement en Afrique du Sud.

Les maisons ZenKaya existent en différentes tailles, «du S au XL». Elles sont intégralement préfabriquées puis acheminées par camion sur le terrain à bâtir. C'est pourquoi leur largeur est standardisée à 3,40 m et la hauteur sous plafond est de 2,40 m. Seule leur longueur les différencie: la version la plus petite, le «ZenKaya Studio» (20,4 m²) présente, sur une longueur de 6 m, une pièce à tout faire – avec kitchenette sur demande – et une salle de bains séparée. Sur près de 18 m de longueur, la «ZenKaya Two Bedrooms» (56,7 m²), le plus grand modèle, abrite un salon-salle à manger et une cuisine, deux chambres à coucher et une salle de bains.

Aussi sobre que dynamique, son aspect extérieur a valu à la maison ZenKaya les louanges de la critique d'architecture: sur l'un des côtés étroits, plafond et plancher se rejoignent pour former une bande blanche continue, entourant la maison tel un U blanc couché sur le côté. L'apparence de la façade reprend la division intérieure des pièces: aveugle, le mur extérieur de

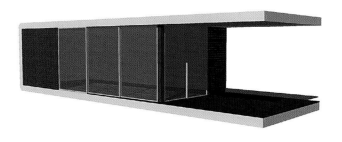

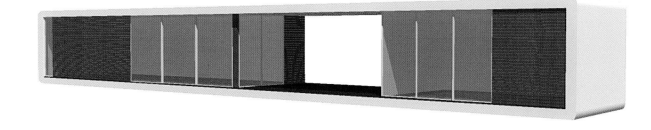

12000

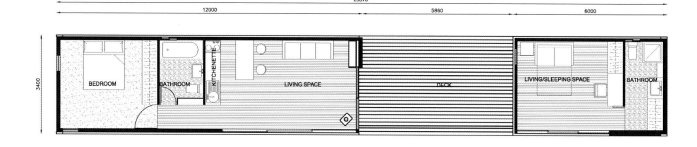

23870

12000   5860   6000

3400

BATHROOM   KITCHENETTE   LIVING/SLEEPING SPACE   DECK

SHOWER

3400

BEDROOM   BATHROOM   KITCHENETTE   LIVING SPACE   DECK   LIVING/SLEEPING SPACE   BATHROOM

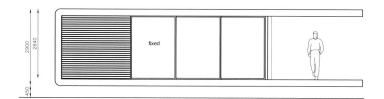

2900
2640

fixed

450

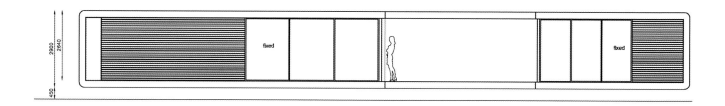

2900
2640

fixed   fixed

450

The drawings show the ZenKaya loft layout (left) and one bedroom and studio layout (right)

Zeichnungen der Raumanordnungen des Zenkaya Loft (links), Anordnungen von Schlafzimmer und Studio (rechts)

Les dessins montrent les dispositions de la ZenKaya Loft (à gauche) et de la chambre et de l'atelier (à droite)

There are not only two types of wall construction, using different types of insulation, but also numerous surfaces to choose from.

Es stehen nicht nur zwei Versionen für den Wandaufbau mit unterschiedlicher Isolierung, sondern auch zahlreiche Oberflächen zur Auswahl.

Il existe non seulement deux variantes de murs avec différents types d'isolation, mais aussi de nombreuses surfaces au choix.

form by virtue of the overhanging roof and extended floor structure. The main room and the veranda are only separated by a sliding-glass door that can also be completely opened.

Bigot describes this as "responsible design". "When a designer is forced to meet all the program requirements on a defined space, the result is often a pure and logical design, leaving unnecessary bells and whistles behind." However, if the client wishes to do so, he can choose a different fit out for the kitchen and bath, walls and floors.

öffnen, wodurch der Innenraum mit dem Außenbereich verschmilzt. Der Schmalseite vorgesetzt und durch Dach und Bodenplatte in die Kubatur des Hauses eingebunden ist eine Veranda. Hauptraum und Veranda sind durch eine Schiebetür aus Glas getrennt, die ebenfalls vollständig geöffnet werden kann.

Bigot nennt seinen Entwurf „responsible design": „Wenn ein Designer gezwungen ist, alle Ansprüche auf einem vorgegebenen Raum zu erfüllen, ist das Resultat oft klar und logisch – was nicht wirklich nötig ist, wird fortgelassen." Wenn der Bauherr es wünscht, kann er folglich auch andere Ausstattungselemente für Küche und Bad, Wände und Boden wählen.

la salle de bains présente ici un revêtement de bois, tandis que le mur de la pièce principale fait place à une baie vitrée qu'il est possible d'ouvrir totalement, permettant ainsi la fusion de l'intérieur et de l'extérieur. Devant le côté étroit, intégrée au cubage de la maison par le toit et le radier, se trouve une véranda. La pièce principale et la véranda sont séparées par une porte coulissante en verre qui peut également être ouverte en grand.

Bigot qualifie son projet de «responsible design» (création responsable): «Lorsqu'un designer doit respecter toutes les exigences d'un programme en un espace très limité, le résultat obtenu est souvent un design pur et logique: ce qui n'est pas absolument nécessaire passe à la trappe.» Lorsque le maître d'ouvrage le souhaite, il peut donc aussi choisir d'autres éléments d'ameublement pour la cuisine et la salle de bains, les murs et les planchers.

FREEDOM HOUSE

Prebuilt Pty Ltd., Kilsyth, Victoria, Australia
2005–

Opposite page: Three-bedroom, two bath model with 1200 sq.ft. of floor space in a rural setting

Rechte Seite: Die Ausführung mit drei Schlaf- und zwei Badezimmern und 111 m² Wohnfläche in ländlicher Umgebung

Page de droite: Modèle de 111 m² avec trois chambres et deux salles de bains, installé à la campagne

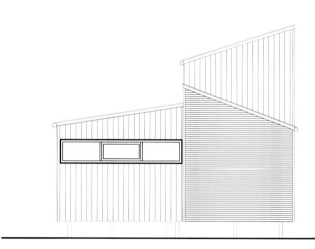

The Freedom House has been produced in series since 2005. The house is a wooden skeleton structure clad in corrugated sheet metal, which, as a material that has traditionally been popular in Australia because of its flexibility and weather resistance, is a central element of its design. The mass of the building is set on low footings of steel or wood and can therefore be just as easily built on a slope as on flat building sites.

The Freedom House offers enough space for a family and is delivered in five different sizes, each with a fully equipped kitchen and bathroom. At a cost of between AU$165,000 and AU$266,000, the most spacious luxury version offers three bedrooms, two bathrooms, and a study in addition to the living area. The open floor plan creates a loft-like atmosphere, the hardwood floors feature radiant heating, and the windows have thermal glazing. Prebuilt specifically constructed the building components of the house so that they can be completely delivered in one truckload. Unlike the usual, often boxy prefabricated houses on the market, the Freedom House with its monopitch roofs at opposing angles emits a sculptural quality all its own.

Das Freedom House ist 2005 in Serie gegangen. Zentrales Gestaltungselement des Hauses ist die Wellblechverkleidung der Holzskelett-Konstruktion – ein Material, das in Australien seiner Wetterbeständigkeit und Flexibilität wegen traditionell gern verwendet wird. Der auf Stahl- oder Holzfüßen leicht aufgeständerte Baukörper kann auf abschüssigem Hanggelände ebenso gut installiert werden wie in der Ebene.

Das Freedom-Haus bietet genügend Platz für eine Familie und ist in fünf verschiedenen Größen lieferbar, jeweils mit voller Küchen- und Badausstattung. Die Kosten liegen zwischen 165000 und 226000 AU$. In der 134 m² großen Luxus-Variante „Freedom 15600 Deluxe" bietet es neben dem Wohnbereich drei Schlafzimmer, zwei Badezimmer und ein Arbeitszimmer. Der offene Grundriss erzeugt eine loftartige Atmosphäre, der Holzfußboden ist beheizt und die Fenster sind doppelt verglast. Prebuilt hat die Baukomponenten des Hauses eigens so konstruiert, dass sie in einer LKW-Ladung komplett angeliefert werden können. Anders als die oft boxartig konstruierten, marktüblichen Fertighäuser hat das Freedom-Haus mit seinen gegeneinander verschobenen Pultdachelementen eine eigene skulpturale Qualität.

La Freedom House est produite en série depuis 2005. L'élément formel central de la maison est son revêtement de tôle ondulée sur ossature en bois – un matériau qui, en raison de sa résistance aux intempéries et sa flexibilité, est traditionnellement utilisé en Australie. Ce bâtiment légèrement surélevé sur des pieds d'acier ou de bois peut être aussi bien monté sur une pente abrupte que sur un terrain plat.

La Freedom House offre suffisamment d'espace pour une famille. Elle est disponible en cinq tailles, avec cuisine et salle de bains équipées. À des prix compris entre 165000 AU$ et 226000 AU$, sa version de luxe « Freedom 15600 Deluxe » de 134 m² comprend, outre l'espace séjour, trois chambres, deux salles de bains et un bureau. Le plan ouvert lui donne des airs de loft. Le sol en bois est chauffé et les fenêtres sont à double vitrage. Prebuilt a fabriqué les éléments constructifs spécialement pour qu'ils puissent être livrés intégralement par camion. À la différence des maisons préfabriquées aux allures cubiques répandues sur le marché, la Freedom House dégage un effet sculptural propre grâce à la juxtaposition de ses divers appentis.

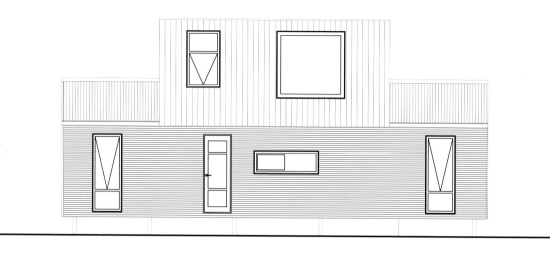

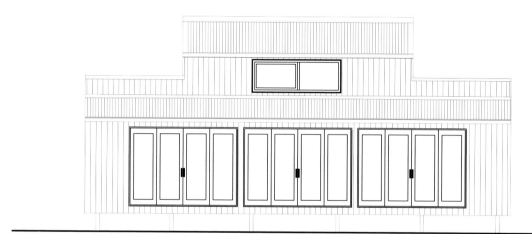

Elevations of the house; decks can be added as desired

Ansichten des Hauses mit je nach Wunsch hinzufügbaren Terrassen

Élévations de la maison, possibilité d'ajouter des terrasses

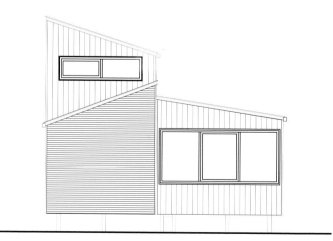

The house is delivered with built-in closets and kitchen cabinets–they are practical because they make the best use of space.

Einbauschränke und Küchenzeile gehören zum Lieferumfang – eine sinnvolle Lösung, da diese den knappen Raum am besten ausnutzen.

La maison est livrée avec placards et cuisine intégrés, une solution idéale pour optimiser l'utilisation de l'espace limité.

MOD HOUSE

Prebuilt Pty Ltd., Kilsyth, Victoria, Australia
2005–

"The Prebuilt Mod House Range is for those who like their homes clean and crisp with a modernist edge." Thus the characterization of the Mod House, which Prebuilt offers as one of six prefabricated houses designed by various architects for this company located in a Melbourne suburb. The Mod House was designed by the Melbourne architectural office of Pleysier Perkins.

The Mod House is based on a highly flexible system of pavilion modules, which can be as large as 52 ½ ft. by 18 ft.—transporting anything larger by truck is prohibited in Australia. The individual modules can be combined at will: in the form of an "I", an "L", or a "U", and as one-, two-, or three-story dwellings; the client can also determine the location of the doors and windows. Houses ranging in size from a one-bedroom for AU$ 175,000 to a three-module house with four bedrooms and two living rooms for AU$ 437,000.

Hence, the Mod Houses that have been built are highly divergent in terms of their floor plans, exteriors, the way they extend into their surroundings, i.e. by means of pergolas or terraces, and whether they stand on or off the ground. A characteristic feature of the Mod Houses is a flat roof, the lateral orientation of the overall layout and the individual parts, and the clear modern lines and austerity of the external view.

The Mod Houses are, like all of the houses by Prebuilt, wood-frame structures. They are produced entirely in a factory, delivered by truck, and set down on a foundation made of steel or on wooden footings—on ground level or as high as six meters off the ground. The assembly and installation of a house takes only a few hours. They use solar energy and have a water recycling system.

„Das Prebuilt Mod House ist ideal für Bauherren, die ihr Haus sauber und makellos mögen – und mit modernem Flair." So charakterisiert die Firma Prebuilt das Mod House, einen von derzeit sechs Fertighaustypen, die von verschiedenen Architekten entworfen wurden und von der in einem Vorort von Melbourne beheimateten Firma gebaut und vertrieben werden. Der Entwurf zum Mod House stammt vom Melbourner Architekturbüro Pleysier Perkins.

Das Mod-Haus basiert auf einem sehr flexiblen System von „Pavillon-Modulen", die bis zu 16 x 5,50 m messen können – Güter mit größeren Abmessungen dürfen in Australien auf einem LKW nicht transportiert werden. Die einzelnen Module können beliebig kombiniert werden: in I-Form, L-Form, U-Form, ein-, zwei- oder dreigeschossig; auch kann der Bauherr die Lage der Türen und Fenster selbst bestimmen. Zur Auswahl stehen Größen vom Haus mit einem Schlafzimmer für 175 000 AU$ bis hin zum Drei-Module-Haus mit vier Schlaf- und zwei Wohnzimmern für 437 000 AU$.

In der Tat unterscheiden sich die bisher gebauten Mod-Häuser erheblich voneinander, in ihren Grundrissen, in der Gestaltung des Äußeren, in der Art und Weise, wie sie durch Pergolen und Terrassen in die Umgebung ausgreifen, ob sie auf dem Boden stehen oder auf Stützen. Gemeinsam ist allen Mod-Häusern das Flachdach, die Längsausrichtung der Gesamtanlage oder einzelner Teile sowie eine moderne Klarheit und Sachlichkeit im Äußeren.

Die Mod-Häuser sind, wie alle Häuser der Firma Prebuilt, Holzrahmenkonstruktionen. Sie werden komplett in der Fabrik hergestellt, per LKW an den Standort geliefert und dort auf ein Fundament aus Stahl- oder Holzstützen gesetzt – ebenerdig oder aufgeständert auf maximal 6 m. Aufstellung und Anschluss eines Hauses dauern nur wenige Stunden. Sie nutzen Solarenergie und verfügen über ein Wasser-Recycling-System.

« La série Prebuilt Mod House est idéale pour les maîtres d'ouvrage amateurs de maisons aux contours nets et impeccables, teintées de modernisme. » C'est ainsi que la société Prebuilt décrit sa Mod House, l'un des six autres modèles de maisons préfabriquées conçus par différents architectes, puis construits et distribués par une société située dans une banlieue de Melbourne. Le projet de la Mod House vient de l'agence d'architectes de Melbourne Pleysir Perkins.

La Mod House repose sur un système très flexible de modules de pavillon, pouvant mesurer jusqu'à 16 m x 5,50 m, car il est interdit de transporter des marchandises de dimensions supérieures par camion en Australie. Les modules individuels peuvent être combinés à volonté : en forme de I, de L, de U, à un, deux ou trois étages. Le maître d'ouvrage peut également déterminer l'emplacement des portes et des fenêtres. Le choix des possibilités s'étend de maisons à une chambre pour 175 000 AU$ à des modèles jusqu'à trois modules avec quatre chambres et deux salons pour 437 000 AU$.

En réalité, les Mod Houses construites jusque-là se distinguent considérablement les unes des autres par leurs plans, la conception extérieure, le style avec lequel elles s'inscrivent dans leur environnement avec leurs pergolas et terrasses, qu'elles soient de plain-pied ou sur pilotis. Les Mod Houses ont en commun le toit plat, l'alignement longitudinal du plan d'ensemble ou des différents éléments, ainsi qu'une clarté et une sobriété extérieure.

Les Mod Houses sont, tout comme les autres maisons de la société Prebuilt, des constructions à ossature de bois. Elles sont entièrement fabriquées à l'usine, puis acheminées par camion sur le site de construction et installées sur des fondations constituées de poteaux d'acier ou de bois, de plain-pied ou surélevées de 6 m au plus. Le montage et les raccords d'une maison ne nécessitent que quelques heures. Elles utilisent l'énergie solaire et disposent d'un système de recyclage de l'eau.

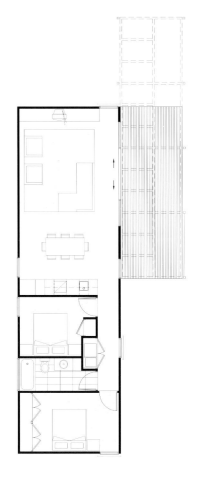

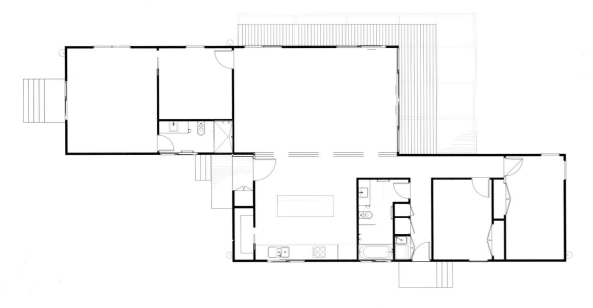

MARC ASMUS, BRYAN MEYER, PAUL STANKEY

HIVE MODULAR B-LINE

Hive Modular LLC, Minneapolis, Minnesota, USA
2005–

The two-story versions B-Line
Medium 001 (opposite page) and
B-Line Medium 003 (right) are
particularly well suited for urban
building sites.

Die zweistöckigen Ausführungen
B-Line Medium 001 (rechte Seite)
und B-Line Medium 003 (rechts) sind
vor allem für städtische Grundstücke
geeignet.

Les modèles à deux étages B-Line
Medium 001 (page de droite) et
B-Line Medium 003 (à droite) sont
particulièrement adaptées à des sites
urbains.

In 2004, the architects Marc Asmus and Bryan Meyer founded Hive
Modular LLC along with the interior decorator Paul Stankey in order to develop "cool" prefabricated houses. In professional practice, all three of the
partners had frequently encountered the discrepancy between their concept of good architecture, on the one hand, and the constrained financial
means of most clients, on the other. In 2005, the first prototype of the Hive
Modular House was erected in Minneapolis; in the meantime, the office offers an extensive assortment of designs and styles. The original B-Line is
now flanked by three additional product lines, and each of the house types
is available in three sizes, with varying details. And in cases where the
client finds these choices insufficient, Hive Modular also drafts individual
designs. The only thing that all Hive buildings have in common is the use
of prefabricated modules. However, even the size of the wall, floor, and
ceiling modules can be varied. The only limits to size are set by the
Department of Transportation's regulations for highway load sizes. The
width of the modules is limited to 16 ft. and the length to 62 ft. The standard house models have 9-ft. ceilings; however, one module can be stacked
on top of another for a 20-ft. ceiling.
Hive Modular houses are wood frame structures with fiberglass insulation
in the walls. The basic shape of the "B-Line" is a simple single-story "bar",
thus the "B" in the name, which can be expanded as needed. The client can
choose between three sizes, determine the arrangement of the windows
and doors, opt for a flat or a pitched roof, as well as various packages for the

2004 gründeten die Architekten Marc Asmus und Bryan Meyer und der
Innenarchitekt Paul Stankey die Firma Hive Modular LLC, um „coole" Fer-
tigbau-Häuser zu entwickeln. Alle drei hatten in ihrer Berufspraxis immer
wieder die Diskrepanz zwischen ihren Vorstellungen von guter Architektur
einerseits und dem engen finanziellen Rahmen vieler Bauherren andererseits erlebt. 2005 wurde der erste Hive-Modular-Prototyp in Minneapolis
aufgebaut, inzwischen bietet das Büro ein umfangreiches Sortiment an
Entwurfs- und Ausführungsvarianten an. Zur ursprünglichen „B-Line" sind
drei weitere Produktlinien hinzugekommen, alle Haustypen werden in drei
Größen und in unterschiedlichen Detailvarianten angeboten. Und wenn
auch das dem Kunden noch zu wenig an Auswahl ist, bietet Hive Modular
die Erarbeitung eines ganz individuellen Entwurfs an. Was die Hive-Bau-
ten verbindet, ist allein die Verwendung vorgefertigter Module. Doch
selbst die Größe der Wand-, Boden- und Deckenmodule ist variabel. Grenzen nach oben setzen allein die Transportvorschriften auf den US-amerikanischen Straßen. Die Breite der Module ist auf 4,90 m (16 Fuß) beschränkt
und deren Länge auf 18,90 m (62 Fuß). Die Standardhausmodelle haben
2,74 m (9 Fuß) hohe Räume; es können aber auch zwei Module aufeinander
gebaut werden, wodurch sich eine Raumhöhe von 6,1 m (20 Fuß) ergibt.
Hive Modular-Häuser sind Holzrahmenkonstruktionen, die Wände sind
mit Fiberglaswolle isoliert. Grundfigur der „B-Line" ist ein simpler eingeschossiger „Riegel" (englisch „bar", daher das B im Namen), der bei Bedarf
erweitert werden kann. Der Bauherr kann zwischen drei Größenmodellen

En 2004, les architectes Marc Asmus et Bryan Meyer et l'architecte d'intérieur Paul Stankey fondèrent l'entreprise Hive Modular LLC, afin de développer des maisons préfabriquées «cool». Au cours de leur pratique profes-
sionnelle, tous trois avaient constaté le décalage entre leurs propres
conceptions d'une belle architecture et les limites financières de nombreux
maîtres d'ouvrage. En 2005, le premier prototype Hive Modular fut
construit à Minneapolis. Depuis, l'agence offre une vaste palette de projets,
dans de nombreuses variantes. Aux B-Line d'origine s'ajoutent trois gam-
mes de produits supplémentaires. Tous les types de maisons sont disponibles en trois tailles avec diverses options. Et dans le cas où le client trouve
l'offre trop restreinte, Hive Modular propose l'élaboration d'un projet totalement personnalisé. L'utilisation de modules préfabriqués est le seul déno-
minateur commun aux bâtiments Hive. En effet, même la taille des modules de murs, de planchers et de plafond est variable. Seules les normes de
transport en vigueur sur les routes américaines fixent la limite à ne pas dé-
passer. La largeur du module ne doit pas excéder 4,90 m (16 pieds), et sa
longueur 18,90 m (62 pieds). Les modèles standard ont une hauteur sous
plafond de 2,74 m (9 pieds), bien qu'il soit possible d'empiler deux modules,
portant la hauteur d'une pièce à 6,1 m (20 pieds).
Les maisons modulaires Hive sont des constructions à ossature de bois; les
murs sont isolés avec de la laine de verre. Le modèle de base «B-Line» est
une simple «barre» («bar» en anglais, d'où le B du nom) de plain-pied qui
peut être agrandie en fonction des besoins. Le maître d'ouvrage a le choix

Below: Plan of the B-Line
Medium 001 with 1,780 sq.ft.
of floor space

Unten: Grundrisse des B-Line
Medium 001 mit 165 m²

En bas: Plans de la B-Line
Medium 001 avec 165 m²

Since the pitched roof can be replaced by a mono-pitched roof, the building can be adapted to different building codes and personal tastes.

Durch die Möglichkeit, das Flachdach gegen ein Sattel- oder Pultdach auszutauschen, lassen sich die Gebäude den Bauvorschriften bzw. dem Geschmack anpassen.

La possibilité d'échanger le toit plat contre un toit en pente ou en appentis permet d'adapter le bâtiment à la réglementation de la construction ainsi qu'aux goûts personnels.

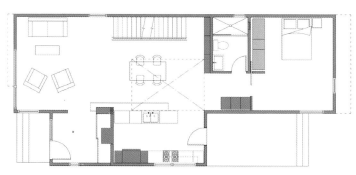

interior design, and must decide how the exterior should look. The external walls are made of fiber cement. They can be produced in various colors or painted later. External wall modules clad in metal or wooden shingles are also available.
The small version was designed mainly as a second or weekend home. With 990 sq.ft. of floor space, it offers an open living space, two bedrooms, and one bathroom. In the B-Line Medium there is an upper story, a central room with a metal stairway, and a separate bathroom for each bedroom. Additional features found in the B-Line Large, which offers 2,400 sq.ft. of floor space, include a master bedroom on the ground floor, three bedrooms upstairs, a foyer, and small functional rooms.

wählen, kann die Anlage von Fenstern und Türen bestimmen, hat die Wahl zwischen Flach- und Satteldach, kann unter verschiedenen „Paketen" für die Innenausstattung wählen und muss entscheiden, wie sein Haus von außen aussehen soll. Die Außenwände sind aus Faserzement gefertigt. Sie können gleich in verschiedenen Farben hergestellt oder später angestrichen werden. Auch stehen Außenwand-Module aus Metall oder Holzschindeln zur Wahl.
Die kleine Version ist vor allem als Zweit- oder Wochenendhaus gedacht. Sie birgt auf 92 m² ein Wohn-/Esszimmer, zwei Schlafzimmer und ein Bad. In der „Medium"-Größe kommen ein Obergeschoss, ein zentraler Raum mit einer Metall-Treppe und die Anlage von separaten Badezimmern je Schlafzimmer hinzu. Die große Version der „B-Line" bietet als Besonderheiten auf 223 m² einen großen Schlafraum im Erdgeschoss, drei Schlafräume im Obergeschoss, eine Eingangshalle und kleine Funktionsräume.

entre trois tailles, peut déterminer l'endroit où pratiquer portes et fenêtres, choisir entre un toit plat et un toit en pente, ainsi qu'entre plusieurs « kits » pour l'aménagement intérieur, et doit se prononcer sur l'apparence extérieure de la maison. Les murs extérieurs sont en fibre de ciment. Ils peuvent être directement fabriqués en diverses couleurs, ou être peints ultérieurement. Il existe également des modules de murs extérieurs en métal ou en bardeaux de bois. La petite version a surtout été pensée comme une résidence secondaire ou une maison de week-end. Sur 92 m², elle accueille une salle de séjour-salle à manger, deux chambres et une salle de bains. Dans sa version « Medium », un étage, une pièce centrale avec escalier métallique et des salles de bains séparées pour chaque chambre viennent se rajouter. Sur 223 m², la version spacieuse de la B-Line offre comme particularités une grande chambre à coucher au rez-de-chaussée, trois chambres à l'étage, un hall d'entrée et des petits cagibis.

Below: Floor plans of the B-Line Medium 003 with 2,000 sq.ft.

Unten: Grundrisse des B-Line Medium 003 mit 186 m²

En bas: Plans de la B-Line Medium 003 avec ses 186 m²

Right: The living room in the B-Line Medium 003 (right above) and in the B-Line Medium 002 (right below) in comparison.

Rechts: Der Wohnraum im B-Line Medium 003 (rechts oben) und im B-Line Medium 002 (rechts unten) im Vergleich.

À droite: Le séjour dans la B-Line Medium 003 (en haut à droite) et dans la B-Line Medium 002 (en bas à droite) pour comparaison.

MARMOL RADZINER PREFAB

Marmol Radziner Prefab, Los Angeles, California, USA
2005–

Opposite page: The orientation of the Desert House is designed to capture the best to best capture views of San Jacinto peak and the surrounding mountains.

Rechte Seite: Das Wüstenhaus ist so ausgerichtet, dass es beste Sicht auf den Gipfel des San Jacinto und die umgebenden Gebirgszüge bietet.

Page de droite: La Desert House est orientée de façon à bénéficier de la plus belle vue sur le sommet de San Jacinto et les montagnes environnantes.

The architectural office of Marmol Radziner + Associates, which employs a staff of over 100 in Los Angeles, originally gained experience with the use of prefabricated modules in office buildings. In 1996, the Californians built the first office building using prefabricated steel-frame structures, then, in 2005, the first residential building made of prefabricated modules: the Desert House is located outside of Palm Springs; it belongs to the head of the company Leo Marmol and served as a model for a continually increasing range of prefabricated houses by the company.

In the Desert House there is no longer a clear separation between indoors and outdoors. The house is not defined by its exterior walls, but instead by the span of the roof landscape into which large areas beyond the walls of glass and wood are integrated. Rooms are thus formed that one is inclined to furnish with chairs or a dining table, and which are protected from the sun and heat by the continuous roof, although not necessary by walls on all sides. These open areas, under the roof, connect the main volume of the building to a second wing, in which a guest apartment and a studio are located. The slightly staggered "L" shape of the overall complex creates a sort of interior courtyard with a swimming pool and a fire pit.

The Desert House is a steel frame structure, i.e. the frames of the floors and

Das Architekturbüro Marmol Radziner + Associates, das in Los Angeles über 100 Mitarbeiter beschäftigt, sammelte zunächst an Bürobauten Erfahrungen für die Anwendung vorproduzierter Module. 1996 bauten die Kalifornier das erste Bürohaus mit Hilfe vorgefertigter Stahlrahmen-Konstruktionen, 2005 dann das erste aus Fertig-Modulen zusammengesetzte Wohnhaus: das außerhalb von Palm Springs gelegene Wüstenhaus für Firmenchef Leo Marmol, das nun Pate steht für das stetig wachsende Fertighaus-Angebot der Firma.

Beim Wüstenhaus ist die klare Trennung von Innen und Außen aufgehoben. Das Haus wird nicht durch die Außenwände definiert, sondern durch die Dachlandschaft, die auch Bereiche außerhalb der großen Glas- und Holzwände einbindet. Diese Räume, die zur Möblierung mit Sesseln oder auch einer Esstisch-Gruppe einladen, sind durch das durchlaufende Dach gegen Sonne und Hitze geschützt, nicht aber – zumindest nicht nach allen Seiten – durch Wände. Diese offenen überdachten Bereiche verbinden den Hauptbaukörper mit einem zweiten Flügel, in dem eine Gästewohnung und ein Studio untergebracht sind. Durch die versetzte L-Form des Gesamtkomplexes ergibt sich eine Art Innenhof mit einem Swimming Pool und einem Feuerplatz.

L'agence d'architecture Marmol Radziner + Associates, qui emploie aujourd'hui plus de cent collaborateurs à Los Angeles, s'est tout d'abord forgé une expérience dans l'utilisation de modules préfabriqués avec la construction de bâtiments de bureaux. En 1996, les Californiens bâtirent le premier immeuble de bureaux avec l'aide de structures à ossatures d'acier préfabriquées. En 2005, ils construisirent la première maison d'habitation à partir de modules préfabriqués assemblés, la Desert House, située en dehors de Palm Springs, pour le chef d'entreprise Leo Marmol, désormais parrain de l'offre sans cesse croissante de maisons préfabriquées par la société.

Dans la Desert House, la claire séparation entre l'intérieur et l'extérieur a été supprimée. La maison n'est pas définie par ses murs extérieurs, mais par le paysage de ses toits qui couvre également des zones situées au-delà des grandes baies vitrées et des murs de bois. Ces espaces, qui invitent à disposer des fauteuils ou un coin repas, sont protégés du soleil et de la chaleur par un toit continu, mais pas par des murs – tout au moins pas de tous les côtés. Ces zones ouvertes, mais couvertes, relient le corps du bâtiment principal à une deuxième aile dans laquelle se trouvent un appartement d'hôte et un studio. La forme en L décalée de l'ensemble

The Desert House consists of four house and six roof modules, the room within the walls measures roughly 2,000 sq.ft.

Das Wüstenhaus ist aus vier Haus- und sechs Dach-Modulen zusammengesetzt, der Raum innerhalb der Wände misst knapp 185 m².

La Desert House est composée de quatre modules de maison et six de toiture; l'espace dans l'enceinte des murs est d'environ 185 m².

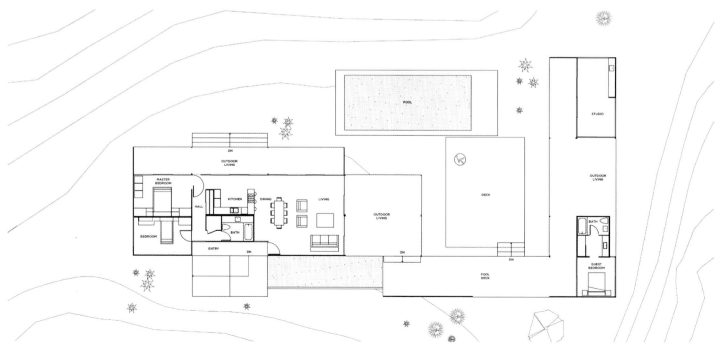

The Palms House is a customized prefab home with 3 bedrooms, 2 ½ bathrooms and 2,800 sq.ft. of floor space, built using 14 modules.

Das Palms Haus ist ein individuell anpassbares Fertighaus mit drei Schlafzimmern, 2½ Badezimmern und 260 m² Wohnfläche aus insgesamt 14 Modulen.

La Palms House est une maison préfabriquée personnalisée, avec 3 chambres, 2 salles de bain et demi et 260 m² de surface habitable composée de 15 modules.

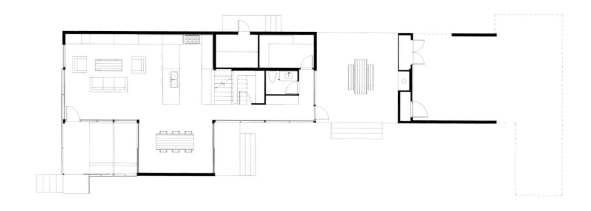

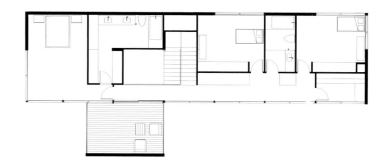

Wooden blinds for privacy and solar protection regulate the relationship between the external and internal space.

Hölzerne Sicht- und Sonnenschutz-blenden regulieren das Verhältnis zwischen Innen- und Außenraum.

Des brise-soleil en bois protègent du soleil et des regards indiscrets tout en régulant le rapport entre l'espace extérieur et intérieur.

ceilings and the supports are made of steel. Metal plates covered with a layer of concrete are fitted into the floor frames—in the cooler months they store heat. The edges of the roof are designed to provide protection against sun from the south and the west. All of the energy required in the house is produced by solar panels.

In the meantime, Marmol Radziner has built at least a dozen prefabricated residential buildings. Another model project is the two-story Palms House, which consists of 14 modules; it includes three bedrooms and two bath-rooms on 2,800 sq.ft. of floor space. The standard ceiling height of all of Marmol Radziner houses is 9 ft.; but it can be increased to 14 ft. by adding a hat module.

Das Wüstenhaus ist eine Stahlrahmen-Konstruktion, d.h. die Rahmen der Böden und Decken und die Stützen sind aus Stahl gefertigt. In die Boden-rahmen sind Metallplatten eingelassen, auf die eine Betonschicht aufgetra-gen ist – sie speichert in kühleren Monaten die Wärme. Nach Süden und Westen sind die Dachkanten als Sonnenschutz ausgebildet. Die im Haus benötigte Energie wird ausschließlich über Solarpaneele gewonnen.

Mittlerweile hat Marmol Radziner gut ein Dutzend Fertig-Wohnhäuser ge-baut. Ein weiteres Vorzeige-Modell ist das zweigeschossige Palms Haus, das aus 14 Modulen zusammengesetzt ist und auf 260 m² drei Schlaf- und zwei Badezimmer beherbergt. Die Standard-Raumhöhe beträgt bei den Marmol Radziner-Häusern 2,74 m (9 Fuß); sie kann aber durch ein „Hut-Modul" auf 4,27 m (14 Fuß) erhöht werden.

forme une sorte de cour intérieure avec piscine et coin barbecue.

La Desert House est une construction à ossature d'acier, c'est-à-dire que les cadres des planchers et des plafonds ainsi que les poteaux sont en acier. Des panneaux métalliques sont fixés sur les cadres du plancher sur lesquels une couche de béton est coulée. Elle garde la chaleur pour les mois plus froids. Sur les côtés sud et ouest, les bordures de toit font office de brise-soleil. L'énergie nécessaire à la maison est exclusivement obte-nue par des panneaux solaires.

Entre-temps, Marmol Radziner a construit une bonne douzaine de mai-sons d'habitation préfabriquées. La Palms House est un modèle d'exposition de 260 m² composé de 14 modules assemblés sur deux niveaux, avec trois chambres et deux salles de bains.

KIP HOUSE

M2 A/S, Aarhus, Denmark
2005–

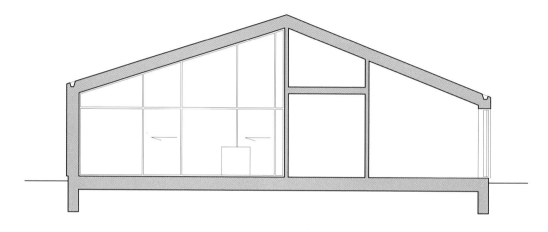

"The same boring prefabricated houses have ruined our cities," says Kim Herforth Nielsen, artistic director of the architectural office 3XN. "We have attractive inner cities in Denmark, but all around them it always looks the same." Hence, he did not hesitate when the prefabricated house company M2 asked him to design a house. A number of other famous offices in Denmark also agreed, and thus began M2's campaign to "revolutionize" the Danish domestic prefabricated housing market: with unusual houses, designed by the most interesting architects in the country, offered at the same prices as "traditional" prefabricated houses—that means square meter prices of roughly € 1,700 for standard versions. M2 offered 16 houses in 2009—in different versions that could be individually finished according to the clients' choices of materials and interior design. Equipped with features such as Boform kitchens, Philippe Starck fittings, and sound systems from Bang & Olufsen, highest quality design is guaranteed. A house designed by a star architect, ready for occupation for a guaranteed price is an attractive offer: roughly 50 of the 3XN Kip houses alone have already been built. 3XN designed a total of four residential and holiday home models for M2, a welcome reprieve from the large projects all over the world with which the 160 employees in Aarhus and Copenhagen are usually engaged at this point. In 1986, three architects by the name of Nielsen joined forces, hence the name of the office. Now only one of them is still there; Kim Herforth Nielsen, who is the "head architect" within a team of five partners.
The Kip House is a minimalistic design that gives rise to exciting views and spatial effects through simple means. It is basically a single-story house with a rectangular floor plan and a pitched roof. However, the middle axis of the rectangle is shifted to one side, thereby creating an arrow-shaped layout. At the same time, the pitched roof also soars to a dramatic

„Die langweiligen, immergleichen Fertighäuser haben unsere Städte kaputt gemacht," sagt Kim Herforth Nielsen, künstlerischer Chef des Architekturbüros 3XN. „Wir haben schöne Innenstädte in Dänemark, aber drumherum sieht es überall gleich aus." So musste er nicht lange überlegen, als ihn die dänische Fertighausfirma M2 um einen Entwurf bat. Weitere namhafte dänische Büros sagten ebenfalls zu, und so trat M2 im Herbst 2005 an, den heimischen Fertighaus-Markt zu „revolutionieren": mit ungewöhnlichen Häusern, entworfen von den interessantesten Architekten des Landes, zum Preis von „traditionellen" Fertighäusern – und das heißt: zu einem Quadratmeterpreis von etwa 1700 € je Standardversion. 16 Häuser bot M2 im Jahr 2009 an – jeweils in verschiedenen Varianten und, was Materialien und Einrichtung angeht, individuell vom Bauherrn zu gestalten. Ausstattungselemente wie Boform-Küchen, Philippe-Starck-Armaturen und Hifi-Anlagen von Bang & Olufsen bürgten für hohe Design-Qualität. Ein von einem Star-Architekten entworfenes Haus schlüsselfertig zu einem garantierten Preis – ein verlockendes Angebot: Allein von 3XNs Kip House wurden rund 50 Stück gebaut.
Vier Wohn- und zwei Ferienhaus-Typen hat 3XN insgesamt für M2 entworfen, für die 160 Mitarbeiter in Aarhus und Kopenhagen eine willkommene Abwechslung zu den Großprojekten in aller Welt, mit denen sie sich inzwischen beschäftigen. Es waren drei Architekten namens Nielsen, die sich 1986 zusammentaten, daher der Büroname. Nur einer ist mittlerweile übrig geblieben; Kim Herforth Nielsen ist heute der „leitende Architekt" unter fünf Partnern.
Das Kip House ist ein minimalistischer Entwurf, der mit einfachsten Mitteln spannende Ansichten und Raumwirkungen erzeugt. Die Grundfigur ist ein eingeschossiges Haus auf rechteckigem Grundriss mit Satteldach.

« Ces ennuyeuses maisons préfabriquées monotones ont détruit nos villes », déclare Kim Herforth Nielsen, directeur artistique du bureau d'architectes 3XN. « Au Danemark, nous avons de jolis centres-villes, mais tout autour, c'est partout pareil. » Il n'eut donc pas à réfléchir très longtemps lorsque l'entreprise de maisons préfabriquées M2 lui commanda un projet. D'autres agences danoises de renom répondirent également présent, et c'est ainsi que M2 entreprit de « révolutionner » le marché national des maisons préfabriquées à l'automne 2005 avec des maisons hors du commun, projetées par les architectes les plus intéressants du pays, au prix de maisons préfabriquées « traditionnelles », à savoir à un prix du mètre carré d'environ 1700 € la version standard. En 2009, M2 proposa 16 maisons, chacune dans différentes versions. Quant aux matériaux et à l'aménagement, ils étaient laissés à l'appréciation individuelle du maître d'ouvrage. Une maison clé en main conçue par un architecte renommé à un prix garanti : telle était l'offre alléchante. 50 maisons Kip House de 3XN ont ainsi été bâties.
Au total, 3XN a projeté quatre types de maisons d'habitation et deux maisons de vacances pour M2, offrant aux 160 collaborateurs d'Aarhus et Copenhague une diversion bienvenue aux grands projets internationaux dont ils s'occupent entre-temps. Trois architectes dénommés Nielsen – d'où leur nom – qui s'étaient associés en 1986 en sont à l'origine. Aujourd'hui, il n'en reste plus qu'un : Kim Herforth Nielsen, « chef architecte » parmi cinq partenaires.
La Kip House est un projet minimaliste, qui, avec des moyens élémentaires, offre des vues et des effets d'espace saisissants. La forme de base est celle d'une maison de plain-pied à plan rectangulaire et toit en pente. Cependant, d'un côté, le centre du rectangle est en renfoncement, ce qui engendre un plan sagittal et fait que le toit en pente s'élève très haut au niveau de la

Im Rahmen des M2-Programmes zur Entwicklung einer schlüsselfertigen Villa entwarf 3XN nicht nur das Kip House, sondern auch noch das Flower House (auf dem kleinen Bild rechts im Hintergrund), das X House, das Twist House und das Basic House, sowie die Sommerhäuser KipUp und Trapez.

In the M2 turn-key villa development program 3XN designed not only the Kip House, but also the Flower House (in the background to the right in the small picture), the X House, the Twist House and the Basic House, as well as the KipUp House and Trapez House summer cottages.

Dans le cadre du programme M2 de développement d'une villa clé en main, 3XN conçut la Kip House, mais aussi la Flower House (sur la petite photo, à droite), la X House, la Twist House et la Basic House, ainsi que les maisons de campagne KipUp House et Trapez House.

height at the tip of the arrow. The exterior walls are clad in blackened wood or completely glazed, the roof is covered with black roofing paper.
The basic idea behind the arrangement of the rooms is the separation between "active" and "passive" areas, with three or four bedrooms located in the latter (depending on the client's wishes). The two parts are separated by the kitchen area—which is part of the living and dining area—and by two bathrooms, as well as three "bridges" that connect the two parts of the house. There is no continuous hallway.
The bedrooms receive light through floor-to-ceiling windows, the dining and living area is illuminated through a glass wall on one side and an additional triangular window on the other. The back section can be separated as an office area, if needed. All of the interior walls are painted white. The house is available in four variations, with living spaces of either 1,668 or 1,873 sq.ft., half of which can be foreseen with a cellar, if desired.

Die Mitte des Rechtecks ist jedoch zu einer Seite hin verschoben, wodurch ein pfeilförmiger Grundriss entsteht und das Satteldach an der Pfeilspitze geradezu dramatisch hoch aufragt. Die Außenwände sind mit schwarzgefärbtem Holz verkleidet oder in Glasflächen aufgelöst, das Dach ist mit schwarzer Dachpappe gedeckt.
Grundgedanke der Raumanlage ist die Trennung in eine „aktive" Aufenthaltsseite und eine „passive" Seite, auf der sich (je nach Bauherrenwunsch) drei oder vier Schlafzimmer befinden. Getrennt werden beide Teile durch die Küchenzeile – als Teil des Wohnzimmers mit Essbereich –, zwei Badezimmer und drei „Brücken", die beide Hausteile verbinden. Es gibt keinen durchgehenden Flur.
Die Schlafzimmer werden durch raumhohe Glasfenster belichtet, das Ess- und Wohnzimmer erhält durch eine Glaswand und ein weiteres Dreiecksfenster von beiden Seiten Licht. Der hintere Teil kann bei Bedarf als Büroraum abgetrennt werden. Alle Innenwände sind weiß gestrichen. Das Haus ist in vier Varianten lieferbar, mit Wohnflächen von 155 oder 174 m² und, wenn gewünscht, zur Hälfte unterkellert.

pointe de la flèche. Les murs extérieurs sont parés de bois de couleur noire ou disparaissent dans des parois vitrées. Le revêtement de la toiture est en carton bitumé noir.
L'idée sur laquelle repose l'aménagement de l'espace est la séparation entre la partie de séjour «active» et la partie «passive» dans laquelle se trouvent trois ou quatre chambres, en fonction des souhaits du maître d'ouvrage. Ces deux parties sont séparées par la cuisine intégrée – partie intégrante du séjour avec coin salle à manger – deux salles de bains et trois «ponts» qui relient les deux parties de la maison. Il n'y a pas de couloir continu.
Les chambres sont éclairées par des baies vitrées toute hauteur. Les sources lumineuses de la salle de séjour-salle à manger proviennent d'une paroi vitrée d'un côté, et d'une autre fenêtre, triangulaire, de l'autre. Au besoin, la partie arrière peut être isolée et utilisée comme bureau. Tous les murs intérieurs sont peints en blanc. La maison est disponible en quatre modèles, avec des surfaces habitables de 155 m² ou 174 m² et, sur demande, dotées de cave sur la moitié.

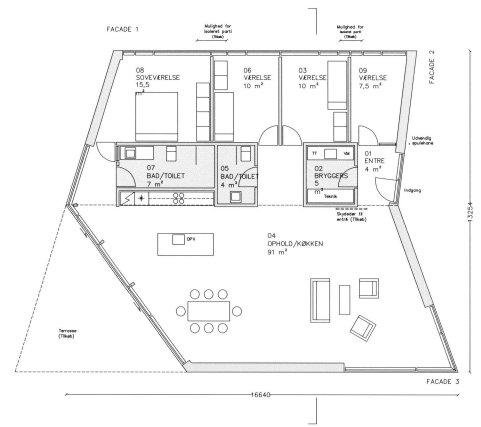

Floor plan (above), and view of the neighboring Flower House from the living area (opposite page)

Grundriss (oben), Ausblick vom Wohnbereich auf das benachbarte Flower House (rechte Seite)

Plan (ci-dessus) et vue sur la Flower House voisine depuis le séjour (page de droite)

MARIANNE CUSATO

KATRINA COTTAGES

Cusato Cottages LLC, New York, New York, USA
2006–

Opposite page: Cottage Square in Ocean Springs, Mississippi. The cottages in this photo are KC 308 and KC 544, with a cottage by Eric Moser in between.

Rechte Seite: Cottage Square in Ocean Springs, Mississippi. Bei den abgebildeten Cottages handelt es sich um die Modelle KC 308 und KC 544, dazwischen das Haus von Eric Moser.

Page de droite: Cottage Square à Ocean Springs, Mississippi. Les cottages de cette photo sont les modèles KC 308 et KC 544, avec un cottage d'Eric Moser au milieu.

In August 2005 Hurricane Katrina ravaged the Gulf Coast of the United States causing extensive damage in Florida, Louisiana, Mississippi, Alabama and Georgia. In New Orleans nearly 80% of the city was submerged under up to 15 ft. of water after two levees burst. At the time, the idea of abandoning the city altogether was even considered.
Only a few days after this natural catastrophe, however, the movement for Katrina Cottages formed around the architect and city planner Andres Duany with the goal of rebuilding the destroyed areas while preserving the Old Southern settlement patterns.
Hence, the Katrina Cottages are executed in the historical cottage style: with pitched roofs, a veranda out front and traditional decorative elements. And since they are prefabricated, they can be built within a few days at low cost. Thus, they serve as an alternative to the anonymous emergency trailers that lined the streets in the affected areas and became so loathsome to the inhabitants over time. The Katrina Cottages are now sold in a growing number of variations produced by diverse manufacturers. Thus, the home improvement product company Lowe's currently offers 19 different Katrina Cottages in sizes ranging between 308 and 1,807 sq.ft., based on designs by Marianne Cusato, Andres Duany, W. A. Lawrence, Eric Moser and Geoffrey Mouen.
One of the first cottages was designed by the New York architect Marianne Cusato. She presented her KC 308 at the International Builders' Show in Orlando in January 2006. With a footprint of 308 sq.ft., it is so small that it can be assembled elsewhere and delivered to its destination by truck. The KC 308 is a simple wood frame structure with a corrugated metal roof and foam-filled two-layer cladding. The larger model, KC 544 with 544 sq.ft. of

Im August 2005 wütete der Hurrikan Katrina an der US-amerikanischen Golfküste und verursachte in Florida, Louisiana, Mississippi, Alabama und Georgia verheerende Schäden. Vor allem in New Orleans standen durch den Bruch zweier Deiche nahezu 80 % des Stadtgebietes meterhoch unter Wasser. Zeitweise wurde gar erwogen, die Stadt teilweise oder gänzlich aufzugeben. Nur wenige Tage nach dieser Naturkatastrophe jedoch formierte sich um den Architekten und Städteplaner Andres Duany die Architekten-Bewegung der Katrina Cottages, die den Wiederaufbau der zerstörten Gebiete unter Rekonstruktion des alten südstaatlichen Siedlungsbildes zum Ziel hatte.
Die Katrina Cottages sind dementsprechend im historischen Cottage-Stil gehalten: mit Satteldach, einer dem Eingang vorgelagerten überdachten Veranda und traditionellen Dekor-Elementen. Und da sie vorfabriziert sind, lassen sie sich kostengünstig und binnen weniger Tage errichten. Somit dienen sie als Gegenentwurf zu den auf Dauer für die Bewohner unattraktiven, anonymen Wohnwagen-Notunterkünften, die zu Tausenden die Straßen der betroffenen Gebieten säumen. Die Katrina Cottages werden in einer stetig wachsenden Anzahl von Varianten über verschiedene Hersteller vertrieben. So bietet etwa die US-amerikanische Firma Lowe's derzeit 19 unterschiedliche Katrina Cottages in Größen zwischen 28 m² und 163 m² an, die auf Entwürfen von Marianne Cusato, Andres Duany, W. A. Lawrence, Eric Moser und Geoffrey Mouen basieren.
Eines der ersten Cottages stammte von der New Yorker Architektin Marianne Cusato. Auf der International Builders' Show in Orlando stellte sie im Januar 2006 ihr KC 308 vor. Es ist mit einer Grundfläche von ca. 28 m² (308 Quadratfuß) so klein, dass es anderswo zusammengebaut und dann

En août 2005, l'ouragan Katrina dévasta la côte américaine du golfe du Mexique et fit des ravages en Floride, Louisiane, Alabama, Géorgie et dans le Mississippi. En raison de la rupture de deux digues, près de 80 % de la zone urbaine de la Nouvelle-Orléans se retrouva sous les eaux. Il fut même envisagé d'abandonner partiellement, voire totalement, la ville. Toutefois, quelques jours à peine après cette catastrophe naturelle, le mouvement des architectes des Katrina Cottages se forma sous la direction de l'architecte et urbaniste Andres Duany, mouvement qui avait pour objectif la reconstruction des zones sinistrées selon la reconstitution de l'ancien lotissement dans le style des États du Sud.
Les Katrina Cottages sont conformes au style historique des cottages, avec leur toit en bâtière, leur véranda couverte précédant l'entrée et leurs éléments décoratifs traditionnels. Comme ils sont préfabriqués, il est possible de les construire en l'espace de quelques jours à peu de frais. Ils constituent ainsi une alternative aux logements provisoires anonymes et peu engageants en mobile homes qui bordent par milliers les rues des secteurs touchés. Les Katrina Cottages sont vendus par divers fabricants dans des variantes en nombre croissant. À titre d'exemple, l'entreprise américaine Lowes propose actuellement 19 types différents de Katrina Cottages basés sur des modèles de Marianne Cusato, Andres Duany, W. A. Lawrence, Eric Moser et Geoffrey Mouen dans des tailles allant de 28 m² à 163 m².
Un des premiers cottages fut celui de l'architecte new-yorkaise Marianne Cusato. Elle présenta son KC 308 lors de l'International Builders' Show (Exposition des constructeurs internationaux) à Orlando en janvier 2006. Avec sa surface d'environ 28 m² (308 pieds carrés), il est si petit qu'il peut être assemblé hors site puis acheminé vers sa destination par camion. Le

MASTER SUITE
11'-10" x 14'-0"

BED 1
14'-6" x 10'-0"

BED 2
10'-1" x 9'-2"

OPTIONAL STAIR
TO ATTIC

PORCH
8'-0" x 23'-6"

STUDY
9'-0" x 11'-7"

LIVING/DINING
19'-0" x 15'-6"

22'-0"

26'-0"

12'-6"   35'-0"

47'-6"

Living room, floor plan, elevations
and exterior (opposite page) of the
Katrina Cottage 910/1185

Wohnbereich, Grundriss, Ansichten
und Außenansicht (rechte Seite) des
Katrina Cottage 910/1185

Séjour, plan, élévations et vue
extérieure du Katrina Cottage
910/1185

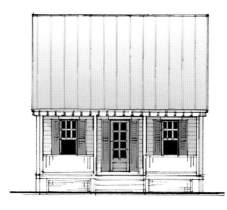

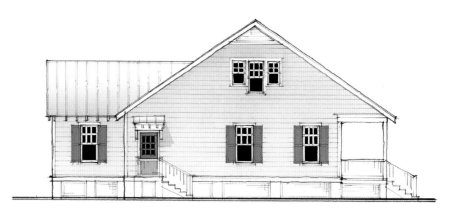

floor space, was also designed by Cusato and encompasses two bedrooms and a bathroom. The steel frame structure uses prefabricated panels that are attached on site. Other cottages are erected directly on the building site.

The houses designed by the Katrina Cottage Architects are, in the meantime, so popular, that they are even bought by people in other areas for use as first or second homes. This is partly due to the fact that they take account of an important lesson taught by the catastrophe, one that is also of importanca beyond the Gulf Coast: they are designed to withstand gusts of up to 125 miles per hour.

per LKW an den Ort seiner Bestimmung geschafft werden kann. Das KC 308 ist eine einfache Holzrahmenkonstruktion mit Wellblechdach und einer ausgeschäumten, zweischaligen Verkleidung. Das mit rund 50 m² (544 Quadratfuß) etwas größere KC 544, ebenfalls von Cusato entworfen, umfasst zwei Schlafzimmer und ein Bad. Die Stahlrahmenkonstruktion verwendet vorgefertigte Paneele, die vor Ort montiert werden. Andere Cottages werden direkt auf der Baustelle errichtet.

Die Häuser der Katrina-Cottage-Architekten sind mittlerweile so begehrt, dass sie selbst von Bewohnern anderer Regionen gekauft werden, die sie als Haupt- oder Zweitwohnung nutzen. Denn nicht zuletzt ziehen sie eine Konsequenz aus der Katastrophe, die auch abseits der Golfküste von Relevanz ist: Sie sind so stabil konzipiert, dass sie Windböen von über 200 km pro Stunde standhalten können.

KC 308 se présente comme une simple construction à ossature de bois avec un toit de tôle ondulée et un revêtement de panneaux sandwiches à remplissage en mousse. Avec ses quelque 50 m² (544 pieds carrés), le KC 544 un peu plus grand, également conçu par Marianne Cusato, comprend deux chambres et une salle de bains. La construction à ossature d'acier se compose de panneaux préfabriqués à monter sur site. D'autres cottages sont directement bâtis sur le chantier.

Entre-temps, les maisons des architectes des Katrina Cottages sont devenues si prisées que même des habitants d'autres régions les achètent afin d'en faire leur résidence principale ou secondaire. D'autant plus qu'ils tirent une conséquence de la catastrophe, qui importe aussi au-delà de la côte du Golfe : ils sont d'une robustesse telle qu'ils résistent à des rafales de vent supérieures à 200 km/heure.

The Katrina Cottage 308 at Cottage Square in Ocean Springs, Mississippi, floor plan and elevations

Katrina Cottage 308 am Cottage Square in Ocean Springs, Mississippi, Grundriss, Ansichten

Katrina Cottage 308 au Cottage Square à Ocean Springs, Mississippi, plan, élévations

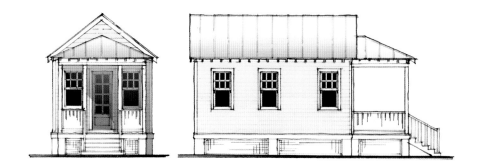

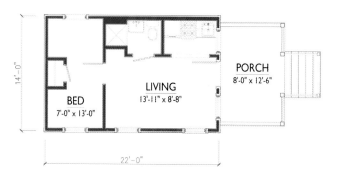

BED
7'-0" x 13'-0"

LIVING
13'-11" x 8'-8"

PORCH
8'-0" x 12'-6"

14'-0"

22'-0"

The Katrina Cottage 544, a
2-bedroom house, in Ocean Springs,
Mississippi, floor plan and elevations

Katrina Cottage 544 – ein Haus mit
zwei Schlafzimmern – in Ocean
Springs, Mississippi, Grundriss und
Ansichten

Katrina Cottage 544 – maison avec
deux chambres – à Ocean Springs,
Mississippi, plan et élévations

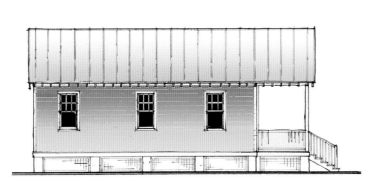

LIVINGHOME RK1

LivingHomes, Los Angeles, California, USA
2006–

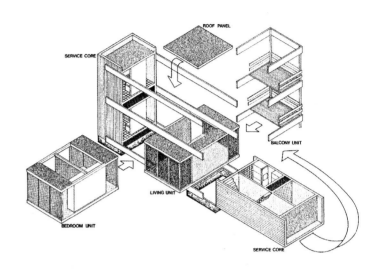

Right: The modular concept
Rechts: Das modulare Konzept
À droite: Le concept modulaire

It comes as no surprise that the LivingHome RK1 was developed by an architect who has long been considering the problem of site-specific design: tower-like modules produced on the basis of steel structures provide the basic framework and ensure that the buildings withstand earthquakes. The horizontal elements suspended within this framework forge connections while remaining as open as possible. This principle, originally conceived for student dormitories, has now been applied to a prefabricated house. It consists of eleven modules and has 2,500 sq.ft. of living space. The initial prototype was erected in Santa Monica with the help of a mobile crane within a period of eight hours; notable characteristics of the house are the two-story living room, onto which galleries open, extensive floor-to-ceiling glazing, and terraces on various levels. Closets serve as room dividers and allow for a great degree of flexibility in terms of interior decorating. The LivingHome RK1 was the first house to receive the Leadership in Energy and Environmental Design (LEED) Award. This award for energy efficient and ecological buildings has been awarded in the United States since 1998. The LivingHome RK1 earned the LEED award by including a number of features: rain water collection for use in the garden, photovoltaic cells to improve the energy balance, some polycarbonate glazing, and even optimal ventilation of the bathrooms. An essential part of the concept is the greening of the interior, since plants help to improve the indoor air and climate. Yet what is most remarkable is the fact that, despite all of these measures, the house still remains elegant and residents do not feel constrained by dogmatic building theories.

Es ist kein Zufall, dass das LivingHome RK1 von einem Architekten entwickelt wurde, der sich schon lange mit standortgerechtem Entwerfen beschäftigt: Turmartige Module, aus einer Stahlkonstruktion gefertigt, bilden das tragende Gerüst und sorgen für erdbebensichere Bauweise. Zwischen ihnen werden horizontale Verbindungselemente eingehängt, die so offen wie möglich gestaltet werden. Dieses einst für ein Studentenwohnheim erdachte Prinzip wurde nun auf ein vorgefertigtes Haus übertragen. Es besteht aus elf Modulen und verfügt über 230 m² [2500 Quadratfuß] Wohnfläche. Der erste Prototyp wurde mit Hilfe eines Autokrans in acht Stunden in Santa Monica aufgebaut; besondere Kennzeichen sind hier der zweistöckige Wohnraum, auf den sich Galerien im Obergeschoss öffnen, eine großzügige, deckenhohe Verglasung und die Außenterrassen auf verschiedenen Ebenen. Schränke dienen als Raumteiler und ermöglichen große Flexibilität in der Einrichtung der Räume.

Das LivingHome RK1 war das erste Haus, das mit der Leadership in Energy and Environmental Design (LEED) ausgezeichnet wurde. Diese Auszeichnung für energie- und umweltgerechtes Bauen wird seit 1998 in den Vereinigten Staaten verliehen.

Die LEED hat sich das LivingHome RK1 mit einer Reihe von Errungenschaften verdient: Regenwasser wird zur Gartenbewässerung gesammelt, Solarzellen verbessern die Energiebilanz, die Verglasung ist teilweise aus Polycarbonat und sogar die Badezimmerentlüftung ist optimiert. Wesentlicher Teil des Konzepts ist auch die Begrünung des Innenraums, die Pflanzen tragen zur Luft- und Klimaverbesserung bei. Das Erstaunlichste ist aber, dass trotz all dieser Maßnahmen ein derart filigran wirkendes Haus entstanden ist, in dem sich der Bewohner nicht durch eine rigide Baudogmatik eingeengt fühlt.

Ce n'est pas un hasard si la LivingHome RK1 a été conçue par un architecte qui s'intéresse depuis longtemps à l'adéquation des projets à leurs sites: fabriqués à partir d'une structure d'acier, des modules en forme de tour constituent l'ossature porteuse d'un type de construction garanti antisismique. Des éléments d'assemblage horizontaux aux formes aussi ouvertes que possible les relient. Ce principe développé au départ pour une résidence universitaire est désormais appliqué à une maison préfabriquée. Il consiste en onze modules et dispose d'une surface de 230 m². Le tout premier prototype a été assemblé en huit heures à Santa Monica avec l'aide d'une grue mobile. Ce bâtiment se caractérise tout particulièrement par son séjour de deux étages sur lequel s'ouvrent des galeries au niveau supérieur, une immense baie vitrée toute hauteur et des terrasses extérieures sur différents niveaux. Des placards font office de cloisons et favorisent une grande flexibilité dans l'aménagement des pièces.

La LivingHome RK1 a été la première maison à recevoir la distinction Leadership in Energy and Environmental Design (LEED). Cette dernière est décernée aux États-Unis depuis 1998 pour les constructions respectueuses de l'environnement et de l'énergie. Vu sa panoplie de nouveautés, la LivingHome RK1 a mérité la LEED: l'eau de pluie est récupérée pour l'arrosage du jardin, les photopiles améliorent le bilan énergétique, le vitrage est partiellement en polycarbonate, et même la ventilation de la salle de bains est optimisée. Les espaces verts inclus dans les intérieurs constituent également un élément essentiel du concept, les plantes contribuant à l'amélioration de l'air et du climat. Malgré toutes ces mesures, il est étonnant de voir apparaître une maison donnant une impression de légèreté, dans laquelle les habitants ne se sentent pas oppressés par un dogmatisme architectural strict.

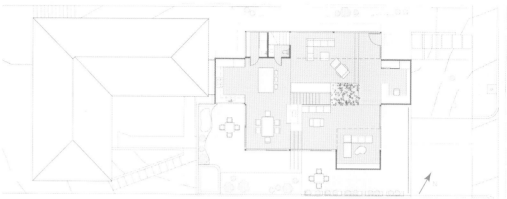

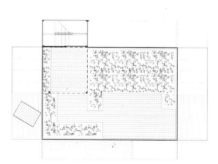

Plans of the ground floor (above), upper level (middle) and top level (below)

Grundrisse des Erdgeschosses (oben), Obergeschosses (Mitte) und Dachgeschosses (unten)

Plans du rez-de-chaussée (en haut), du premier étage (au milieu) et du dernier étage (en bas)

A special highlight is the gallery over the living room.

Ein besonderes Highlight ist die Empore über dem Wohnraum.

La galerie surplombant le séjour est particulièrement remarquable.

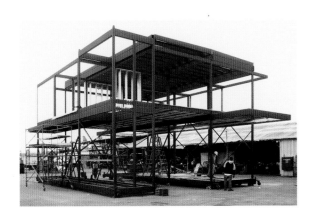

The spacious living room is divided
into various functional areas.

Der große Wohnraum teilt sich in
unterschiedliche Funktionsbereiche
auf.

Le grand salon se divise en plusieurs
zones fonctionnelles.

Below: The glass-ceiling of the bathroom opens the small room in an unexpected manner.

Unten: Das Glasdach im Bad öffnet den kleinen Raum in unerwarteter Weise.

En bas: Le toit vitré de la salle de bains ouvre la petite pièce d'une manière inattendue.

Closets serve as room dividers and ensure flexibility in interior decorating.

Schränke dienen als Raumteiler und ermöglichen große Flexibilität in der Einrichtung.

Les placards font office de cloisons et favorisent une grande flexibilité dans l'aménagement.

332

LOFTCUBE

Loftcube GmbH, Munich, Germany
2007–

Opposite page: Installation within the context of the Berlin *Designmai* exhibition in 2003 on the roof of a former cold storage warehouse on the banks of the Spree River

Rechte Seite: Aufbau im Rahmen der Berliner Ausstellung „Designmai" 2003 auf dem Dach eines ehemaligen Kühlhauses an der Spree

Page de droite : Installation dans le cadre de l'exposition berlinoise « Designmai » en 2003 sur le toit d'un ancien entrepôt frigorifique des rives de la Spree

The basic idea behind the Loftcube designed by Werner Aisslinger was the development of a living capsule that could be set down on the flat roofs of typical post-war urban buildings. For him, an important source of inspiration was the roof landscape on Le Corbusier's Unité d'habitation in Marseille.

The Loftcube, which rests on four stilts measuring nearly 5 ft. in height, is available in two sizes: 420 and 600 sq.ft. Both versions can be connected by gangways to form larger residential landscapes. The outer skin of the cube, which can be assembled in two to three days, is made of white glass-fiber reinforced plastic panels, reminiscent of a 1970s design. Wooden louvers in front of the windows provide protection both against the sun as well as observation by potential neighbors. Access to the interior is gained via a gangway made of powder-coated steel with hardwood steps. Most of the interior is made of highly flexible acrylic polymer elements that can be adapted to the needs of the inhabitants. It also features sliding partitions. The wall panel between the kitchen area and the bathroom includes a water faucet that swivels in either direction, so that it can be used both for the kitchen sink and the washbasin. The bathroom floors are made of white, washed pebbles for a feeling similar to standing on a beach. The mobile house draws water and electricity from the building that supports it. "It is parasitic architecture," according to Aisslinger, "a smaller object that is docked onto a larger one."

Since 2007, the Loftcube has been produced in series with a complete interior program. One can imagine the capsule, which is available in two sizes priced at € 99,000 and € 139,000, not only on the wasteland of unused flat roofs, but also as a futuristic weekend house on a lake.

Die Grundidee des Loftcube von Werner Aisslinger war, eine bewegliche Wohnkapsel zu entwickeln, die sich auf die Flachdächer großstädtischer Nachkriegsbauten aufsetzen lässt. Eine wichtige Inspirationsquelle war für ihn vor allem die Dachlandschaft auf Le Corbusiers Unité d'habitation in Marseille.

Den Loftcube, der in einer Höhe von 1,50 m auf vier Stelzen ruht, gibt es in zwei Größen: 39 und 55 m². Beide Ausführungen lassen sich durch brückenartige Übergänge zu größeren Wohnlandschaften verbinden. Die Außenhaut des in zwei bis drei Tagen montierbaren Würfels ist aus weißen glasfaserverstärkten Kunststoff-Clips, die an das Design der 1970er Jahre denken lassen. Holzlamellen vor den Fenstern schützen vor Sonneneinstrahlung oder auch den Einblicken der Nachbarn. Zugang zum Innenraum erhält man über eine „Gangway" aus pulverbeschichtetem Stahl mit Hartholzstufen aus Bankirai. Die Interieurs bestehen zum großen Teil aus Acrylpolymer, sind flexibel und lassen sich an die Bedürfnisse des Bewohners anpassen: Es gibt verschiebbare Raumtrenner, in das Wandpaneel zwischen Küchenbereich und Bad ist ein durchschwenkbarer Wasserhahn eingelassen, der sowohl für die Spüle als auch das Waschbecken verwendet werden kann. Der Badezimmerboden aus weißem, gewaschenem Kiesel vermittelt bloßen Füßen das Gefühl, man sei am Strand. Strom und Wasser bezieht das mobile Haus von seinem Trägergebäude. „Es ist eine parasitäre Architektur", sagt Aisslinger, „ein kleines Objekt, das an ein großes andockt."

Seit 2007 wird der Loftcube mit komplettem Interieurprogramm in Serie produziert. Über die eigens gegründete Loftcube GmbH ist die Kapsel, die man sich nicht nur auf Flachdächern vorstellen kann, sondern auch als futuristisches Wochenendhäuschen am See, in zwei Größen zum Preis von 99 000 bzw. 139 000 € erhältlich.

L'idée de départ du Loftcube de Werner Aisslinger était de développer une capsule d'habitation mobile, pouvant être rajoutée sur les toits plats des bâtiments construits après-guerre dans les grandes villes. Il s'est surtout inspiré du paysage du toit-jardin de l'Unité d'habitation de Le Corbusier à Marseille.

Le Loftcube est disponible en deux tailles : 39 m² et 55 m². Haut de 1,50 m, il repose sur quatre pilotis. Ces deux modèles peuvent être reliés par des couloirs pour former un espace intérieur plus vaste. L'enveloppe extérieure du cube assemblable en deux à trois jours est constituée de panneaux de plastique blanc renforcé de fibres de verre, rappelant le design des années soixante-dix. Des lamelles de bois placées devant les fenêtres protègent du rayonnement du soleil ou des regards de voisins éventuels. L'accès à l'intérieur s'effectue par une passerelle d'acier peint par poudrage avec des marches en bois dur de Bangkirai. Essentiellement constitués d'éléments de polymère acrylique, les espaces intérieurs sont modulables et peuvent s'adapter aux besoins des habitants : on y trouve des cloisons mobiles, un robinet orientable intégré au panneau mural entre l'espace cuisine et la salle de bains, utilisable aussi bien pour l'évier que pour le lavabo. Le sol de la salle de bains recouvert de galets blancs lavés donne la sensation d'être sur une plage. L'eau et l'électricité de la maison mobile proviennent du bâtiment porteur. « C'est une architecture parasite, explique Aisslinger, un petit objet qui s'arrime à un grand. »

Depuis 2007, le Loftcube est produit en série avec la totalité de l'équipement intérieur. Disponible en deux tailles aux prix respectifs de 99 000 € et 139 000 €, la capsule peut aussi être imaginée comme petite maison de week-end futuriste en bord d'un lac, et non pas uniquement sur des toits en terrasse. Elle est disponible auprès de la Loftcube GmbH, créée spécialement.

Sketch of a group of Loftcubes for
combined studio and residential use

Skizze zu einer Gruppe von
Loftcubes mit kombinierter Studio-
und Wohnnutzung

Croquis d'un groupe de Loftcubes
utilisés comme atelier et résidence

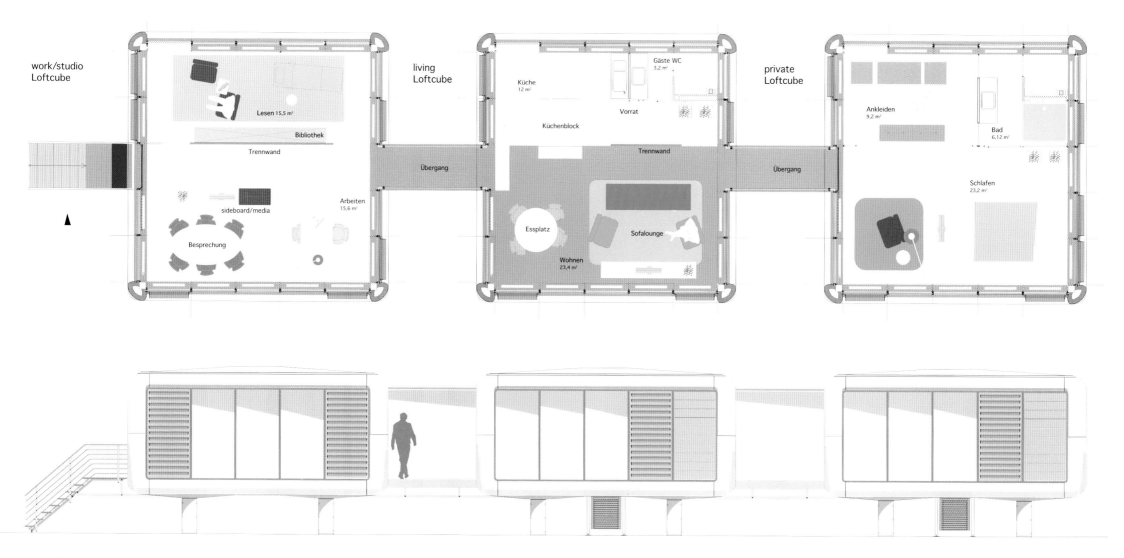

work/studio
Loftcube

Lesen 15,5 m²

Bibliothek

Trennwand

sideboard/media

Arbeiten
15,6 m²

Besprechung

living
Loftcube

Küche
12 m²

Gäste WC
3,2 m²

Vorrat

Küchenblock

Trennwand

Übergang

Essplatz

Sofalounge

Wohnen
23,4 m²

private
Loftcube

Ankleiden
9,2 m²

Bad
6,12 m²

Übergang

Schlafen
23,2 m²

Decorating suggestions for the
house that was presented. Notable
in this context is the use of thick,
light-colored carpet.

Einrichtungsvorschläge für das
vorgestellte Haus. Auffallend ist
hier die Verwendung von hellem,
dicken Teppichboden.

Suggestions de décoration pour
la maison présentée. À noter
l'utilisation de moquettes claires
et épaisses.

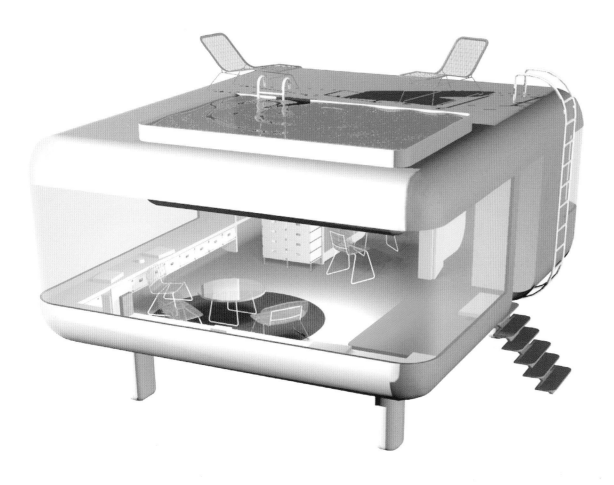

Illustration of a design with a pool on the roof

Konzeptdarstellung mit Pool auf dem Dach

Illustration d'un projet avec piscine sur le toit

Opposite page: A photomontage featuring a Norwegian landscape

Linke Seite: Fotomontage mit norwegischer Landschaft

Page à gauche: Montage photo avec un paysage norvégien

BOXHOME

Prototype in Oslo, Norway
2007

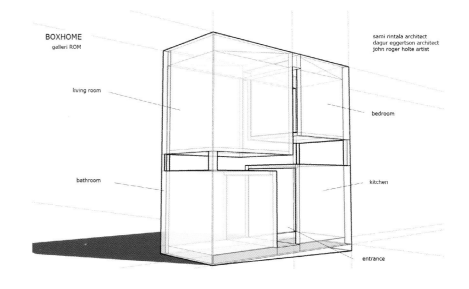

BOXHOME
galleri ROM

sami rintala architect
dagur eggertson architect
john roger holte artist

living room

bedroom

bathroom

kitchen

entrance

The Boxhome is a wooden cube characterized by extreme formal reduction with windows cut into its façade clad in sheet aluminum.

Das Boxhome ist ein aufs Äußerste reduzierter Holzkubus, in dessen mit Aluminiumblechen verkleidete Fassaden Fenster eingeschnitten sind.

La Boxhome est un cube de bois réduit à l'extrême, avec des fenêtres découpées dans ses façades à revêtement de tôles d'aluminium.

This is as small as it gets: this experimental house built in 2007 by the architectural office Rintala Eggertsson, which operates in Oslo and Bodö, is only 18 ft. long, 7 ½ ft. wide, and 19 ft. high. Yet the architects have still succeeded in combining four different living areas on 205 sq.ft. of living space: the kitchen, which includes a dining table, and the bathroom are on the lower level, the living room and the bedroom are on the upper level, which is reached by climbing a ladder. All of the interior areas and the built-in furniture are made of different kinds of wood, which, in turn, define the various zones of the house: pine and birch in the kitchen, spruce in the bathroom, oak in the living room, and walnut in the bedroom.
Sami Rintala and Dagur Eggertsson believe their building expresses an attitude that should also be applied to larger single-family houses: the reduction to the most essential does not mean forfeiting sensuality.
The Finnish-Icelandic architectural duo provides four arguments underlining the need for such a house: first of all because it makes economic and ecological sense to build small houses that use fewer resources and less energy, and which can also be completed in a shorter period of time, since the climatic conditions in Northern Europe require heating for more than half of the year, while construction now accounts for a third of the world's energy consumption. Secondly, housing construction should no longer be entrusted to "an uncontrolled group of actors interested only in maximizing income"—but that people should instead take charge of building their own homes. Thirdly, in Western society we should be clear about the consequences of our consumer culture. The most important goal, however, is the fourth one: "to create a peaceful, little home, a kind of urban cave, into which a person can withdraw when they need to forget the intensity of the surrounding city for a while."

Kleiner geht's nicht: 5,50 m lang, 2,30 m breit und 5,70 m hoch ist das 2007 in Oslo gebaute Experimentalhaus des in Oslo und Bodö arbeitenden Büros Rintala Eggertsson. Und doch haben die Architekten auf den 19 m² Wohnfläche vier separate Wohnbereiche untergebracht: die Küche mit Esstisch und das Badezimmer im Erdgeschoss, das Wohnzimmer und das Schlafzimmer auf der oberen Ebene, die über eine senkrecht an der Wand stehende Leiter zu erreichen ist. Alle Innenflächen und Einbauten sind aus Holz von unterschiedlichen Bäumen gefertigt, wodurch das spartanische Innere in Zonen gegliedert wird: Kiefer und Birke in der Küche, Fichte im Bad, Eiche im Wohnzimmer und Nussbaum im Schlafzimmer.
Sami Rintala und Dagur Eggertsson verstehen ihren Bau als Statement für eine Haltung, die auch bei größeren Einfamilienhäusern Anwendung finden soll: die Reduktion auf das Nötigste, ohne auf Sinnlichkeit zu verzichten.
Das finnisch-isländische Architektenduo liefert gleich vier Gründe, warum man ein solches Haus braucht: Erstens sei es ökonomisch und ökologisch sinnvoll, kleine, mithin wenig Rohstoff und Energie verbrauchende und obendrein in kurzer Zeit zu errichtende Häuser zu bauen, da aufgrund der klimatischen Bedingungen im Norden Europas über die Hälfte des Jahres geheizt würde und Bauarbeiten zudem heutzutage mehr als ein Drittel des gesamten Energieverbrauchs in der Welt ausmachten. Zum Zweiten sollte man den Wohnungsbau nicht weiterhin „einer unkontrollierten Gruppe von Akteuren, die an einem Maximum an Einkommen interessiert sind", überlassen – sondern den Bau seines Hauses selbst in die Hand nehmen. Zum Dritten sollten wir uns in den westlichen Gesellschaften darüber klar werden, welche Folgen unsere Konsumkultur hat. Das wichtigste Ziel aber ist das vierte: „ein friedliches, kleines Heim zu schaffen, ein Art städtische Höhle, in die sich eine Person zurückziehen und – je nach Wunsch – für eine Weile die Intensität der umgebenden Stadt vergessen kann."

Difficile de faire plus petit : 5,50 m de longueur, 2,30 m de largeur et 5,70 m de hauteur. Telles sont les dimensions de la maison expérimentale construite en 2007 à Oslo par l'agence Rintala Eggertsson basée à Oslo et Bodö. Et malgré cela, les architectes ont réussi à découper la surface habitable de 19 m² en quatre zones séparées : la cuisine avec une table et la salle de bains au rez-de-chaussée, le salon et la chambre à l'étage auquel on accède par une échelle posée verticalement contre le mur. Toutes les surfaces intérieures et les éléments encastrés sont en bois provenant d'arbres différents, l'intérieur spartiate étant divisé en diverses zones : celle du pin et du bouleau dans la cuisine, de l'épicéa dans la salle de bains, du chêne dans le salon et du noyer dans la chambre.
Sami Rintala et Dagur Eggertsson considèrent leur construction comme une affirmation d'une attitude qui devrait également s'appliquer aux maisons unifamiliales plus spacieuses : la réduction à l'essentiel, sans renoncement à la sensualité. Le duo d'architectes finno-islandais énumère quatre raisons qui font qu'une telle maison est nécessaire : il est tout d'abord logique d'un point de vue économique et écologique de construire des maisons petites, donc peu consommatrices de matières premières et d'énergie et, de surcroît, assemblables en peu de temps, étant donné qu'au nord de l'Europe, on chauffe plus de six mois par an et que les travaux représentent aujourd'hui plus d'un tiers de la consommation d'énergie totale mondiale. En second lieu, la construction de logements ne devrait pas être confiée à « un groupe d'acteurs incontrôlés intéressés par un profit maximum », mais la construction de sa propre maison devrait être prise en charge personnellement. Troisièmement, on devrait être conscient des conséquences qu'entraîne la culture de la consommation des sociétés occidentales. L'objectif le plus important reste toutefois le dernier : « Créer un petit foyer paisible, une sorte de grotte urbaine dans laquelle la personne puisse se retirer et, si elle le souhaite, oublier un instant l'intensité de la ville environnante. »

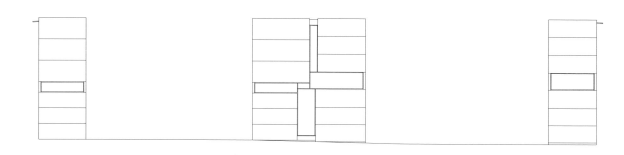

Construction of the model house in
Oslo, elevations

Aufbau des Musterhauses in Oslo,
Ansichten

Construction de la maison-témoin
à Oslo, élévations

Interior, floor plans, section
Innenraum, Grundrisse, Schnitt
Vue intérieure, plans, coupe

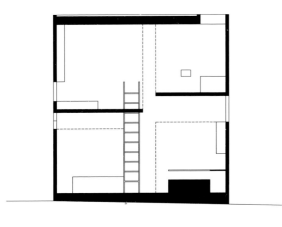

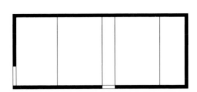

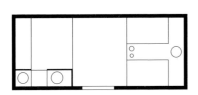

CLAESSON KOIVISTO RUNE

PLUS HOUSE

Arkitekthus, Stockholm, Sweden
2007–

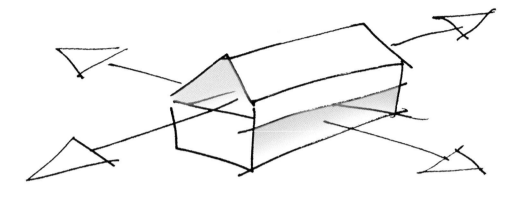

In Sweden, where prefabricated houses are quite popular, architecturally successful and affordable alternatives to the standard catalogue models have been available for a number of years now. One of the leaders in this context is the Stockholm company Arkitekthus. The supporting walls, floors, and roofs of their houses are prefabricated, all the other elements— the inner workings and the external walls—are built on a concrete foundation on site. Arkitekthus cooperates with four prestigious architectural offices in Sweden, two of their prefabricated house models were designed by Claesson Koivisto Rune.

The Plus House, designated as AH#001 in the Arkitekthus catalogue, was created in 2007, the reference model is located in Tyresö, southeast of Stockholm. The two-story wooden building is a modern variation developed on the basis of the classic Swedish country house. In this case, the house has no windows in the usual sense—instead, some of the walls are entirely glazed: the two long sides on the ground floor, and the gable ends of the upper story under the pitched roof. The two visual axes that result intersect each other, forming a plus sign, thus the name of the house. The glass walls are slightly retracted and divided into smaller fields by mullions and transoms. The other external walls are austerely clad in vertical wooden boards. The pitched roof is covered with zinc sheeting. The glass walls not only allow ample daylight into the house, they also integrate it into the natural surroundings—an effect that is enhanced by the terraces located in front of it.

The Plus House is available in two sizes, with either 1,800 sq.ft. or 2,000 sq. ft. of living space. The height of the larger version is 26 ft., and the height of the smaller one is 24 ft. The ground floor is a continuum of space from which only two small rooms, the toilet and a utility room, are separated. In the larger version they are located in the middle of the house next to the stairway, and thus divide the remaining space into a living room and a dining room with a kitchen. In the smaller version the two smaller rooms are located on the narrow side, the remaining space is only divided into two areas by a stairway leading straight upstairs. On the upper floor, where the rooms in the larger version can be nearly 9 ft. high, three separate bedrooms and one bathroom are foreseen. The larger variation is offered for roughly € 415,000, and the smaller one costs approximately € 385,000.

Auch in Schweden, wo Fertighäuser sehr beliebt sind, gibt es seit einigen Jahren architektonisch gelungene und gleichwohl erschwingliche Alternativen zu den üblichen 08/15-Modellen aus dem Katalog. Führend ist hier die Stockholmer Firma Arkitekthus. Die tragenden Wände, Böden und Dächer der Häuser werden vorproduziert, alles andere – das Innenleben und die Außenwände – entsteht erst vor Ort, auf einem Fundament aus Beton. Arkitekthus arbeitet mit vier der renommiertesten schwedischen Architekturbüros zusammen, zwei ihrer Fertighaus-Modelle wurden von Claesson Koivisto Rune entworfen.

Das Plus House, im Arkitekthus-Katalog AH#001 genannt, entstand 2007, das Referenzmodell steht in Tyresö südöstlich von Stockholm. Der zweigeschossige Holzbau entwickelt den Grundtyp eines traditionellen schwedischen Landhauses in modernen Formen weiter. So weist das Haus kein einziges Fenster im herkömmlichen Sinne auf – statt dessen sind ganze Wände komplett in Glas aufgelöst: im Erdgeschoss die beiden Längsseiten, im Obergeschoss die Stirnseiten unter dem Satteldach. Beide Sichtachsen ergänzen sich auf dem Grundriss zu einem Plus-Zeichen – daher der Name des Hauses. Die Glaswände sind leicht eingezogen und durch Stützen und Streben in kleinere Flächen gegliedert. Die übrigen Außenwände sind schmucklos vertikal mit Holzlatten verkleidet. Das Satteldach ist mit Zinkblechen belegt. Die Glaswände bringen nicht nur viel Tageslicht ins Haus, sie binden auch die Natur ringsum ein – ein Effekt, der durch die vorgelagerten Terrassen noch verstärkt wird.

Das Plus House gibt es in zwei Größen, mit 162 m² und mit 187 m² Wohnfläche. Die größere Version ist 7,85 m hoch, die kleinere 7,20 m. Das Erdgeschoss bildet ein Raumkontinuum, von dem nur zwei kleine Räume, die Toilette und ein Funktionsraum, abgetrennt sind. In der größeren Version liegen sie in der Mitte des Hauses neben der Treppe und teilen dadurch den übrigen Raum in ein Wohnzimmer und ein Esszimmer mit Küche. In der kleineren Version sind die beiden kleinen Räume an eine Schmalseite gerückt, der verbliebene Raum wird nur durch die geradläufige Treppe in zwei Bereiche geteilt. Im Obergeschoss, dessen Räume in der größeren Variante bis zu knapp 4 m hoch sind, sind drei separate Schlafzimmer und ein Badezimmer vorgesehen. Die größere Variante wird für rund 415 000 €, die kleinere für ca. 385 000 € angeboten.

Même en Suède – où les maisons préfabriquées sont très prisées – il existe aussi depuis quelques années des alternatives réussies d'un point de vue architectonique, et toutefois abordables, aux habituels modèles 08/15 du catalogue. Dans ce domaine, l'entreprise de Stockholm Arkitekthus est à la pointe. Les murs porteurs, les planchers et les toits des maisons sont préfabriqués tandis que tout le reste (l'aménagement intérieur et les murs extérieurs) est produit sur site, sur les fondations de béton. Arkitekthus travaille en partenariat avec quatre agences d'architecture suédoises parmi les plus réputées. Deux de ses modèles de maisons préfabriquées ont été conçus par Claesson Koivisto Rune.

La Plus House ou AH#001 dans le catalogue d'Arkitekthus, a été créée en 2007: le modèle de référence se trouve à Tyresö, au sud-est de Stockholm. Cette construction de bois à deux niveaux constitue la version moderne de la maison de campagne suédoise traditionnelle. La maison ne comporte aucune fenêtre dans le sens classique du terme, mais des murs intégralement vitrés les remplacent: sur les deux côtés longitudinaux du rez-dechaussée et sur les façades du premier étage sous le toit incliné. Les deux angles de vue se complètent en un signe plus sur le plan au sol, d'où le nom de la maison. Les baies vitrées sont légèrement renfoncées et divisées en petites surfaces par des poteaux et des supports. Les murs extérieurs restants sont sobrement habillés de lattes de bois verticales. Le toit en pente est recouvert de tôles de zinc. Les baies vitrées constituent non seulement une importante source de lumière naturelle pour la maison, mais intègrent également la nature environnante, un effet encore renforcé par la présence des terrasses. La Plus House existe en deux tailles, avec des surfaces habitables de 162 m² et de 187 m². Le rez-de-chaussée constitue un espace continu dans lequel seules deux petites pièces, les toilettes et un cagibi, sont séparées. Dans la version la plus spacieuse, elles se trouvent au milieu de la maison, à côté de l'escalier et divisent ainsi la pièce restante en une salle de séjour et une salle à manger avec cuisine. Dans la version la plus réduite, les deux petites pièces sont reléguées du côté d'une aile étroite et l'escalier droit divise la pièce restante en deux espaces. À l'étage, dont les pièces de la version spacieuse atteignent quasiment 4 m, trois chambres séparées et une salle de bains sont prévues. La version spacieuse est vendue 415 000 €, la petite, 385 000 €.

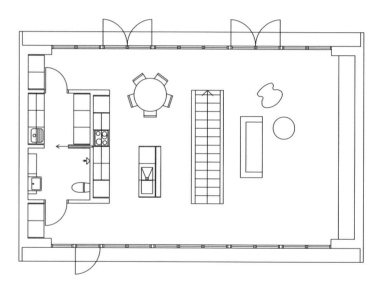

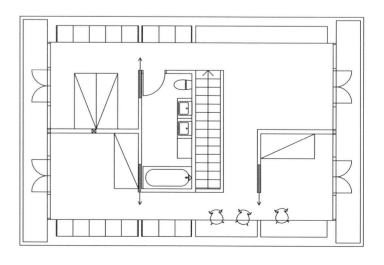

The glass walls are each slightly recessed, so that a narrow balcony is created on the upper level.

Die Glaswände sind jeweils etwas eingezogen, so dass im Oberge-schoss ein schmaler Balkon entsteht.

Les baies vitrées sont en léger renfoncement, de sorte qu'un étroit balcon se forme au niveau supérieur.

The realization of the stairway
without risers contributes to the
spacious effect.

Die Ausführung der Treppe ohne
Setzstufen dient der großzügigen
Wirkung.

La réalisation de l'escalier sans
contremarches contribue à la
sensation d'espace.

FOLDED ROOF HOUSE

Arkitekthus, Stockholm, Sweden
2008–

Opposite page: The house is augmented here by a sauna (right foreground) and a guest house (left).
Rechte Seite: Das Wohnhaus ist hier durch eine Sauna (vorne rechts) und ein Gästehaus (links) ergänzt.
Page de droite: La maison d'habitation a été dotée d'un sauna (devant, à droite) et d'une maison d'amis (à gauche).

A year after the development of the Plus House, Claesson Koivisto Rune created a second design for the prefabricated house company Arkitekthus: the Folded Roof House (AH#002), which was first built on Muskö, an island south of Stockholm, in 2008. It is a one-story wooden house with an asymmetrically folded butterfly roof made of rust-free steel.

The entrance to the house is located on one of the long sides, which creates the impression of a closed block, due to the fact that it has no windows and is clad in vertical wooden boards. Hence, the visitor is all the more surprised by the brightness and openness of the house. As was already the case with the Plus House, large wall areas are executed entirely in glass. A large living and a dining room with a kitchen form the center of the house, with three bedrooms and two bathrooms on the two narrow sides. The two narrow sides and one entire side of the main room are completely glazed—and provide a view of the sea surrounding the island of Muskö. The glass walls are set back slightly into the cubic volume of the house, thus the terraces in front of them are partially protected by overhanging roofs; this enhances the correspondence between the interior and the exterior spaces.

The house with 1,500 sq.ft. of living space costs roughly € 340,000, a smaller version with 1,200 sq.ft. of space costs € 300,000. The house on Muskö has two separate additions, a guest house and a sauna, which are not included in the standard model.

Arkitekthus clients are able to make a number of particularly interesting choices. People interested in the house are asked, "Are you more the modern or the classic type?" with a familiarity similar to the tone adopted by

Ein Jahr nach der Entwicklung des Plus House lieferten Claesson Koivisto Rune der Fertighausfirma Arkitekthus einen zweiten Entwurf: das Folded Roof House (AH#002), das erstmals 2008 auf Muskö, einer Insel südlich von Stockholm, realisiert wurde. Es handelt sich um ein eingeschossiges Holzhaus mit einem asymmetrisch gefalteten Schmetterlingsdach aus rostfreiem Stahl.

Der Hauseingang befindet sich an einer der Längsseiten, die, weil ohne Fenster und mit vertikalen Holzlatten verkleidet, blockhaft und verschlossen wirkt. Um so mehr wird der Besucher dann im Inneren von der Helligkeit und Offenheit des Hauses überrascht. Wie schon im Plus House sind auch hier große Wandflächen in Glas aufgelöst. Das Zentrum des Hauses bildet ein großer Wohn- und Essraum mit Küche, an den beiden Schmalseiten sind drei Schlaf- und zwei Badezimmer angelegt. Der Hauptraum ist in ganzer Länge durch eine Glaswand zu einer Seite hin – auf Muskö ist sie zum Meer hin gelegen – geöffnet, ebenso die beiden Schmalseiten. Die Glaswände sind etwas in die Kubatur des Hauses eingerückt, sodass die vorgelagerten Terrassen zu einem Teil Loggia-artig überdacht sind; dadurch wird ein stärkeres Ineinandergreifen zwischen Innen- und Außenraum hergestellt.

Das 140 m² Wohnfläche umfassende Haus kostet ca. 340 000 €, eine kleinere Variante von 114 m² Fläche 300 000 €. Beim Muskö-Haus entstanden auf Bitten des Bauherrn zwei separat gelegene Bauteile: ein Gästehaus und eine Sauna. Beides gehört nicht zum Standard-Modell.

Interessant ist die Wahlmöglichkeit, die die Firma Arkitekthus ihren Bauherren bei der Innenausstattung ihrer Häuser einräumt: „Bist Du ein

Un an après la conception de la Plus House, Claesson Koivisto Rune livra un deuxième projet à l'entreprise de maisons préfabriquées Arkitekthus, la Folded Roof House (AH#002), qui fut réalisée pour la première fois en 2008 sur l'île de Muskö, au sud de Stockholm. Il s'agit d'une maison en bois de plain-pied, à toit papillon asymétrique en acier inoxydable. La porte d'entrée se trouve sur l'un des côtés longitudinaux qui, dépourvu de fenêtres et habillé de lattes de bois verticales, procure une impression de bloc fermé. Une fois à l'intérieur, le visiteur sera d'autant plus étonné par la luminosité et l'ouverture de la maison. Tout comme dans la Plus House, de grandes surfaces murales sont ici aussi vitrées. Le centre de la maison est occupé par une grande salle de séjour-salle à manger avec cuisine; trois chambres et deux salles de bains se trouvent des deux côtés étroits de la maison. Sur toute sa longueur, la pièce principale s'ouvre d'un côté par une baie vitrée. Il en est de même pour les côtés étroits de la maison. Les baies vitrées sont en léger renfoncement dans le cubage de la maison, de sorte que les terrasses situées devant sont partiellement couvertes, à la façon de loggias. Ceci accentue l'effet d'interpénétration de l'espace intérieur et extérieur.

La surface habitable de 140 m² coûte environ 340 000 €. La version plus petite, avec une surface de 114 m², 300 000 €. Pour la maison de Muskö, à la demande du maître d'ouvrage, deux éléments séparés ont été préfabriqués: une maison d'invités et un sauna. Ces deux derniers ne font pas partie du modèle standard.

La diversité de choix que l'entreprise Arkitekthus accorde à ses maîtres d'ouvrage en matière d'aménagement intérieur de ses maisons est à noter: « Es-tu plutôt moderne ou classique? » demande-t-on à l'intéressé sur le

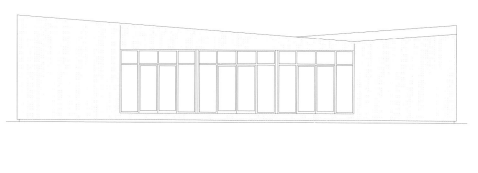

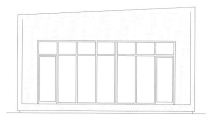

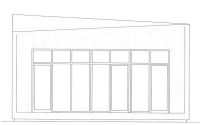

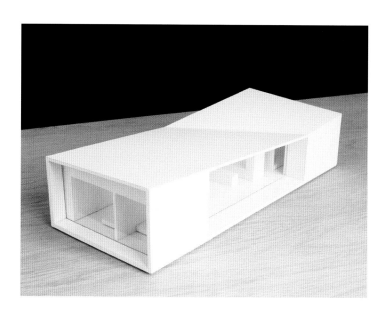

IKEA. Every house is available in two interior variations, which are then completely styled by the architect involved—ensuring that the final product takes on a more coherent appearance. According to the company, the designs in the "classic" line use oak to evoke a "warm" character, while in the "modern" line contrasts between light-colored wood and dark stone are characteristic. However, even the classic version seems more modern than conservative. In this context the conviction that architects have complete control over their designs is alive and well. Arkitekthus also emphasizes the ample storage space in all of their houses indicating that these ambitious prefabricated houses from Sweden are geared towards people's practical needs.

Moderner oder ein Klassiker?", wird der Interessent im schwedischen IKEA-Du gefragt. Jedes Haus gibt es in zwei Interieur-Varianten, die dann aber von den jeweiligen Architekten komplett durchgestaltet sind – damit am Ende ein Haus „aus einem Guss" entsteht. Bei der Designlinie „Classic" verleiht die Verwendung von Eichenholz dem Haus einen „wärmeren" Charakter, die Designlinie „Modern" ist geprägt von den Kontrasten zwischen hellem Holz und dunklem Stein – so die Firma. Aber auch die Klassik-Variante wirkt viel eher modern als konservativ. Hier lebt er noch, der Glaube an die unbedingte Entwurfshoheit des Architekten. Besonders herausgestellt wird von Arkitekthus, dass es in allen Häusern dank zahlreicher Einbauschränke viel Stauraum gibt – ein Zeichen für die Praxisnähe dieser ambitionierten schwedischen Fertighäuser.

mode du tutoiement suédois façon IKEA. Il existe deux possibilités d'aménagement intérieur pour chaque maison, qui sont ensuite complètement remaniés par les architectes respectifs, afin d'obtenir une maison formant une unité. D'après Arkitekthus, l'utilisation de bois de chêne pour la série des modèles « Classic » confère à la maison un caractère « chaleureux », tandis que la série « Modern » se caractérise par les contrastes entre bois clair et pierre sombre. Toutefois, même la version classique apparaît bien plus moderne que traditionnelle. On retrouve ici encore la croyance en la souveraineté créatrice absolue de l'architecte. Arkitekthus insiste particulièrement sur la possibilité de rangement qu'offrent toutes les maisons grâce aux nombreux placards – emblématique de la connaissance du terrain de ces ambitieux constructeurs de maisons préfabriquées suédoises.

Right: The terrace in front of the sauna
Rechts: Freiplatz vor der Sauna
À droite: La terrasse devant le sauna

The living room, kitchen, and hallway have been combined to form one
large room from which the bathroom
and the bedrooms can be reached.

Wohnraum, Küche und Flur sind zu
einem großen Raum verschmolzen,
von dem aus sich das Bad und die
Schlafzimmer erreichen lassen.

Séjour, cuisine et entrée se fondent
en un grand espace d'où l'on accède
à la salle de bains et aux chambres.

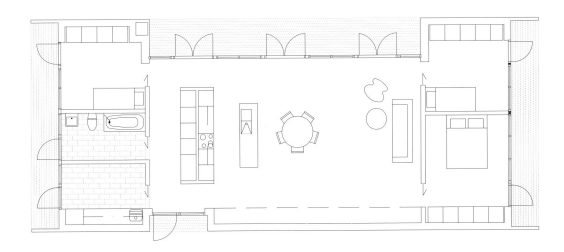

BRIAN DONOVAN, TIMOTHY HILL

DHAN SERIES HOUSE

Happy Haus, Fortitude Valley, Queensland, Australia
2008–

The external walls are made of plywood and can be chosen in various colors.

Die Außenwände sind aus Sperrholz gefertigt und in verschiedenen Farben wählbar.

Les murs extérieurs sont en contreplaqué et sont disponibles en plusieurs couleurs.

The name of these houses is not "Happy House", but instead, in perfect Gerglish, "Happy Haus". Yet, they come from Australia—more precisely from Brisbane, Queensland. They are produced in individual modules in a factory in South Queensland and assembled on site.

The company offers two models: the "White Series" by the Brisbane architectural office of Owen and Vokes and the "DHAN Series", which was developed by Brian Donovan and Timothy Hill—who operate one of the most successful architectural offices in Australia.

Donovan and Hill's express intention was to develop a type of house that would be relevant for Australians. They cite "open-plan living and connectivity" as their design principles; and it is indeed a characteristic of their houses.

The DHAN series consists of three building elements: the "base", the "expander", and the "shed". The "base" is an elongated rectangular module, which is available in four different floor plans. It encompasses a kitchen, a bathroom, and a living room, which can be divided into a living room and bedroom by a wardrobe unit. This base can stand alone or be augmented by an "expander" module. They are available in sizes ranging from one to three bedrooms. A "studio", which is an independent living unit with a bedroom, bathroom, kitchen, and living area, is also available. The third building element is the "shed" module: a shelter open on two sides, which will mainly be used as a garage.

Using these three modules, the house can be configured and expanded at will. However, the extensions are not directly docked onto the base—each element stands alone and is connected to others via a common roof that spans the space in between them. The houses are raised slightly off the ground. Asymmetrical butterfly roofs and solar protection elements on the windows are characteristic for the houses of the DHAN series.

Die Häuser heißen nicht etwa „Happy House", sondern gut denglisch „Happy Haus". Trotzdem kommen sie aus Australien – genauer gesagt aus Brisbane, Queensland. Sie werden in einzelnen Modulen in einer Fabrik in Süd-Queensland vorgefertigt und vor Ort zusammengesetzt.

Zwei Modelle bietet die Firma an: die „White Series" des Brisbaner Architekturbüros Owen and Vokes und die „DHAN Series", die von Brian Donovan und Timothy Hill entwickelt wurde – sie führen eines der erfolgreichsten Architekturbüros Australiens.

Erklärtes Ziel von Donovan und Hill war es, eine „Haustypologie" zu entwickeln, die für alle Australier passend sei. Als ihre Entwurfsprinzipien nennen sie frei fließende Räume und Verbindungsfähigkeit. Und das charakterisiert in der Tat ihre Häuser.

Die DHAN-Serie besteht aus drei Bauteilen: „Base", „Expander" und „Shed" (Basis, Erweiterung, Unterstand). Die „Basis" ist ein längsrechteckiges Modul, das es in vier verschiedenen Grundrissen gibt. Es umfasst eine Küche, ein Badezimmer und einen Wohnraum, der durch eine Schrankwand in Wohn- und Schlafzimmer geteilt werden kann. Diese Basis kann für sich stehen oder durch „Expander"-Module erweitert werden. Sie gibt es in Größen zu ein, zwei oder drei Schlafzimmern. Angeboten wird auch ein „Studio", eine unabhängige Wohneinheit mit Schlafzimmer, Bad, Küche und Wohnbereich. Drittes Bauteil ist das „Shed"-Modul: ein zu den Seiten offener Unterstand, der vor allem als Garage genutzt werden dürfte.

Mit diesen drei Modulen kann man das Haus beliebig konfigurieren und erweitern. Die Erweiterungen werden allerdings nicht direkt an die Basis angedockt – alle Elemente bleiben für sich, die Verbindung erfolgt mittels überdachter Bereiche. Die Häuser sind leicht aufgeständert. Charakteristisch für die Häuser der DHAN-Serie sind die asymmetrischen Schmetterlingsdächer und die Sonnenschutzelemente an den Fenstern.

Les maisons ne se dénomment pas « Happy House », mais bien « Happy Haus », mélange d'anglais et d'allemand. Et pourtant elles sont originaires d'Australie – ou plus exactement de Brisbane, dans le Queensland. Elles sont fabriquées en modules dans une usine du sud de cet État puis assemblées sur le site.

L'entreprise propose deux modèles : la « White Series » du bureau d'architectes Owen and Vokes et la « DHAN Series » conçue par Brian Donovan et Timothy Hill qui sont à la tête d'une des agences les plus prisées d'Australie.

L'objectif avoué de Donovan et Hill était de développer une « typologie de maison » adaptée à tous les Australiens. Les principes de vastes espaces décloisonnés et de connectivité constituent leur credo créatif, et caractérisent effectivement leurs maisons.

La série DHAN se compose de trois éléments préfabriqués : « Base », « Expander » et « Shed » (base, extension, abri). La « base » est un module rectangulaire décliné en quatre plans différents. Il comprend une cuisine, une salle de bains et une salle de séjour qui peut être divisée en salon-salle à manger par des éléments de rangement. Cette base peut être utilisée seule ou bien être augmentée d'un module « Expander ». Elle existe en trois tailles : avec une, deux ou trois chambres. Un « Studio » est également proposé, une unité d'habitation indépendante avec chambre, salle de bains, cuisine et salle de séjour. Le troisième élément est le module « Shed », un abri ouvert sur les côtés, généralement utilisé comme garage.

Sur la base de ces trois modules, il est possible d'agencer et d'agrandir la maison à volonté. Toutefois, les extensions ne se fixent pas directement à l'élément de base. Touts les éléments restent indépendants et sont ensuite reliés par des zones couvertes. Les maisons sont légèrement surélevées. Les toits papillons asymétriques et les éléments pare-soleil des fenêtres sont caractéristiques des maisons de la série DHAN.

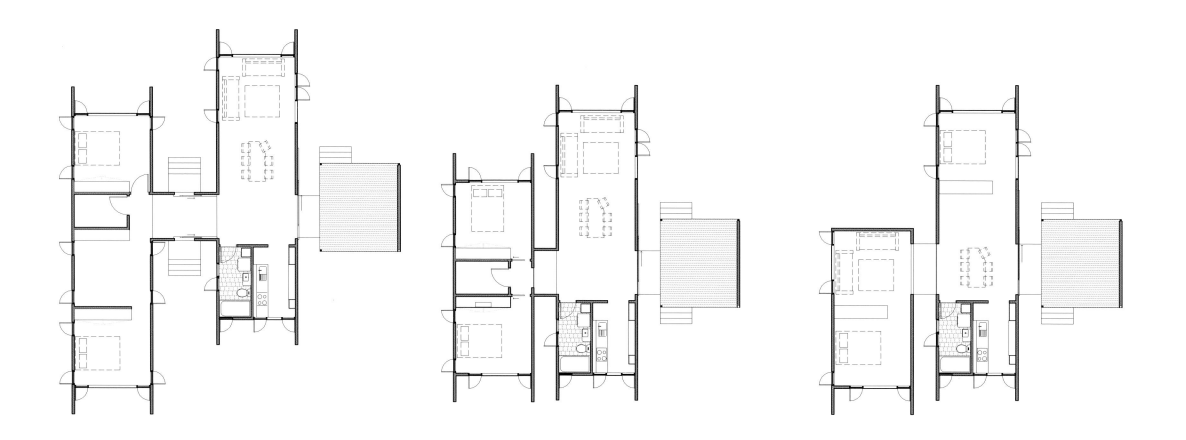

Above: Floor plans of three variations with two or three bedrooms

Oben: Grundrisse von drei Varianten mit zwei oder drei Schalfzimmern

En haut: Plans de trois variantes à deux ou trois chambres

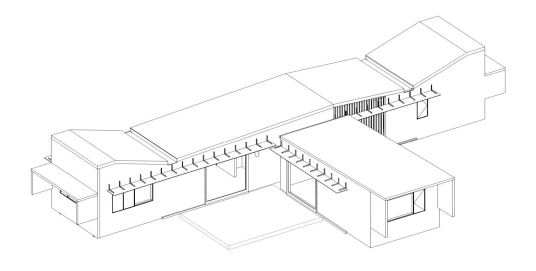

Characteristic of the interior decoration is the contrast between the walls, which are painted white, and the natural wood of the windows, doors, and moldings under the ceilings. Lighting is installed in the molding, which also serves to hang pictures.

Charakteristisch für die Innengestaltung ist der Gegensatz zwischen den weiß gestrichenen Wänden einerseits und den hölzernen Fenstern, Türen und Leisten unter der Decke andererseits; letztere bergen die Beleuchtung und dienen darüber hinaus zum Aufhängen von Bildern.

Le contraste entre les murs, peints en blanc, d'une part, et le bois naturel des fenêtres, des portes et des moulures sous le plafond d'autre part, sont caractéristiques de la décoration intérieure. Les moulures dissimulent les éclairages et servent également à suspendre des tableaux.

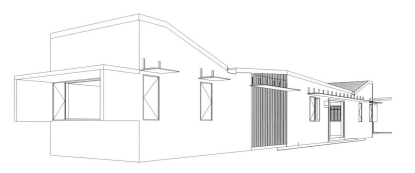

SYSTEM 3

Oskar Leo Kaufmann | Albert Rüf, Dornbirn, Austria
2008–

Opposite page: The presentation of
the house in New York City, 2008
Rechte Seite: Das Haus auf der
Präsentation in New York City, 2008
Page de droite: La maison lors de sa
présentation à New York City, 2008

In 2008, the Museum of Modern Art in New York staged an exhibition on prefabricated architecture and invited five architectural offices to present a project on site. Among those invited were Oskar Leo Kaufmann and Albert Rüf from Vorarlberg, who impressively demonstrated how quickly a prefabricated house could be assembled. One morning a truck with a shipping container rolled into the courtyard of the MoMA. First the "serving unit" was unloaded. An hour later the building crew began to assemble the wall, floor, and roof elements of the "naked space". After four and a half hours the 722-sq.ft. house, complete with furniture, was ready for the inhabitants to move in. In the meantime, the prototype has been developed further and is now suited for mass production. In early 2010, potential builders will be able to place the first orders for the house.

The ingenious idea behind "System 3" is basically a very simple one that was developed on the basis of previous projects; in terms of building technology, the house is divided into two separate areas. All of the complex building elements and installations are combined in the "serving space", which includes the kitchen, bathroom, electrical installations, heating, ventilation, Internet connection, and a stairway leading up to the flat roof. This segment is completely prefabricated. The dining room, living room, and bedrooms are docked onto this functional core, requiring only wall, floor and ceiling elements. This is the "naked space", which only becomes living space through individual furnishings.

Through processes controlled by computers, it is possible to create openings anywhere in the wall elements and in any shape desired to accommodate large windows, doors, or a number of small oculi, as Kaufmann and Rüf demonstrated on the example of the prototype in New York. In order to

Im Jahr 2008 zeigte das Museum of Modern Art in New York eine Ausstellung zur Fertighausarchitektur und lud fünf Architekturbüros ein, jeweils ein Projekt vor Ort zu präsentieren. Eingeladen waren auch die Vorarlberger Oskar Leo Kaufmann und Albert Rüf, die eindrucksvoll demonstrierten, wie schnell man ein Fertighaus aufstellen kann: Eines Morgens rollte ein LKW mit einem Überseecontainer auf den Hof des MoMA. Zunächst wurde die „Service Unit" entladen, eine Stunde später begann die Aufbaumannschaft, die Wand-, Boden- und Dachteile des „Naked space" aneinander und an die „Service Unit" zu montieren. Es dauerte viereinhalb Stunden, dann stand das 53 m² große Haus samt Möbeln schlüsselfertig zum Einzug bereit. Inzwischen wurde der Prototyp zur Serienreife weiterentwickelt, Bestellungen von Bauherren sollen ab Anfang 2010 möglich sein. Clou des aus älteren Projekten weiterentwickelten „Systems 3" ist die ebenso simple wie geniale Idee, das Haus bautechnisch in zwei Bereiche zu teilen: Im „Service Space" sind alle aufwendigen Bauteile und Installationen zusammengefasst: Küche, Bad, Stromversorgung, Heizung, Lüftung, Internetanschluss sowie eine Treppe auf das Flachdach. Dieser Teil wird komplett vorgefertigt. Die Ess-, Wohn- und Schlafzimmer werden an diesen Funktionskern angedockt, und dafür braucht man nur Wand-, Boden- und Deckenelemente: Dies ist der „Naked Space", der erst durch die individuelle Möblierung zum Wohnraum wird.

Computergesteuert können die Wandelemente an beliebigen Stellen in beliebigen Formen geöffnet werden, für große Fenster, Türen oder eine Vielzahl von kleinen runden Lichteinlässen, wie Kaufmann und Rüf es am New Yorker Prototyp demonstrierten. Um einen problemlosen Transport zu gewährleisten, entspricht das Maximalmaß der Service Unit dem

En 2008, le Museum of Modern Art (MoMA) de New York accueillit une exposition sur l'architecture des maisons préfabriquées et invita cinq agences d'architectes à présenter chacune un projet sur place. Également invités, les architectes originaires du Vorarlberg Oskar Leo Kaufmann et Albert Rüf firent grande impression en démontrant avec quelle rapidité il était possible de monter une maison préfabriquée. Un matin, un camion fit son entrée dans la cour du MoMA chargé d'un container maritime. La « Service-Unit » fut tout d'abord déchargée, puis, une heure plus tard, l'équipe de montage s'attela à l'assemblage des éléments de murs, de planchers et de toiture du « Naked space » et de la « Service-Unit ». Il fallut quatre heures et demi pour obtenir une grande maison de 53 m² meublée, clés en main.

L'idée aussi simple que géniale consistant à diviser structurellement la maison en deux parties est le clou du « System 3 »: dans le « Service Space », tous les éléments et autres installations techniques, à savoir la cuisine, la salle de bains, l'alimentation électrique, le chauffage, la ventilation, la connexion Internet, ainsi qu'un escalier menant au toit plat, se trouvent regroupés. Cette partie fait l'objet d'une préfabrication complète. La salle à manger, le salon et les chambres sont fixées à ce noyau fonctionnel, ce qui nécessite uniquement des éléments de murs, de planchers et de toiture. Il s'agit là du « Naked Space » qui ne devient salle de séjour qu'une fois l'ameublement personnel terminé. À l'aide d'un outil d'assistance par ordinateur, il est possible de placer les éléments de murs à l'endroit choisi et de pratiquer des ouvertures de toutes formes pour grandes fenêtres, portes, voire pour une multitude de petits oculus comme Kaufmann et Rüf en firent la démonstration sur le prototype new-yorkais. Afin de garantir un transport sans problème, les dimensions maximum de la « Service-Unit »

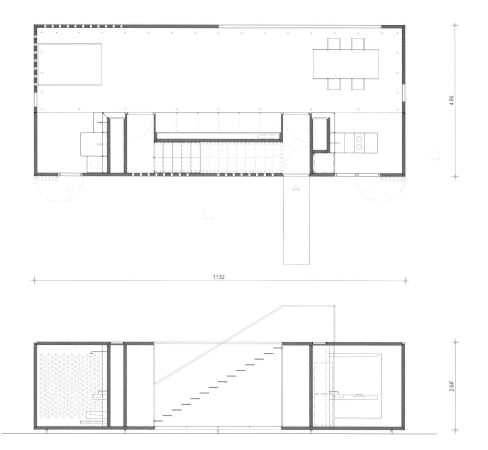

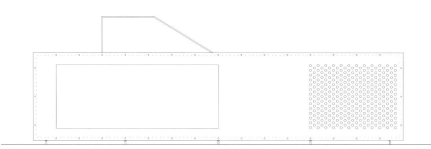

ensure problem-free transport, the maximum size of the service unit corresponds with international container standards, and the elements used to construct the naked space are also oriented on these dimensions. In the case of the New York prototype, the functional core and all of the other building components fit into a single container.

The size, features, and configuration of the service unit can be individually determined by the client, however there are also maximum dimensions for the wall, floor, and ceiling elements: 9.5 x 38 ft. These wall elements are nearly 5 in. thick and made of plywood. They are fitted out with prefabricated windows and doors on site. In New York, the external walls were protected by marine varnish, but alternative "skins" can also be chosen. It is also possible to install solar cells. The architects offer metal furniture for the interior, lighting can be installed by means of cables and hooks anyplace that it is required. The internal walls can be painted in any color chosen by the client. This system, which is both simple and—due to its production method—cost-effective, is also extremely flexible. Every service unit can be augmented on either of the long sides by naked spaces or additional service units as desired. Multi-story buildings are also possible.

internationalen Container-Standard, und daran orientieren sich auch die Elemente des Naked Space. Beim New Yorker Prototyp passten der Funktionskern und sämtliche anderen Bauteile in einen einzigen Container. Größe, Ausstattung und Anlage der Service Unit können vom Bauherrn individuell bestimmt werden, und auch für die einzelnen Wand-, Boden- und Deckenelemente gibt es allenfalls Maximalmaße: 2,88 x 11,64 m. Dabei handelt es sich um 12 cm dicke aus Sperrholz gefertigte Wandelemente, in die vor Ort die ebenfalls vorgefertigten Fenster und Türen eingesetzt werden. In New York waren die Außenwände durch Bootslack geschützt, es kann aber auch eine andere „Haut" gewählt werden. Auch die Installation von Solarzellen ist möglich. Für die Einrichtung bieten die Architekten Metallmobiliar an, Lampen können durch Kabel und Haken überall da angebracht werden, wo man sie braucht. Die Innenwände werden auf Wunsch in Farben nach Wahl bemalt.

Das so einfache und durch die Produktionsweise sehr kosteneffektive System ist zudem extrem flexibel: Jede Service Unit ist zu beiden Längsseiten hin durch Naked Spaces oder weitere Service Units beliebig erweiterbar. Auch mehrgeschossige Gebäude sind möglich.

correspondent à celles du container standard international, tout comme les éléments du « Naked Space ».

La taille, l'équipement et les appareils de la « Service-Unit » peuvent être déterminés par le maître d'ouvrage en fonction des besoins individuels. Pour ce qui est des éléments de murs, de planchers et de toiture, les dimensions maximales atteignent tout au plus 2,88 m x 11,64 m. Il s'agit là d'éléments préfabriqués de murs en contreplaqué de 12 cm d'épaisseur, dans lesquels les fenêtres et portes préfabriquées sont encastrées sur site. À New York, les murs extérieurs étaient enduits de vernis pour bateaux; il est toutefois possible de choisir une autre « peau ». L'installation de cellules photovoltaïques constitue également une option. Pour l'ameublement, les architectes proposent du mobilier métallique; les lampes peuvent être fixées à tout endroit à l'aide de câbles et de crochets, à la convenance du client. De même, les murs intérieurs sont peints de la couleur souhaitée.

Ce système présente par ailleurs une grande flexibilité : chaque « Service Unit » est extensible à volonté des deux côtés longitudinaux par l'adjonction d'autres « Naked Spaces » ou « Service Units ». Il est également possible de monter des bâtiments de plusieurs étages.

The "System 3" skin is like a jacket. It can be removed, changed and washed. The skin is made of different membranes and foils and includes thermal insulation, waterproofing, and a vapor barrier.

Die „System 3"-Außenhaut wirkt wie eine Jacke: Sie ist entfernbar, austauschbar und waschbar. Die Außenhaut besteht aus verschiedenen Membranen und Folien und bietet Wärmedämmung, ist wasserdicht und feuchtigkeitshemmend.

L'enveloppe extérieure du « System 3 » s'apparente à une veste : on peut l'enlever, la changer et la laver. Constituée de diverses membranes et feuilles, l'enveloppe renferme l'isolation thermique, est étanche et anti-humidité.

The furniture and all of the interior elements are made of blank metal. Shelves, lockers, and hooks can be fastened to the wood panels with screws, without worrying about electric cables.

Die Möbel und alle Elemente der Inneneinrichtung sind aus blankem Metall. Regale, Spinde und Haken können einfach ohne Gefährdung darunterliegender Kabel auf die Wandpaneele geschraubt werden.

Les meubles et tous les éléments de décoration intérieure sont en métal pur. Les étagères, armoires métalliques et crochets peuvent être facilement fixés aux panneaux sans se préoccuper des câbles électriques.

Each unit fits into a shipping container, giving them a characteristic "long and narrow" format.

Jede der Einheiten im charakteristischen Format „Lang und schmal" passt in einen Schiffscontainer.

Chaque unité au format long et étroit si caractéristique rentre dans un container maritime.

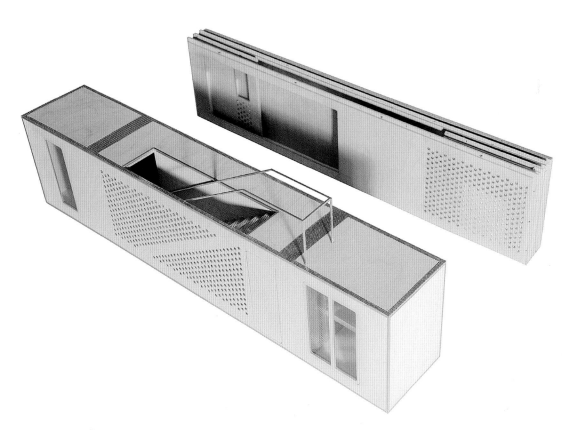

367

SOE KER TIE HOUSE

Noh Bo Tak, Thailand
2008–2009

The use of bamboo has a long
tradition in the region.
Der Einsatz von Bambus hat in der
Region eine lange Tradition.
L'utilisation de bambous est une
longue tradition dans la région.

Should architects from the West provide developmental aid to Third World countries by building houses there? There are many reasons for not doing so, according to the home page of the architects from the Norwegian TYIN Tegnestue (which means drafting room)—but there are even more reasons for doing so. The non-profit organization, which is operated by five architectural students from the University of Trondheim and sponsored by over 60 Norwegian companies and private donors, embraced the task of building houses for and with people in the Third World: at low cost, adapted to local structures and traditions, and with the goal of training people to build better houses on their own in the future. The express interest of the Norwegians in this context is that the participants learn from each other. In August of 2008, three of the Norwegian architecture students traveled to Noh Bo, a little village near the boarder between Thailand and Burma, mainly populated by Karen, who are refugees from the oppression to which they are subjected in Burma. Since 2006, a Norwegian named Ole Jørgen Edna has been running an orphanage in this village, which he was desperately seeking to expand. The students from Trondheim designed and built six dormitories for 24 children in three months in collaboration with local laborers. The basic idea was "to create an atmosphere similar to what the children would have experienced in a more normal situation". Every child was to be ensured their own private sphere, a house, and neighbors to play with. The six sleeping places per house were distributed over three levels arranged in alternation.
The local laborers referred to the designs as "Soe Ker Tie Hias", butterfly

Sollen Architekten aus der westlichen Welt in der Dritten Welt Entwicklungshilfe leisten, indem sie dort Häuser bauen? Es gibt viele Gründe, die dagegen sprechen, sagen die Architekten der norwegischen TYIN Tegnestue (zu Deutsch: „Zeichenstube") auf ihrer Homepage – aber noch mehr Gründe, es doch zu tun. Die Non-Profit-Organisation, die von fünf Architektur-Studenten der Universität Trondheim geleitet und deren Arbeit von über 60 norwegischen Unternehmen und Privatleuten gesponsort wird, hat es sich zur Aufgabe gemacht, für und gemeinsam mit Menschen in der Dritten Welt Häuser zu bauen: zu geringen Kosten, angepasst an die lokalen Strukturen und Traditionen und mit dem Ziel, Anleitungen zu geben, wie künftig eigenständig bessere Häuser gebaut werden könnten. Dabei geht es den Norwegern ausdrücklich um ein wechselseitiges Lernen. Im August 2008 reisten drei der norwegischen Architekturstudenten nach Noh Bo, einem kleinen Dorf nahe der thailändisch-burmesischen Grenze, in dem vor allem Karen wohnen, Flüchtlinge eines in Burma unterdrückten Volkes. In diesem Dorf leitet der Norweger Ole Jørgen Edna seit 2006 ein Waisenhaus, das dringend einer Erweiterung bedurfte. Die Trondheimer Studenten entwarfen und bauten in Zusammenarbeit mit einheimischen Bauleuten in drei Monaten sechs Schlafhäuser für 24 Kinder. Die Grundidee war, „eine Atmosphäre zu schaffen, die die Kinder in einer normaleren Situation erlebt hätten". Jedes Kind sollte seine eigene Privatsphäre haben, ein Haus und eine Nachbarschaft zum Spielen. Die sechs Schlafplätze je Haus verteilen sich auf drei versetzt angelegte Ebenen.
Die lokalen Arbeiter nannten die Entwürfe „Soe Ker Tie Hias", Schmetter-

Appartient-il aux architectes des pays occidentaux de fournir une aide au développement des pays du tiers-monde en y construisant des maisons? Aux dires des architectes norvégiens de TYIN Tegnestue sur leur page web, nombreuses sont les raisons qui s'y opposent, mais plus nombreuses encore sont celles qui y incitent. Dirigée par cinq étudiants en architecture de l'université de Trondheim, l'organisation à but non lucratif sponsorisée par plus de 60 entreprises norvégiennes et par des personnes privés s'est fixée pour objectif de construire des maisons pour les habitants du tiers-monde et avec leur aide. Ces projets à bas coûts, adaptés aux structures et traditions locales, ont pour objectif de fournir des directives qui permettront la construction autonome de meilleurs habitats à l'avenir. Pour les Norvégiens, il s'agit clairement d'un échange réciproque de savoirs. En août 2008, trois des étudiants norvégiens en architecture se sont rendus à Noh Bo, un petit village près de la frontière thaïlando-birmane où vivent essentiellement des Karen, réfugiés d'un peuple opprimé de Birmanie. Dans ce village, le Norvégien Ole Jørgen Edna dirige un orphelinat depuis 2006 qu'il était urgent d'agrandir. En collaboration avec des ouvriers du bâtiment locaux, les étudiants de Trondheim ont conçu six maisons-dortoirs pour 24 enfants. L'idée de départ était de « créer une ambiance qu'auraient connue les enfants dans une situation plus normale ». Chaque enfant devait avoir sa sphère privée, sa maison et des voisins pour jouer. Les six couchages par maison se répartissent sur trois niveaux décalés. Les ouvriers locaux ont qualifié les projets de « Soe Ker Tie Hias », maisons papillons. Les façades latérales et arrière sont en bambous tissés,

The arrangement of the houses makes it possible for children to maintain social contacts in the neighborhood, while at the same time offering them an opportunity to spend time alone.

Die Anordnung der Häuser ermöglicht den Kindern soziale und nachbarschaftliche Kontakte, bietet zugleich aber auch Gelegenheit zum Rückzug.

La disposition des maisons permet aux enfants d'avoir des contacts sociaux avec le voisinage tout en leur offrant la possibilité de se retirer.

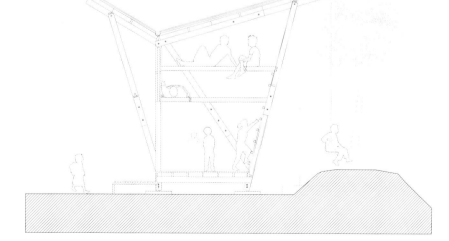

Right: Site plan
Rechts: Lageplan
À droite: Plan du terrain

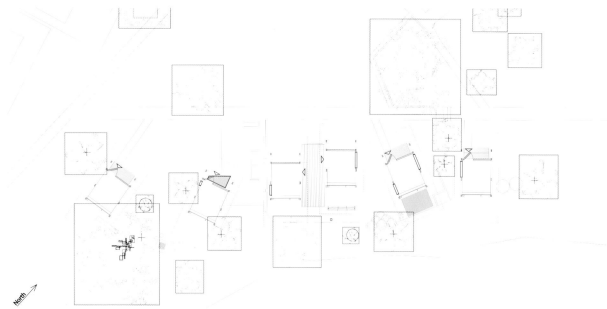

North

houses. The side and back façades are made of woven bamboo—a technique typical of the region. The form of the roof facilitates both natural ventilation and the collection of rainwater. The individual elements of the ironwood structure were prefabricated and connected to each other on site using bolts in order to achieve greater stability. The building is raised slightly off the ground and the four corner footings stand on old tires in order to protect the houses and the footings from dampness.

"After six months of learning from each other in Noh Bo, we hope that we have left something useful behind: important principles such as diagonal bracing, the economical use of building materials, and protection against dampness, will hopefully lead to more sustainable building practices in the future."

lingshäuser. Die Seiten- und Rückfassaden sind aus Bambus gewebt - in einer für die Region typischen Technik. Die Dachform ermöglicht eine natürliche Belüftung und zugleich das Sammeln von Regenwasser. Die einzelnen Elemente der Eisenholzkonstruktion waren vorgefertigt und wurden vor Ort durch Bolzen miteinander verbunden, um mehr Stabilität zu erreichen. Die Häuser sind leicht aufgeständert, die vier Eckpfähle stehen in alten Reifen, um Haus und Pfähle vor Feuchtigkeit zu schützen.

„Nach sechs Monaten beidseitigen Lernens in Noh Bo hoffen wir, dass wir etwas Nützliches hinterlassen: Wichtige Prinzipien wie Schrägversteifung, der ökonomische Umgang mit dem Material und der Schutz vor Feuchtigkeit werden hoffentlich zu einem nachhaltigeren Bauen in der Zukunft führen."

technique typique de la région. La forme du toit permet une aération naturelle en même temps que la récupération de l'eau de pluie. Les différents éléments de cette construction à ossature de bois et de fer étaient préfabriqués et furent assemblés sur site avec des goujons afin d'obtenir une meilleure stabilité. Les maisons sont légèrement surélevées, les quatre poteaux d'angle s'appuient sur de vieux pneus afin de protéger les pilotis et la maison de l'humidité.

« Après six mois d'échanges de savoirs à Noh Bo, nous espérons avoir laissé quelque chose d'utile derrière nous : des principes fondamentaux tels que le contreventement, la gestion économique du matériau et la protection contre l'humidité qui seront la base, nous l'espérons, de constructions durables à l'avenir. »

Various types of walls create an exciting interplay of light and shadow.

Die verschiedenen Arten der Wandausführung erzeugen reizvolle Schattenmuster.

Les différents types de murs produisent de charmants jeux de lumière.

PROF. DIRK DONATH, BAUHAUS-UNIVERSITÄT WEIMAR

UNIVERSAL WORLD HOUSE

Consido AG, Schaffhausen, Switzerland
2009–

The innovative SwissCell® Panels have a honeycomb core made of cellulose soaked in polyurethane resin.

Neuartige SwissCell®-Paneele, die über einen Kern mit einer Wabenstruktur aus kunstharzgetränkter Zellulose verfügen.

Les nouveaux types de panneaux SwissCell® ont une âme à structure en nids d'abeilles trempés dans de la cellulose imprégnée de résine synthétique.

One of the most basic motivations for erecting buildings out of prefabricated elements is the goal of finding quick, low-cost solutions to alleviate an existing shortage of housing. Thus it comes as no great surprise that, in a world increasingly given to thinking in globalized categories, prefabrication is now being employed to create more dignified living conditions in the Third World. And it is against this background that the Consido AG developed the Universal World House, which is intended to replace the sheet metal huts found in the slums of developing countries.

The house was designed between 2007 and 2008 by a professor for architecture at the Bauhaus University in Weimar, Dirk Donath. It has nearly 390 sq.ft. of floor space and costs roughly € 3,600 with basic furnishings. These basic furnishings include integrated single and double beds, a simply equipped kitchen, some built-in furnishings, a veranda with a shower, toilet, and a wash basin for a large family in a separate segment. The wall to the living area can be flipped up in order to both open up the house and provide additional shade.

The cost of the house is so low because of the material used. It consists of honeycomb-core panels made of a substance that, up until now, was hardly considered exemplary for its water resistance, resilience, or even stability: paper. However, when formed in a honeycomb-like structure, it becomes the stable core of a modular building system. Because of their light weight and their high tensile strength, honey comb structures are used in the construction of airplanes and yachts. But instead of using aluminum, or some other material that is costly and energy intensive in its production, as is done in such cases, cellulose soaked in polyurethane resin is used in

Eines der Grundmotive, Häuser aus vorfabrizierten Elementen zu errichten, ist das Bestreben, eine schnelle und preisgünstige Abhilfe für bestehenden Wohnungsmangel zu schaffen. Es liegt daher nahe, dass in einer zunehmend global denkenden Welt die Fertigbauweise auch in den Dienst der Schaffung menschenwürdiger Lebensverhältnisse in der Dritten Welt gestellt wird. Vor diesem Hintergrund hat die Firma Consido AG das Universal World House entwickelt, das die Wellblechhütten der Elendsquartiere ersetzen soll.

Entworfen wurde das Haus in den Jahren 2007 bis 2008 durch den Architekturprofessor Dirk Donath von der Bauhaus-Universität in Weimar. Es verfügt über eine Grundfläche von 36 m² und kostet zusammen mit einer Grundausstattung an Mobiliar etwa 3 600 €. Die Ausstattung bietet mit acht integrierten Einzel- und Doppelbetten, einer rudimentär eingerichteten Küche, einigen Einbaumöbeln, einer Veranda mit einem vom übrigen Wohnbereich getrennten Trakt mit Dusche, Toilette und einem kleinen Handwaschbecken Platz für eine große Familie. Die Wand zum Wohnbereich ist nach außen aufklappbar und dient so zugleich als Schattenspender.

Was das Haus so preisgünstig macht, ist sein Material. Es besteht aus Wabenkernpaneelen, die aus einem Grundstoff sind, der bis dato kaum Inbegriff für Wasserdichte, Beständigkeit oder gar Stabilität war: Papier. Dieses bildet, zu einer wabenähnlichen Struktur verarbeitet, den stabilen Kern eines modularen Bausystems. Wabenstrukturen werden aufgrund ihres leichten Gewichts und der hohen Belastbarkeit vor allem beim Bau von Flugzeugen und Yachten verwendet. Doch statt, wie dort üblich,

L'une des raisons fondamentales à l'édification de maisons en éléments préfabriqués est le souci de trouver un remède rapide et bon marché à la pénurie de logements. Il tombe donc sous le sens que, dans un monde de plus en plus globalisé, les méthodes de constructions préfabriquées soient mises au service de conditions de vie plus humaines dans le tiers-monde. C'est dans cet esprit que l'entreprise Consido AG a conçu la Universal World House, destinée à remplacer les baraques de tôle ondulée des bidonvilles. La maison fut conçue entre 2007 et 2008 par le professeur d'architecture Dirk Donath de l'université du Bauhaus à Weimar. Elle dispose d'une surface de 36 m² et coûte – équipement mobilier de base compris – environ 3 600 €. L'équipement comprenant huit lits individuel et double, une cuisine rudimentaire, quelques placards, une véranda avec une aile séparée du reste du séjour accueillant douche, toilette et petit lavabo offre de la place pour une grande famille. Le mur donnant sur le séjour peut être rabattu et sert aussi à prodiguer de l'ombre.

Le prix de la maison est très abordable en raison du matériau utilisé. Elle est composée de panneaux en nids d'abeilles dont le matériau de base n'a jamais été synonyme d'étanchéité, de résistance ou de stabilité jusqu'à ce jour : le papier. Une fois transformé en une structure similaire aux nids d'abeilles, il constitue le noyau stable d'un système de construction modulaire. En raison de leur poids léger et de leur grande résistance, ces structures en nids d'abeilles sont surtout utilisées dans la construction d'avions et de yachts. Toutefois, au lieu d'utiliser de l'aluminium ou des matériaux chers et énergivores lors de la production – comme il est courant dans ces domaines –, les nouveaux types de panneaux SwissCell® utilisés par

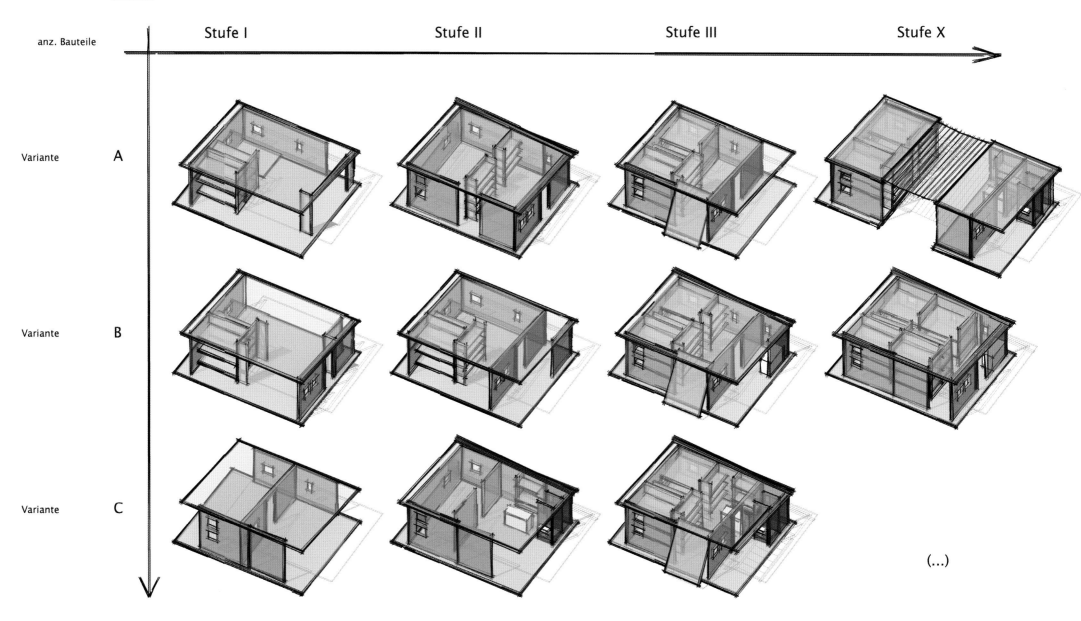

		zweiseitig geschlossener Wetterschutz	dreiseitig geschlossener Wetterschutz	vierseitig geschlossener Wetterschutz	Sonderlösungen
anz. Bauteile		Stufe I	Stufe II	Stufe III	Stufe X
Variante	A				
Variante	B				
Variante	C				(...)

The numerous variations of the house make it suited for diverse uses and family structures.

In der Vielfalt seiner Varianten eignet sich das Haus für die unterschiedlichsten Nutzungen und Familienstrukturen.

Grâce à la variété des modèles, la maison est adaptée aux utilisations et aux structures familiales les plus diverses.

The outer wall can be flipped up to both provide solar protection and to overcome the separation between interior and exterior space.

Das aufklappbare Außenwandelement dient sowohl als Sonnenschutz als auch zur Aufhebung der Trennung zwischen Außen- und Innenraum.

Le mur extérieur peut pivoter, fournissant ainsi une protection contre le soleil et permettant de rompre avec la séparation entre l'espace intérieur et extérieur.

Consido AG's innovative SwissCell® panels, which are transformed into extremely stable, lightweight and water-resistant structures with a thickness of 2 in. through a special process using high pressure and temperatures. The homogenous bond between the outer layer and cell layers ensures a high level of tensile strength, while the combination of materials ensures that the composite is weather resistant.
The intention of this development project is to help people help themselves. That not only means that the house is assembled on site, as is common in prefabricated construction, but that the panels themselves are also produced on site. In order to keep transportation costs to a minimum, and to create new jobs locally, Consido only delivers the raw materials along with the necessary production line in the form of a mobile production unit. A plant was established in the German city of Kiel in order to produce the machines that are required.
In the meantime, interest has been expressed by a number of countries. There have been numerous enquiries from Africa, Asia, South America, and Russia. In addition, contacts to potential customers, including many internationally operating NGOs such as World Vision, Misereor and UN organizations, have also been intensive.

Aluminium oder andere in der Produktion sehr energieintensive und teure Materialien zu verwenden, kommt in den von der Firma Consido AG eingesetzten neuartigen SwissCell®-Paneelen kunstharzgetränkte Zellulose zum Einsatz, die sich in einem speziellen Verfahren unter großem Druck und hohen Temperaturen zu 5 cm dünnen, extrem stabilen und sehr leichten Strukturen verwandelt, die obendrein wasserbeständig sind. Die homogenen Verbindungen der Deck- und Zellschichten sorgen für eine hohe Belastbarkeit, der Materialmix für die Witterungsbeständigkeit der Composite. Das Entwicklungshilfeprojekt dient der Hilfe zur Selbsthilfe. Das bedeutet, dass nicht nur – wie im Fertighausbau sonst üblich – der Zusammenbau vor Ort erfolgen soll, sondern auch die Produktion der Paneele selbst. Um den Transportaufwand zu minimieren und neue Arbeitsplätze vor Ort zu schaffen, liefert das Unternehmen Consido lediglich die Rohstoffe und darüber hinaus die erforderlichen Fertigungsstraßen als mobile Produktionseinheiten. Im norddeutschen Kiel wurde eigens hierfür eine Produktionsanlage errichtet, in der die dafür notwendigen Maschinen hergestellt werden. Mittlerweile ist das Interesse mehrerer Länder geweckt. Es gibt zahlreiche Anfragen aus Afrika, Asien, Südamerika und aus Russland. Darüber hinaus bestehen rege Kontakte zu potenziellen Kunden, vielen weltweit agierenden namhaften NGOs wie World Vision, Misereor sowie UN-Organisationen.

l'entreprise Consido AG sont en cellulose imprégnée de résine synthétique. Soumise à une grande pression et à des températures élevées selon un procédé spécial, elle se transforme en de fines structures extrêmement robustes et légères de 5 cm d'épaisseur, qui, de plus, sont étanches. Les combinaisons homogènes des couches cellulaires et de l'enrobage assurent une grande résistance ; quant au mélange des matériaux, il est garant de la résistance aux intempéries du matériau composite.
Le projet d'aide aux pays en voie de développement vise à les aider à s'organiser par leurs propres moyens. Cela signifie d'une part la construction en commun sur site, tel qu'il est d'usage dans les constructions préfabriquées, et, d'autre part, la production des panneaux. Afin de limiter le temps de transport et de créer de nouveaux emplois sur place, l'entreprise Consido livre uniquement les matières premières et les chaînes de fabrication nécessaires sous la forme d'unités de production mobiles. Dans le nord de l'Allemagne, à Kiel, un site de production a été spécialement construit afin d'y fabriquer les machines indispensables.
Entre-temps, ce projet a suscité l'intérêt de plusieurs pays. De nombreuses demandes arrivent d'Afrique, d'Asie, d'Amérique du Sud et de Russie et il existe des contacts actifs avec des clients potentiels, plusieurs ONG réputées, actives au niveau international, telles que World Vision, Misereor, ainsi que des organisations des Nations-Unies.

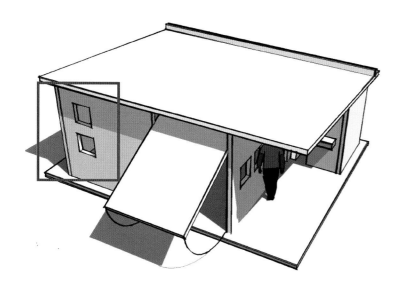

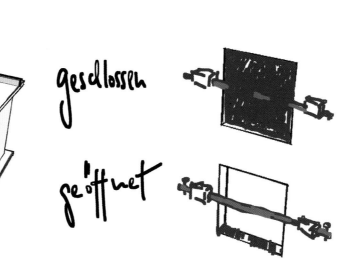

geschlossen

geöffnet

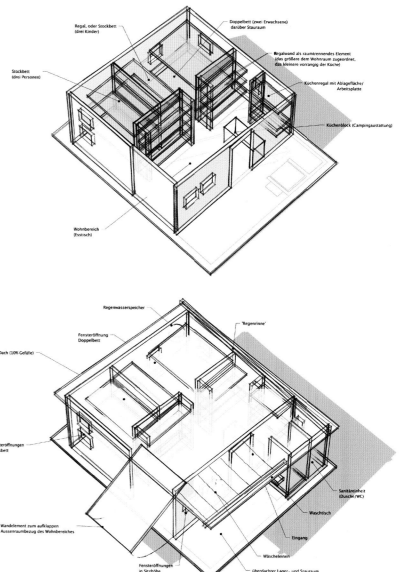

Regal, oder Stockbett (drei Kinder)

Doppelbett (zwei Erwachsene) darüber Stauraum

Regalwand als raumtrennendes Element (das größere dem Wohnraum zugeordnet, das kleinere vorrangig der Küche)

Stockbett (drei Personen)

Küchenregal mit Ablagefläche/ Arbeitsplatte

Küchenblock (Campingausstattung)

Wohnbereich (Esstisch)

Regenwasserspeicher

'Regenrinne'

Fensteröffnung Doppelbett

Dach (10% Gefälle)

Fensteröffnungen Stockbett

Sanitäreinheit (Dusche/WC)

Waschtisch

Wandelement zum aufklappen Aussenraumbezug des Wohnbereiches

Eingang

Wäscheleinen

Fensteröffnungen in Sitzhöhe

überdachter Lager- und Stauraum

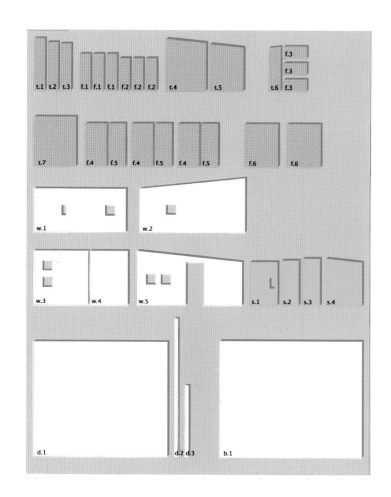

t.1 t.2 t.3   f.1 f.1 f.1 f.2 f.2 f.2   t.4   t.5   f.3 f.3 f.3 f.3 t.6 f.3

t.7   f.4 f.5 f.4 f.5 f.4 f.5   f.6   f.6

w.1   w.2

w.3   w.4   w.5   s.1 s.2 s.3 s.4

d.1   d.2 d.3   b.1

Material from a single tree suffices for the production of a Universal World House. It has an expected life of 50 years and can be completely recycled.

Für die Herstellung eines Universal World House reicht das Material eines einzigen Baumes. Es soll 50 Jahre halten und lässt sich vollständig recyceln.

Pour la fabrication d'une Universal World House, le matériau fourni par un seul arbre suffit. Elle est prévue pour durer 50 ans et est totalement recyclable.

DANIEL LIBESKIND

THE VILLA

Proportion GmbH, Berlin, Deutschland
2009–

Typical characteristics are a zinc facade, large widows, and a wood frame.

Typische Merkmale sind die Zink-Fassade, riesige Fensterflächen und das Gerüst aus Holz.

Les caractéristiques typiques sont la façade en zinc, de grandes baies vitrées et l'ossature en bois.

Daniel Libeskind, who is well known as the architect of the Jewish Museum in Berlin, develops his designs based on the geographical and historical context of the building task. This Polish-American architect designs a building as the hub in an extensive network of relationships which he establishes in his painstaking preliminary work. However, no one ever expected Libeskind to design a model house. Yet he did: on September 29, 2009 the prototype of the "Libeskind Villa" was ceremoniously opened in the North Rhine-Westphalian town of Datteln. The building is to be sold and built 30 times all over the world as a "limited edition" by the Berlin company proportion GmbH. The prototype of this "residential sculpture", the external skin of which is made of zinc like the Jewish Museum in Berlin, is now used as a reception and exhibition building by the Rheinzink company.

The exterior form of this house, which is a wood frame structure, resembles a crystal in its sharp, asymmetric lines. The two-story building, built on an irregular floor plan, is held together visually by three interlocking bands of zinc; in the recessed walls under these bands, there are irregular openings for high windows.

Libeskind cites the question as to what sort of house he would want to live in as the point of departure for this design. He obviously wants it to be spacious. The dimensions of the villa are considerable: overall there are 5,550 sq.ft. of living space on three levels, 2,153 sq.ft. each on the ground floor and the level below. Although there are only three rooms on the ground floor: the hearth room, the guest suite, and the enormous two-story living room measuring over 1,000 sq.ft.—aptly referred to a as the "Grand Room". They can all be accessed from the entry hall. The kitchen island, designed by Libeskind, is also located here. A stairway leads to the upper story, where the master suite with a balcony, two bedrooms, and two bathrooms are located. An outstanding feature of the master bathroom is a rain

Daniel Libeskind, der durch sein Jüdisches Museum in Berlin berühmt geworden ist, entwickelt seine Entwürfe aus den geografischen und historischen Bezügen der Bauaufgabe. Seine Bauten bilden die Mittelpunkte ausgedehnter Beziehungsgeflechte, die der polnisch-amerikanische Architekt in sorgfältiger Vorarbeit knüpft. Dass Libeskind jemals ein Typenhaus entwerfen würde, hätte daher wohl niemand erwartet. Er hat es dennoch getan: Am 29. September 2009 wurde der Prototyp der „Libeskind-Villa" im nordrhein-westfälischen Datteln feierlich eröffnet. 30 mal soll dieser Bau nun in alle Welt verkauft werden, als „limitierte Edition" vertrieben und gebaut von der Berliner Firma proportion GmbH. Der Prototyp der „Wohnskulptur", deren Außenhaut, wie beim Berliner Jüdischen Museum, aus Zink gefertigt ist, wird nun von der Firma Rheinzink als Empfangs- und Ausstellungsgebäude genutzt.

Ausgangspunkt seines Entwurfs, sagt Libeskind, sei die Frage gewesen, in was für einem Haus er selbst am liebsten wohnen würde. Offensichtlich mag er es großzügig.

Die äußere Form des Hauses, eine Holzrahmenkonstruktion, gleicht in ihrer asymmetrischen, spitzen Form einem Kristall. Der zweigeschossige Bau auf unregelmäßigem Grundriss wird von drei Bändern optisch zusammengehalten, in den zurückspringenden Wänden unter diesen Bändern öffnen sich unregelmäßig geschnittene hohe Fenster.

Die Maße der Villa sind beachtlich: Insgesamt bietet sie auf drei Ebenen 515 m² Wohnfläche, davon je 200 m² im Erd- und Untergeschoss. Dabei birgt das Erdgeschoss nur drei Räume: Von der Eingangshalle aus erreicht man das Kaminzimmer, die Gästesuite sowie das zwei Geschosse hohe und mit 95 m² riesige Wohnzimmer, passend „Grand Room" genannt. Hier befindet sich auch die von Libeskind entworfene „Kücheninsel". Eine Treppe führt ins Obergeschoss, wo sich eine „Master Suite" mit Balkon, zwei Schlafzimmer und zwei Badezimmer befinden. Clou des „großen Bade-

Daniel Libeskind, qui a acquis sa notoriété avec le Musée juif de Berlin, développe ses projets en prenant comme point de départ le contexte géographique et historique du programme de construction. Ses bâtiments constituent les centres de vastes réseaux de relations que l'architecte américano-polonais noue soigneusement au préalable. Personne n'aurait d'ailleurs pensé que Libeskind projetterait un jour une maison-témoin, ce qu'il a pourtant bel et bien fait : le 29 septembre 2009, le prototype de la « Villa Libeskind » a été solennellement ouverte à Datteln, en Rhénanie-du-Nord-Westphalie. En tant qu'« édition limitée » construite par l'entreprise berlinoise proportion GmbH, 30 unités de ce bâtiment sont destinées à être vendues à l'international. Ce prototype de la « sculpture à habiter » dont l'enveloppe extérieure est faite de zinc, tout comme le Musée juif, sera utilisé par l'entreprise Rheinzink comme bâtiment d'accueil et d'exposition. Vue de l'extérieur, avec sa forme pointue et asymétrique, cette maison à ossature de bois ressemble à des cristaux. Trois bandes en dessous desquelles des murs en retrait présentent de hautes fenêtres aux formats irréguliers assurent la cohésion optique de ce bâtiment à deux étages et plan irrégulier.

Libeskind raconte s'être posé la question du type de maison dans lequel il aurait aimé vivre afin de s'en inspirer pour concevoir son projet. Apparemment, il les aime spacieuses. Les dimensions de la villa sont considérables : au total, elle présente, sur trois niveaux, 515 m² de surface d'habitation, dont 200 m² respectivement pour le rez-de-chaussée et le sous-sol. Et pourtant le rez-de-chaussée n'accueille que trois pièces : depuis le hall d'entrée, on accède à la salle de la cheminée, aux suites pour les invités ainsi qu'à l'immense salle de séjour de 95 m², haute de deux niveaux, dénommée à juste titre « Grand Room ». On y trouve également l'« îlot cuisine », conçu par Libeskind en personne. Un escalier mène à l'étage supérieur où se trouvent la suite de maître avec balcon, deux chambres à coucher et deux salles

The two interiors, "Libeskind" (left)
and "Casual" (right)

Gegenüberstellung der Interieur-
varianten „Libeskind" (links) und
„Casual" (rechts)

Comparaison entre les intérieurs
Libeskind (à gauche) et Casual
(à droite)

shower falling from a height of over 13 ft. Features foreseen for the lower
level include a fitness room, a wine cellar, and a daylight sauna.
The interior is offered in two variations: in a "warm, natural", casual style
(parquet floors, heated stone in the bathrooms) and in a "cool, sculptural"
Libeskind style (bright white, polished flooring, crisp, hard-edged forms in
the bathrooms). All of the rooms are equipped with radiant heating. The
Libeskind Villa conforms with German low-energy standards. Solar and
geothermal energy sources are used for power, rainwater can also be fed
into the system.

zimmers" ist die 4 m hohe „Regendusche". Im Untergeschoss sind u.a. ein
Fitnessraum, ein Weinkeller und eine mit Tageslicht belichtete Sauna
vorgesehen.
Das Interieur wird in zwei Varianten angeboten: im „warmen, natürlichen"
„Casual Style" (Parkettböden, warme Steinflächen in den Badezimmern)
und im „kühlen, skulpturalen" „Libeskind-Style" (sehr weiße, polierte
Bodenbeläge, scharfe klare Formen in den Badezimmern). Alle Räume sind
mit Fußbodenheizung versehen. Die Libeskind-Villa erfüllt die deutschen
Niedrigenergie-Standards. Zur Energieversorgung werden solar- und
geothermische Energiequellen genutzt, Regenwasser kann ebenfalls ein-
gespeist werden.

de bains. Le clou de la « grande salle de bains » est la « douche pluie » haute
de 4 m. Au sous-sol se trouvent entre autres une salle de gymnastique, une
cave à vins et un sauna éclairé par la lumière naturelle.
L'intérieur est proposé en deux versions : dans le « Casual Style », chaud et
naturel (parquet, surface en pierre chauffée dans les salles de bains), et
dans le « Libeskind Style », froid et sculptural (sols très blancs et polis,
formes claires aux contours très définis dans les salles de bains). Toutes les
pièces sont équipées de chauffages au sol. La villa Libeskind remplit les
normes allemandes de basse consommation d'énergie.
L'approvisionnement énergétique provient de sources d'énergie solaire et
géothermique, et l'eau de pluie peut également être récupérée.

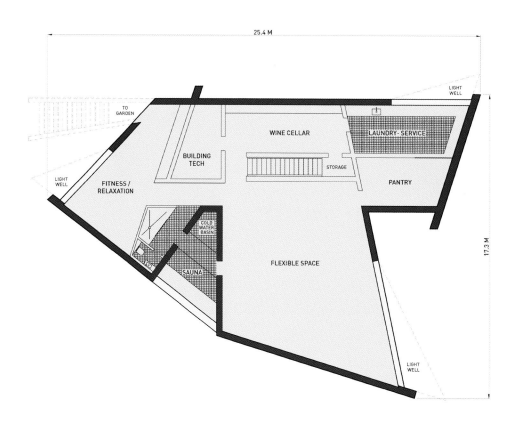

Floor plan labels:

25.4 M

17.3 M

LIGHT WELL

TO GARDEN

WINE CELLAR

LAUNDRY - SERVICE

BUILDING TECH

STORAGE

LIGHT WELL

FITNESS / RELAXATION

PANTRY

COLD WATER BASIN

SAUNA

FLEXIBLE SPACE

LIGHT WELL

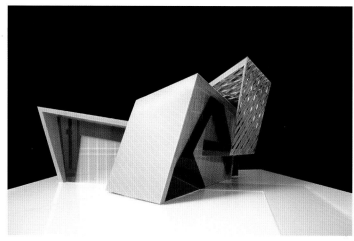

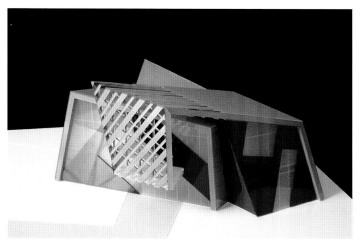

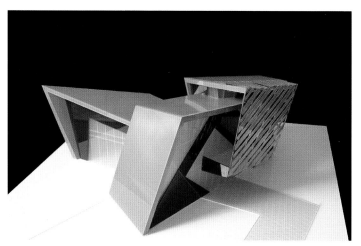

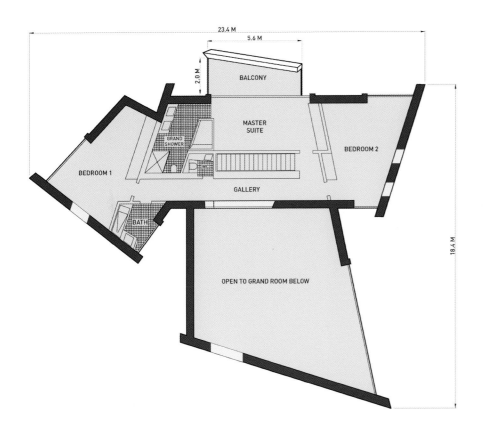

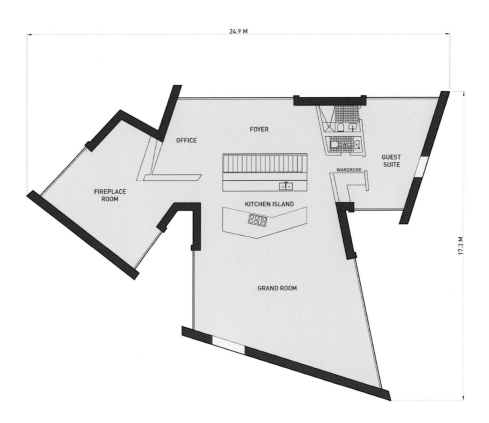

BIBLIOGRAPHY

Arieff, Allison: *Prefab*. Layton, Utah: Gibbs Smith, 2002

Bancilhon, Philippe: *Jean Benjamin Maneval. La Bulle Six Coques*. Paris: Jousse entreprise éditions, 2004

Bemis, Albert Farwel: *The Evolving House*. Cambridge, Mass: MIT, 1936

Broadhurst, Ron (ed.): *Home delivery. Fabricating the modern dwelling* [exhibition at The Museum of Moden Art, New York]. Basel/Boston/Berlin: Birkhäuser, 2008

Cherner, Norman: *Fabricating Houses from Component Parts. How to build a house for $6,000*. New York, New York: Reinhold Publishing, 1957

Cinqualbre, Olivier/Pacquement, Alfred/Rubin, Robert M.: *Jean Prouvé: La maison tropicale/The Tropical House*. Paris: Centre Pompidou, 2009

Cooke, Amanda/Avi Friedman: *Ahead of Their Time. The Sears Catalogue Prefabricated Houses*, in: *Journal of Design History*, 14/1, 2001, pp. 53–70

Davies, Colin: *The Prefabricated Home*. London: Reaktion Books, 2005

Decker, Julie/Chris Chiei: *Quonset Hut. Metal Living for a Modern Age*. New York: Princeton Architectural Press, 2005

Ebong, Ima: *Kit Homes Modern*. New York: Collins Design, 2005

Enjolras, Christian: *Jean Prouvé. Les maisons de Meudon 1949–1999*. Paris: Editions de la Villetta, 2003

Fetters, Thomas L.: *The Lustron Home. The History of a Postwar Prefabricated Housing Experiment*. Jefferson, N.C.: McFarland, 2002

Fuller, Richard Buckminster: *Critical Path*. New York: St. Martin's Griffin, 1982

Genzel, Elke/Voigt, Pamela: *Kunststoffbauten. Teil 1: Die Pioniere*. Weimar: Verlag der Bauhaus-Universität, 2005

Gloag, John/Grey Wornum: *House Out of Factory*. London: George Allen & Unwin, 1946

Graff, Raymond/Matern, Rudolph A./Williams, Henry Lionel: *The Prefabricated House. A Practical Guide for the Prospective Buyer*. Garden City, N.Y.: Doubleday & Co., 1947

Hays, K. Michael/Miller, Dana:

Buckminster Fuller. Starting with the Universe. New York: Yale University Press, 2008

Herbers, Jill: *Prefab Modern*. New York: Harper Design International, 2004

Herbert, Gilbert: *Pioneers of Prefabrication. The British Contribution in the 19. Century*. Baltimore: Johns Hopkins University Press, 1978

Herbert, Gilbert: *The Dream of the Factory-Made House. Walter Gropius and Konrad Wachsmann*. Cambridge, Mass.: Harvard UP, 1984

Home, Marko and Mika Taanila: *Futuro. Tomorrow's House from Yesterday*. Helsinki: Desura, 2002

Institut für das Bauen mit Kunststoffen: *Untersuchung über die Wohn- und Konstruktionsformen von Kunststoffhäusern und Raumzellen in Abhängigkeit von der Rentabilitätsschwelle*, in: *Plasticonstruction*, 5, 1973, pp. 245–257

Jandl, H. Ward, et alii: *Yesterday's Houses of Tomorrow. Innovative American Homes 1850 to 1950*. Washington D.C.: The Preservation Press, 1991

Junghanns, Kurt: *Das Haus für alle. Zur Geschichte der Vorfertigung in Deutschland*. Berlin: Ernst & Sohn, 1994

Koch, Carl/Lewis, Andy: *At Home With Tomorrow*. New York/Toronto: Rinehart & Co., 1958

Krausse, Joachim/Lichtenstein, Claude (eds.): *Your Private Sky. R. Buckminster Fuller: The Art of Design Science*. Baden (AG): Lars Müller, 1999

Meyer-Bohe, Walter: *Vorgefertigte Wohnhäuser*. Munich: Callwey, 1959

Nerdinger, Winfried: *The Architect Walter Gropius: Drawings, Prints, and Photographs from Busch-Reisinger Museum*. Harvard University Art Museums Cambridge, Mass., and Bauhaus-Archiv Berlin (eds.), Berlin: Mann, 1985

Peters, Nils: *Jean Prouvé. The Dynamics of Creation*. Cologne: Taschen, 2006

Pfeiffer, Bruce Brooks: *Frank Loyd Wright. The Complete Works 1943–1959*. Cologne: Taschen, 2009

Rosa, Joseph: *Albert Frey, Architect*. New York: Rizzoli International, 1990

Rubin, Robert M.: *Jean Prouvé: A Tropical*

House. February 14–May 6, 2005, Yale School of Architecture Gallery, New Haven: Yale School of Architecture, 2005

Smith, Elizabeth (ed.). *Blueprints for Modern Living. History and Legacy of the Case Study Houses*. Cambridge, Mass.: MIT Press, 1989

Sprague, Paul E.: *The Origin of Ballooon Framing*, in: *Journal of the Society of Architectural Historians*, 40, 1981, pp. 311–319

Strauch, Dietmar: *Einstein in Caputh. Die Geschichte eines Sommerhauses*. Berlin: Anton Hain Verlag, 2001

Trulove, James Grayson and Cha, Ray: *Prefab Now*. New York: Collins Design, 2007

Touchaleaume, Éric. *Jean Prouvé. Les Maisons Tropicales*. Paris: Galerie 54, 2006

von Vegesack, Alexander (ed.): *Jean Prouvé. Die Poetik des technischen Objekts*. Weil am Rhein: Vitra Design Museum, 2005

PHOTO CREDITS

Courtesy of Wolfgang Feierbach, Altenstadt: 166, 168 all, 169 both, 170 top both, 171 all; Photo Klaus Meier-Ude: 167, 170 bottom, 172, 173 both, 174 both, 175

© Floto + Warner, New York, NY: 243, 244 top left, 244 bottom right, 245, 246

© Renee Flugge: 360 bottom left

Photo Lionel Freedman: 119 bottom left

Courtesy, The Estate of R. Buckminster Fuller: 4, 72, 73, 75 left, 87, 88 both, 89, 90 both, 91 both

Photo Alan Band/Keystone/Getty Images: 2

Photo Express/Express/Getty Images: 21 left

Photo © Arnold Newman/Liaison Agency/Getty Images: 99

Photo John Phillips/Time Life Pictures/Getty Images: 74 left

Photo John G. Zimmerman/Time & Life Pictures/Getty Images: 153, 154, 155, 156, 157 top right

© J. Paul Getty Trust. Used with permission.

Julius Shulman Photography Archive, Research Library at the Getty Research Institute: 22, 93, 94 bottom left, 94 bottom right, 95

© Steve Gleason, Warren, MA: 37 top, 38, 39 all

© David Glomb, Rancho Mirage, CA: 307, 308 top, 309

© Peter Gössel, Bremen: 339 bottom, 375, 377 both, 379 all

© John Gollings, St. Kilda: 297 top right, 299, 300 top left, 300 bottom right, 301

© Pedro Guerrero, Tucson, AZ: 121, 125

Haack + Höpfner, Munich: 278 left

Haack + Höpfner, Munich, Horden Cherry Lee Architects, London: 272, 276 bottom, 278 right

Courtesy of Hanse-Haus GmbH, Oberleichtersbach: 256, 257, 258 both, 259, 260 all, 261 both

Courtesy of Happy Haus, Fortitude Valley, Queensland: 358, 360 top, 360 bottom right, 361 bottom

Special Collections, Frances Loeb Library, Graduate School of Design, Harvard University: 92, 94 top left, 94 top right; Photo Julius Shulman: 96, 97

Courtesy of Architekturbüro Hellmuth: 176, 179 bottom left, 180 both, 182 bottom, 183 bottom both

© Hiroyuki Hirai, Tokyo: 205, 207, 208 left, 209

Courtesy of Hive Moduar LLC, Minneapolis, MN: 302, 303, 304 all, 305 left, 305 bottom right; Photo T. J. Thoraldson 305 top right

E. F. Hodgson Co.: Hodgson portable houses, Boston, Massachusetts, 1908: 34, 37 bottom left, 37 bottom right

E. F. Hodgson Co.: Hodgson portable houses, poultry and pet stock, Boston, Massachusetts, 1920: 13, 36

Horden Cherry Lee Architects, London: 274 both, 275 both

Courtesy of Huf Haus GmbH & Co. KG, Hartenfels: 190, 191, 192 both, 193

© Frank Huster/Robert Hipp-Huster, Neckartenzlingen: 194, 195, 196 top right, 196 bottom left, 196 bottom right, 197, 198, 199 both

Interior Design, November, 1968: 157 left

© Steffen Jänicke, Berlin: 335, 337 all

Courtesy of Ray Kappe, Pacific Palisades, CA: 326

Courtesy of Oskar Leo Kaufmann, Dornbirn: 216 both, 219 left, 362, 364 top right, 364 bottom both, 367

© Tom Kawara, Zurich: 211, 212, 213 right, 214, 215 both

© Sascha Kletzsch, Munich: 273, 276 top, 277, 279 both

Courtesy of Andreas Knitz, Berg/Ravensburg: 146, 150 top

Koch, Carl/Lewis, Andy: At Home With Tomorrow. New York/Toronto: Rinehart & Co., 1958: 116, 118 top left, 118 top right, 119 top

Courtesy of Lazor Office LLS, Minneapolis, MN: 250, 252 all, 253 all, 255 left; Photo Tomm Brown: 254; Photo Randy O'Rourke: 251, 255 right

© David Lena, Santa Monica, CA: 311, 312, 313

Courtesy of the Library of Congress, Prints and Photographs Division: 24; Farm Security Administration/Office of War Information Photograph Collection: 21 right, 23, 35; Historic American Buildings Survey: 18, Photo Jack E. Boucher: 104 right

Life magazin, Nov. 8th 1968: 152

© Åke E:son Lindman, Bromma: 347, 348 top left, 348 bottom, 349, 350 left, 351 both

© Jon Linkins, Enoggera, Queensland: 359, 361 top

Courtesy of LivingHomes, Los Angeles, CA: 328 right, 329 left

Courtesy of LoftCube GmbH, Munich: 334, 336, 338, 339 top

Lustron Home Erection Manual: 100 bottom left, 101 top left, 101 top right

© Ignacio Martinez, Navia: 217, 218, 219 right

MUJI.net Co., Ltd.: 271

Courtesy of Jerry Murbach: 1

Museum Eberswalde: 54, 55, 56 both, 58 both, 60 both, 61 both

Museum of Finnish Architecture, Helsinki: 140, 141, 142, 143 both, 144 both, 163, 165; Photo Carl Gustav Hagström: 164

Courtesy of Kazuhiko Namba + Kai-Workshop, Tokyo: 266, 268 right, 269 left, 270 right

Robert Carrick/National Library of Australia: 7

Frank Hurley/National Library of Australia: 20

Damian McDonald/National Library of Australia: 32

National Trust of Australia (Vic): 33 both

National Trust for Historic Preservation: 103

Ohio Historical Society: 98, 100 top left, 100 right, 101 middle left, 101 middle right, 102, 104 left, 105

picture-alliance/dpa: Photo Ensio Ilmonen/Lehtikuva: 187; Photo Lehtikuva: 185, 186 right, 188, 189; Photo Wilhelm Bertram: 147, 151, 160; Photo Scanpix Gunnar Källström: 161

Courtesy of Pinc House AB, Stockholm: 280, 282 bottom, 284 bottom; Photo Charlie Drevstam: 281, 282 top both, 283 both, 284 top both, 285

Popular Science, March 1946: 5

Courtesy of Prebuilt Pty Ltd., Kilsyth: 292, 293, 294 all, 295, 296, 297 bottom both, 298, 300 top right, 300 bottom left

Courtesy of proportion GmbH, Berlin: 380, 384 top right, 385 top; Photo Klaus Helbig: 381, 382; © Screen ID: 383 both, 385 bottom; © SDL: 384 bottom

Family Prouvé: 108, 109 all, 111 top, 115 top right, 115 bottom right, 129 both, 132 both

Courtesy of Quik Build LLC: 28 both

Courtesy of Marmol Radziner + Associates, Los Angeles, CA: 308 bottom, 310 all

Courtesy of Resolution: 4 Architecture, New York, NY: 242, 244 top right, 244 bottom left, 247 both; Photo Roger Davies: 248, 249 both

Revue de l'Aluminium, no. 185, 1952, page 58: 114 left, 114 bottom right, 115 left

Courtesy of Rintala Eggertsson Architects, Oslo: 340, 342 bottom, 345 left; Photo Sami Rintala: 344 left, 345 right

Courtesy of Rocio Romero LLC, St. Louis, MO: 226 bottom; Photo Ethan: 224; Photo Karl Petzke: 226 top right; Photo Frank Di Piazza: 227 bottom left; Photo Traci Roloff: 225, 227 bottom right, 227 far right; Photo Jennifer Watson: 226 left

© Douglas Royalty/Connecticut College: 62

© Hiro Sakaguchi, Tokyo: 267, 268 left, 269 right, 270 left

Digital image © 2010, The Museum of Modern Art/Scala, Florence: 17

Photo Ben Schnall: 118 bottom

Sears Archives: 10

Sears, Roebuck and Co.: Modern Homes, Chicago, Illinois: 1913: 11

Courtesy of sps-architekten, Thalgau: 262, 265 both

La Trobe Collection, State Library of Victoria: 31

South Australian Record, 27 November 1837: 30

S. P. Luftbild GmbH, Dattenberg: 196 top left

Courtesy of Matti Suuronen, Espoo: 158, 162 both

© John Swain, Sacramento, CA: 229, 231, 232, 233

Courtesy of Mikko Tuovinen: 184, 186 left

Courtesy of TYIN tegnestue, Trondheim: 370 bottom, 372 bottom

United States Patent and Trademark Office: 9, 74 right, 75 right, 86

Albert Frey Collection, Architecture & Design Collection, University Art Museum, University of California, Santa Barbara: 47, 52 left, 53 right

Wachsmann, Konrad: Holzhausbau – Technik und Gestaltung, Ernst Wasmuth Verlag, Berlin, 1930: 43 top right, 43 bottom, 45 top left, 45 top right, 45 bottom left

Wagner, Martin: Das wachsende Haus, Berlin, 1932: 57, 59 top left, 59 top middle, 59 top right

Courtesy of The Wall AG, Schaffhausen: 374, 376, 378 all

Monsanto Company Records, University Archives, Department of Special Collections, Washington University Libraries, St. Louis, MO: 26

Courtesy of WeberHaus, Rheinau-Linx: 221

Courtesy of Larry Weinberg: 117, 119 bottom right

© The Frank Lloyd Wright Foundation, Scottsdale: 120, 122, 124 right

Courtesy of ZenKaya Ecohomes, Pretoria: 286, 288 all

THE AUTHORS

IMPRINT

Arnt Cobbers
Born in Kempen in 1966, he studied art
history, history and music in Berlin before
writing a dissertation on medieval church
architecture. After working as an architectural critic, he is now a freelance author in
Berlin. Among his many publications are
books on architecture in Berlin, as well as
on the work of Karl Friedrich Schinkel,
Frank Lloyd Wright, Erich Mendelsohn,
Ludwig Mies van der Rohe, Marcel Breuer,
Ieoh Ming Pei, and others. He was also the
editor-in-chief of the music magazines
Crescendo and *Partituren*, founder of the
jazz magazin *halb elf*, and is currently
editor-in-chief of the music magazine
Concerti.

Oliver Jahn
Born in Frankfurt am Main in 1970, studied
literature, philosophy, and linguistics. After
many years of working as a freelance author
for newspapers such as *Die Welt*, the
Süddeutsche Zeitung and the *Rheinischer
Merkur*, and as an employee of the Arno
Schmidt Stiftung, an editor and coordinator
at Suhrkamp Verlag, and the editor in
charge of design and architecture at the art
magazine *Monopol* (Berlin), he now works
as the director of the department of architecture and design at the magazine *AD
Architectural Digest*. Jahn's numerous publications on literature, architecture, and
design include *Ähnliches ist nicht dasselbe.
Eine rasante Revue für Ror Wolf*, Oliver
Jahn/Kai U. Jürgens (eds.), Kiel, 2002.

© 2010 TASCHEN GmbH
Hohenzollernring 53, D-50672 Köln
www.taschen.com

Project management: Gössel und Partner,
Bremen
Design and layout: Andy Disl, Cologne
Text edited by: Johannes Althoff, Berlin
English translation: Maureen Roycroft
Sommer, Bergisch Gladbach
French translation: Myriam Ochoa-Suel,
Berlin

Printed in China
ISBN 978-3-8365-0753-0

To stay informed about upcoming
TASCHEN titles, please request our magazine at www.taschen.com/magazine or
write to TASCHEN America, 6671 Sunset
Boulevard, Suite 1508, USA-Los Angeles,
CA 90028, contact-us@taschen.com, Fax:
+1-323-463.4442. We will be happy to send
you a free copy of our magazine which is
filled with information about all of our
books.